An Introduction to Islamic Finance

Theory and Practice

An Introduction to Islamic Finance

Theory and Practice

Zamir Iqbal
&
Abbas Mirakhor

John Wiley & Sons (Asia) Pte Ltd

Copyright © 2007 John Wiley & Sons (Asia) Pte Ltd
Published in 2007 by John Wiley & Sons (Asia) Pte Ltd
2 Clementi Loop, #02-10, Singapore 129809

This publication is designed to provide accurate and authoritative information in regard to the subject matter covered. It is sold with the understanding that the publisher is not engaged in rendering professional services. If professional advice or other expert assistance is required, the services of a competent professional person should be sought.

Neither the authors nor the publisher are liable for any actions prompted or caused by the information presented in this book. Any views expressed herein represent those of the authors and do not represent the views of World Bank Group and of International Monetary Fund (IMF).

Other Wiley Editorial Offices

John Wiley & Sons, Inc., 111 River Street, Hoboken, NJ 07030, USA
John Wiley & Sons Ltd, The Atrium, Southern Gate, Chichester PO19 BSQ, England
John Wiley & Sons (Canada) Ltd, 5353 Dundas Street West, Suite 400, Toronto, Ontario M9B 6HB, Canada
John Wiley & Sons Australia Ltd, 42 McDougall Street, Milton, Queensland 4064, Australia
Wiley-VCH, Boschstrasse 12, D-69469 Weinheim, Germany

Library of Congress Cataloging-in-Publication Data:

ISBN-13: 978-0470-82188-6

Typeset in 11/13 point, Bembo by Superskill Graphics Pte Ltd
Printed in Singapore by Saik Wah Press Pte Ltd
10 9 8 7 6

In the Name of Allah, the All Merciful, the All Beneficent

Contents

Glossary

Akhlaq	Personal, moral, and behavioral disposition of a person.
Al-adl	Justice.
Al-Istihsan	Juristic preference of one alternative to another.
Al-Maslaha	Public welfare.
Amanah	Trust. Placing something valuable in trust with someone for custody or safe-keeping.
Aqidah	Faith and beliefs of a Muslim.
Ariya	Lending for gratuitous use. Lending of an asset takes place between a lender and a borrower with the agreement that the former will not charge anything.
Barakah	Blessings and returns for performing virtuous acts.
Bay'	Sale of a property or commodity for a price.
Bay' al-'Arabun	Payment of a portion of full-sale price paid in good faith.
Bay' al-Istisnah	Sale on order to manufacturer or contractor.
Bay' al-Muajjil	Sale contract where the price of a product or underlying asset is agreed but the payment in lump sum or installments is deferred to a specified future date.
Bay' al-Salam	Sale by immediate payment against future delivery. Similar to conventional forward contract but requires full payment at the time of contract.

Bay' al-Dayn	Sale of debt or liability.
Bay' Bithamin Ajil (BBA)	Sale contract where payment is made in installments after delivery of goods. Sale could be for long-term and there is no obligation to disclose profit margins.
Gharar	Any uncertainty or ambiguity created by the lack of information or control in a contract.
Hawala	Transfer of a debt or an obligation from one debtor to another.
Ibadat	The *Shariah* rules guiding the practicalities of ways to perform rites and rituals.
Iijarah wa 'iqtina'	A hire-purchase contract which is similar to conventional lease-purchase agreements. In addition to regular contract of *Ijarah*, another contract is added which includes a promise by the lessor/owner to sell the leased asset to the lessee at the end of the original lease agreement.
Ijarah	A sale contract which is not the sale of a tangible asset but rather a sale of the *usufruct* (the right to use the object) for a specified period of time.
Ijma'	Consensus on legal opinion.
Ijtihad	The efforts expanded by jurists to extract solutions to problems based on the principles of primary and secondary sources, where rules of behavior are not explicitly addressed by the primary sources, i.e. *Quran* and *Sunnah*.
Jo'ala	Agreement with an expert in a given field to undertake a task for a pre-determined fee or commission (as in a consultancy agreement or contract).
Khilafah	Stewardship.

Khiyanah	Betrayal of trust. Faithlessness.
Kifala	Suretyship. Assuming someone's liability in case the principal fails to meet his/her obligation.
Ma'ad	Believing in returning to *Allah* (swt) for final, definite and complete account of one's actions.
Madhahib	Different schools of thought in understanding, interpreting and formulating the precepts of *Shariah*.
Maysur	Impermissibile games of chance.
Muamalat	Rules of behavior governing practicalities of day-to-day life in social, political, and economic activities.
Mudarabah	An economic agent with capital *(rabbul-mal)* can develop a partnership with another agent *(mudarib)*, with skills to form a partnership, with the agreement to share the profits. Although losses are borne only by the capital owner, the *mudarib* may be liable for a loss, in case of misconduct or negligence on his part.
Mudarib	Economic agent, with entrepreneural and managements skills, who partners with *rabbul-mal* (owner of capital) in a *Mudarabah* contract.
Murabahah	A cost-plus-sale contract where a financier purchases a product, i.e. commodity, raw material or supplied, for an entrepreneur who does not have his/her own capital to do so. The financier and the entrepreneur agree on a profit margin, often referred to mark-up which is added to the cost of the product. The payment is delayed for a specified period of time.

Musharakah Aqed	Granting ownership rights to the partner with value of assets without any specific linkage to any real asset.
Musharakah Mulk	Ownership rights given to a partner to a specific real asset.
Musharakah Mutanaqisah	Contract of diminishing partnership. Usually, one partner buys out share of others over time.
Musharakah	Equity partnership. It is a hybrid of *Shiraka* (partnership) and *Mudarabah*, combining the act of investment and management.
Nafs	Soul, psyche.
Niyya	Intention.
Nubuwwa	Believing that Mohammed (*pbuh*) is the last and the final messenger of *Allah* (swt) bringing to mankind the most perfect set of rules of conduct required for the perfect life in this world.
Qard-e-Hasna	Charitable loans with no interest and low expectations of return of principal.
Qimar	Gambling.
Qiyas	Analogical reasoning.
Quran	The Divine book revealed to Prophet Mohammed (*pbuh*).
Rabbul-mal	Provider of funds/capital in *Mudarabah* contract.
Rahn	The contract of *rahn* or pledge is to secure a property provided by the borrower against a loan so that in case of the borrower's inability to make the payment, liability may be recovered from the value of the pledged property.

Riba	The premium (interest) that must be paid by the borrower to the lender along with the principal amount as a condition for the loan or for an extension.
Riba al-Fadl	*Riba* in a hand-to-hand or barter exchange.
Riba al-Nasiah	*Riba* in a money-to-money exchange provided exchange is delayed or deferred and additional charge is incurred with such deferment.
Sarf	Sale by exchange of money-for-money on the spot.
Shariah	Islamic Law.
Suftaja	Bills of exchange.
Sukuk	Plural of the Arabic word *Sakk* meaning certificate, reflects participation rights in the underlying assets.
Sunnah	The practice of Prophet Mohammed (*pbuh*).
Takaful	Insurance contract through mutual or joint guarantee.
Taqwa	Ever-present consciousness of *Allah* (swt).
Tawhid	The Unity and Oneness of the Creator — *Allah* (swt).
Wadia	Deposit of one's property with another person for safe-keeping with permission to use it without the intention of receiving any return from it.
Wikala	Representation. Entrusting a person or legal entity (*Wakil*) to act on one's behalf or as one's representative.

Introduction

Islam propounds the guiding principles, and prescribes a set of rules, for all aspects of human life, including the economic aspect. How, and to what degree, would an economic and financial system be different from a modern conventional, non-Islamic system, if such a system were to be designed in conformity with the principles of Islam? Would such a system be optimal in the allocation, production, and distribution of economic resources? How can some of its fundamental principles be explained with due analytical rigor? Researchers interested in contemplating or devising a social, economic, and financial system based on the tenets of Islam are familiar with many such questions.

Efforts to explain Islamic financial and economic principles and rules in modern analytical terms are only two decades old. Despite considerable published research, however, there is still some confusion in regard to precisely defining various social sciences prefixed with the term "Islamic", such as "Islamic economics" or "Islamic finance". One of the main reasons of this confusion is the tendency to view different aspects of such a system in isolation, without looking at it in its totality. For example, the term "Islamic finance" is often deemed to denote a system that prohibits "interest", whereas this simple description is not only inaccurate but also a source of further confusion. Unfortunately, also, a number of writers take the liberty of expressing opinions on these issues without sufficient knowledge of Islam, its primary sources, its history and often without even a working knowledge of the language of Islam, i.e., Arabic.[1] Against the backdrop of a politicized atmosphere, such attempts render an understanding of these issues even more difficult.

Systematic thinking by professional economists about Islam and economics has a short history compared to the atrophy that followed a remarkable earlier period of vibrant scholarship in the sciences and humanities in the Muslim world. This "hibernation"[2] occurred after achievements in all areas of thought by Muslim scholars and dynamic economic growth in Muslim societies. After these contributions, discoveries and intermediation by Islamic sciences actually helped facilitate the development and growth of Western societies and economies. From the present-day perspectives, however, and especially when judged against the last three decades of research and development in other disciplines, the published writings on Islamic economics in various languages give a sense of a return of vibrancy and energy in the discipline. These efforts are directed toward the development of a coherent and rigorous explanation of how Islam proposes to organize an economic system by answering the fundamental questions of what should be produced, how and for whom, how decisions should be made and by whom, and, finally, how Islamic institutions could be revived to address the problems of modern societies.

Economic Institutions, Rules and Contracts

Islam postulates a unique nexus of contracts among the Creator, man and society on the basis of the Divine Law that directly affects the workings of the various social, political, economic, and financial systems. Therefore, to understand the way in which economic affairs and financial institutions are to be organized in an Islamic system, it is first necessary to comprehend the nature of this relationship. What differentiates Islam from other systems of thought is its unitary perspective, which refuses to distinguish between the sacred and the profane and which insists that all of its elements must constitute an organic whole. Consequently, one cannot study a particular aspect or part of an Islamic system, say its economic system, in isolation, without a knowledge of the conceptual framework which gives rise to that part or aspect, anymore than one can study a part of a circle without conceptualizing the circle itself.

An economic system is a collection of *institutions* set up by society to deal with allocation of resources, production and exchange of goods and services and distribution of the resulting income and wealth. In the most general sense, *institutions* entail, first, the *existence* of certain sets of formal and informal rules of conduct and, secondly, systems and procedures for the *enforcement* of such rules, designed to achieve a set of objectives. The degree of the effectiveness of such rules and their enforcement, therefore, is determined by the degree to which there is an identity between the objective(s) of institutions and the choices individuals make in that institutional setting.

(a) *Rules of Conduct and the Social Order:* The function of rules of conduct is to provide the means by which individuals can overcome the obstacles presented by their ignorance of particular facts that must exist to determine overall justice in the social order. Rules specify what kind of conduct is appropriate in certain circumstances. Rules are specific means to specific ends. They are, essentially, restrictions on what individual members of society may do without upsetting the social order. All individuals count on the social order in deciding on their individual choices and actions. Therefore, rules should guide individuals in their actions. If emotions and impulses tell them what they want, the rules tell them whether or not they can have it and how they will be able and allowed to get it. Additionally and importantly, observance of rules of conduct integrates individuals into society. Rules serve to prevent conflicts, reconcile differences and facilitate cooperation among individuals. Compliance with them promotes social integration and unity and preserves the intended social order.

Two conditions must exist for preserving the social order; one is necessary and the other sufficient. The former requires that rule compliance be enforced, through persuasion if possible, coercion if necessary. The latter states that the social order will be preserved if it is generally accepted that the rules of conduct will be enforced in all cases irrespective of the particular consequences some may foresee. Only if applied universally, without regard to particular effects, will rules of conduct serve the objective of the permanent preservation of the social order.

(b) *Enforcement Mechanism:* The enforcement characteristics of Islamic rules are that each and every individual is made responsible for knowing the theories for themselves and then for ensuring that others know them as well. The enforcement mechanism in Islam is embodied in the most important of all social duties of Muslims. This duty is the first, and by far the most important, mechanism for ensuring education, training and development of all individuals to become familiar with the rules of just conduct prescribed by Islam. Secondly, this mechanism ensures that individuals comply with the rules once they know them.

If these rules are not generally known or understood because both individuals and their collectivities have avoided their duty, rule compliance will be lacking or fundamentally weak. In that case, imposition by fiat of an Islamic economic superstructure, whatever that may mean under the circumstances, will not produce the desired result. But once the rules are known and understood, individuals, the government and society at large — all have the duty and the responsibility to ensure compliance and enforcement.

(c) *Contracts and Ideology*: Not only do individuals, as members of society, make choices for themselves, but they also interact with other members of society through transactions facilitated by explicit and implicit contracts entered into within the bounds specified by the institutional setting of a given society. A contract is a time-bound instrument with an objective. It stipulates the obligations that each party is expected to fulfill in order to achieve the objectives of the contract.

The conformity and enforcement of contracts can be costly, mainly because information is costly and is held asymmetrically by the parties to a contract. For this reason, ideology matters. The strength of enforcement of rules of conduct in general, and of contracts in particular, depends on ideology. Ideology consists of a "subjective" model that individuals possess to evaluate and explain the world around them. Ideology is important because it is a key to individual choices that affect the performance of an economic system. Economic performance is affected by institutions (rules) as well as technology — which together determine transformation (production) and transaction costs.

With this background, let us examine the ideological principles that lay the foundation of Islam's social, economic and financial systems.

Islamic Ideology

The core and fundamental axioms of Islamic ideology are the belief in (1) the Unity and Oneness of the Creator (*Tawhid*), (2) the prophethood (*Nubuwwa*), and (3) the ultimate return of everything to the Creator for the final judgement (*Maad*).

> The first and the most important axiom of Unity and Oneness of the Creator requires one to believe that all creation has only one omniscient and omnipresent Creator — *Allah* (swt) — who has placed man on this earth to pursue his own felicity and perfection.[3] Further, it becomes incumbent upon each believer to believe that the orbit of man's life is much longer, broader and deeper than the material dimension of life in this world.

The second axiom requires believing that Mohammed (*pbuh*) is the last and the final messenger of *Allah* (swt) bringing to mankind the most perfect set of rules of conduct required for the perfect life in this world.[4] The significance of this axiom is that one has to believe that he (the Prophet) lived a life in which his own actions and words personified a prototype model of the perfect state of human perfection that a believer has to strive for.

The third axiom requires believing that at some point in this cycle of life, *Allah* (swt) will call forth all of mankind for a final, definite and complete account, followed by a judgement. At that point each person will see his/her actions and will receive the just reward or punishment due. This axiom highlights the significance of the role that the concept of the "life hereafter" plays, thus extending the planning horizon of a believer beyond the short span of life on this earth.

Concomitant with the acceptance of Islam, the individual agrees to observe the rules of Islamic Law (*Shariah*) in private and public affairs. This acceptance and agreement represents a contract between the individual and the Creator, which symbolizes the primordial covenant between *Allah* (swt) and man, according to which man agreed to serve and worship no one but *Allah* (swt).[5]

Based on this ideology, the rules of conduct are structured and prescribed around the axis of the principle of Unity and Oneness (*Tawhid*). These rules are comprehensive and govern all of man's actions and decisions, and constitute an integrated, consistent and unified whole; compliance with these rules leads, in turn, to unity of human society. A corollary of the axiom of the Unity is that not only that the Creator is One, but that all His creation constitutes a unity as well. The *Quran* — the Divine Book revealed to Prophet Mohammed — calls attention to the fact that despite all apparent multiplicity, human beings are fundamentally of one kind; they were created as one being (*nafs*) and will ultimately return to *Allah* (swt) as one (*nafs*) as well. The *Quran* says:

"Neither your creation nor your resurrection is possible other than as one united *nafs*" (31:28)

In a series of verses, the *Quran* exhorts man to take collective and unified social action as well as to preserve and protect the collectivity from all elements of disunity.[6] These and many other verses order human beings to work hard toward social unity and cohesion, construct their societies, and preserve and defend that unity. Unity and social cohesion are so central among the objectives of the *Quran* for mankind, that it can be argued that all conducts prohibited by Islam are those that ultimately will lead to disunity and social disintegration. Conversely, all righteous conducts prescribed by Islam are those that lead to social integration, cohesiveness and unity. As a result, Islam is a call to the collectivity and has given the collectivity an independent personality and identity, which will be judged on its own merits or demerits separately from the individuals that constitute the collectivity. The final judgement on individual actions will have two dimensions, one as the individual and the other as a member of the collectivity.

Why Ideology Matters

The strength of ideology determines the strength of rule-compliance, and therefore the strength of institutions, which, together with technology, determine the performance and efficiency of an economic system. Efficiency is measured by the cost of a given level of economic performance. The stronger the ideology, the less the divergence between the choices individuals make and those expected of them by the objectives of institutions, and, consequently, the lower the cost of enforcement of contracts and rules of conduct. By implication, in an ideal situation, with a strong ideology, in which all rules of conduct are complied with and are universally enforced, there will be no divergence between what institutions expect of individual choices and the actual choices. Therefore, in the ideal situation, asymmetry and moral hazard are minimized since a large part of uncertainty will be eliminated with rule compliance. The remaining risks will become insurable.

(i) The Model of Man

It is important to understand the model of man according to the ideology of Islam, so that man's rights and responsibilities, as also man's relationship with society, are understood. Whereas *Allah* (swt) is the One and the Only Creator and the Sustainer of the Universe and of man, man himself is unique within the created order as he is the objective and the "synthetic fruit" of the process of creation, and possesses a dual dimension. His body constitutes his cosmic dimension, which is the essence of all that exists in the world of matter and through which he is connected to the material world. He also possesses a cosmic dimension through his soul, which is in a state of ceaseless journey and *Allah* (swt) is the goal to which it is oriented. This journey is a becoming process and an evolutionary process toward perfection, which for man, contains the potential of entrance into all levels of intellectual and spiritual achievements leading to the final meeting with *Allah* (swt).

For man, the recognition and constant reminder that everything in the Universe is contingent upon *Allah* (swt) entails a simultaneous understanding that the proper relationship between man and *Allah* (swt) is the relationship of "the servant and the served." The sole declared purpose of man is to "serve" *Allah* (swt) and to do so in accordance with His commands. This service is the implementation of the divine imperative for man and is for his own benefit. The notion of service, i.e., *ibada* indicates the act of the removal of barriers (material and otherwise) which exist on the path to *Allah* (swt).

The unique position of man among all created order stems from the fact that he has been designated as *Allah*'s vicegerent on earth. This designation is a Divine trust which bestows on man particular responsibilities which are composed of developing his own potentialities and, concomitantly, struggling for the creation of a just and moral social order on earth. To discharge the responsibilities with which he is charged, man is provided with the material and extra-material means to assist him in discharging his duties. First, he has been endowed with a theomorphic nature composed of the powers of cognition, intellect volition and speech to recognize and accept *Allah* (swt) as the Supreme Creator. Through his intelligence and will, man can discern and then choose between right and wrong, between just and unjust, between true and false, and between the real and the illusory. Although this power of discernment has been imprinted on his soul, to help man remember his purpose and his responsibilities, he is provided with guidance and remembrance in the form of the *Quran* and with reminders in the persons of the prophets as well as other human beings, to show him the "right path."

Man is also provided with the criteria by which his actions will be judged by his Creator; and he is reminded of the retributions that his transgressions will bring him and rewards that his efforts, obedience, and service to *Allah* (swt) will earn him in this life and in the hereafter. Through the *Quran* and the Reminders, man is told that there will come a day of reckoning, "the Hour," and a moment when every human will be shaken into a unique self-awareness of facing his/her deeds and misdeeds and accepting the judgement upon them. Through these means, he is constantly reminded of the transitory nature of this world and the permanence of the next, of what he must do to earn happiness in this life and felicity in the next, of his purpose, and of his responsibilities. Finally, all created phenomena in the material world have been subjected to man's use in order to provide him with the necessary material means to perform his responsibilities. Through his intelligence man is charged with the power to discover the knowledge which is necessary to utilize the natural resources to the fullest possible extent in order to remove material obstacles which may prevent him, and his kind, from actualizing their full potential.

Thus, *Allah* (swt) creates, preserves, guides, and finally judges man vis-à-vis the performance of his responsibilities. Hence, man's purpose is defined, his responsibilities are designated, necessary means of discharging these responsibilities are provided, guidance and reminders are constantly made available and the promise and criteria of the final judgement, as well as the rewards and retributions commensurate with obedience and transgression, are made known; it is, then, man's free will and choice which determine which path he, in fact, chooses.

Islam, then, models man as a being whose behavior, including its economic dimension, is teleological in nature. Whatever he thinks or does is accomplished with his final purpose in mind. His behavior is oriented toward his final destination. Things of this world, including material possessions, represent only the means by which he can come closer to his final goal. In his thought and behavior he is constantly aware of the presence of *Allah* (swt), who is "closer to him than his jugular vein."[7] This awareness extends not only to the individual's own affairs, but, particularly, also to his day-to-day dealings with others. This ever-present consciousness, called "*taqwa*," is a crucial concept in the *Quran* and represents an "awe," a "fear," or a "heeding," which a believer feels when fully conscious of *Allah*'s presence in his daily life and in his dealings with others. The concept carries with it the recognition by man that his actions will be judged in the Hereafter. It represents a defense mechanism, an "inner torch" by which man can distinguish between right and wrong, seeming and real, ephemeral and lasting. It is by this mechanism that he can defend himself against the temptations of the lower instincts. The becoming process and the evolutionary process toward perfection take place through the constant strengthening of this inner torch (i.e., *taqwā*). It is this defense mechanism that will assure man of his real and final success.

(ii) Society

The central aim of Islam is to establish a just, moral, and viable social order through the agency of man. Hence, the individual and the society are viewed as correlates. The position of vicegerent and its concomitant responsibilities are conferred upon all of mankind. It is the entire humanity that has the collective responsibility of ensuring that every human being has the opportunity to tap their dormant potential and of removing all obstacles from the individual's path to their ultimate goal. It is this collective view that evokes the matter of the unity of mankind, which leads to the equality (i.e., before the Law) of its members. Islam enunciates the principle that all mankind has been endowed with the same nature. It assumes, affirms, and confirms the equality of the entire human race and equalizes all men as creatures of *Allah* (swt); all endowed with the same cosmic status and the same essential qualities of creaturely humanity. It obliterates all basis of distinction except goodness, virtue, and service to *Allah* (swt). The principle of the Unity (in face of apparent diversity) of mankind is derived from the central doctrine of Unity and Oneness of *Allah* (swt) around which every aspect of Islam revolves. This principle leads to the conclusion that Islamic society is an open-ended community whose limit is the entire humanity.

Islamic community was brought into existence as a "community of the middle," "justly balanced," a "witness" to all nations, whose chief characteristic is the belief in the certainty of the Absolute and His Oneness.[8] The central function of this community is to "command the good and forbid the evil;" and whose members are fully conscious of their purpose and ultimate goal and possess the moral consciousness to fully realize their obligations to their fellow men and to the society.[9] This community is a "fraternity" of the faithful, which serves as a nucleus for the dissemination of its universal values.

Islam regards communities as having rights and responsibilities distinct from those of the aggregation of their individual members and which, like individuals, are accountable for their actions and suffer the consequences of disobedience. The *Quran* asks Muslims to consider the fate of communities and civilizations that went before them and see how they, through the operations of immutable laws that govern the rise and fall of peoples, received what they deserved and take lessons from it.[10]

The Islamic community, as well as each of its members, is charged with the responsibility of preserving, promoting, and propagating Islamic values and laws if it is to flourish and successfully accomplish its missions and objectives. Islam considers the existence of an Islamic community indispensable for the achievement of the Divine purpose recognizes that all individuals exist in a cultural and sociological environment and owe much of their perception of the world, and many of their reactions to its phenomena, to this environment and other individuals who share it. Much of the significance of this community relates to the need for acquisition, acculturation, and inculcation of the basic Islamic values, which, *ipso facto*, represent the growth of a Muslim personality. The well-knit way of life in the Islamic community molds individual behavior in its own design. Islamic principles, which deal with the formation, preservation, and continuation of the Islamic community, reflect the dialectic interaction of psycho-physiological requirements of individuals, on the one hand, and the necessary socio-economic order envisioned by Islam, on the other. It is this interaction that shapes the wants of the members of the community as well as the pattern of their preferences. This interaction, patterned in accordance with the teachings of Islam, is absolutely crucial to the development of behavior, including its economic dimension, of the individual and the collectivity envisioned by Islam.

Inasmuch as Islam's greatest emphasis is on the development of the individual's active moral consciousness in all his/her social interactions, the existence of political authority in society does not absolve the individual of the performance of duties with which he/she is charged. Adherence to moral principles and the doctrinal antecedence logically predispose a Muslim to an active and assertive political role in society. It is the active moral consciousness of the individual and the duty of "commending the good" and "forbidding of evil" along with the divine exhortation of consultation which gives the individual Muslim the right and the obligation of participating in the affairs of the community.

(iii) Concept of Justice

As was earlier mentioned, the central aim of Islam is to establish a just and moral social order through the agency of man. This all-embracing desideratum of the Islamic system is the ruling principle from which man's thought and behavior, the substantive and regulative rules of the *Shariah*, the formation of the community and the behavior of polity and of political authority derive their meaning and legitimacy. It can be claimed that it is the emphasis on justice that distinguishes the Islamic system from all other systems. It is via the concept of justice that the *raison d'etre* of the rules governing the economic behavior of the individual and economic institutions in Islam can be understood. What gives the behavior of a Muslim its orientation, meaning, and effectiveness is acting with the knowledge that justice evokes *Allah*'s pleasure and injustice, His displeasure. Whereas justice in Western thought is a quality of the behavior of one man with another and his actions can be perceived as unjust only in relation to the "other," in Islam it has an implication for the individual as well. That is, even when one does injustice to someone else, there is always reciprocity, in that through injustice to others, ultimately, one also does injustice to oneself and receives its results both here and in the hereafter.

Justice in Islam is a multifaceted concept, and several words or terms exist for each aspect. The most common word in use, which refers to the overall concept of justice is the word *Adl*. This word and its many synonyms imply the concepts of "right," as an equivalent of "fairness," "putting things in their right place," "equality," "equalizing," "balance," "temperance," and "moderation." These last few concepts are more precisely expressed as the principle of the "golden mean," according to which the believers are not only individually urged to act in conformity with this principle, but also the community is called upon, by the *Quran*, to be a "nation in the middle."[11] Thus, justice in Islam is the conceptualization of an aggregation of moral and social values, which denotes fairness, balance, and temperance. Its implication for individual behavior is, first of all, that one should not transgress one's bounds and, secondly, that one should give others, as well as oneself, what is due.

In practice, justice is operationally defined as acting in accordance with the Law, which, in turn, contains both substantive and procedural justice. Substantive justice consists of elements of justice contained in the substance of the Law, while procedural justice consists of rules of procedure assuring the attainment of justice contained in the substance of the Law. The underlying principles which govern the distinction between just and unjust acts determine the ultimate purpose of the *Shariah*, which includes: the establishment of the "general good" of society (considered to be the intent of the *Quran* and the *Shariah* is the path by which it is achieved), building the moral character of individual Muslims, and finally the promotion of freedom, equality, and tolerance, which are often stated as important goals of the *Shariah*. Of these, protection of the interests of society is considered to be the most important principle. Although there can be no contradiction between justice for the community as a whole and justice for the individual, the interest of the individual is protected so long as such interest does not come into conflict with the general interest of the community.

(iv) The Polity

Islam considers justice as the foundation of the polity. The Unity of Religion and the Law, which exists in principle, must be carried out in practice. Without an organized political authority the existence of both Religion and the Law may be endangered; without the constraints of the *Shariah*, the polity will degenerate into an unjust and tyrannical political order. Only in pursuit of justice can the polity be expected to fulfill the ends for which it was established. The pursuit of justice results in a convergence between the interests of the ruler and the ruled, leads to the improvement of social and economic conditions, and enhances the power of Islam in society. Two factors are necessary for this: the moral consciousness of the individual in not transgressing the limits set on their behavior by the *Shariah* and the faithfulness of the political authority to the terms of its contract in ensuring that the rules of the *Shariah* are implemented.

Shariah — The Law

Islam legislates for man according to his real nature and the possibilities inherent in the human state. Without overlooking the limited and the weak aspects of human nature in any way, Islam envisages man in light of his primordial nature as a theomorphic being, the vicegerent of the Creator on earth and a theophany of *Allah*'s attributes, with all the possibilities that this implies. It considers man as having the possibility of being perfect, but with a tendency to neglect his potentialities by remaining only at a level of sense perception. It asks, therefore, that in turn for all the blessings with which man is provided, he remember his real nature, keep in mind his terrestrial journey, seek to realize the full potential of his being, and remove all the obstacles which bar the right functioning of his intelligence. To order human life into a pattern intended for it by its Creator, man is provided with a network of injunctions and rules, which represent the concrete embodiment of the Divine Will in terms of specific codes of behavior by virtue of acceptance — through the exercise of his free choice — by which a person becomes a Muslim and according to which he lives his private and social life. This network of rules — called the *Shariah*, which is etymologically derived from a root meaning "the road" — leads man to a harmonious life here and felicity hereafter.

The emphasis on the axiomatic principle of Unity forms the basis for the fundamental belief that Islam recognizes no distinction between the spiritual and the temporal, between the sacred and the profane, or between the religious and the secular realms. Islam seeks to integrate all of man's needs, inclinations, and desires through the all-embracing authority of the *Shariah*, Life is considered as one and indivisible. Therefore, the rules of the *Shariah* hold sway over economic life no less than over social, political, and cultural life; they persuade, determine, and order the whole of life. It is through the acceptance of and compliance with the rules of the *Shariah* that the individual not only integrates themselves into the community, but also into a higher order of reality and the spiritual center. Violations of these rules will have a disintegrative effect upon the life of the individual and that of the community.

Table 1.1 Basics of the *Shariah*

The life of a Muslim at the individual and the societal level is governed by different sets of rules. The first set concerns the core relationship between man and the Creator. This set of rules, known as *Aqidah* (faith), deal with all matters of the faith and beliefs of a Muslim. The second set of rules deals with transforming and manifesting the faith and beliefs into action and daily practices and is formally known as *Shariah* (Law). Finally, the third set is *Akhlaq* (personal moral behavioral disposition), which concerns behavior, attitude, and work ethics according to which a Muslim lives in society. *Shariah*, being the practical aspect, is the one which every member of the society looks up to, to seek answers for issues concerning everyday life. *Shariah* is further divided into two components; *Ibadat* (rituals) and *Muamalat* (transactions). *Ibadat* is concerned with the practicalities of ways to perform rites and rituals and to understand and explain man's relationship with *Allah* (swt) and *Muamalat* is concerned with the practicalities of day-to-day life by defining the rules governing social, political, and economic activities. As a result, a significant subset of *Muamalat* defines the conduct of economic activities within the economic system, which ultimately lays down the rules for commercial, financial and banking systems.

Although the *Quran* and the *Sunnah* are the primary sources of the *Shariah*, *Ijtihad* (from the same root as *Jihad*) plays a critical role. *Ijtihad* refers to the efforts of individual jurists to extract solutions to problems and is the vehicle by which rules of behavior not explicitly addressed to problems that arise as human societies evolve are determined. *Ijtihad* is exercised through the earlier consensus of jurists (*Ijma*), anology (*qiyas*), judicial preference (*istihsan*), public interest (*maslaha*), and customs (*urf*). Secondary sources of the *Shariah* have to satisfy the condition that they do not introduce any rules that are in conflict with the main tenets of Islam.

(i)   *Ijma*, meaning in-agreement or consensus, refers to a group having or holding the same opinion.

(ii) *Qiyas* or analogical reasoning is a method of forming legal opinion or precedent for a situation or incident for which there is no direct ruling in the primary sources of Law, i.e., *Quran*, *Sunnah*, and *Ijma*, by drawing similarities with another or earlier situation or incident, which is clear according to these sources.

(iii) *Al-Istihsan* or juristic preference applies where a *mujtahid* prefers one alternative to another, although the former may not have an explicit argument in its favor.

(iv) *Al-Masalaha*, literally means "to bring about utility and fend off damage or injury for public good."

Over the course of history, different theories of interpreting and formulating the *Shariah* have evolved depending upon different approaches and schools of thought. These approaches, or methods (*Madhahib*), are ways of describing belief, religious practices and laws within a certain framework. The most commonly practiced methods are *Hanafi, Maliki, Shafi'i, Hanbali,* and *Jafari.* The difference between the schools of thought is primarily due to the way each source of Law, i.e., the *Quran,* the *Sunnah, Ijma',* and *Qiyas* are assigned different weights in decision-making. For example, the *Jafari madhhab* does not accept analogical reasoning (*qiyas*) in its entirety as a legitimate method to derive rules of *Shariah.* Moreover, this school of thought greatly emphasizes the principle of *Ijtihad* (expert investigation and provision of solutions to new problems arising from the dynamic nature embedded in the evolutionary process of human society by jurists).

The *Shariah* is the guide for human action, which encompasses every aspect of human life and, hence, sanctifies and gives religious significance to activities that may appear mundane. This blueprint for an ideal life operationalizes the understanding of the Divine Will in terms of human action by providing a scale by which actions can be measured in accordance with their correspondence with the Will of *Allah* (swt). Hence, all human actions are valued in terms of the weight of their merits and demerits through their classification into the five categories of obligatory, recommended, indifferent, reprehensible, and forbidden. Through this scale of valuation, the worth of and the return for/on human acts or actions are defined, so that man can distinguish between the "straight path" and those which will lead him astray. It is then through the exercise of the individual free will that the individual chooses the path to follow.

The *Shariah* consists of constitutive and regulative rules. Individual Muslims, as well as their collectivity, must conduct their affairs in accordance with these rules. In Islam, the basic source of the Law is the *Quran.* The central reality of the *Quran* in the life of Islam and its influence upon the life of individual Muslims cannot be overemphasized. It includes all the necessary constitutive rules of the Law as "guidance for mankind." It, however, contains many universal statements that needed further explanation before they could become specific guides for human action.

The principles enunciated in the *Quran* were explained, amplified, practiced, and exemplified by the Prophet (*pbuh*), who is considered a symbol of the perfection of the human person; the best prototype and the "best model."[12] The Prophet (*pbuh*) participated in social life in its fullest possible sense and demonstrated how life, in all its dimensions, can be integrated into a spiritual center. His career, so intently devoted to the construction of the Islamic community, exemplifies the *Quranic* concepts of *Allah*'s Will and man's duties. His personality, actions, and sayings, which are closely bound to the *Quran*, leave an indelible mark on the consciousness of the individual Muslim. Hence, after the *Quran*, the Prophet's sayings, and his actions are the most important sources of the Law and a fountainhead of Islamic life and thought.

Compliance with the rules of the *Shariah* is essential for the preservation of the community and this is ensured by two factors. Firstly, the behavior of the individual being constrained by the duty of adherence to the binding norms of the socio-economic order. Secondly, by the coercion exercised by the collectivity. The rules deal with:

- the individuals' body and their state of consciousness
- governing individuals' relationships with other members of the society
- guiding individuals' relationship with the collectivity, and
- the code of conduct necessary for the community as a whole.

One of the critical implications of *Shariah* rules governing the economic system is that each and every activity of an economic agent implicitly and indirectly finds its roots in the greater scheme of things between man and the Creator. Consequently, this link gives high priority to applying morality and ethics vigorously in all business and commercial matters.

The *Shariah* rules are derived through a rigorous process of investigation and thinking across time and geographical regions. The expansion of the rules of Law and their extension to new situations, resulting from the growth and progress of the Islamic community, is accomplished with the help of consensus in the community, analogical reasoning — which derives rules by discerning an analogy between new problems and those existing in the primary sources — and through independent human reasoning of those specialized in the Law. As a result, *Shariah* is invested with great flexibility in handling problems in diverse situations, customs, and societies and therefore has a wide-range of solutions and precedents, depending on different circumstances.

History has *not* recorded instances when Muslim jurists were unable to provide Islamic solutions to new problems. Their opinions covered all aspects of life. They laid down brilliant theories, exemplary rules and solutions. Unfortunately, however, with the decline of Islamic rule in Muslim countries, the significance of the *Shariah* in running day-to-day life also declined. Gradually, civil and commercial law based on French, Italian or British Law was adopted — a practice still in effect in almost every Muslim country. During this period, development of the *Shariah* remained dormant. In the last few decades, however, the reawakening among Muslims has generated enormous demands for the development of *Shariah*-based rules addressed to the problems of modern society.

A Case for Islamic Economic and Financial Systems

Given our understanding of the role of institutions, rules, Law (*Shariah*) and the ideology of Islam, one can make the following propositions regarding the economic system: (Core principles of Islamic economics are discussed in detail in Chapter 2)

- Islam has a view on how to organize political, social, and economic systems based on a set of ontological and epistemological propositions regarding individuals and their collectivities.
- Defining an economic system as a collection of institutions dealing with production, exchange, distribution and redistribution and defining institutions as defined by Douglas North as rules and norms, Islam proposes a distinct economic system that differs in many important respects from those recommended by other schools of thought regarding how an economy is to be organized.
- The behavioral rules and norms of an Islamic system — once clearly, rigorously, and analytically articulated in a way intelligible to economists — can yield empirically testable propositions which, in turn, could lead to policy analysis and recommendation on solutions to the problems of modern societies.

There is a consensus among Islamic scholars on the objective of Islam for the economy, on the sources, i.e., *Shariah*, and on the idea that Islamic economics is capable of providing a paradigm different from traditional economics. They believe that such an Islamic economic paradigm be successfully constructed to propose solutions to society's problems — such as distorted income distribution, external diseconomies accompanying growth, unemployment and poverty, environmental problems.

The paradigm shift advocated by the Islamic economics system in its teachings challenges the conventional thinking in several areas, such as following:

(a)   There is no doubt that the foremost priority of Islam and its teachings on economics is about "**Justice and Equity**." The notion of justice and equity from production to distribution is embedded deep in the system. As an aspect of justice, social justice in Islam consists of the creation and provision of equal opportunities and the removal of obstacles equally for every member of the society. Legal justice, too, can be interpreted as meaning that all members of the society have equal status before the Law, equal protection of the Law, and equal opportunity under the Law. The notion of economic justice, and its attendant concept of distributive justice, as an aspect of the overall principle of justice in Islam, is particularly important as an identifying characteristic of the Islamic economic system, because the latter's rules governing permissible and forbidden economic behavior on the part of the consumers, producers, and government, as well as questions of property rights and of production and distribution of wealth, are all based on the fundamental Islamic concept of justice.

(b)   The Islamic paradigm incorporates a spiritual and moral framework that values human relations above material possessions. In this way, it is concerned about not only the material needs but also about establishing a balance between material and spiritual fulfillment of the human being.

(c)   The Islamic system creates a balanced relationship between the individual and the society. Self-interest and private gains of the individual are not denied, but they are regulated for the larger betterment of the collectivity.

(d)   The individual's pursuit of maximum profit in enterprise and maximum satisfaction in consumption are not the sole objectives of society and any wasteful consumption is discouraged.

(e)   Recognition and the protection of property rights of all members of the society is the foundation of a stakeholder-oriented society, preserving the rights of all and reminding them of their responsibilities.

In addition to the abovementioned characteristics, Islam's unconditional prohibition of *Riba* (interest) (discussed in detail in Chapter 3) changes the landscape of the Islamic financial system. Prohibition of interest by Islam is actually an indirect prohibition of pure debt security. Instead of debt, other modes of financing based on the principle of sharing of profit and loss are recommended. The desire to eliminate interest and the promotion of risk-sharing modes of financing are the rationale behind Islamic banking practiced today. While acknowledging the expressions of skepticism, and even cynicism, regarding the present practices of Islamic banking, it can be reasonably hypothesized that there is a consensus among scholars on two fundamental propositions regarding the Islamic financial system: (i) interest is *Riba*, and (ii) risk- and profit-sharing is the Islamic alternative.

As soon as there was a mention of a system operating without the notion of interest and debt, the challenge came from Western analysts who suggested the folly of adopting such a system. Here, we summarize their arguments in six propositions:

1.   Zero interest means infinite demand for loanable funds and zero supply;
2.   Such a system would be incapable of equilibrating demand for and supply of loanable funds;
3.   Zero interest rate means no savings;
4.   Zero interest rate means no investment and no growth;
5.   In this system, there could be no monetary policy, since no instruments of liquidity management could exist without a fixed pre-determined rate of interest; and, finally,
6.   In conclusion zero interest means a one-way flight of capital.

By 1988, this challenge was met when research, using modern analytical financial and economic theory, showed the following:

- A modern financial system can be designed without the need for an *ex ante* determined positive nominal fixed interest rate. In fact, it was shown by Western researchers that there was no satisfactory theory that could explain the existence of a positive nominal *ex ante* interest rate;
- Moreover, it was shown that not assuming a nominal fixed *ex ante* positive interest rate, i.e., no debt contract, did not necessarily mean that there would have to be zero return on capital;
- The basic proposition of Islamic finance was that the return on capital would be determined *ex post*, and that the magnitude of the return on capital was determined on the basis of the return to the economic activity in which the funds were employed;
- It was the expected return that determined investment;
- It was also the expected rate of return, and income, which determined savings. Therefore, there is no justification for assuming that in such a system there would be no savings and investment;
- It was shown that in such a system there would be positive growth;

- That monetary policy in such a system would function as in the conventional system, its efficacy depending on the availability of instruments which could be designed to manage liquidity;
- Finally, it was shown that, in an open-economy macroeconomic model without an *ex ante* fixed interest rate, but with returns to investment determined *ex post*, there was no justification to assume that there would be a one-way flight of capital.

Therefore, the system which prohibited a fixed *ex ante* interest rate and allowed the rate of return on capital to be determined *ex post*, based on the returns to the economic activity in which the funds were employed, was theoretically viable.

In the process of demonstrating the analytical viability of such a system, research also clearly differentiated it from the conventional system. In the conventional system, based on debt contracts, risks and rewards are shared asymmetrically, with the debtor carrying the greatest part of the risk, and with governments enforcing the contract. Such a system has a built-in incentive structure that promotes a moral hazard and asymmetric information and requires close monitoring. Costs can be managed if monitoring is delegated to an institution acting on behalf of the collectivity of depositors/investors; hence the reason for the existence of banking institutions.

In the late 1970s–early 1980s, it was shown, mostly by *Minsky*, that such a system was inherently prone to instability because there would always be maturity mismatch between liabilities (short-term deposits) and assets (long-term investments). Because the nominal values of liabilities were guaranteed, but not the nominal values of assets; when the maturity mismatch became a problem, banks would go into liability management mode by offering higher interest rates to attract more deposits. There was always the possibility that this process would not be sustainable, resulting in an erosion in confidence and runs on banks. Such a system, therefore, needed a "lender of last resort" and bankruptcy procedures, restructuring processes, and debt workout procedures to mitigate the contagion.

During the 1950s–60s, *Lloyd Metzler* of the University of Chicago had proposed an alternative system in which contracts were based on equity rather than debt, and in which there was no guarantee of nominal values of liabilities since these were tied to the nominal values of assets. *Metzler* showed that such a system did not have the instability characteristic of the conventional banking system. In 1985, in his now classic article in the IMF staff papers, *Mohsin Khan* showed the affinity of *Metzler's* model with Islamic finance. Using *Metzler's* basic model, *Mohsin Khan* demonstrated that this system is more stable than the conventional system.

By the early 1990s, it was clear that an Islamic financial system was not only theoretically viable, but also had desirable characteristics that rendered it superior to a debt-based conventional system. The phenomenal growth of Islamic finance during the 1990s demonstrated the empirical and practical viability of the system.

The crises we have been witnessing in the international financial system since 1997 have set the stage for Islamic finance to demonstrate its viability as potentially a genuine alternative global financial system. The present international system is deficient in many ways, of which the two most important are:

- A debt-based system needs an effective lender of last resort, and the present international financial system does not have one and it is not likely that one will emerge anytime soon; and
- A debt-based system needs bankruptcy proceedings, debt restructuring, and workout mechanisms and processes that the present international financial system lacks. There are preliminary discussions underway for an international **sovereign debt restructuring mechanism** to be established, but there are many complications. While such a mechanism, if and when it comes into being, will help reduce the risk of moral hazard and lead to better distribution of risk, it will not address the inherent and fundamental fragility of a system largely based on debt contracts.

Meanwhile, there is no guarantee that the international financial system has witnessed its last crises with huge domestic costs that, at times, have threatened the foundation of societies. For example, Indonesia; it took this country 25 years to reduce poverty by 50%, but it took a year of severe financial crisis to wipe out most of this gain. Countries with an otherwise viable economic system have paid dearly because of the crises generated by a debt structure whose nominal values and maturities were out of line with the ability of the economic structure to service them.

There are many analyses of financial crises and a long list of their causes, but surprisingly, little is said about the one underlying common denominator of all of them: debt contracts that are by nature out of sync with, and unrelated to, the income flows that the underlying productive and capital assets of these countries can generate to serve them. There is still debate on the reasons why Malaysia did not suffer from the contagion as much as the other crisis countries. While capital controls may have played a role, some analysts believe its liability structure and its general reliance on non-debt-creating flows made Malaysia less vulnerable to the crisis.

While the financial innovations of the 1990s in the conventional system have led to a mobilization of financial resources in astronomical proportions, they have also led to the equally impressive growth of debt contracts and instruments. According to the latest reports, there are now US$32 trillion of sovereign and corporate bonds alone. Compare this (plus all other forms of debt, including consumer debt in industrial countries) to the production and capital base of the global economy and one observes an inverted pyramid of huge debt piled up on a narrow production base that is supposed to generate the income flows that are to service this debt. In short, this growth in debt has nearly severed the relationship between finance and production. Analysts are now worried about a "debt bubble." For each dollar worth of production there are thousands of dollars of debt claims. An Islamic financial system has the potential to redress this serious threat to global financial stability because of its fundamental operating principle of a close link between financial and productive flows and because of its requirement of risk sharing.

The IMF currently advises developing countries to ensure the following:

- They should avoid debt-creating flows;
- They should rely mostly on Foreign Direct Investment (FDI);
- If they have to borrow, they should ensure that their debt obligations are not bunched toward the short end of maturities;
- If they have to borrow, they should ensure that their economy is producing enough primary surplus to meet their debt obligations;
- They should ensure that their sovereign bonds incorporate clauses (such as majority action clause, engagement clause, initiation clause) that make debt workout and restructuring easier. That is, to make sure that there exists better risk-sharing mechanisms to avoid the moral hazard; and finally,
- They should put in place an efficient debt management structure.

As this architecture emerges, Islamic finance has to develop its own genuinely Islamic financial instruments. So far, we have been "free riding" on financial theories and instruments developed within the context of the conventional debt-and-interest-based system. Unless Islamic finance develops its own genuinely Islamic financial instruments, it cannot achieve the dynamism of a system that provides the security, liquidity, and diversity needed for a globally accepted financial system, which would be a genuine alternative to the present debt-interest-based international financial system.

Unfortunately, there is, at present, nothing in the Muslim world that resembles large endowment institutions, such as the National Science Foundation, the Ford Foundation, and the Rockefeller Foundation, to support research in Islamic banking, finance, and economics. There is, therefore, an urgent need for scholarly foundations, institutions, colleges, and universities that can train Islamic financial engineers in economic and financial theory and methods, on the one hand, and Islamic *Shariah*, on the other.

Islamic finance possesses the basic instruments that can be channelled into creating a wide, and varied menu of financial instruments. There is a theory developed in the 1980s referred to as the spanning theory, which asserts that if there is one basic financial instrument it can be spanned into an infinite number of instruments. Islamic finance has at least 14 basic instruments and financial experts can span these into a much larger menu to provide greater security, liquidity, and diversity to meet the demand of investors on a global scale. To reiterate, there is an urgent need for rich endowments to be established solely for the purpose of financially supporting institutions that can train the kind of research scholars and experts mentioned.

Let us conclude by mentioning a very important function of Islamic finance that is seldom noted: it is the ability of Islamic finance to provide the vehicle for financial and economic empowerment. For example, the Agricultural Development Bank of Iran, through partnerships with farmers, helps them to convert their physical possessions into assets that can generate additional capital. Similarly, Islamic finance can be used in other Muslim and developing countries to convert dead capital into income-generating assets to financially and economically empower the poor.

Modern History of Islamic Banking and Financial Services

Although Islam has provided a blueprint of how a society is to be organized and how the affairs of its members are to be conducted in accordance with its prescriptions, the system itself has not been applied in its entirety, with the exception of a brief period at the inception of Islam. The level of complexity in the economy at that time was relatively less, compared to the economies of modern times. As stated earlier, the business practices were conformed to the principles of Islam and the element of "interest" was minimized. Since the practice of "interest" was condemned by other major religions of the time as well and the institution of "interest" was yet to be developed, the need to be conscious of system-wide compatibility with

Islam was not felt on an urgent basis. Only in the recent decades when the element of "interest" became an integral part of the economy, were the Muslims prompted to be more conscious of the existence of "interest" and they also became more interested in society-wide implementation of Islamic teachings.

For the sake of minimizing the historical details, further discussion on the history of Islamic economics and finance is limited to the developments since the nineteenth century. One can divide the developments and efforts made toward implementing a *Shariah*-compliant economic, financial, and banking system into three phases; pre-1950, 1950–1990, and from 1990 to the present.

Phase I: Pre-1950

Throughout the nineteenth century and through a good part of the twentieth century, several Muslim countries were under colonial rule of different rulers. During the colonial period, these Muslim societies had considerably lost touch with their old values and heritage, including the belief in tradition and traditional practices. Old tradition was often given a low priority compared to the emerging values of the colonial powers, who were looked upon as the symbol of modern success. Although there is evidence of resistance to the imposition of colonial values and a desire to return to the Islamic tradition, such efforts were not widespread. It was only after the end of the colonial period that Muslims began to re-discover their identities and manifested the desire to regain the lost values in all aspects of life, especially concerning the economic system.

A formal critique and opposition to the element of "interest" started in Egypt in the late nineteenth century when Barclays Bank was established in Cairo to raise funds for the construction of the Suez Canal. The establishment of such an interest-based bank in a Muslim country evoked opposition from its inception. Further, a formal opposition to the institution of "interest" can be found as early as 1903 when the payment of interest on post office saving funds was declared contrary to Islamic values and therefore illegal by *Shariah* scholars in Egypt. In India, a minority community of Muslims in southern India took the first step toward their desire to pursue an Islamic mode of economic activities by establishing interest-free loans as early as in the 1890s. This was mainly a welfare association collecting donations and skins of animals sacrificed during festivals from the public and providing interest free loans to the poor. Another such institution called "*Anjuman Imdad-e-Bahmi Qardh Bila Sud*" (Interest Free Credit Society) was also established in Hyderabad in India in 1923.

During the first half of the twentieth century, there were several attempts to highlight the differences between the emerging conventional economic system and the areas where it conflicted with Islamic values. The need for an alternative economic system conforming to the principles of Islam soon came to the fore and economists began to lay out alternatives to the conventional banking system by exploring *Shariah*-compliant contracts, especially equity partnerships. Some of the early Muslim intellectuals and jurists (*fuqaha*) who made significant contributions in highlighting and realizing the need for an economic and banking system based on the tenets of Islam include Maulana Syed Abul Ala Maudoodi (Pakistan), Imam Muhammad Baqir al-Sadr (Iraq), Anwar Iqbal Qureshi (Pakistan), Mohammad Nejatullah Siddiqi (India), Muhammad Uzair (Saudi Arabia), Umer Chapra (Saudi Arabia), and Ahmad al-Najjar (Egypt).[13] By 1953, Islamic economists had offered the first description of an interest-free bank based on two-tier *Mudarabah* and *Wakala* (agency) basis. By the end of 1950s, Islamic scholars and economists started to offer theoretical models of financial intermediation as a substitute to interest-based banking.

Phase II: 1960s–1980s

By the start of the 1960s, there was enough demand for Shariah-compliant banking and it resulted in the establishment of the *Mit Ghamr* Local Savings Bank in Egypt in 1963 by the noted social activist Ahmad-al-Najjar. It is widely considered to be the first modern Islamic bank. *Mit Ghamr* bank borrowed some ideas from the German savings banks with the principle of rural banking within the general framework of Islamic values. Unfortunately, this experiment lasted for four years only. Around the same time, there were parallel efforts in Malaysia to develop a saving scheme for Muslims to perform the Pilgrimage. This effort was motivated by the idea that money saved for pilgrimage should be free of any contamination of "interest," since regular commercial banks were operating on the basis of interest. The Pilgrims' Savings Corporation was established in 1963, which was later incorporated into the Pilgrims' Management and Fund Board (popularly known a *Tabung Haji*) in 1969.

The Nasir Social Bank was established in Egypt in 1971 by a Presidential decree. It is the first example of state sponsorship in the establishment of an interest-free institution. The establishment of the Dubai Islamic Bank by some traders in 1975 is considered to be one of the earliest private initiatives in the U.A.E. The 1970s witnessed a rise in the price of oil leading to an accumulation of oil revenues in several oil-rich Muslim countries, especially in the Middle East. Oil revenues of the 1970s, sometimes referred to as

"Petro-dollars," offered strong incentives for creating suitable investment outlets for Muslims wanting to comply with the *Shariah*. Interest-free or Islamic banking, which was a conceptual idea by the early 1970s, found a strong business case to be explored further. This business opportunity was exploited by both domestic and international bankers, including some of the leading conventional banks.

In 1975, the Islamic Development Bank (IsDB) was established on the lines of regional development institutions with the objective of promoting economic development in Muslim countries as well as offering development finance according to the rules of the *Shariah*. The Jeddah-based IsDB has played a key role in expanding Islamic modes of financing and in undertaking valuable research in the area of Islamic economics, finance and banking. During the 1970s, the concept of a financial *Murabahah* (trust financing) was developed as the core mechanism for the placement of Islamic banks' funds. Academic and research activities were launched with the First International Conference on Islamic Economics, held in *Makkah*, Saudi Arabia in 1976. The first specialized research institution, namely, the Centre for Research in Islamic Economics was established at the King Abdul Aziz University of Jeddah, Saudi Arabia, in 1978.

The 1980s proved to be the beginning of a trend of rapid growth and expansion of an emerging Islamic financial services industry. This growth became steady through the 1990s. The major developments of the 1980s include continuation of serious research work at the conceptual and theoretical level, constitutional protection in three Muslim countries and the involvement of conventional bankers in offering *Shariah*-compliant services. The Islamic Republics of Iran, Pakistan and Sudan announced their intentions to transform their overall financial systems to make them compliant with the *Shariah*. Other countries such as Malaysia and Bahrain started Islamic banking within the framework of the existing system. The International Monetary Fund (IMF) initiated research in the macroeconomic implications of an economic system operating without the basis of interest. Similar research was conducted to understand the issues of profit–loss sharing contracts and the financial stability of a system based on the sharing of profit and loss. The significance and contribution of this research was recognized in 2004 when two IMF economists, Mohsin Khan and Abbad Mirakhor were awarded IsDB's highest prize in Islamic Economics. Organization of Islamic Countries (OIC) Fiqh Academy and other *Shariah* scholars engaged themselves in the discussions for reviewing financial transactions.

During the early stages of Islamic financial market growth in the 1980s, Islamic banks faced a dearth of quality investment opportunities, which created business opportunities for the conventional Western banks to act as

Table 1.2   Development of Islamic Economics and Finance in Modern History

Pre-1950s	• Barclays Bank opens its Cairo branch in the 1890s to process the financial transactions related to the construction of the Suez Canal. Islamic scholars challenge the operations of the bank, in relation to its dealings with interest. This critique also spreads to other Arab regions, and to the Indian sub-continent where there was a sizeable Muslim community. • Majority of *Shariah* scholars declare that interest in all its forms amounts to the prohibited element of *Riba*.
1950s–60s	• Initial theoretical work in Islamic economics begins. By 1953, Islamic economists offer the first description of an interest-free bank based either on two-tier *Mudaraba or Wakala basis*. • Mitghamir Bank in Egypt and Pilgrimage Fund in Malaysia are established.
1970s	• First Islamic commercial bank, Dubai Islamic Bank opens in 1974. • Islamic Development Bank (IsDB) is established in 1975. • Accumulation of oil revenues and Petro-dollars increases demand for *Shariah*-compliant products.
The 1980s	• Islamization of economies in Islamic Republics of Iran, Pakistan and Sudan where banking systems are converted to interest-free banking systems. • Increased demand attracts Western intermediation and institutions. • The Islamic Research and Training Institute (IRTI) is established by the Islamic Development Bank (IsDB) in 1981. • Countries like Bahrain and Malaysia promote Islamic banking parallel to the conventional banking system.
The 1990s	• Attention is paid to the need for accounting standards and regulatory frameworks. Accounting and Auditing Organization for Islamic Financial Institutions (AAOIFI) is established. • Islamic insurance (*Takaful*) is introduced. • Islamic Equity Funds are established. • Dow Jones Islamic Index and FTSE Index of *Shariah*-compatible stocks are developed.
2000–Recent	• Islamic Financial Services Board (IFSB) is established to deal with regulatory and supervisory, and corporate governance issues of the Islamic financial industry. • *Sukuks* (Islamic bonds) are launched.

Source: Khan (1996) and IDB (2005)

intermediaries to deploy Islamic banks' funds according to the guidelines given by the Islamic banks. Western banks helped Islamic banks place funds in commerce and trade-related activities by arranging a trader to buy goods on behalf of the Islamic bank and to resell them at a mark-up. Gradually, Western banks realized the importance of the emerging Islamic financial markets and started to offer Islamic products through "Islamic windows" in an attempt to attract the clients directly, without having an Islamic bank as intermediary. Islamic windows are not independent financial institutions, but are specialized set-ups within conventional financial institutions that offer *Shariah*-compliant products for their clients. Meanwhile, due to the growing demand for Shariah-compliant products and fear of losing depositors, non-Western conventional banks also started to offer "Islamic windows." In general, Islamic Windows are targeted at "high net-worth" individuals who represent the wealthiest segment of investors — who want to practice Islamic banking — approximately 1–2% of the world Muslim population.

The number of conventional banks offering "Islamic windows" is growing, as several leading conventional banks, such as the Hong Kong and Shanghai Banking Corporation (HSBC), are pursuing this market very aggressively. Citibank was one of the early Western banks to establish a separate Islamic bank — Citi Islamic Investment Bank (Bahrain) in 1996. More recently, another well-known Western bank, Union Bank of Switzerland (UBS), established Noriba Bank and the trend is followed by a number of Gulf banks which are establishing Islamic subsidiaries. HSBC has a well-established network of banks in the Muslim world. With the objective of promoting Islamic asset securitization and private equity and banking in OECD countries, HSBC Global Islamic Finance (GIF) was launched in 1998. The list of Western banks keeping "Islamic windows" includes, among others, American Express Bank Ltd., American Bank, ANZ Grindlays, BNP-Paribas, Chase Manhattan, UBS, and Kleinwort Benson. The leading non-Western banks with a significant size of "Islamic windows" are National Commercial Bank of Saudi Arabia, United Bank of Kuwait, and Riyadh Bank.

Phase III: 1990s–Present

By the early 1990s, the market had gained enough momentum to attract the attention of public policy makers and of institutions interested in introducing innovative products. The following are some of the noteworthy developments:

- Recognizing the need for standards, a self-regulatory agency — Accounting and Auditing Organization for Islamic Financial Institutions (AAOIFI) was established. AAOIFI was instrumental in highlighting the special regulatory needs of Islamic financial institutions. AAOIFI was successful in defining accounting and Shariah standards which were adopted or recognized by several countries. However, with the growth of the market, the regulatory and supervisory authorities with the help of the IMF established a dedicated regulatory agency, the Islamic Financial Services Board (IFSB) in the early 2000s to address systemic stability and various governance and regulatory issues relating to the Islamic financial services industry. IFSB took on the challenge and started working in the area of regulation, risk management and corporate governance.
- Further progress was made in developing capital markets. Islamic asset-backed certificates, *Sukuks*, were introduced in the market. Different structures of *Sukuks* were launched successfully in Bahrain, Malaysia and other financial centers. Among the issuers were corporations, multilaterals and sovereign entities such as the Islamic Development Bank, the International Bank for Reconstruction and Development and the Governments of Bahrain, Qatar and the Islamic Republic of Pakistan. During the equities market boom of the 1990s, several equity funds based on *Shariah*-compatible stocks emerged. Dow Jones and *Financial Times* launched Islamic indices to track the performance of Islamic equity funds.

Several institutions were established to create and support a robust financial system. These institutions include the International Islamic Financial Market (IIFM), the International Islamic Rating Agency (IIRA), the General Council of Islamic Banks and Financial Institutions (CIBAFI) and the Arbitration and Reconciliation Centre for Islamic Financial Institutions (ARCIFI).

Endnotes

1 For example, see writings of Kuran, Timur (1995) "Islamic Economics and the Islamic subeconomy," *Journal of Economic Perspectives*, Fall 1995, 9:4, pp. 155–173.

2 Chapra, M. U. (2000), "The Future of Economics," The Islamic Foundation, UK.

3 The ultimate Creator (God) of all universes is named Allah in Islamic tradition. The term (swt) is abbreviation for *subhana-wa-ta'ala* meaning The Exalted One.

4 The term (*pbuh*) is an abbreviation invoking peace and blessings of *Allah* (swt) on the Prophet, asking that peace be upon him and is often stated after the name of the Prophet to show one's respect.

5 *Quran* (7:172).

6 Following are some of the verses emphasizing the principle of unity:

"And indeed this is my straight path therefore follow it — and do not follow other ways because that will lead to disunity amongst you" (6:153)

"Grab hold of the rope of Allah collectively and do not disunite" (3:103)

"Cooperate with one another unto righteousness and piety and do not cooperate with one another unto unrighteousness and enmity" (5:2)

7 *Quran* (50:16).

8 *Quran* (2:143, and 21:92).

9 *Quran* (3:104, 3:110).

10 *Quran* (2:141–143; 5:66; 6:42; 6:108; 7:164; 16:63; 40:5).

11 *Quran* (2:143).

12 *Quran* (33:21).

13 Ahmad Khurshid, "Islamic Finance and Banking: The Challenges and Prospects," *Review of Islamic Economics*, The Islamic Foundation, Leicester, UK. No 9, July 2000. p. 59.

CHAPTER

2

The Economic System

At the core of the Islamic economic system lies a body of immutable rules, defined by the *Shariah*, which affect economic behavior and outcomes and which are both time-and-place-invariant. On the periphery of the system, there are rules which impact economic behavior, but which are subject to change depending on the circumstances. These latter are results of decisions taken by legitimate authorities in an Islamic society in pursuit of policies, e.g., deliberate interventions in economic affairs, to further their aims. These policies and actions taken in pursuit of specific objectives, must, nonetheless, be *Shariah*-compatible. While Islamic economic systems adopted in various localities may vary with respect to these peripheral economic rules and institutions, they cannot differ with respect to their core rules and institutions. For example, while one Islamic country may differ from another with respect to its foreign trade policies, the institution of inheritance cannot be totally different from one Islamic society or country to another.

To understand the economic system of Islam, we need to discuss some of its key characteristics. Before that, however, a general statement regarding the Islamic economy is necessary. It can be categorically stated that Islam requires, as one of its specific objectives, a "healthy," dynamic, and growth-oriented economy, without which the higher aims of Islam cannot be accomplished. A dynamic and growing economy is considered "healthy," only when its rules, institutions, organizations and their operations, as well as the behavior of the individual and the collectivity, are in conformity with the *Shariah*.

An economic system is a collection of institutions set up by society to deal with allocation of resources, production and exchange of goods and services, and distribution of the resulting income and wealth. What has been said can be directly applied to Islam with only a single exception, i.e., instead of the word "society" in the definition of an economic system, we insert the words "the Law-Giver" to have a definition for an Islamic economic system as:

> "… a collection of institution, i.e., formal and informal rules of conduct and their enforcement characteristics, designed by the Law-Giver, i.e., *Allah* (swt) through the rules prescribed in the *Quran*, operationalized by the *Sunnah* of the Prophet (*pbuh*) and extended to new situations by *ijtihad* — to deal with allocation of scarce resources, production and exchange of goods and services and distribution of resulting income and wealth."

Core Principles of the Islamic Economic System

(i) Property Rights

The conventional definition of the word "property" is that it is a bundle of rights, duties, powers, and liabilities with respect to an asset. In most societies, this bundle buttresses the economy. Private property, in the Western conception, is the right of the individual to use, enjoy, and dispose of material things and exclude others from their use or enjoyment. The notion of property is two-fold, which suggests that the right to private property is the right of the individual to exclude others, while the right to common property is the right of the individual not to be excluded by others, from the use and enjoyment of an asset.

Perhaps the most significant characteristic of the Western conception of private property is that it is interpreted to mean the exclusive and inalienable right of disposing of the property. This notion is considered to be a matter of course to such an extent, that it may be surprising to realize that this narrow conception of private property right is a relatively recent development, only a few centuries old. Before the market society came to prevail in the West, a great part of the property right in land and other assets was a right to use and enjoy the asset, but not a right to dispose of it. For example, the right to use or enjoy the revenue from a parcel of land, a corporate charter or a monopoly granted by the State did not carry with it the right of disposing of the property. The development of the market society necessitated a revision of this notion of property, since it was thought that the right not to be excluded from the use or enjoyment of something was not marketable. It was deemed impossible to reconcile this particular right with a full market economy. Hence, of the two earlier kinds of property rights — the right to exclude others and the right not to be excluded by others — the second was abandoned and the conception of the right to property was narrowed to cover only the right to exclude others. In Islam, however, this right is retained without in any way diminishing the role of the market as a resource-allocating and impulse-transmitting mechanism.

The first basic principle of property in Islam is that *Allah* (swt) is the ultimate owner of all property. In order that man becomes materially able to perform his duties and obligations, he has been given the right of possession. The second principle of property, therefore, establishes the right of the collectivity to the resources at man's disposal. Based on the principle of justice, and the recognition of man's natural tendencies, rights, and obligations, individuals are allowed to appropriate the products resulting from the combination of their labor and some of these resources — without the collectivity losing its original rights, either to the resources or to the products resulting from the individual's creative labor applied to these resources — in accordance with the rules specified by the *Shariah*. In addition, the *Shariah* determines which natural resources will be retained as the exclusive property of the collectivity and which resources — and in what proportions — will be at the disposal of individual members of the society.

The second principle relates to the connection between laboring and owning, which is central in Islam. This principle recognizes two ways in which an individual can obtain rights to property: (i) through his own creative labor and/or (ii) through transfer — via exchange, contract, grants, or inheritance — of property rights from another individual who has gained title to the property or asset through *his* own labor. Work, therefore, is the basis of acquisition of right to property. Work, however, is not only performed for the purpose of satisfaction of needs and wants, but it is considered a duty and an obligation required from every member of the society. Similarly, the use of natural resources for producing goods and services for the society is also everyone's right and obligation. So long as the person has the ability, they have both the right and the obligation to apply their creative labor to resources. But if they lack the ability, they no longer have an obligation to work and produce, but their right to resources is retained. This constitutes the third principle and is referred to as the principle of "invariance of ownership."[1]

Before any work is performed on or with natural resources, all members of the society have equal rights to these resources. However, when individuals apply their creative labor to these resources, they gain a right of priority in the use and enjoyment of the resulting product, without the rights of others being nullified. The right of the collectivity to the property is protected by the *Shariah* through the limitations imposed on the right of disposing of the property by the person who has gained priority in the use and enjoyment of that property. Hence, while the right of use and enjoyment of the property is affirmed by the *Shariah*, the exclusive and absolute right of disposing of the property is rejected.

(ii) Property Obligations

The *Shariah* outlines private property obligations concomitant with property rights. Among the obligations is, first, the responsibility of sharing — the proceeds in monetary terms if the product is sold and an income is earned, sharing in the use otherwise — and, secondly, the obligation, severely incumbent upon the individual, not to waste, destroy, squander, or to use the property for purposes not permitted by the *Shariah*. To do so would be to transgress the limits set on one's rights and an encroachment on the rights of the collectivity. This position of the *Shariah* is in conformity with the Islamic conception of justice and the rights and responsibilities of the individual and the community.

Islam recognizes that the Divine Providence has endowed individuals with unique and unequal abilities and that some individuals have greater mental and/or physical capacities and consequently, are capable of obtaining title to a larger amount of property and assets. But this only means that such individuals' responsibilities and obligations are greater than those of others. However, once these individuals have discharged their duties of sharing, in accordance with prescribed manner and in the prescribed amount, and provided they are not in violation of the rules of *Shariah*, their rights to their possessions are held inviolate and no one has any right to force appropriation (or expropriation) of that person's property to anyone else. This right is held so sacred that even when rules had to be developed for emergency case of expropriation for projects of public utility it was called "legitimate violation" (*ikrah hukmi*). Even in this case, such actions could be taken only after adequate compensation was paid to the owner of the property. To violate the legitimate property rights of a person is considered to be "oppression" and "exploitation," just as there is "discord and corruption on earth" when individuals do not discharge their private property obligations.

While the individual's right to property affirms the natural tendency in man to possess — particularly something resulting from his own creative labor — the concomitant private property obligations, from the point of view of justice, are designed to give effect to the interdependence of the members of the community, with a view to recognizing explicitly that they cannot live in isolation. The private property obligations, therefore, reject the notion that a person does no harm to members of his group if as a result of his effort he is better off and others are no worse off than they would otherwise be. These obligations write the principle of sharing into the delineation of interests in property and consider private ownership subject to a trust, or a duty, in order to effect sharing. Hence, private initiative, choice, and reward are recognized in Islam in its conception of property rights, but such recognition is not allowed to subvert the property obligation principle of sharing or to lead to violations of the rights of the community. If, as a result of the growth of the society, division of labor, or increasing complexities of markets, either the obligation to share is shirked or the rights of the society and the cohesion of the community are undermined, an intervention by the legitimate authority to take corrective measures would be deemed justified.

(iii) Contracts

In any economic system, individuals not only make choices for themselves, but they also interact with other members of the society through transactions facilitated by explicit and implicit contracts entered into within the bounds specified by the institutional setting of the society. A contract is a time-bound instrument with an objective. The contract stipulates the obligations that each party is expected to fulfill in order to achieve the objectives of the contract.

The concept of contracts in Islam is not only important in the legal aspect of exchange, as an institution necessary for the satisfaction of legitimate human needs, but it is also a concept upon which the *Shariah* is based. The whole fabric of the Divine Law is contractual in its conception, content and application. The foundation of the *Shariah* is the covenant between *Allah* (swt) and man, which imposes on man the duty of being faithful to his word. On *Allah*'s side, the *Quran* often states that "*Allah* (swt) will not fail in His Promise."

Muslims are constantly reminded of the importance of contractual agreement, as they are required by their faith to honor their contracts. In a very terse, direct, and forceful verse, the *Quran* exhorts "O you who believe, fulfill contracts." The Prophet (*pbuh*) also said, "Muslims honor their covenants." The *Quran* directs Muslims to reduce their contracts to writing and have witnesses to the conclusion of their agreements. The purpose of documenting a contract is to clear any misunderstanding or ambiguity about the responsibilities of the parties to the contract. This also ensures that all parties to the contract have full knowledge of what they are committing to and what their respective responsibilities would be. *Shariah* scholars often point out that one of the reasons why the Islamic system of *mu'amalat* (transactions) is so highly articulated is that it is based on solid principles of contracts and the rights and obligations of the parties to the contract. The dynamic of contracts and the process of *ijtihad* inherent to *Shariah* have ensured that Muslim jurists continue to comment and build upon the theoretical constructs.

Throughout the legal and intellectual history of Islam, a body of rules constituting a general theory of contracts — with explicit emphasis on specific contracts, such as sales, lease, hire, and partnerships — was formulated on the basis of the *Shariah*. Contracts are considered binding, and their terms are protected by the *Shariah*, no less securely than the institution of property. This body of rules established the principle that, in matters of civil and economic dealings, any agreement not specifically prohibited by the *Shariah* is valid and binding on the parties and can be enforced by the courts, which treat the parties to a contract as complete equals.

The freedom to enter into contracts and the obligation to remain faithful to their stipulations have been emphasized in Islam so that a characteristic which distinguishes a Muslim is considered to be his faithfulness to the terms of his contracts. The maxim that "Muslims are bound by their stipulations" is a traditional rule, the importance of which is recognized by all schools of Islamic thought.

(iv) Trust

Trust is considered the most important element of social capital in Islam and the cornerstone of the relationship of individuals with *Allah* (swt) and with others in society. Islam places a strong emphasis on trust and considers being trustworthy as an obligatory personality trait. The root of the word "belief" — *Iman* — is the same as that of trust — *Amanah*. Moreover, abiding by one's contracts and remaining faithful to promises with other members of the society derives from the need to remain faithful to the original, primordial covenant between human beings and *Allah* (swt), as stated in the *Quran* (7:172). Accordingly, the *Quran*, in a number of verses, insists that a strong signal of true belief is faithfulness to contracts and promises made. Moreover, the *Quran* makes clear that performing the obligations one has contracted or promised is mandatory for a believer. Indeed, fidelity to one's promises and to the terms of contracts one enters into, as well as maintaining trust, are considered important characteristics of a true believer.

In the chapter of the "Faithful" — Chapter 23, Verses 1-8 — keeping trust and promises are two of the major characteristics of the faithful. In the first verse of Chapter 5 of the *Quran*, the faithful are ordered to abide by the terms of contracts that they have entered into. Similarly, in Verse 34 of Chapter 17, the faithful are commanded to keep their promises, for they will be asked about their faithfulness to their promises. There are other verses of the *Quran* that emphasize the duty of the faithful to remain fully conscious of *Allah* (swt) while entering into a contract or making promises, or being trustworthy when they are entrusted with objects for safekeeping (see, for example, Verse 58 and Verse 283 of Chapter 2). The *Quran* also identifies a chief characteristic of prophets and messengers of *Allah* (swt) as trustworthiness (for example, see Chapter 42; Verses 107, 125, 143, 162, 178, 193) and deprecates betrayal of trust (see Chapter 8, Verse 58 and Chapter 12, Verse 52). In short, Islam has made trust and trustworthiness — as well as keeping faith with contracts and promises — obligatory and has rendered them inviolable, except in the event of an explicitly permissible justification.

The life of the Prophet (*pbuh*) is a shining illustration of the implementation of guidance of *Allah* (swt) in maintaining trust and remaining trustworthy in his own life, both individually and within the community. Regarded as eminently trustworthy even before his divine appointment, the community conferred upon him the title of *Al-Ameen* (Trustworthy). The Prophet expended a great deal of effort, from his divine appointment until his passing, in modifying when possible and changing when necessary, the behavior of the members of community toward trustworthiness. There are numerous statements, actions, and circumstances attributed to him in which trust was the preeminent concern. For example, in a few short, but significant statements, (quotations from Payandeh, 1984), he declares:

"The person who is not trustworthy has no faith, and the person who breaks his promises has no religion;"

"Maintaining promises perfectly is a sign of faith;"

"There are three (injunctions) that no one is allowed to violate: treating parents kindly regardless of being Muslim or non-believer; keeping a promise whether to a Muslim or to a non-believer, and returning what is entrusted for safekeeping — regardless of whether the person entrusting is a Muslim or a non-believer;"

"Return what is placed in your trust for safekeeping to the person who has trusted you and do not betray even the one who has betrayed you;"

Finally, he (*pbuh*) specifies the chief characteristics of hypocrites as follows:

"Three (behavioral traits), if found in a person, then he is a hypocrite even if he fasts, prays, performs bigger and smaller pilgrimages, and says 'I am a Muslim:' when he talks, he lies; when he promises, he breaches; and, when trusted, he betrays."

In *Shariah*, the concept of justice, faithfulness (called *Amanah* whose antonym is *khayan* meaning betrayal, faithlessness, and treachery), reward and punishment are linked with the fulfillment of obligations incurred under the stipulations of the contract. Justice links man to *Allah* (swt) and to his fellow men. It is this bond that forms the contractual foundation of the *Shariah*, which judges the virtue of justice in man not only by his material performance, but also by the essential attribute of his intention (*niyya*) with which he enters into every contract. This intention consists of sincerity, truthfulness, and insistence on rigorous and loyal fulfillment of what he has consented to do (or not to do). This faithfulness to one's contractual obligations is so central to Islamic belief that when the Prophet was asked "who is the believer?," He replied that "a believer is a person in whom the people can trust their person and possessions." He is also reported to have said that "a person without trustworthiness is a person without religion." So basic is the notion of contracts in Islam that every public office is regarded, primarily, as a contract and an agreement which defines the rights and obligations of the parties. The highest temporal office, that of *khalīfa*, is inaugurated by "*mubāya'a*" which is a contract between the ruler and the Muslim community that he will be faithful in discharging of his duties.

(v) Individual Obligations, Rights and Self-interest

In Islam, human freedom is envisaged as a personal surrender to the Divine Will rather than an innate personal right. Man is ontologically dependent on *Allah* (swt) and can only receive what is given to him by the Source of his being. Human rights are a consequence of human obligations and not their antecedent. Man is charged with certain obligations toward his Creator, nature, himself, and other humans, all of which are outlined by the *Shariah*. When these obligations are fulfilled, certain rights and freedoms, which are also delineated by the *Shariah*, are gained. Limitations that are imposed by the *Shariah* on the rights and freedom of individual are in the direction of removing negative possibilities from human life. The obligations, rights, and limitations defined by the *Shariah* must be observed if the individual and the system are to have an Islamic identity.

Within the framework of the *Shariah*, and as a result of the Islamic conception of justice, individuals have natural rights that are guaranteed, among which is the right of the individuals to pursue their economic interests. Islam considers natural rights of the individual as the same rights granted to him by *Allah* (swt). Pursuing one's economic interests, within the framework of the *Shariah*, is first an obligation and a duty, then a right that no one can abrogate. So long as the individual has the ability, the obligation and the right pursue, economic interests are, concomitantly, extended to them. What is, however, significant is the fact that if power and ability to pursue one's economic interests are lacking, the obligation is no longer incumbent upon the person, even as their rights are still preserved. The right to economic benefits is never negated as a result of a lack of ability in the individual to undertake their duty of pursuing their economic interests. The potential right remains even if a person is unable to actualize it. Conversely, if the person is able but does not perform their obligations, their rights are also negated.

In Islam, contrary to popular opinion, self-interest is not negated. Islam, in fact, considers it a primary factor in its incentive-motivation system; a necessity in any organized society if the individual is to find it utility-maximizing to follow behavioral rules prescribed by the system. Provided that self-interest is defined to cover spiritual and temporal or temporary and eternal interests, there is not one rule in the *Shariah* that does not carry with it its own justification in terms of individual self-interest. It is for his own benefit, material and spiritual, in this world and for his ultimate salvation and felicity in the next, that the individual is invited to follow the rules of the *Shariah*. This is made clear by the *Quran* in which all injunctions are generally coupled with the assertion that compliance with them by the individual is for his own benefit. Often the incentives and the rewards for compliance and the retribution for non-compliance, both here and in the hereafter, are enumerated. It is in the context of the pursuit of self-interest that individual obligations and rights as well as the limits and accountabilities to these rights are specified by the *Shariah*.

(vi) Work

The concept of work in Islam (called *Al-Amal*) is far broader than, and has different characteristics and objectives than, those understood in the Western economic tradition. In Islam, the work ethic is defined by the *Quran* itself, which mentions the word *al-amal* (narrowly translated as work) in over 360 verses. A closely related concept of *al-fi'l* (also translated as work) is mentioned in an additional 109 verses. All these verses stress the need for work and action by human beings. It is because of this emphasis on work that Islam is considered "the ideology of practice and the practice of ideology" and "a religion of action." The *Quran* exalts work and raises it to the level of worship, and considers it as an inseparable dimension of faith itself. Conversely, it considers idleness — or squandering of time in pursuit of unproductive and non-beneficial work — as the manifestation of lack of faith and of unbelief.

Man is called upon to utilize time in pursuit of work by declaring that *Allah* (swt) has made the day as a means of seeking sustenance. A person who, through hard work seeks *Allah*'s "bounty" — which includes all appropriate means of earning one's livelihood — is most highly praised. All able-bodied persons are exhorted to work in order to earn their living. No one, who is physically and mentally able, is allowed to become a liability for one's family or for the State, through idleness and voluntary unemployment. The work which everyone is required to perform must be "good" or "beneficial" (*Al-Amal As-Sālih*), but no work is considered inconsequential in terms of its rewards or punishments in this world and in the next. One will have to reap whatever rewards or retributions are due as a result of his work.

Work, therefore, is regarded not only as a right, but also as a duty and an obligation. Hence, based on its notion of individual rights and responsibilities, Islam extends to the individual the right to choose the type of work they desire, but along with this freedom comes the obligation to consider the needs of the society as well as the selection of the type of work permitted by the *Shariah*.

Since all class distinctions are negated by Islam, no line of work permissible by the *Shariah* is considered demeaning by Islam, which countenances only diversification on the basis of natural talents, skills and technology — which are considered to be a grace or blessing (*fadl*) from *Allah* (swt) and which all Muslims are urged to acquire — or personal inclinations. Based on its concepts of justice and contracts, Islam makes it an obligation for the worker to perform the tasks, which he has contracted, to the best of his ability. But since individuals are endowed with different abilities and talents, this productivity will differ. Justice, however, demands that the return for every individual's work must be commensurate with his/her productivity.

While Islam, in no uncertain terms, has decried laziness, idleness, and socially unproductive work, it maintains that those who are physically or mentally unable to work still retain a right to what the society, individually and collectively, produces. This conclusion is based on the principle of invariant claim to ownership, which maintains that all human beings have a right to the resources which *Allah* (swt) has provided for mankind. Since the source of physical and mental abilities in human beings is also *Allah* (swt), due to which some members of the society are able to possess more than others, the right of ownership of those less able to the original resources remains valid. This follows from the fact that *Allah*'s (swt) original right of ownership of resources, which He has created, is not negated when they, along with the creative labor of individuals are transformed into products, property and wealth.

(vii) Wealth

Islam encourages man to utilize, to the fullest extent possible, all the resources that *Allah* (swt) has created and entrusted to man for his use. Non-utilization of these resources for his benefit, and for that of the society, is tantamount to ungratefulness to *Allah* (swt)'s provision of these resources. Wealth is considered an important means by which man can pave the way for the attainment of his ultimate objective. Islam refers to wealth as "good," an object of delight and pleasure and a support for the community. Conversely, involuntary poverty is considered to be undesirable and a basis of unbelief. This particular conception of wealth, however, is qualified in terms of the means employed in its earning, possession, and disposal.

Its "earning" is qualified through the emphasis that wealth is only a means for the achievement of man's ultimate objective and not an end in itself. It must be earned through "good," "productive," and "beneficial" work. This type of work is specified by the *Shariah*, which defines the methods of lawfully earning wealth. Not only are lawful methods of earning wealth specified, but the types of economic activity that are prohibited are also outlined. The *Shariah* specifies non-permissible professions, trade and economic activity, which may lead to unlawfully acquired wealth. Even within each profession, the *Shariah* specifies proper and improper practices. Just as wealth, rightfully earned and purposefully disposed of, is considered a blessing, wealth acquired or accumulated unlawfully for its own sake is condemned as "corruption" and retrogression to the basest of all human negative qualities, i.e., greed.

Islam regards wealth as the life-blood of the community, which must be constantly in circulation; therefore, its possession excludes the right of hoarding.[2] The implication is that wealth, lawfully earned, must be invested within the community to improve its economic well-being. Investing the wealth is not only measured by the monetary gain associated with it, but also by the benefits that accrue to the society. The needs of the society, therefore, must be a consideration for an owner of wealth.

Disposal of wealth is subject to the rules of the *Shariah* as well. The first and foremost among these rules is the recognition of the rights of others in this wealth resulting from the principle of invariant claim to ownership. Among these are levies whose amounts are specified and also those levies whose amounts are left to be determined by the wealth-owner. These levies fall due when wealth exceeds a specific minimum amount (called *Nisāb*). After these obligations are met, the remainder of wealth belongs to the owner, but it must be used in accordance with the rules of the *Shariah*. Among these are rules that forbid extravagance, opulence, waste, or general abuse of wealth. It cannot be used to harm others, or to acquire political power or to corrupt the polity.

While Islam treats wealth, lawfully acquired, possessed, and disposed of, to be sacred and subject to the protection of the *Shariah*, it regards the wealth-owner as a trustee who holds his wealth as a trust on behalf of *Allah* (swt) and the community. Hence, his inability to use his wealth properly provides the basis for the forfeiture of his right to his wealth. Extravagance, waste, and general abuse of wealth is the basis upon which the community can consider him a *safih*, a person of weak understanding, and one in possession of "weak intellect" and a person who, along with his own financial and a moral loss, is damaging the interests of the community. There is a principle *hajr,* according to which such a person's wealth is made the ward of the community, or of its legitimate representatives, who may limit his right to the use only of a part of his property to meet his basic needs. Therefore, only that wealth is considered "good" and a "support" for the community, in the attainment, possession, and disposal of which all rules of the *Shariah* are or have been observed.

(viii) The Concept of *Barakah*

An important aspect of the analysis of an economic system relates to the incentive-motivation structure which the system embodies. The purpose in considering this aspect is to determine whether or not an individual within the system will find it utility-maximizing to follow the behavior rules prescribed by the system. If the answer is in the affirmative, then the system as a whole will operate according to its rules. If the rules are not incentive-compatible, there will be deviations from its rules. The above presentation has described some of the key characteristics of the Islamic system as well as rules of behavior along with their accompanying incentive-motivation considerations, which Islam has provided for its followers. The incentive-motivation aspects of the system have their origin in the basis of belief in Islam, which considers adherence to its rules of behavior as primarily serving the best interests of the individual, both in this world and the next, as well as those of the society as a whole. Islam has provided these rules without negating either the drives or the self-interests of the individual. At the same time, its Law has provided methods and procedures whereby the interests of the community can be protected, should the individual feel it utility-maximizing to violate the rules and thereby damage the interests of the society.

An important factor in the incentive system of Islam is the concept of *barakah*, which serves as the material inducement for the individual to follow the path of proper conduct. This notion refers to an invisible "but material" blessing whose results can be observed by any believer who engages in righteous conduct. It encompasses the whole spectrum of man's conduct, including, most importantly, his economic behavior. The concept maintains that righteous conduct, i.e., behavior whose motivation and objective is to please *Allah* (swt), will have returns with an increasing rate. The more righteous the conduct, the greater is the presence of *barakah*. This concept asserts that expending one's wealth in the "cause of *Allah* (swt)" (without expecting a return from the receiver directly) will not lead to its diminution, but to its expansion. Such actions will, in fact, bring manifold returns to the giver. The concept establishes a positive correlation between the system's conduct and prosperity. It encourages Muslims to go beyond the minimum requirements of the *Shariah* in "pleasing *Allah* (swt)." The converse of the concept holds as well. That is, unrighteous conduct in earning, possessing, or disposing of wealth will rob its holder of its *barakah*. It not only applies to individual behavior, but also holds true for the community as a whole: "a society prospers if it preserves a keen perception of the Message (and acts according to its rules); its prosperity departs if it declines in morality (and acts against the rules of the *Shariah*)." Because the results of the operation of *barakah* are observable, it serves as an incentive for compliance with rules.

(ix) Risk Sharing

Another core principle of Islamic economics is the notion of risk-sharing. This is based on the principle of liability, which states that profit is justified on the basis of one's taking responsibility, possibly even becoming responsible for the loss and the consequences. This legal maxim, said to be derived from a saying of the Prophet (*pbuh*) that "profit comes with liability" implies that *Shariah* distinguishes lawful profit from all other forms of gain and one becomes entitled to profit only when one bears the liability, or risk, of loss.

(x) Competition and Cooperation

In the Islamic conception of man's ultimate end, economic life plays a purely instrumental role. Even in this role, economic affairs are meant only to provide the institutions and mechanisms needed for satisfying man's economic needs, as man's essence as the supreme creature of *Allah* (swt) is allowed to be manifested in this world. Thus, the economic system designed in accordance with the fundamental principles of Islam assures that man can exercise his eminent dignity, freedom, responsibilities and rights in the conduct of economic affairs. The economic system must be so ordered as not to assign to man a purely instrumental role in achieving the goals of the economy or the State. Islam seeks to guide man to direct individual action and responsible participation in economic affairs in a manner that commits him to community solidarity and cooperation, resulting in a dynamic and growing economy. Thus, the individual is made accountable for the moral effects of his social actions, including those in economic affairs, so that his own inner personal-spiritual transformation and growth is bound to the progress of the community.

Hence, Islam utilizes cooperation and competition in structuring the ideal society through harmonization and reconciliation between these two opposite, but equally primeval and useful forces at every level of social organization. From this perspective, one can argue that one of the greatest distinguishing characteristics of Islam is its forceful emphasis on the integration of human society as a necessary consequence of the unity of *Allah* (swt). To this end, the personality of the Prophet (*pbuh*) is inseparable from what the *Quran* considers as the optimal approach necessary for the emergence of solidarity in the human society. Every dimension of the personality of the Prophet (*pbuh*), manifested in his various social roles in the community, is directed toward maximum integration and harmony in the society. Moreover, every rule of behavior, including those in the economic area, is designed to aid the process of integration. Conversely, all prohibited practices are those, which, one way or another, lead to social disintegration.

The *Quran* and the traditions of the Prophet (*pbuh*) make clear references to the dual nature of competition and cooperation, that is, human beings can cooperate and compete for good or evil. It is this that leads to integration or disintegration of human society. The fundamental sources, however, emphasize that competition and cooperation must be utilized in probity and piety rather than in evil and enmity. Thus in Verse 2, Chapter 5, the *Quran* declares, "cooperate with one another unto righteousness and piety. Do not cooperate with one another unto sin and enmity." Similarly, Muslims are urged to compete with one another in beneficial and righteous deeds. There is no evidence in these sources that would allow suppression of one of these forces in favor of the other when they are used within the framework of the rules specified by the *Shariah*. Rather, all of the regulatory and supervisory authority invested in the legitimate political authority is directed toward a balanced and constructive utilization of these forces. The *Shariah* rules regarding the structure of the market and the behavior of market participants are an example of such balance. Although the rules of the *Shariah* regarding economic affairs demarcate limits and boundaries of desirable competitive and cooperative behavior necessary for the provision and preservation of the solidarity of society, the individual always remains the identifiable agent through whose action (and on whose behalf) all economic activities take place.

Economic Justice

A just economy is part of a just, healthy, and moral society, which is the central objective of Islam for the human collectivity. What underpins all the rules of behavior prescribed by Islam is its conception of justice, which maintains that all behavior, irrespective of its content and context, must, in its conception and commission, be based on just standards as defined by the *Shariah*. Islam considers an economy, in which the behavior of its agents is so conceived, as an enterprising, purposeful, prosperous, and sharing economy in which all members of society receive their just rewards. Such an economy is envisioned as one in which economic disparities that lead to social segmentation and divisiveness are conspicuously absent. Another important rule is the prohibition against taking (i.e., receiving) interest. This issue is covered in detail in a later chapter of this book.

Components of economic justice in an Islamic society are (i) equality of liberty and opportunity for all members of the society with respect to utilization of natural resources, (ii) justice in exchange, and (iii) distributive justice — all accomplished within the framework of the *Shariah*. In this conception, liberty means that a person is not prevented by others from combining his creative labor with resources which are designated by the *Shariah* for the use of the individual members of the society. Opportunity, on the other hand, represents a favorable conjunction of circumstances, which gives the individual the chance to try it. Whether one succeeds or not depends on one's efforts and abilities. This equality of opportunity must be secured deliberately by the collectivity. It not only denotes free and equal access to physical resources, but, generally, also extends to technology, education, and environmental resources. The basis for this equality of access to resources and equality of opportunity in their use is Islam's position that natural resources are not of human creation but are provided by *Allah* (swt) for all members of the society, therefore, liberty and opportunity to use these resources must be distributed equally to all. Even if the opportunity to use these resources is not available to some members of the society, either naturally or due to some other circumstances, their original claims to resources remain intact and are not nullified. They must be remunerated for these claims, at some point in time, by the other members who happen to have "or get" greater opportunity to use them.

The idea is that, by mixing their creative labor with resources, individuals create a claim of equity to the possession of the assets thus produced, by virtue of which they can participate in exchange. To allow exchange to take place on the basis of just standards, Islam places a great deal of emphasis on the market and its moral, just — and based on these two factors — its efficient operation. To assure justice in exchange, the *Shariah* has provided a network of ethical and moral rules of behavior, which cover, to the minutest detail, the behavior of all participants in the market. It requires that these norms and rules be internalized and adhered to by all participants before they enter the market. A market that operates on the basis of these rules, which are intended to remove all factors inimical to justice in exchange, yields prices for factors and products that are considered "fair" and "just." Unlike the scholastic notion of "just price," which lacks an operational definition, the Islamic concept of just price refers to the price prevailing as a result of interaction of economic forces operating in a market in which all rules of behavior specified by the *Shariah* are observed and adhered to by all participants. It is an *ex-post* concept meaning that a just price has been paid and received.

The rules governing exchange in the market cover *Shariah*-compatible sources of supply and demand for factors and products before they enter the market, Shariah-based behavior on the part of the buyers and sellers and a price-bargaining process free of factors prohibited by the *Shariah*. Hence, market imperfection refers to the existence of any factor considered non-permissible by the *Shariah*. The rules regarding supply and demand not only govern the permissibility of products demanded and supplied, but also look beyond these phenomena to their origin. Not all demands for products are considered legitimate, nor all acts of supplying products in the market, permissible. The means by which the purchasing power that gives effect to demand is obtained and the manner in which the production of commodities for their supply takes place, must have their origin based on just standards. Rules governing the behavior of participants in the market are designed to ensure a just exchange. The freedom of contract and the obligation to fulfill them, the consent of the parties to a transaction, non-interference with supplies before their entry into the market, full access to the market to all buyers and sellers, honesty in transactions, provision of full information regarding the quantity, quality, and the prices of the factors and products to buyers and sellers before the start of negotiation and bargaining and provision of full weights and measures, are prescribed. On the other hand, behaviors such as fraud, cheating, monopoly practices, coalitions, and combination of all types among buyers and sellers, underselling products, dumping actions, speculative hoarding, and bidding-up of prices without the intention to purchase are forbidden. All in all, any form of behavior leading to the creation of instantaneous property rights without a commensurate equity created by work, is forbidden. A market in which all these conditions are fulfilled, produces fair and just prices for the factors and products, which are just or equitable not on any independent criterion of justice, but because they are the result of bargaining between or among equal, informed, free, and responsible men.

Islam's emphasis on moral and just conduct in the market place is remarkable in its vigor. A producer or a businessman whose behavior complies with Islamic rules is said to be like the prophets, martyrs, and the truthful friends of *Allah* (swt). He is ranked with the prophets because he, like the prophets, follows the path of justice; like martyrs because they both fight with heavy odds in the path of honesty and virtue; and like the truthful because both are steadfast in their resolves. Islam asks the participants to go beyond the rules of the *Shariah* in the market place and extend beneficence to one another as a safeguard against injustice. Beneficence implies helping others in ways not required by justice. It is thus different from justice, which prescribes just limits to selfishness. While justice regulates and limits selfishness, beneficence rises above it. Moreover, participants in the market are not only responsible for their own just behavior, but due to the obligation of "enjoining the good and forbidding the evil" they are also made responsible for the behavior of their fellow participants. Islam maintains that when a man sees another committing an injustice toward a third and fails to attempt to remove that injustice, by reason of this failure he becomes a party to that injustice. If the person failing to help is himself a beneficiary of this injustice, then his failure is considered tantamount to supporting it. Although provisions are made for coercive and corrective action by legitimate authorities, the clear preference is for self-management of the market. Any interference in the operations of such a market, e.g., through price controls, is considered unjust, a transgression and a sin.

It was in response to the rules of market behavior imposed by the *Shariah* that led the Muslims early in their history to structure their markets in the form of bazaars which looked almost the same all over the Muslim world and possessed characteristics that promoted the observance of and compliance with the rules ordained by the *Shariah*. Physically, bazaars were structured to guarantee maximum compliance with these rules. Each physical segment of the market was specialized with respect to specific products and the prices showed little variation from one part of the market to the next. The institution of guilds made self-regulation of each profession and trade possible. Additionally, markets were inspected for compliance with the rules of the *Shariah* by a market supervisor (called *Muhtasib*) who was appointed by local judges. Unfortunately, the institution of bazaars did not have the opportunity to evolve in order to meet the requirements of an expanding economy or the growing complexity in economic relations. The bazaars that still exist in many parts of the Muslim world, while maintaining their underdeveloped physical and infrastructural nature — most are centuries old and have not been expanded — lack many of the Islamic characteristics and requirements in their operations.

The last component of Islamic economic justice, i.e., distributive justice, is the mechanism by which equal liberty and equity are reconciled without the least possible infringement of either. The first market for Muslims was founded by the Holy Prophet in Madīna. Insofar as the pattern of the distribution of resources is just and equal access to these resources, as well as equal opportunity in their use, is guaranteed, the claim to equity on the basis of reward and effort is just. The moral basis of property is the primacy given to equity and it is derived directly from human efforts and achievements. The bases of private property in Islam are: (i) property which is derived from personal ability and effort, including material property made or obtained from natural resources by combining them with personal skills, ability, and technology, income from self-made capital, assets acquired in exchange for the product of owner's labor, (ii) property acquired by transfers from the producer, and (iii) property acquired through inheritance from the producer. Rules regarding distributive justice operate through (ii) and (iii).

Assuming equal liberty and opportunity, whenever work has to be performed for production of wealth, the output of different people may vary greatly both in quality and quantity. Equity then demands that, commensurate with their productivity, different people receive different rewards. Hence, starting from the equality of liberty and opportunity of access to resources, equity may lead to inequality. Moreover, the allocation of resources arising from the operation of the market will reflect the initial distribution of wealth as well as the structure of the market. Assuming that both the operation and the structure of the market are just, there is no logical reason to assume that market outcome, by and of itself, will lead to equal wealth distribution. Consequently, the result may be (and often is) that inequalities equitably created, will have inter- as well as intra-generational implications. It is here that the distributive mechanisms of Islamic economic justice attempt to modify inequalities equitably created.

Contrasted with claims to equity, Islam recognizes claims based on equality of liberty and opportunity which are reflected in the degree of access to resources, degree and extent of the ability of persons to actualize his potential liberty and opportunity, and finally the right of prior ownership, i.e., the principle of invariance of ownership rights. Thus, Islam recognizes the right that the less able have in the wealth of those who have greater ability and opportunity to produce greater wealth. This right has the first claim on the surplus wealth produced by individuals. Various levies (such as *Zakat*, *Khums*, *"Ushr*, *Kharaj*, *Sadaqa*, *Nafaqa*, etc.) are ordained in order that such rights may be redeemed. The payment of these levies cannot be regarded as beneficence, because beneficence is giving others some product, service, benefit, or benefaction from the motive of helping them and it is radically different from justice. The payment of the levies ordained by Islam is considered fulfillment of a right that others have in one's wealth; it is a contractual obligation that must be met. Islam also encourages beneficence over and above these obligatory dues, but these levies are in the nature of returning to others what rightfully belongs to them. Shirking from this obligation causes misdistribution of wealth, which Islam considers as the major source of poverty.

Islam asserts unambiguously that poverty is neither caused by scarcity or paucity of natural resources, nor is it due to a lack of proper synchronization between the modes of production and distribution, but that it is a result of waste, opulence, extravagance, and non-payment of what rightfully belongs to less able segments of the society. This position is illustrated by the Prophetic saying that: "Nothing makes a poor man starve except that with which a rich person avails a luxury." This is why waste, abuse of wealth, extravagance, and excessive consumption are condemned as unjust, particularly when they occur in conjunction with poverty that they can help to alleviate. In the morality of property, Islam unequivocally considers all individuals entitled to a certain standard of life; and it is this entitlement that entails the satisfaction of their claim as a matter of equity and justice and not as a matter of beneficence.

To modify patterns of distribution of wealth to the next generation, Islam has instituted its rules of inheritance, which break up and distribute a person's accumulated wealth. This institution is based on the principle that the right of the owner to his wealth ceases upon his death. Before his death, the power of the person to bequeath his wealth as he wishes is recognized, but is basically restricted to a maximum of one-third of his net assets. The central core of the system consists of the compulsory rules of inheritance which, according to the *Shariah*, are regarded as the consideration for the duties of protection and support owed to the deceased during his life-time that, in turn, reflect another rule that the duty of a person to maintain his needy collateral relatives is dependent upon, and proportionate to, his right to inherit from that relative.

The basis of the Law of inheritance is the *Quran*, which clearly specifies the exact manner in which the shares of heirs are to be determined in the inheritance.[3] Among the same category of heirs there is neither preferential treatment nor discrimination. Men and women are all heirs, though a woman's share is generally one-half of a man's share in the same category of heirs. The reason for this seemingly discriminatory rule is the fact that, under the rules of the *Shariah*, the whole responsibility for the maintenance of the family rests upon the husband and not upon the wife. Even if the wife has a larger income and greater wealth (due to her own work or due to inheritance from father, brother and other relatives), as is sometimes the case, she is not required to share that wealth or income with her husband — and the husband has no claim on her property or income — and still the legal responsibility for the maintenance of the family rests upon the husband; the wife is under no legal obligation to make any contribution toward her family. Considering the nature of the (extended) family ties and mutual responsibilities exhorted by Islam, its institution of inheritance breaks up the wealth of each generation and redistributes it to the next. The objective is that a large number should receive a modest portion of such wealth, rather than a single heir, or a small number receiving wealth in large blocks.

Role of the State

Islam considers economic relations and behavior as the means of integration of society and the integration of man into a higher order of reality. For this purpose, man is asked to consider his economic attainments as means and not as ends in themselves. All the rules of behavior regarding economic matters are addressed to individuals and their collectivity. This collectivity is considered to be organized into a polity, which is represented by the State. The State is regarded as a basic institution, indispensable for the orderly organization of social life, the achievement of legitimate objectives, the creation of material and spiritual prosperity, and the defense and propagation of faith. Hence, all responsibilities directed at the collectivity are assumed by the *Shariah* to be incumbent upon the State, which is primarily a vehicle for implementing the *Shariah*; The legitimacy of the State is derived from its enforcement of the rules of the *Shariah*. The State is assumed to be empowered to use, within the limits of the Law, all available means at its disposal to achieve the objectives and duties prescribed for the collectivity, including the synchronization of individual and public interests.

Foremost among the collective duties is to ensure that justice prevails in all walks of social life. Thus, the establishment of a judiciary or judicial system, with all the apparatus necessary for carrying out the verdicts of the courts, free of any charges and available to all, is regarded as an indispensable duty of the State. Guarantee of equal liberty and opportunity in terms of access to and use of resources, identified by the *Shariah* for the use of individuals, is another duty specified for the State. This requires provision of education, skills and technology, available to all. Once both equal liberty and equal opportunity are provided, then production of wealth, its possession and exchange become matters of equity. All infrastructure necessary for markets to exist and operate has also been traditionally the responsibility of the State. The first market for the Muslim community was built in *Madīna* at the direction of the Prophet (*pbuh*) who required that trade be allowed to take place in that market freely, without any charges or fees imposed on the participants and appointed supervisors for the market. On this basis, jurists have recognized market supervision, and its control only when necessary, as a duty of the State.

As was stated earlier, while Islam recognizes equity on the basis of effort and rewards, it declares an inviolable right for those unable to actualize their potential equal liberties and opportunities in the wealth of those more able. Thus Islam, as praxis for the believer, requires a balance between libertarian and egalitarian values. The libertarian principle of the inviolability of the right of individuals to their property and wealth is respected, so long as the individuals remit the claims specified earlier. This is the concession of libertarianism to egalitarianism, and of enterprise to distributive justice. Islam leaves no doubt that the preference is for voluntary actions of individuals in payment of the levies incumbent upon them. The larger the extent of shirking on the part of the individual, the heavier becomes the duty of the State to correct the resulting misdistribution. The more the individuals conform their behavior in production, exchange, and distribution to the rules of the *Shariah*, the weaker is the State's justification to interfere. When these rules are violated, interference becomes a duty of the State.

Eradication of poverty is undoubtedly one of the most important of all duties made incumbent upon the State, second only to the preservation and propagation of faith, whose very existence is considered threatened by poverty. Islam regards poverty primarily as a result of shirking on the part of the more able and wealthy members of the society from performing their prescribed duties. Hence, commitment to distributive justice, which normally constitutes a large portion of governments' budgets in other systems, is placed squarely on the shoulders of the individuals with the financial and economic capability to meet it. Not only does the *Shariah* specify who must pay, but it also designates explicit categories of the recipients.

To summarize, the role of the State in an Islamic economy relates, firstly, to ensuring that everyone has equal access to natural resources and means of livelihood; secondly, to ensuring that each individual has equal opportunity including education, skills, and technology — to utilize these resources ; thirdly, to ensuring that markets are supervised in such a manner that justice in exchange can be attained; fourthly, to ensuring that transfer takes place from those more able to those less able in accordance to the rules of the *Shariah*; and, finally, to ensuring that distributive justice is done to the next generation through the implementation of the laws of inheritance. The State is then empowered to design any specific economic policy that is required in order to guarantee the attainment of these objectives. To meet the necessary expenditures associated with the performance of its duties, the *Shariah* has given the control, utilization, and management of a portion of natural resource endowment of the society, e.g., underground mineral resources, to the State. According to a consensus of opinion among jurists, it has also empowered the State, to impose taxes whenever there is a gap between the resources it can command and its expenditures. Borrowing by the State, when it does not involve paying interest, is permitted when and if necessary.

Endnotes

1   This concept, in a narrower sense, was originally articulated by As-Šahīd As-Sadr in Iqtisāduna. Along with the first two principles of property, this provides the justification for the *Quranic* dictum that in the property of the rich there is a right for the poor and serves the basis for legislation empowering transfer of income and wealth as well as rules against waste and extravagance in consumption.

2   *Quran* (9:34).

3   *Quran* (4:11–12).

CHAPTER

3

Financial Contracting and *Riba* (interest)

As stated in the previous chapters, the Islamic economic system is a rule-based system founded on the principles of preservation of property rights and sanctity of contracts. Beginning from the notion of property as a sacred trust, the *Shariah* ensures its protection from any exploitation through unjust and unfair dealings. Prohibition of *Riba* (interest) and the elimination of contractual ambiguity (*Gharar*) and other forms of exploitation are some of the implications of these core principles.

The significance of contracts and the related obligations cannot be overstated. In this context, financial transactions are no different from any other set of contracts that are subject to compliance with *Shariah* principles. Primarily, a financial transaction is considered valid if it fulfills the basic requirements of a valid legal contract and, in addition, does not contain certain elements such as *Riba* (interest), *Gharar* (lack of information disclosure), *Qimar* (gambling) and *Myisur* (games of chance involving deception). While the prohibition of *Riba* is the most critical and gets the most attention, one cannot dispute the criticality of *Gharar* and other elements. Historically, jurists or *Shariah* scholars did not cause unnecessary interference in the economic activities and gave various economic agents full freedom to contract, provided certain basic requirements, i.e., prohibition of *Riba*, (interest) were met.

The prohibition of *Riba* (interest) is not confined to Islam only, but has a much longer history spanning over several traditions and civilizations. Appendix I provides a detailed discussion of similar prohibition throughout the history. The prohibition of *Riba* is not due to any formal economic theory as such, but is directly prohibited by the Divine order in *Quran*. Verses of *Quran* clearly prohibit dealing with *Riba*, but *Riba* is not precisely defined at the time of revelation. Such omission is often attributed to the fact that the concept of *Riba* was not in vogue in society at the time of the prohibition and therefore there was no need to provide a formal definition. Defining the term in modern times in any language other than Arabic adds further complexity. For example, unfortunately, there is no single word in a contemporary English dictionary, which can suffice to be an equivalent and accurate translation of the term *Riba*. This has caused much of the confusion in explaining the concept of *Riba* to the lay person as much as to the scholars.

Although the term *Riba* is discussed in detail in this chapter, an introductory and simple definition of *Riba* could be "the practice of charging financial interest or a premium in excess of the principal amount of a loan." Through the prohibition of *Riba*, *Allah* (swt) has prohibited paying or receiving more than the principal on the money lent as loan irrespective of whether the rate is simple or compounded.

The Concept of *Riba* in Islam

Although the term *Riba* is referred to in the *Quran*, no detailed explanation is available in the practice of the Prophet (*pbuh*). This is attributed to two reasons. First, that the verses concerning *Riba* were revealed toward the end of the Prophet's life and therefore there is very little history or knowledge of cases where people asked him concerning the term and he provided the explanation. The second and more plausible reason is that *Riba* was already a well-developed and well-known term at the time of the revelation and therefore, the Prophet (*pbuh*) did not feel any need for any further details, explanation or elaboration. This argument is supported by an incident relating to the repairs to the *Ka'bah* (Sacred House in Mekkah) in pre-Islamic times where contributions from *Riba* money were rejected because such earnings were considered impure.

Literally, the Arabic term *Riba* refers to excess, addition and surplus, while the associated verb implies "to increase, to multiply, to exceed, to exact more than was due, or to practice usury." Lane's Lexican presents a comprehensive meaning, which covers most of the earlier authentic definitions of *Riba*. According to Lane, the term *Riba* meant:

> *"to increase, to augment, swellings, forbidden 'addition', to make more than what is given, the practicing or taking of usury or the like, an excess or an addition, or an addition over and above the principal sum that is lent or expended"*

Early Muslim scholars considered money to be a medium of exchange, a standard of value and a unit of account, but rejected its function as a store of value. Lending on interest was prohibited because it was an act of ungratefulness and considered to be unjust, since money was not created to be sought for its own sake, but for other objects. Verses of the *Quran* emphasized engaging in trade and commerce rather than earnings through *Riba* (interest). When some questioned the difference between the trade and *Riba* arguing that both are the same, Verse 2:275 ("... However, God permits commerce, and prohibits **usury** (interest)....") was revealed to reiterate that the two are different and one is prohibited while the other is not. The concept of *Riba* was clear in the minds of early jurists, scholars and practitioners. For a long time and before the introduction of paper currency, *Shariah* scholars always considered the question of *Riba* in the context of an exchange contract (*Sarf*), i.e., sale or exchange of currency or money or as a sub-heading under discussion of trade. Only a few scholars discussed the subject under the heading of loan (*Qard*).

Literally meaning "increase," *Riba* was interpreted by classical scholars, such as Ibn Arabi, Mujahid, and Tabari, as increase which has no wealth (*mal*) corresponding to it (Ibn Arabi) or as reward for waiting (Mujahid) or that increase which accrues to the lender on account of deferred payment due to an extension in the actual period of loan (Tabari). At the time of the prohibition, it was a common practice for people to lend money on the condition that a specific amount would be payable periodically as interest and that the principal amount will remain to be paid. At the expiry of the loan, if the borrower was unable to meet the obligation for any reason, the lender will offer to extend the lending period subject to an increased rate of interest. The concept of *Riba* is not confined to money lending only, but extends to exchange of goods as well. *Shariah* recognizes two forms of *Riba* — *Riba al-Nasiah* and *Riba al-Fadl*.

> **Riba al-Nasiah:** *Riba al-Nasiah* deals with *Riba* in money-to-money exchange, provided the exchange is delayed or deferred and additional charge is associated with such deferment. The term *Nasi'ah* comes from the root *nasa'a* which means to postpone, defer, or wait, and refers to the time that is allowed to the borrower to repay the loan in return for the "addition" or the "premium." This kind of *Riba* is the basis of the prohibition of interest as practiced in today's financial transactions. The prohibition of *Riba al-Nasi'ah* essentially implies that the fixing in advance of a positive return on a loan as a reward for waiting is not permitted by the *Shariah*. It makes no difference whether the return is a fixed or variable percentage of the principal, or an absolute amount

to be paid in advance or on maturity, or a gift or service to be received as a condition for the loan.

Riba al-Fadl: *Riba al-Fadl* is more subtle and deals with hand-to-hand or barter exchange. Such prohibition is derived from the sayings of the Prophet (*pbuh*) who required that commodities are exchanged for cash instead of barter since there may be differences in the quality to ensure that no exploitation takes place due to any mismatch in the quantity and the quality of the exchanges. Otherwise, it may give rise to an unjust increase, i.e., *Riba*. The concept of *Riba al-Fadl* is remarkably similar to the prohibition of increase in lending victuals in the Old Testament (Leviticus 25:37). Whereas the Old Testament prohibits quantitative increases, *Riba al-Fadl* prohibits qualitative increases as well. Considering that in today's markets, exchange takes place through the medium of money, the relevance of *Riba al-Fadl* has diminished, but the essence of the concept remains applicable to similar situations.

Definition of *Riba*

Focusing on *Riba* in financial transaction, now we can construct a more formal definition of the term. According to the *Shariah*, *Riba* technically refers to the "premium" that must be paid by the borrower to the lender along with the principal amount as a condition for the loan or for an extension in the duration of loan. At least four characteristics define the prohibited interest rate: (1) it is positive and fixed *ex-ante*; (2) it is tied to the time period and the amount of the loan; (3) its payment is guaranteed regardless of the outcome or the purposes for which the principal was borrowed; and (4) the state apparatus sanctions and enforces its collection.

This definition of the term "*Riba*" is generally accepted by all and is clear, straight-forward, and unambiguous. One would not find any dispute in the literal or the obvious meaning of the term *Riba*, but it is the interpretation and scope of the prohibition and its applicability to practical life which raise several questions for *Shariah* scholars who have dealt with them over a period of time and each time a new situation arises. Four most commonly asked questions are whether the prohibition is limited to consumer loans only, whether only excessive interest or compounding of interest is prohibited, whether adjustment for inflation or any indexation in any form falls within the definition of *Riba*, and finally whether prohibition of interest denies time value of money.

These questions need further exploration and therefore are discussed further.

Commercial versus Productive Loans

A distinction based on the purpose of the loan is often highlighted to argue that the prohibition of *Riba* in Islam was meant for *Riba* on consumer loans only, since the institution of *Riba* was used by moneylenders to exploit poor people in the time of need. The logic of the argument is that there were no organized markets for commercial and production financing and the bulk of the lending by individuals was for personal consumption. Charging *Riba* on the lendings for consumption was deemed unfair, unjust, and exploitive, and therefore, like other traditions, Islam also prohibited it. Borrowing of money for productive purposes should not fall into the same category.

However, this weak argument is based on a lack of knowledge of the history of the early Islamic period. There is considerable evidence to show that lending for commercial and business ventures existed and the practice to charge interest on such loans was prevalent at the time of the prohibition. First, the practice of lending on the basis of *Riba* for agricultural purposes is well documented. Considering that the economy during that time was primarily an agricultural economy, it is reasonable to conclude that *Riba*-based loans for non-consumption purposes existed and were subject to the prohibition. Second, it is a historical fact that the business community of Mecca was part of a sophisticated network of traders and it is known that some of these trades would borrow on the basis of *Riba* to finance their trade expeditions. It was a common practice to raise funds to purchase local products before embarking on a trade journey. In some cases, such trade journeys were undertaken and financed by *Riba*-based loans. The Prophet (*pbuh*) signed a pact with the people of Taif who were well-known for their moneylending business, including lending to the traders of Mecca, with the condition that *Riba*-based businesses be abolished. After the prohibition of *Riba*, the trade journeys continued, but the mode of financing was changed from loans to partnerships.

Common Lending Practices Prior to Prohibition of *Riba*

- A person would sell goods to another on the understanding that the price would be paid within an agreed period. If the price was not paid within that period, an amount was added to the price and the period of repayment was extended.

- A person would lend money to another on the understanding that a fixed additional amount would be paid besides the principal, within a fixed period.
- A rate would be agreed between the borrower and the lender according to which the principal along with the additional amount would be repaid. If a further period for repayment was required, then the rate was increased for the extended period.

Source: SIDDIQUE (1995)

There is clear and sufficient evidence that at the time of the prohibition, borrowing and lending was for both commercial and productive purposes and therefore prohibition was intended for all forms of lending.

Does *Riba* Refer to Excessiveness or Compounding of Interest Only?

As mentioned earlier, the literal meaning of the word "usury" has changed from simple interest of any kind and at any level to excessive interest or interest rate above a certain legal limit. This has become the source of confusion for some researchers who take the contemporary definition of usury to be its original meaning and therefore wrongly come to the conclusion that only excessive interest rate is prohibited. Similarly, out-of-context interpretation of Verse 3:130 ("Do not devour interest doubled and redoubled") often leads to the misunderstanding that the prohibition is for excessive or compounded rate of interest and that therefore it excludes other forms of simple, fair or legal rates.

In refuting the claims that prohibition was meant for excessive interest only, Muslim scholars argue that:

- The verses concerning the prohibition (2:275-81, 3:130-2, 4:161 and 30:39) do not make any distinction between exorbitant or reasonable rate of interest. The verse mentioning doubling and re-doubling of interest is an intermediate verse, while the final injunction 2:279 ("... *and if you repent then ye have your principal*" ...) is a clear indication that interest is not acceptable at any level.
- Doubling and redoubling of interest is a phenomenon that takes place at any rate of interest. With the help of a simple mathematical formula, one can show that doubling and re-doubling of the principal can take place even at a very low interest rate. For example, based

on daily compounding (a common practice in today's financial markets), a $1 loan will be doubled in 15 years at the rate 4.6%.

• The prohibition of interest is associated with the notion of injustice. Researchers refer to Verse 2:279 ("*… neither should you commit injustice nor should you be subjected to it …*") to argue that *Riba* is categorically linked in its totality with injustice and there is no mention of excessive or exorbitant rate. Similarly Verse 2:279 ("*… And if you repent, then you have your principal …*") is often quoted to support this argument that the verse protects the principal lent but does not offer any protection of any *Riba*, i.e., simple or excessive.

Is Adjustment for Inflation or Indexation Allowed?

Whereas the issues of consumer versus productive loans and excessive interest are relatively easy to resolve, the question of any adjustment or compensation for "inflation" or "deflation" is not that straightforward. The question is often raised if the money lent without *Riba* (interest) should be adjusted for any decrease or increase of value over the period of lending. Indexation of financial obligation refers to an adjustment in value over a period of time to compensate for the change in the value due to inflationary or deflationary pressures. Indexing wages to inflation is a widely common practice, but indexing investments or financial obligations is also growing fast in the conventional financial markets. In the case of financial assets, inflation-linked securities link the returns to the consumer prices index or to the cost of living index. The adjustments are often in the form of *ex-post* adjustments and the objective is to guarantee a return equal to the real interest rate instead of nominal interest rate.

Indexation is justifiable in the eyes of the *Shariah* for wages, salaries and pensions, the social security payments, etc, but the Shariah does not support indexation of financial assets. Some scholars argue that Islam's notion of justice is a ground for compensation when lending without *Riba*, while others argue that the prohibition is absolute and any compensation or indexation would amount to *Riba* (interest). Opponents of any adjustments base their arguments on moral, legal, economic and financial grounds. Some of the arguments against indexation are based on finding solutions to the sources of fiscal imbalance and price instability, rather than making any adjustments through indexations. Common arguments against indexations are briefly discussed here.

Firstly, it is argued that the verses of *Quran* (2:275) clearly protect only the principal amount of the loan and consider anything in excess of it as *Riba*. It is understood that this prohibition covers all transactions that may make any adjustments similar to *Riba* (interest), such as deferred exchange of currency, devaluation or revaluation, and change in the unit of currency at the time of repayment of loans. Since lending of money is a currency transaction that is treated as similar to exchange of commodity, any compensation for the fall in the value of money is not justifiable.

Secondly, Muslim scholars also argue that by virtue of the presence of inflation in the economy, the investor's or lender's purchasing power would be at stake irrespective of whether money is lent as loan on non-*Riba* basis or is invested in a return-bearing security. In either case, the net loss to the lender is a real interest rate or real return. Even if money was not lent but was kept for consumption purposes, the same loss of purchasing power will occur. Therefore, it seems unreasonable to expect the borrower to bear all the loss, which is likely to occur to the lender in any case.

Thirdly, it is argued that even if some form of indexation is allowed, it may not be in consonance with the notion of justice and therefore may not serve its intended purpose. While it is recognized that inflation is the loss of purchasing power and indexation is a compensation for such loss, the problem is how to clearly identify and hold responsible a certain party for its share. There are several contributing factors leading to inflation and the contributing magnitude of each factor and party cannot be determined. Therefore, it is unjust to ask one party to take the entire burden, while others are burden-free. For example, if only the borrower is asked to compensate for the loss, which was caused by factors beyond the borrower's control, i.e., irresponsible policies of the government, it would imply that a person who is not responsible for inflicting loss is made to compensate and the party responsible is not held responsible.

Fourthly, some scholars have also discussed the practice of indexation by arguing that there is no perfect index that can fully capture the loss of the value. The constituents of the index representing the cost of living may not serve as a good proxy for the loss in purchasing power. Also, the cost of living index represents the consumption habits of an average person in an economy and since the cost of living may differ from region to region and from city to city, it would not be possible to measure it accurately. This inaccuracy can lead to an unjustified transfer of wealth from the borrower to the lender or vice versa. Similarly, inflation indices are based on a lag and therefore are not readily available to be used in daily financial transactions. All these factors make indexation less practical and prone to biases, which may open a back door for unjustified charges.

Finally, *Shariah* scholars and economists raise the issue that indexation is not the answer but, indeed, price stability and fiscal discipline are to be achieved to combat inflation. In this respect, the role of the State in causing inflation leading to disequilibrium in the economy should receive serious attention. Some economists argue that it is the responsibility of an Islamic State to take effective steps to check inflation in order to minimize the depreciation in the value of money and when the government policies are the source of inflation, the government should compensate the borrower.

Irrespective of the causes and sources of inflation, indexation is not accepted by scholars; however, other remedies have been suggested. For example, if the lender and the borrowers are concerned about inflation, then the loan can be denominated in terms of a commodity, i.e., gold. The lender can lend a certain quantity of gold to the borrower who is obligated to return the same quantity at the expiry of the loan. It is also pointed out that the partnership and profit-and-loss sharing instruments of the Islamic economic system provide a built-in compensation for inflation because the profit is shared in the agreed ratio whereas the losses are borne in the ratio of respective capitals.

Does Prohibition of *Riba* deny "Time Value of Money?"

It is a common misunderstanding and a myth that by prohibiting interest on loans, Islam denies the concept of the time value of money. Islamic scholars have always recognized the time value of money, but maintain that the compensation for such value has its limitations. Recognition of an indirect economic value of time does not necessarily mean acknowledging any right of equivalent material compensation for this value in all cases. According to the *Shariah*, compensation for the value of time in sales contracts is acknowledged, but in the case of lending, increase (interest) is prohibited as a means of material compensation for time.

The Islamic notion of opportunity cost of capital and time value of money can be clearly understood by reviewing the distinction between investment and lending. Time by itself does not give a yield, but can only contribute to the creation of value when an economic activity is undertaken. Given a sum of money, it can be invested in a business venture or it can be lent for a given period of time. In case of investment, the investor will be compensated for any profit and loss earned during that time and Islam fully recognizes this return on the investment as a result of an economic activity. On the other hand, if money is in the form of a loan, it is an act of charity where surplus funds, are effectively being utilized to promote economic development and social well-being.

In response to the contemporary understanding that interest on a loan is a reward for the opportunity cost of the lender, Islamic scholars maintain that interest fixed *ex ante* is certain, while profits or losses are not and to take a **certain** as a compensation for the **uncertain** amounts to indulging in *Riba* and is therefore unlawful. The element of uncertainty diminishes with time and the resultant return on investment is realized, rather than the accruing of return due to passage of time. In short, Islam's stand on the time value of money is simple and clear. Money is a medium of exchange; time facilitates completion of economic activity, and the owner of capital is to be compensated for any return resulting from economic activity. Lending should be a charitable act without any expectation of monetary benefit.

Rationale for the Prohibition of *Riba*

The fundamental sources (*Quran* and *Sunnah*) do not provide any detailed rationale for the prohibition against *Riba* (interest) beyond asserting, axiomatically, that charging interest is an act of injustice. Contemporary Muslim scholars, particularly the economists among them, have provided various rationales for this prohibition by alluding to the consequences of the existence of interest in modem societies, or by arguing that modem economic theory has not provided any justification for the existence of even the necessity of interest rates. Some also argue that human wisdom and comprehension are limited compared to the Knowledge of *Allah* (swt) and therefore any exercise to fully understand the rationale of the prohibition of *Riba* may not yield any optimal comprehension.

Riba and Economic and Social Injustice

One of the primary and the most frequently articulated rationales by Muslim scholars is that the existence of *Riba* (interest) in the economy is a form of social and economic exploitation, which violates the core Islamic teaching of social justice. Therefore, the elimination of interest from the economic system is intended to promote economically just, socially fair, and ethically and morally correct economic behavior.

The logic as to why the Holy *Quran* has given such a severe verdict against interest is that Islam is against all forms of exploitation and is for an economic system that aims to secure extensive socio-economic justice. Islam, therefore, condemns all forms of exploitation, particularly the injustice continued in the form of a lender being guaranteed a positive return without assuming a share of the risk with the borrower, whereas the borrower takes upon himself all sorts of risks in addition to putting in his skills and labor. Considering that the wealth an individual possesses is actually a trust held for *Allah* (swt), like a person's life (also a trust from the Creator) the trust of wealth is sacred as well.[1] Then, if that wealth is taken unjustly, an injustice is done to the sanctity of a human being.

It is also argued that the existence of *Riba* is not compatible with Islam's value system, which prohibits any form of "unjustified" enrichment (*akl amwal alnas bi al-batil*). *Riba*, which represents unequal and therefore unjustified monetary benefit, is differentiated from trade, which promotes exchange of counter-values in a more just fashion. By eliminating *Riba*, each party to the contract gets a fair and equitable reward, which ultimately leads to more equitable returns distribution and therefore to a more just economic system.

Riba Violates Islam's Principles of Property Rights

The *Quran* clearly and strongly condemns acquisition by individuals of each other's property through wrongful means (see Verses 2:188, 4:29, 4:161 and 9:34). Islam recognizes two types of individual claims to property: (a) the property rights that are a result of the combination of an individual's labor and natural resources, and (b) rights or claims to the property that is obtained through exchange, remittances of what Islam recognizes as the rights of those less able to utilize the resources to which they are entitled, outright grants, and inheritance. Money represents the monetized claim of its owner to the property rights created by assets that were obtained or received through (a) and/or (b). Lending money is, in effect, a transfer of these rights from the lender to the borrower and all that can be claimed in return for it is its equivalent and no more. Interest on money loaned represents an unjustifiable and instantaneous property rights claim. It is unjustifiable because interest is a property right claimed outside the legitimate framework of individual property rights recognized by Islam and instantaneous because as soon as the contract for lending upon interest is concluded, a right to the borrower's property is created for the lender, regardless of the outcome of the enterprise for which the money is used.

Money lent on interest is used either productively in the sense that it creates additional wealth, or unproductively, in the sense that it does not lead to incremental wealth produced by the borrower. In the former case, that is, when the funds are used in combination with the labor of the entrepreneur to produce additional wealth, the money lent cannot have any property rights claim to the incremental wealth because the lender, when lending money, does not bargain for a proportion of the additional wealth but for a fixed return, irrespective of the outcome of the enterprise. He, in effect, transfers the right to his property to the borrower. In the latter case, since no additional wealth, property or assets are created by the borrower, the money lent — even if legitimately acquired — cannot be used to claim any additional property rights since none is created.

Promotion of Profit-and Risk-Sharing

When the Arabs argued that "trade is but like *Riba*" (2:275), *Allah* (swt) did not deny that apparent similarity, but decisively informed that "but *Allah* has permitted trade and forbidden *Riba*" (2:275). The legal differences between the two are clear, and have been detailed over the centuries by capable Muslim jurists. However, the fact remains that the sophisticated Arab traders of Makkah did not at first see any discernible difference between the Islamic model and the one based on *Riba*. The sharing of risks and uncertainties of the enterprise is an extremely important characteristic of Islamic financial contracts, since the *Shariah* condemns even a guarantee by the working partner to restore the invested funds intact, not only because it removes the element of uncertainty needed to legitimize the agreed distribution of expected profits, but also because the lender will not be remunerated to the extent of the productivity of his financial capital in the resulting profit.

In Islam, the financial instruments for trade and production purposes are based on risk-and-profit sharing as a return for the entrepreneurial effort and on financial capital. The lender who advances money for trade and production can contract to receive a share of the profit. In doing so, he becomes part owner of capital and shares in the risk of the enterprise, and is not a creditor. This is a fundamental difference between a shareholder and a creditor. The shareholder is one of the proprietors of the enterprise, liable for its debts to the extent of his investment, and receives a return (a dividend) only when a profit is earned. The creditor, as a debenture holder, lends money without the risk of owning and operating capital goods and claims interest regardless of the profit or loss position of the enterprise. The creditor runs a risk, but it is the risk of the solvency of the borrower, not of the success or failure of the enterprise.

Lack of Theory of Interest

Islamic scholars advocating the elimination of interest from the economy highlight the fact that there is no satisfactory theory of interest in the conventional economic theory. This criticism is especially levied on having a fixed rate of interest. Muslim writers see the existing theories of interest as attempts to rationalize the existence of an institution that has become deeply entrenched in modern economies and not as attempts to justify, based on modern economic analysis, why the moneylender is entitled to a reward on the money he lends.

Typical justifications for interest in any economy include the arguments that interest is a reward for saving, a marginal productivity of capital, and an inevitable consequence of the difference between the value of capital goods today and their value after some time, hence the following points:

- When argued that interest is a reward for saving, Muslim scholars respond that such payments could only be rationalized if savings were used for investment to create additional capital and wealth. According to them, the mere act of abstention from consumption should not entitle anybody to a return;
- When argued that interest is justified as marginal productivity of capital, Muslim scholars respond that although the marginal productivity of capital may enter as one factor into the determination of the rate of interest, interest, per se, has no necessary relation with the productivity of capital. Interest, they argue, is paid on money, not on capital, and has to be paid irrespective of capital productivity. In distinguishing between interest as a charge for the use of money and a yield from the investment of capital, Muslim scholars argue that it is an error of modern theory to treat interest as the price of, or return on, capital. Money, they argue, is not capital, it is only "potential capital," which requires the service of the entrepreneur to transform the potentiality into actuality; the lender has nothing to do with the conversion of money into capital or with using it productively.
- When argued that interest arises as the time value of money, Muslim scholars respond that this only explains its inevitability and not its "rightness." Even if the basis for time preference is the difference between the value of commodities this year and the next, Muslim scholars argue, it seems more reasonable to allow next year's economic conditions to determine the extent of the reward.

It is argued that when a person lends funds, the funds are used to create either a debt or an asset (i.e., through investment). In the first case, Islam considers that there is no justifiable reason why the lender should receive a return simply through the act of lending per se. Nor is there a justification, either from the point of view of the smooth functioning of the economy, or that of any tenable scheme of social justice, for the State to attempt to enforce an unconditional promise of interest payment regardless of the use of borrowed money. If, on the other hand, the money is used to create additional capital wealth, the question is raised as to why the lender should be entitled to only a small fraction (represented by the interest rate) of the exchange value of the utility created from the use made of the funds; the lender should be remunerated to the extent of the involvement of his financial capital in creating the incremental wealth.

Act of Lending is an Act of Charity

Many Muslim scholars point out that Islam's prohibition of *Riba* has two dimensions; one is to promote more equitable risk-sharing contracts for business and commercial purposes and the other, to consider lending as a benevolent act with a view to helping someone in need. If someone needs capital for commercial purposes, then capital should be given on a risk-sharing basis and if someone needs funds to overcome some short-term need, then such need should not be exploited and the borrower should not be put under undue burden. The benevolence and philanthropic elements of the prohibition of *Riba* are supported by the *Quran* and the traditions of the Prophet (*pbuh*).

The *Shariah* considers a loan a gratuitous contract, encourages Muslims to offer charitable loans (*Qard-e-Hasna*), and condemns accumulation of wealth for the sake of wealth. Granting a loan without *Riba* is considered a charitable act worthy of bringing blessings (*Barakah*); conversely, lending on the basis of *Riba* has far-reaching consequences. Verses 57:11 ("*Who is he that will lend unto Allah a goodly loan, that He may double it for him or his may be a rich reward …*") and 64:17 ("*If you lend unto Allah a goodly loan, He will double it for you and will forgive you, for Allah is Responsive, Clement*") are examples of the charitable nature of lending in the form of *Riba*-free loans and the associated rewards. Economists argue that such acts of charity can play a critical role in economic development.

Verse 30:39 ("*… which ye give in usury in order that it may increase on (other) people's property hath no increase with Allah; but that which ye give in charity seeking Allah's countenance, hath increase manifolds …*") offers an interesting proposition stating that an act of charity (including lending without interest) is more valuable in the eyes of *Allah* (swt) as compared to increase in wealth through *Riba* (interest). According to a tradition, Prophet (*pbuh*) said that "*Riba* (or *Riba*-based economy) seems to have flourished but the ultimate result is scarcity and contractions." On another occasion, the Prophet (*pbuh*) said that "debauchery and *Riba* lead a nation to ruin." (Imam Ahmad Musnad)

Other Prohibited Element in Financial Contracting: *Gharar*

After *Riba*, *Gharar* is the most important element in financial contracts. In simple terms, *Gharar* stems from informational problems and refers to any uncertainty created by the lack of information or control in a contract. *Gharar* can be thought of as ignorance in regard to an essential element in a transaction, such as the exact sale price, or the ability of the seller to actually deliver what is sold, etc. Existence of *Gharar* in a contract makes it null and void.

Gharar can be defined as a situation when either party to a contract has information regarding some element of the subject of the contract, which is withheld from the other party, and/or the subject of contract is something over which neither party has control. Classic examples include transactions involving birds in flight or fish not yet caught, an unborn calf in its mother's womb, or a runaway animal, etc. All such cases involve the sale of an item that may or may not exist. More modern examples include transactions where the subject is not in the possession of one of the parties and there is uncertainty even about its future possession.

Keeping in mind the notion of fairness in all Islamic commercial transactions, the *Shariah* considers any uncertainty as to the quantity, quality, recoverability, or existence of the subject-matter of a contract as existence of the element of *Gharar*. However, it leaves the judgement to the jurists to determine the extent of *Gharar* in a transaction and depending on the circumstances, one may or may not invalidate the contract. By prohibiting *Gharar*, the *Shariah* prohibited many pre-Islamic contracts of exchange considering them subject to either excessive uncertainty or not being known to one or both parties to the contract causing unnecessary disputes and injustice. In many cases, *Gharar* can be eliminated from contracts by carefully stating the object of the sale and the price to eliminate unnecessary ambiguities. A well-documented contract will eliminate *Gharar* as well.

Considering *Gharar* as excessive uncertainty, one can associate *Gharar* to the element of risk. Some argue that prohibition of *Gharar* is one way of managing risks in Islam, as a business transaction based on profit-and-loss sharing will encourage parties to conduct due diligence before committing to the contract. Prohibition of *Gharar* will force parties to avoid contracts with a high degree of informational asymmetry and with extreme pay-offs, and will make parties more responsible and accountable. However, treating *Gharar* as risk has its consequences. By prohibiting *Gharar*, the *Shariah* prohibits trading of *Gharar* as well. This prohibition of trading *Gharar* is considered to be the prohibition of risk or the prohibition of derivative instruments in today's financial markets, which are designed to transfer risks from one party to another.

One of the implications of the prohibition of *Gharar* is the prohibition of pure speculation and gambling activities, which involve asymmetric information, excessive uncertainty, risk and lack of control. Although some of the earlier researchers raised concerns about the permissibility of trading in the stock markets on the ground that it amounted to speculation, the issue was immediately resolved by arguing that trading in the stock market is based on some fundamental analysis of economic variables and is subject to a reasonable level of uncertainty rather than pure speculation. Another area where the prohibition of *Gharar* has raised concerns in contemporary financial transactions is the area of insurance. Some argue that writing an insurance contract on the life of a person falls within the domain of *Gharar* and, therefore, the contract is not valid. The issue is still under review and not fully resolved.

Appendix I

Usury, *Riba* and Interest: A Historical Perspective

A historical review of the term "usury" further brings to light and explains a consistent pattern of prohibition of interest. Usury was defined originally as charging a fee for the use of money, which meant interest on loans irrespective of the level of interest rate. After moderate interest loans became an accepted part of the business world in the Middle and early modern ages, the word "usury" came to refer to the charging of unreasonable or above-legal rate or relatively high rates of interest. Until the fifteenth century, the only substitute in English for any amount of increase on loan was the term usury, which is synonymous with the modern meaning of interest. According to the Oxford dictionary, the term took its new meaning somewhere between the sixteenth and seventeenth centuries.

Considering "usury" as the practice of lending money on interest, its roots can be traced back approximately four thousand years and since its early incarnation, the practice has been repeatedly condemned, prohibited, and restricted, mainly on moral, ethical, religious, and legal grounds. Throughout history, there is substantial evidence of intense criticism by various traditions, institutions, and social reformers. The rationale employed by these wide-ranging critics has included arguments about work ethic, social justice, economic instability, and inter-generational equity. Among the religious traditions, explicit and implicit prohibition of interest is mentioned in Hinduism, Buddhism, Judaism, Christianity, and Islam.

Greek philosopher Aristotle considered money as a means to facilitate exchange and therefore was of the view that a piece of money cannot beget another piece. He rejected the justification for charging interest on this ground, arguing that money is sterile. In Hinduism, the Vedic texts of Ancient India (2000-1400 BC) the "usurer" (*kusidin*) is mentioned several times and interpreted as any lender at interest. Further details about and references to "interest" are found in the later Sutra texts (700-100 BC), as well as the Buddhist *Jatakas* (600-400 BC). It is during this latter period that the first sentiments of contempt for usury are expressed. According to Jain (1929), Vasishtha, a well known Hindu law-maker of that time, made a special law which forbade the higher castes of *Brahmanas* (Hindu priests) and *Kshatriyas* (warriors) from being usurers or lenders at interest. Also, in the

Jatakas, usury is referred to in a deprecating manner, claiming that "hypocritical ascetics are accused of practicing it."

Judaism and Interest

In Judaism, the Old Testament clearly disallowed dealing with interest as implied by the Hebrew words "*neshekh*" (literally meaning "a bite") and "*turbith*." Similar to *Riba*, the Hebrew word "*neshekh*" referred to any gain, whether from the loan of money or goods or property of any kind. The term "*neshekh*" was not defined explicitly, but was commonly referred to as the practice of the exaction of interest from the debtor by the creditor. In the relevant Exodus and Leviticus texts, the term applies to lending to the poor and destitute, while in Deuteronomy, the prohibition is extended to include all money lending, excluding only business dealings with foreigners. In addition to the direct mention of interest, there are several references to derivatives — or indirect interest known as *avak ribbit*, literally "the dust of interest" — which apply, for example, to non-financial transactions and include certain types of sales, rent agreements and work contracts.

Reference to Usury (interest) in Judaic Scriptures

"If thou lend money to any of my people that is poor by thee, thou shalt not be to him as an usurer, neither shalt thou lay upon him **usury** (interest)." (**Exodus 22:25**)

"Take thou no **usury** (interest) of him, or increase: but fear thy God; that thy brother may live with thee." (**Leviticus 25:36**)

"Thou shalt not give him thy money upon **usury** (interest), nor lend him thy victuals for increase." (**Leviticus 25:37**)

"Thou shalt not lend upon **usury** (interest) to thy brother; **usury** (interest) of money, **usury** of victuals, usury of any thing that is lent upon usury." (**Deuteronomy 23:19**)

"Unto a stranger thou mayest lend upon **usury** (interest); but unto thy brother thou shalt not lend upon **usury** (interest): that the LORD thy God may bless thee in all that thou settest thine hand to in the land whither thou goest to possess it." (**Deuteronomy 23:20**)

Christianity and Interest

In Biblical times, all payments for the use of money were forbidden. There are several references to prohibition of an increase on the amount lent out. Charging interest was condemned throughout the early history of Christianity. In *The Divine Comedy*, Dante places the usurers in the inner ring of the seventh circle of hell, below even suicides.

By the second century AD, usury had become a more relative term which meant charging interest beyond the legal rate, but that did not prevent the Church from continuing to condemn the practice. By the fourth century, the Roman Catholic Church maintained the prohibition of the taking of interest by the clergy and this rule was extended to the laity in the fifth century. In the eighth century, under Charlemagne, the Church declared usury to be a general criminal offence. During Medieval times, lending was considered a gratuitous act and lending on interest, morally wrong. In the early Middle Ages, Popes and Councils continued to oppose all forms of payments for the use of money lent, as money was mainly for the purpose of exchange and its principal use was its consumption. Such anti-usury movement continued to gain momentum during the early Middle Ages and in 1311, Pope Clement V made the ban on usury absolute and declared all secular legislation in its favor null and void.[2]

The end of the thirteenth century saw the decline of the influence of the Orthodox Church and the rise of secular powers and, as a result, despite clear prohibition of the charging of interest by the Church, the practice of charging interest gained some acceptance and tolerance. During the Mercantile Era (1500–1700 AD) when money began to play a critical role in large scale commercial transactions and money was treated as capital, the arguments were put forth to equate interest as rent on capital similar to the charging of rent for physical factors of production. With the emergence of the Protestant Reformation movement and the rise of capitalism, usury or interest was accepted on the grounds that usury is sinful only if it hurts one's neighbor, and charity and natural equity alone can decide in what particular cases a charge for a loan does hurt a neighbor, since each believer is guided by his own conscience.

Factors such as changing business practices, the rise of capitalism and pro-usury movements such as the Reformation, led, sometime around 1620, to the practice of usury making a transition from an offence against public morality, which a Christian government was expected to suppress, to being a matter of private conscience. At the same time, a new generation of Christian moralists redefined usury as excessive interest. For example, the teachings of Reformist John Calvin (1509–64) led to the emergence of the

Calvinist bankers in Geneva, who were free to develop their financial interests without any feelings of guilt, provided that they observed the Christian teaching on justice to the poor, and that they were totally honest in their dealings. The Catholic Church continued to condemn usury (interest) despite several pro-usury movements and the growing spread of usurious transactions. It is worth mentioning that issuance of a bond at a low rate of 4% by the city of Verona in 1740, was severely detested by the Pope. This also indicates that as late as the eighteenth Century, the Christian understanding of usury was that it was equivalent to any form and level of interest and not excessive interest only.

Prohibition of Usury (interest) in Biblical Scriptures

"He that by **usury** (interest) and unjust gain increaseth his substance, he shall gather it for him that will pity the poor." (**Proverbs 28:8**)

"He that putteth not out his money to **usury** (interest), nor taketh reward against the innocent. He that doeth these things shall never be moved." (**Psalm 15:5**)

"Woe is me, my mother, that thou hast borne me a man of strife and a man of contention to the whole earth! I have neither lent on **usury** (interest), nor men have lent to me on **usury** (interest); yet every one of them doth curse me." (**Jeremiah 15:10**)

"He that hath not given forth upon **usury** (interest), neither hath taken any **increase**, that hath withdrawn his hand from iniquity, hath executed true judgment between man and man ..." (**Ezekiel 18:8**)

"In thee have they taken gifts to shed blood; thou hast taken **usury** (interest) and **increase**, and thou hast greedily gained of thy neighbours by extortion, and hast forgotten me, saith the Lord GOD." (**Nehemiah 5:7**)

"Then I consulted with myself, and I rebuked the nobles, and the rulers, and said unto them, Ye exact **usury** (interest), every one of his brother. And I set a great assembly against them." (**Ezekiel 22:12**)

Islam and Interest

The practice of *Riba* (interest) was prevalent at the dawn of Islam and when the prohibition was proclaimed, it did not require any further clarification.

A minor incident that occurred in 605 AD, just years before the revelation of Islam, is worth mentioning. The sacred House of God, *Kabbah*, was damaged due to a fire and contributions from the public were requested for repairing the damage. However, it was emphasized that only pure, clean, and honestly earned money should be donated and as a result prostitutes and usurious moneylenders were specifically debarred from contributing anything. This incident is an indication that even the pagans of Arabia did not consider money earned through lending to be from a clean and ethical source.

Several verses of the *Quran* mention and prohibit *Riba* (interest). In one of the earliest verses (30:39), earning through *Riba* is compared to the blessings and pleasure of *Allah* (swt) through lending as an act of charity. This verse was followed by another verse (4:161), which severely condemned dealing in *Riba* with a reminder that it was prohibited by earlier scriptures of the Jews and Christians as well. In the next set of verses (3:130-2), Muslims were told that avoiding *Riba* was for their own welfare. Finally, the last revelation about *Riba* came through Verses (2:275-81) giving severe warning about *Riba* and recommending to forgive *Riba* due on loans but providing protection to the principal amounts.

Prohibition of Interest in Quran

"The **usury** (interest) that is practiced to increase some people's wealth, does not gain anything at God. But if you give to charity, seeking God's pleasure, these are the ones who receive their reward many fold." (*Ar-Rum* **30:39**)

"And for practicing **usury** (interest), which was forbidden, and for consuming the people's money illicitly, We have prepared for the disbelievers among them painful retribution." (*Al-Nisa* **4:161**)

"O you who believe, you shall not take **usury** (interest), compounded over and over. Observe God that you may succeed." (*Al-'Imran* **3:130**)

"Those who charge **usury** (interest) are in the same position as those controlled by the devil's influence. This is because they claim that usury is the same as commerce. However, God permits commerce, and prohibits **usury** (interest). Thus, whoever heeds this commandment from his Lord, and refrains from usury, he may keep his past earnings, and his judgment rests with God. As for those who persist in usury, they incur Hell, wherein they abide forever." (*Al-Baqarah* **2:275**)

"God condemns **usury** (interest), and blesses charities. God dislikes every disbeliever, guilty. O you who believe, you shall observe God and refrain from all kinds of **usury** (interest), if you are believers. If you do not, then expect a war from God and His messenger. But if you repent, you may keep your capitals, without inflicting injustice, or incurring injustice. If the debtor is unable to pay, wait for a better time. If you give up the loan as a charity, it would be better for you, if you only knew." (*Al-Baqarah* **2:276-280**)

The prohibition of *Riba* (interest) was so explicit and clear that its meaning was rarely challenged. With the introduction of debt securities and commercial banking which further strengthened the institution of interest, the question has been raised more frequently in modern times. Muslim scholars have always maintained that interest is the prohibited element of *Riba*. Like Judaism and Christianity, from time to time, there have been attempts to justify the practice of interest. Throughout Islamic history, questions regarding interest have been posed to *Shariah* scholars and they have predominantly upheld the prohibition. However, in rare cases, there have been exceptions in the form of minority opinions, which often did not last long. Such minority opinions were often under political influence or due to a lack of understanding — either of the traditional Law or of the contract in question.

In recent history, a controversy was created when in 1989 a legal opinion (*fatwa*) was issued by Egypt's highest legal scholar, Sheikh-al-Azhar Muhammad Sayyid al-Tantawi. His opinion was that banks may fix the rate to be paid to the depositors. This opinion was supported by Egypt's prestigious seminary Al-Azhar Islamic Research Institute. While the legal opinion may have been valid given a specific situation, it was never meant to be extended to lead to a general acceptance of the practice of paying or receiving bank interest. Unfortunately, this legal opinion gave the banking industry an excuse to claim that interest was permissible. The same legal opinion resurfaced in late 2002, but was immediately refuted by the Council of Islamic Jurisprudence Academy (IJA), which categorically declared all forms of bank interest illegal from the *Shariah*'s point of view. In both cases — of 1989 and 2002 — the attempts to justify bank interest were met with strong opposition and rejection, with the majority of *Shariah* scholars upholding the prohibition of bank interest.

Interest and Modern Economics

The majority of modern economists do not question the practice of interest and accept the institution of interest as an essential ingredient of the modern economic system. However, from time to time, the notion of charging interest on money is challenged. Silvio Gesell, a successful merchant during the early years of the twentieth century, condemned interest on the basis that his sales were more often related to the price of money (i.e., interest) than the consumers' needs or the quality of his products. His proposal of making money a public service subject to a use fee was not welcomed by the banking community and therefore did not gain any popularity. More recently, an economist, Margrit Kennedy of Germany, has criticized the institution of interest and has advocated an interest- and inflation-free money. Overall, among modern economists, critics of interest are rare exceptions.

More recently, this challenge has come mainly from Islamic scholars. The notable Islamic scholar, Shaikh Mahmud Ahmad, searched through several theories of interest, developed since the time of Adam Smith, to show that there has been no satisfactory explanation of the existence of a fixed and pre-determined rate of return on financial assets. He further analyzed the writings of economists such as Keynes, Bohm Bowerk, Cassels, and Samuelson, to argue that an objective assessment of these writings would lead one to believe that all of these writers held a reasonably strong conviction that the existence of a fixed and pre-determined rate of interest was an impediment to the process of economic growth and development.

By the mid 1980s, economic and financial theory had demonstrated that there were disadvantages in the fixed pay off contracts that dominated interest-based banking, because the following conclusions were drawn for fixed pay off contracts:

- These contracts create inefficient defaults on financial obligations or non-performing assets.
- In the presence of asymmetric information, debt contracts suffer from adverse selection effects and moral hazard effects.
- Fixed fee contracts create a fundamental conflict between the interests of the borrowers and the lenders.
- Socially desirable sectors with low profitability will not get finance; moreover, new entrepreneurs with good projects may not get finance in the absence of security required.

Endnotes

1   According to one of the sayings of the Prophet Mohammad (*pbuh*), "a person's wealth is as sacred as a person's blood."

2   Birnie, A. (1952), *The History and Ethnics of Interest*.

CHAPTER

4

Financial Instruments

The economic activities in any economic system can be viewed as contracts between economic agents. A financial instrument is also a contract, whose terms and conditions define the risk and return profile of the instrument. The whole fabric of Divine Law in Islam is contractual in its conception, content and application. Islam forcefully places all economic relations on the firm footing of "*contractus*" — as discussed in Chapter 2. Preservation of property rights and the commitment to obligations and responsibilities associated with a contract are vital in determining the standards of behavior expected of the economic agents and, ultimately, the nature of the economic system in Islam.

In Islam, a contract is deemed legal and lawful by the *Shariah* if the terms of the contract are free of any prohibition. In other words, if a contract does not have or involve any of the prohibited elements, such as *Riba* or *Gharar*, then it is considered valid, provided it does not violate any other rule or law. For example, although a contract to invest in a company producing alcohol may be valid because or if it is free of *Riba* (interest) and *Gharar* (asymmetrical information), it would still be invalid in the eyes of the *Shariah*, since it deals with production of alcohol, which is prohibited in Islam. Several commercial contracts have their roots in the pre-Islamic period. Post-Islam, they were further developed and widely practiced after their compatibility with the principles of *Shariah* was ascertained and confirmed.

The Islamic economic system has a set of core contracts, which serve as building blocks for designing more sophisticated and complex financial instruments.[1] There is no established classification of contracts in the Islamic legal system as such, but from a business and commercial point of view, one can group certain contracts according to their function and purpose in the economic and financial system. Contracts dealing with commercial and business transactions can be classified into four broad categories as shown in Figure 4.1. These categories are:

1.   Transactional contracts
2.   Financing contracts
3.   Intermediation contracts
4.   Social Welfare contracts

This demarcation and classification based on the function and purpose of contracts give us a framework to understand the nature of credit creation, types of financing instruments, intermediation and the different roles each group plays in the economic system. In other words, theoretically, Islamic commercial law would be able to satisfy the needs of economic agents through various phases of economic activity, right from the purchase or sale of goods, to arrangements for collaterals and guarantees, to arrangements for credit or finance and finally to creation of opportunities for investment.

Transactional contracts deal with the real sector economic transactions that facilitate the exchange, sale and trade of goods and services. The core transactional contracts are based on trade or exchange-based activities. Exchange could be on the spot or on a deferred basis and could be of goods for goods, or of goods for price, or goods for promise to pay. These contracts create assets, which further become the basis of financing and investment opportunities; thus they form the very core of an extended economic and financial system.

Financing contracts offer ways to create and extend credit, facilitate financing of transactional contracts, and provide channels for capital formation and resource mobilization between investors and entrepreneurs. The distinguishing feature of such financing contracts is the absence of a debt contract. Financing contracts are meant either for the financing of transactional contracts in the form of trade finance or asset-backed securities, or for providing capital through equity partnership, which can take several forms, such as partnership, co-ownership, or diminishing partnership.

The role of **intermediation contracts** is to facilitate an efficient and transparent execution of transactional and financial contracts. Intermediation contracts provide the economic agents with a set of tools to perform financial intermediation as well as to offer fee-based services for economic activities. These contracts include *Mudarabah* (a trustee finance contract), *Musharakah* (equity partnership), *Kifala* (guarantee), *Amanah* (trust), *Takaful*

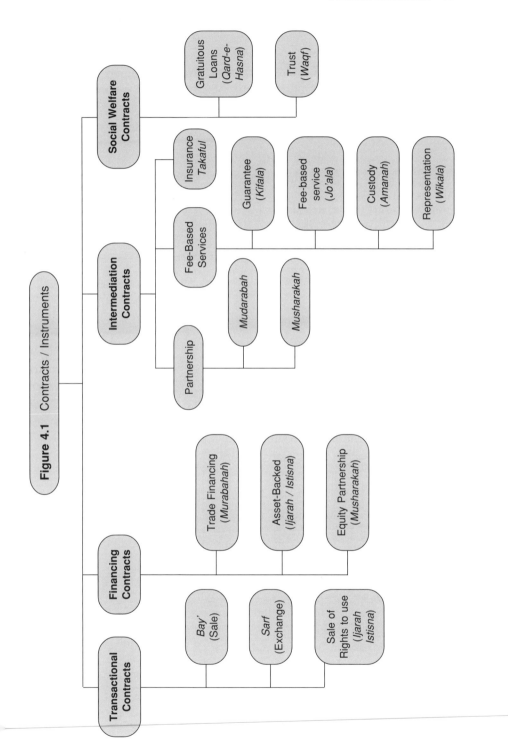

Figure 4.1 Contracts / Instruments

(insurance), *Wikala* (agency) *and Jo'ala* (fee-based service). In a *Mudarabah* contract, an economic agent with capital (*Rabb-ul-mal*) can form a partnership with another agent with skills (*mudarib*), with an agreement to share the profits. Although losses are borne by the capital owner only, the *mudarib* may be liable for a loss resulting from any misconduct or negligence on his part. Intermediation contracts are discussed in detail in the next chapter on financial intermediation.

Finally, **social welfare contracts** are contracts between individuals and the society to promote the well-being and welfare of the less privileged. Although facilitation of social welfare contracts is beyond the scope of intermediation, an intermediary can certainly offer community services by institutionalizing social welfare contracts.

Transactional Contracts

Islam lays great emphasis on promoting trade and gives preference to trading over other forms of business. Trade is not only trading of physical assets but could also be trading of rights to use the physical assets. The basic contracts are therefore the contracts of exchange, sale of an asset or sale of rights to utilize an asset. Whereas contracts of exchange and sale result in the transfer of ownership, contracts for utilization of assets transfer only the right to use a property from one party to another. These two types of contracts lay the foundation of the principal commercial activities in the economy, as all other types of contracts are derived from these basic contracts. Figure 4.2 shows the hierarchy of transactional contracts.

Contracts of Exchange and Sale

A contract of exchange is primarily concerned with trading as well as selling and buying activities, inclusive of their derivatives such as cash sale, deferred payment sale, deferred delivery sale, sale on order, sale on debt, sale on currency, auction sale, etc. Contracts of exchange include a variety of contracts, which differ from one another in terms of the specific legal requirements, rights, obligations and liabilities involved in or connected with them, but are similar to each other in terms of the result of the contract, namely the transfer of ownership from one party to another. There are specific rules for the exchange of specific types of assets; for example, exchange of currency and exchange of debt can only take place on the spot and any deferment of exchange or payment is not allowed.

Figure 4.2 Transactional Contracts

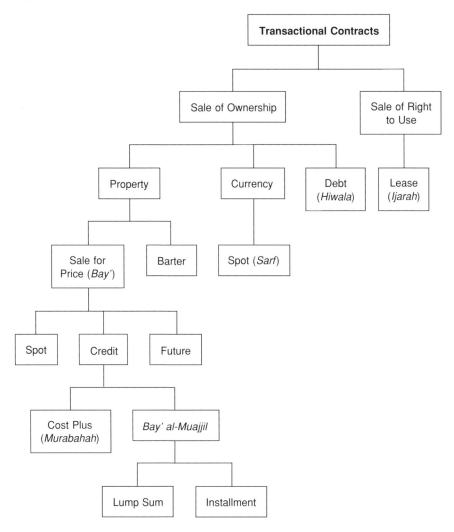

There is no concrete way to classify the contract of sale, but it can be viewed from different angles depending on the underlying asset and/or the modes of payment and delivery.

When sale contracts are viewed considering the subject of sale or the underlying asset, sale can be of five types:

    (i)   *Bay'* — sale of a property or commodity (moveable or immoveable) to another person for a price;

(ii)   *Sarf* — sale by exchange of money for money on the spot;

(iii) sale by barter i.e., exchange of goods for goods, in which neither is a money payment;

(iv)   *Bay' al-Dayn* — sale of debt or liability;

(v)   *Bay' al-Salam* (sale by immediate payment against future delivery) and *Bay' al-Istisnah* (sale on order). The main feature of such sale is that the item for sale is yet to come into existence at the time of contract.

Similarly, when viewed from the point of view of the mode of payment, sales contracts fall into the following categories:

(i)   Spot cash sale: The purchaser is under an obligation to pay the purchase price agreed upon, at the time of concluding the contract.

(ii)   Installment sale: Where payment is deferred and is to be made in installments.

(iii) Lump sum payment payable in the future: This mode of payment is valid if the date of payment is pre-determined. It is applicable to all types of sales except *Bay' al-Salam*.

(iv)   *Bay' al-Arabun*: This means payment of a portion of the full sale price paid in good faith as earnest money. In case the buyer decides not to complete the sale, this advance payment is forfeited to the seller.

In some cases, the sale contract can result in a credit sale where the payment is deferred, but there is a cost involved in deferring the payment. Such sale contracts, the *Murabahah*, are discussed in more detail under financing contracts.

Bay' al-Muajjil (Deferred Payment Sale)

This contract allows the sale of a product on the basis of deferred payment in installments or in a lump-sum payment. The price of the product is agreed upon between the buyer and the seller at the time of the sale and cannot include any charges for deferring payments.

Bay' al-Salam (Purchase with Deferred Delivery)

Bay' al-Salam is similar to conventional forward contracts in terms of function, but is different in terms of the payment arrangements. In the case of *Bay' al-Salam*, the buyer pays the seller the full negotiated price of a specific product which the seller promises to deliver at a specified future date. The main difference between *Bay' al-Salam* and a conventional forward contract is that the full negotiated price is payable at the time of the contract, as opposed to the latter, where the full payment is not due in advance. This forward sale is beneficial to both the seller and the buyer. The seller gets cash to invest in the production process and the buyer eliminates the uncertainty in the future price.

Bay' al-Salam was permitted as a special case by the Prophet (*pbuh*) as pre-payment of the price allowed the farmers to buy seeds and raw materials, and for personal consumption in order to be able to produce the fruits and crops. Due to the prohibition of *Riba*, farmers and traders could not take usurious loans and therefore, they were permitted to sell the agricultural products in advance. Similarly, the traders of Arabia who were engaged in importing and exporting goods could not borrow funds on usurious basis to finance their trade expeditions. In such cases, they were permitted to sell the goods in advance and finance the business through the proceeds.

The permissibility of *Bay' al-Salam* was an exception to the general rule that prohibits forward sales. Therefore, it was subjected to some strict conditions such as the following:

- The transaction is limited to products whose quality and quantity can be fully specified at the time when the contract is made. If the quality or quantity of a product cannot be so specified, it cannot be sold through the contract of *Bay' al-Salam*. For example, precious stones would not qualify for *Bay' al-Salam*, since every piece is normally different from another either in quality or in size or weight and their exact specification is not generally possible.
- Full payment of the purchase price is due at the time of the contract. If payment is not made, it may be misused to create a debt for the sake of selling a debt against debt, which is prohibited.
- The exact date and place of delivery must be specified in the contract.
- It is permissible to take a mortgage and a guarantor on a *Bay' al-Salam* obligation to guarantee that the seller performs their obligation, by delivering the commodity sold, on the due date.
- The commodity intended to be sold must be in the physical or constructive possession of the seller.

In the modern economy, *Bay' al-Salam* can be utilized for several purposes, particularly for the financing of agricultural operations, where the farmers can go through a financial intermediary such as an Islamic bank to buy or sell the produce in the forward market. The bank makes a valuable contribution to economic development by providing financing to farmers and a hedge against price volatility to the users of the produce. In the case of commercial and industrial activities, use of this contract can help finance small-medium enterprises (SMEs) in providing necessary capital to buy inputs and raw material for the production process.

Ijarah (Lease)

The contract of *Ijarah* or leasing means to give something on rent. Technically, an *Ijarah* contract is a contract of sale, but it is not the sale of a tangible asset; rather, it is a sale of the *usufruct* (the right to use the object) for a specified period of time. The word *Ijarah* conveys the sense of both hire and lease. In general, *Ijarah* refers to the lease of tangible assets such as property and merchandise, but it is also meant to denote the hiring of personal services for a fee. Renting of an asset also comes under the contract of *Ijarah*. In the case of the renting of an asset, the asset is leased for a much shorter period than its actual useful life, which also means that the asset can be rented to multiple users over its life.

Compared to the conventional form of financing, where financing is generally in the form of debt, leasing results in financing against a particular asset. In a sense, it combines financing and collateral, because the ownership of the asset serves as collateral and security against any future loss. The title of the ownership of the asset remains with the lessor and in the case of default the equipment is repossessed by the lessor. In addition, the financing is not dependent on the capital base of the lessee but depends on their creditworthiness to service the rental cash flow payments.

One of the major advantages of *Ijarah* is that it resembles the conventional lease agreement. There are some differences between the two, but they are alike in terms of their function. One difference is that in case of *Ijarah*, the leasing agency must own the leased object for the duration of the lease. Another difference is the absence of compound interest that may be charged under conventional leases in the event of default or delay in the installment payments. Similarities with conventional leasing make this contract attractive to conventional investors and borrowers as well.

Ijarah — Features and Conditions

- **The Lessor's Responsibilities:** The lessor must be the owner of the asset to be leased. It is the responsibility of the lessor/owner to maintain the property leased, so that it continues to generate benefit for the lessee. The lessor is expected to protect the property by arranging for adequate insurance against any loss or damage to the asset. The lessor/owner is responsible for certain costs and liabilities arising from leasing, such as damage to the asset, payment of any insurance premium cost and basic maintenance. The cost must be borne by the lessor/owner, but for the sake of efficiency, the lessor/owner may authorize the lessee to administer it on his/her behalf.

- All terms of the *Ijarah* contract should be stipulated in detail. These terms include the asset being leased, the rental amount, schedule of payment and the purpose for which the asset may be used.
- The leased asset should be treated as a trust in the hands of the lessee.
- The *Ijarah* contract is intended for utilization of the asset and not for consumption of the asset. Therefore, one of the conditions of the *Ijarah* contract is that the object leased must not be perishable or consumable.
- In case of any default by the lessee in making rental payment, the lessor is entitled to revoke the contract and claim the contract price for the remaining period.[2] The lessor/owner may claim compensation for any damage caused to the leased assets as a result of negligence on the part of the lessee.

Recently, Muslim jurists have also provided another contract *Iijarah wa "qtina" "or hire-purchase agreement"* which is similar to the conventional lease-purchase agreements. According to this contract, in addition to the regular contract of *Ijarah*, an additional contract is added, which includes a promise by the lessor/owner to sell the leased asset to the lessee at the end of the original lease agreement. The price for the residual value of the asset is pre-determined. The second contract is an option given to the lessee similar to the option available to a conventional lessee by which the lessee can purchase the asset at the conclusion of *Ijarah* contract or can simply return the asset.

The *Ijarah* contract has great potential for developing advanced financial instruments to meet the demands of investors and entrepreneurs. One of the main attributes of leasing practiced today is that the rental flows can differ, i.e., it can be a fixed amount or a floating amount, which makes it suitable for different needs of the investors. Leasing constitutes a large portion of the portfolios of Islamic banks. However, this share could be higher. One of the reasons why Islamic banks do not increase their lease portfolio is that by becoming the lessor/owner of the asset, Islamic banks take on additional responsibilities of administering the lease, which is not their main business.

An *Ijarah*-based model to provide mortgages for housing is already operating in North America. In addition, the *Ijarah* contract has been used in the successful launch of Islamic bonds or *Sukuk* (discussed further in Chapter 8).

Istisna (Partnership in Manufacturing)

The contract of *Istisna* is suitable to facilitate the manufacturing or the construction of an asset at the request of the buyer. Once the manufacturer undertakes to manufacture the asset or property for the buyer, the transaction of *Istisna* comes into existence. Both parties, namely the buyer and the manufacturer, agree on fixing a price and also agree on the specification of the asset intended to be manufactured. At the time of delivery, if the asset does not conform to the specifications, the party placing the order has the right to retract the contract.

One of the important features of *Istisna* relates to the mode and timing of the payment. There is enough flexibility with regard to the payment. It is not necessary that the price be paid in advance. It is also not necessary that it be paid at the time of the delivery. Both parties can agree on the schedule of the payment convenient to both and the payment can also be made in installments.

After *Bay' al-Salam*, the contract of *Istisna* is the second kind of sale contract where an asset is bought or sold before it comes into existence. However, the main differences between *Bay' al-Salam* and *Istisna* are (i) the underlying asset in case of *Istisna* is required to be manufactured or constructed; (ii) there is no requirement to pay the full price at the time of the contract; (iii) whereas *Istisna* can be cancelled before the manufacturer undertakes manufacturing, *Bay' al-Salam* cannot be cancelled unilaterally; and finally (iv) there is flexibility in the time of delivery in case of *Istisna*.

Like *Ijarah*, *Istisna* also has great potential for application in the area of project finance in different sectors and industries. Successful applications of *Istisna* include aircraft manufacturing, locomotive and ship building industries, and the manufacturing of heavy-duty machinery. The *Istisna* contract is suitable in the construction industry for building infrastructure such as roads, dams, housing, hospitals, and schools.

Financing Contracts

Looking at financing contracts from the perspective of their relative risk, at one end of the risk continuum, the system offers low-risk asset-backed securities while at the other extreme it promotes risky equity financing, including venture capital and private equity. In between, there are other collateralized securities originating from the *Ijarah* (leasing) or *Istisna* contracts attached to real assets which can cater to the needs of investors looking for short to medium-term maturity.

Murabahah (Cost-plus sales)

The *Murabahah* contract is one of the most popular contracts of sale used for purchasing commodities and other products on credit. The concept is that a financier purchases a product, i.e., commodity, raw material, etc, for supplying to an entrepreneur who does not have his own capital to do so. The financier and the entrepreneur agree on a profit margin, often referred to as "mark-up," which is added to the cost of the product. The payment is delayed for a specified period of time during which the entrepreneur produces the final product and sells it in the market. To be a valid contract, *Shariah* requires that a *Murabahah* contract should be the result of an original sale and should not be used as a means of financing any existing inventory. In addition, the financier must take the ownership of the item on sale.

Murabahah was originally a sale transaction in which a trader would purchase a product required by an end-user and then will sell the product to the end-user at a price that is calculated using an agreed profit margin over the costs incurred by the trader. With the emergence of financial intermediaries such as banks, the trader's role as financier has been taken over by the bank.

Mechanics of *Murabahah*:

A typical *Murabahah* transaction as practiced today takes place between three players — the financier or the Islamic bank, the vendor or the original seller of the product, and the user of the product requiring the bank to purchase and finance on their behalf. The transaction is explained in detail in the following steps:

Step 1: First, the bank's client seeking financing describes to the vendor the goods they intend to obtain, and asks the vendor to quote the price.

Step 2: After obtaining the quotation from the vendor, the bank's client contacts the bank promising to buy the goods from the bank if the bank buys the same from the vendor and resells them to the client at a price inclusive of the original cost in the quotation, plus a profit to be agreed upon mutually. At this stage, the bank would consider entering into a *Murabahah* contract, and would set the conditions and guarantees for the acceptance.

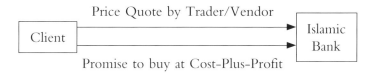

Step 3: At the next stage, the bank purchases the product from the vendor by making payment. In order to avoid getting involved with accepting the delivery and making arrangements to store the product, often banks appoint the client their agent to accept the delivery on their (the banks') behalf.[3] Since the bank is still the owner of the product, a *Murabahah* contract is drawn between the client and the bank indicating the profit or mark-up to be charged and other relevant details. The contract is finalized by agreeing on the mode of payment, i.e., lump sum or through installments. In addition to the *Murabahah* contract, the bank also accepts the goods or other assets as collateral against the credit risk or the risk of default in payment by the client.

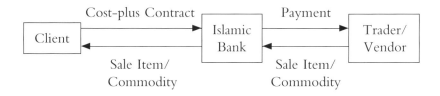

Step 4: At the time of payment, the client makes the payment to the bank. This payment includes the cost of the product to the bank plus a profit margin for the bank.

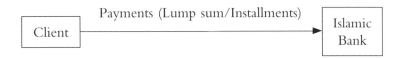

Payments (Lump sum/Installments)

Client → Islamic Bank

Features and Conditions:

(i)   *Murabahah* must be based on a sale and should not be used for financing purposes. This type of transaction cannot be used in cases where the client wants to get funds for a purpose other than purchasing a product, such as working capital, payment of wages and salaries, or settlement of accounts payables. To make it a valid sale transaction, the *Shariah* makes it necessary that the sale item is really purchased by the financier who takes its ownership and possession.

(ii) In the event of default by the end user, the financier only has recourse to the items financed and no further mark-up or penalty may be applied to the outstanding liability. As opposed to conventional loans where interest keeps accruing, no such accrual takes place in case of *Murabahah*. It is common practice among Islamic banks to consider non-payment of two consecutive payments as default, at which stage the bank is entitled to declare that all the other installments are due immediately. In some cases, *Shariah* scholars allow the financier to recover additional amounts to off-set any loss or damage due to the default.

(iii) The financier is allowed to ask for security to protect itself against any non-payment in the future. Often an asset other than the item being financed through *Murabahah* is taken as security, but when no such asset is available, the financer takes the item itself as security. This may require additional claims by the financier on the item financed such as naming the financier as a beneficiary in the insurance policy.

(iv) The mark-up rate charged by the financier is influenced by the type of product financed, type of security and collateral, the creditworthiness of the client, and the length of time for which the financing takes place.

(v)   Another distinct feature is that the resulting financial claim resembles conventional debt security characterized by a pre-determined pay-off. The difference is that Islamic instruments are clearly and closely linked to and are collateralized against a real asset and are consummated by a transactional contract. As a result, a financial claim is created against a real asset with a short-term maturity and relatively low risk.

Although *Murabahah* financing is allowed by the *Shariah* and is very popular with Islamic banks, there are some misconceptions about the instrument among those who do not fully understand the contract. The misunderstanding stems from the question of what is the difference between the mark-up and interest since *Murabahah* results in a financial claim like a zero-coupon bond with a fixed rate of interest. This misunderstanding gets further compounded when an outsider observes a close relationship between the mark-up and the prevailing interest rate in the market, such as LIBOR. Researchers have addressed both of these questions.

In distinguishing *Murabahah* from a loan, it is pointed out that in case of *Murabahah*, no money is loaned but a specific asset is purchased for the client to ensure that the financing is linked to an asset. In addition, whereas in lending money as a loan, the financier is exposed to credit risk only. In the case of *Murabahah*, the financier is first exposed to the price risk when the product is acquired for the client and before the client decides to purchase the product. The client retains an option to decline to take delivery of the product.[4] Therefore, it is argued that by engaging in buying and selling the product, the bank is exposing itself to certain risks, as also it leads to trading of real asset; hence, a *Murabahah* transaction is different from a simple loan.

The confusion in equating *Murabahah* with a loan is not a new one. Early Arab traders during the time of the Prophet (*pbuh*) posed the same question. They stated that "trade is like *Riba*" [*Quran* (2:275)] to which it was answered that "but *Allah* has permitted trade and forbidden *Riba*" [*Quran* (2:275)]. The legal difference between *Murabahah* and an interest-based loan is clear — whereas the former is a sale contract in which the price is increased for deferment of payment, the latter is an increase in the amount of a debt for deferment. The first is permitted, but the second is not.

The practice of using an interest rate index to determine the mark-up rate has been the source of confusion and the focus of much criticism. Islamic banks often argue that the mark-up rate is the function of interest rate index because there is no Islamic bench mark which could provide an indication of what is the prevailing rate of return in the economy. This necessitates the creation of an index to track the expected cost of capital and the rate of return which can be used to price financial instruments.

Bai' Bithamin Ajil (BBA)

In Malaysia and some other South East Asian countries, a form of *Murabahah* in which payment is made in installments some time after delivery of goods is referred to as *Bai' Bithamin Ajil*. *Bai' bithaman Ajil* has features similar to *Murahabah* in terms of the financier undertaking to buy the asset required for resale to the client at a higher price as agreed to by the parties involved. The difference from *Murahabah* is that *Bai' bithaman Ajil* is used for long-term financing and the seller is not required to disclose the profit margin that is included in the selling price.

Tawarruq

Tawarruq, also known as "reverse *Mudarabah*" is a mechanism of borrowing cash by undertaking two separate transactions. In a typical *Tawarruq* transaction, a person buys a commodity or some goods from the seller on credit with an understanding of paying back the price either in installments or in full in the future. Once the commodity is purchased, it is immediately sold to a third party at spot price which is lower than the purchase price. In this way, a loophole is created to borrow money by using two legitimate *Shariah* transactions. In the financial terms, this mechanism amounts to the creation of a zero-coupon loan where the cost of borrowing money (interest rate) is at the same rate which the original seller might be charging to defer the payment, ignoring any transaction costs.

The practice of *Tawarruq* is a recent development in the Middle East market, especially in Saudi Arabia, but it has not received a wide acceptance and there is considerable resistance to the practice. Technically, from the *Shariah*'s point of view, the practice is legitimate, but several scholars have condemned its wide-spread practice stating that it opens up the door for borrowing money on the basis of *Riba* (interest) and without creating any real economic activity, as the same commodity or product might be sold to several borrowers. The practice is disliked by scholars, particularly where the borrower of the money sells the commodity or goods back to the original seller.

Musharakah (Partnership)

The *Musharakah* contract is a versatile contract with different variations to suit different situations. This partnership contract is a pre-Islamic contract and was widely accepted and promoted by the Prophet (*pbuh*). *Musharakah* is a hybrid of *Shirakah* (partnership) and *Mudarabah*, combining the act of investment and management.[5] In the absence of debt security, the *Shariah* promotes the *Musharakah* form of financing. The *Shariah* is fairly comprehensive in defining different types of partnerships, in identifying rights and obligations of the partners, and in stipulating the rules governing the sharing of profits and losses.

Musharakah or *Shirkah* can be defined as a form of partnership where two or more people combine either their capital or labor, to share the profits and losses, and where they have similar rights and liabilities. A special case of partnership of capital and labor is known as *Mudarabah*, which is the cornerstone of Islamic financial intermediation. In general, the term *Musharakah* is commonly used to refer to partnership, but there are further sub-classifications of partnerships with respect to the levels of the partners' authority and obligations, and the type of their contributions, i.e., management skills or goodwill, etc. For the sake of our discussion, we will refer to *Musharakah* as partnership based on capital contribution.

Features and Conditions:

- The partnership agreement need not necessarily be formal and written; it can be informal and oral.
- Every partner is an agent of and for the other, as all the partners benefit from the *Musharakah* business.
- Every partner enjoys equal rights in all respects, in the absence of any condition to the contrary.
- Every partner has a right to participate actively in the affairs of *Musharakah* if they so wish. However, in case of formal legal entities such as limited companies and cooperative societies, partners delegate their rights to participate in the management to professional managers.
- The share of every partner in the profits is to be determined as a proportion or percentage and no fixed amount can be pre-determined. The ratios or percentage of sharing profits should be pre-determined.
- There is unanimity among *Shariah* scholars that the loss shall be borne by the partners according to their contributed capitals. The *Shariah* is very clear that if a party has not invested any capital in the partnership, they are not liable for the loss. This implies that any capital investment is subject to the risk of loss of capital, but any investment of labor or time is limited to the loss of the time invested and the loss of capital is not required to be shared by such a partner.

- The *Shariah* recognizes the limited liability of shareholders in a *Musharakah*-based legal entity, such as a joint stock company or a corporation. Shareholders cannot be held liable for more than their share of capital invested.
- Whereas a partner can withdraw from a partnership after discharging their liabilities as agreed by the partners, a shareholder in a company cannot withdraw from the partnership. They can exit the partnership by selling their share in the market.
- The loss during one period is allowed to be carried forward to the next period and to be offset against the profits of the next period, if any. However, until the total loss has been written off, any distribution of "profit" will be considered as an advance to the partners. In order to avoid such a situation, the practice of building reserves from profits against future losses is recommended.

In modern times, Islamic banks have developed a special kind of partnership known as "consecutive partnership," which considers depositors during a full financial year as partners in the proceeds of that financial year, regardless of the full usage of their funds during this period. Similarly, adjustments are made in the profits for proceeds accrued, but not realized, during a financial period. This was necessary to overcome the accounting problems with the determination of the profit and loss of each depositor based on the deposit period and also to prevent withdrawals from investments funded by the depositor when the depositor wishes to withdraw their funds.

Another form of *Musharakah* is being used to provide housing mortgages by forming a *Musharakah* between the financier and the customer who own the real estate jointly. This contract is commonly known as *Musharakah Mutanaqisah* or "diminishing partnership." As compared to an *Ijarah*-based mortgage where the ownership of the house remains with the lessor/owner for the entire lease period, ownership in a diminishing partnership is explicitly shared between the customer and the financier. As indicated by the name, the ownership of the financier diminishes over time as the customer purchases a share with each monthly payment. The periodic payments of the customer can be divided into two parts; one paying a proportionate rental to the financier based on the financier's share of the property and the other, equity contribution to buy out the financier's share of the equity. Gradually, over time, the customer is able to buy out the financier's share and thus acquires complete ownership of the property.

Islamic Instruments: Historical Background

The Arabian peninsula in particular and the Middle East in general had, for centuries, a sophisticated tradition of trade and business partnerships which can be traced back to the pre-lslamic period. The Prophet (*pbuh*) himself was an honest and successful trader. The mercantile communities of the Middle East followed well-developed customs and traditions, some of which did not have any conflict with the principles of Islam. With the introduction of Islam, the examination of common business practices began, with a view to identifying those practices which were in direct conflict with the teachings of Islam. This process is continuing to this day. However, one of the major contributions of Islam was to codify, systematize, and formalize traditional trade and business practices into a formal legal system of standardized contracts, leading to a mercantile law in complete harmony with Islam. This transformation took place after a rigorous process of eliminating those aspects of the old tradition that were in conflict with the teachings of Islam and retaining those in conformity with it.

As Islam spread out of Arabia to other geographical regions, new situations, business practices, cultures and customs were put to the same test of conformity to the tenets of Islam. Islamic practices and contracts became well-known from one corner of the globe to another. As a scholar noted:

> "Through their trade and commerce in the Middle Ages, Muslims spread over the continents of Asia and Africa and into Europe, bringing with them their religion and their cultures. From the earliest days of the expansion of Islam to the present day, Muslim businesses have been models of success and integrity. Islamic business in history is an exotic and dynamic panorama that ranges from gem merchants in Ceylon, to caravan traders in Mali, to dealers of saffron in Muslim Spain, to sellers of aromatic oils in the deserts of Arabia, to colorful cotton markets in Turkey, to spice markets in India, to the hardwood merchants of Malaysia, to the plantations and industry of Indonesia, to carpet makers in Kashmir, to the great merchant houses of the Levant, to the oil of the Arabian Peninsula, North Africa, and Brunei. The business practices and ethics in all of these places, and from the moment that Muslims arrived there, are derived from the same source."[6]

During the period referred to as "the age of the commercial revolution" (Lopez, 1976), trade flowed freely across the then-known world, supported by the risk-sharing methods of finance, which were developed in the

Muslim countries consistent with the *Shariah*. Information regarding the basic features of these methods was spread through Spain, from the Muslim world to Egypt, Europe, India, and North Africa. These new financial techniques were also transmitted by Muslim merchants to Eurasia, Russia and China, as well as to East Asia.[7]

There is little doubt that the institutions of *commenda* and *maona* — two popular financing instruments in the Europe of the Middle Ages — originated in the Islamic world.[8] *Commenda* was identical to *Mudarabah*, and *maona* partnerships were either *Musharakah* or *Mudarabah*, depending on the nature of activities undertaken by the partners. These institutions, along with financial instruments such as *Hawala* and *Suftaja*, were transmitted to Europe and to other regions by Jewish scholars and merchants throughout the Jewish Diaspora and via Spain through trade and scholastic borrowing from Islamic sources.

Thanks to the latest research conducted on the Geniza archives of Cairo, our understanding of historical Biblical writings and translations, ancient Jewish liturgies, communal records and of the relations between Jews and Arabs in medieval Islamic society has increased enormously. Goitein (1964) refers to Geniza archives as "a treasure of manuscripts written mainly during the *Fatimid* and *Ayyubid* periods and originally preserved in a synagogue in Old Cairo." Further, he indicates that "Geniza (pronounced: Gheneeza), as may be remarked in passing, is derived from the same Persian word as Arabic "*Janazah*," burial, and has almost the same meaning. It is a place where discarded writings were buried so that the name of God, which might have been written on them, might not be discarded. Thus, *Geniza* is the opposite of an orderly archive." He further informs us that "… the documents discussed in this paper, albeit mostly written in Hebrew characters, are in Arabic language."

Based on the Geniza records as well as Islamic *Fiqh* sources, we can draw the following conclusions:

(i)   "There is remarkable symmetry between the *Hanafite* legal formulations of the late-eighth century and the documented commercial practices of the eleventh and twelfth century Geniza merchants"[9];

(ii)   "In the extensive commercial records of the Geniza, we found comparatively little evidence of usurious transactions";

(iii)   Moreover, research by medieval historians demonstrates the extensive use of *commenda* and *maona*;

(iv)   Trade in the Middle Ages was both extensive and intensive, financed by risk-sharing partnerships;

(v)   Partnership was used in industrial, commercial, and in public administration projects;

(vi) Even a cursory examination of the Geniza material proves that lending money for interest was not only shunned religiously, but was also of limited significance economically;

(vii) The practice of *Mudarabah* is well-documented in the westward trade made between Egypt and Tunisia. Based on the same sources, *Musharakah* (equity partnership) being practiced in the north-south trade between Egypt and Syria as well as between Egypt and Jeddah during the eleventh century.[10]

Similarly, 32 *Mudarabah* contracts from the seventeenth century were discovered in the Turkish city of Bursa and were clearly the most important type of business partnerships being practiced in Bursa at this relatively late period. Interestingly, these seventeenth century Turkish partnerships were, for all practical purposes, identical with the classical ones observed in the Geniza archives. Another successful example is discovery of *Mudarabah* and *Musharakah* from the Crimean war period in Palestine. To the East of the Arabian Peninsula, lively trade exchanges took place between the Arabian Peninsula and India. Goitein, for instance, has found 315 documents in the Geniza archives dealing specifically with trade in the Indian Ocean. Islamic partnerships were observed even further East, for instance, in Indonesia, which is at the other end of the Indian Ocean.[11]

Before the beginning of the twentieth century, most economic historians of the Middle Ages ignored the importance of trade and financial relations between Europe and the rest of the world, which were crucial to the economic development of the West before the fifteenth century. Abu-Lughod (1994) contends that this was due to the belief held by the Eurocentric scholarship that globalized trade became relevant only after the "rise of the West" in the late fifteenth century. According to Abu-Lughod, an advanced globalized system of trade "already existed by the second half of the thirteenth century, one that included almost all regions (only the "New World" was missing). However, it was a world-system that Europe had only recently joined and in which it played only a peripheral role." She maps growing global trade flows between 737 and 1478 AD, demonstrating that trade flows first centered in Mesopotamia and spread rapidly over the next eight centuries throughout the then-known world to become global.

There is ample evidence that Islamic modes of financing and intermediation were widely used in several regions of the world. What is even more important to note is that the available evidence is scattered not only across geographical space but also across time, thereby demonstrating to us the universality as well as the tremendous resilience of these institutions. It is important to note that the charging or payment of interest in business transactions was avoided as far as possible and, on the other hand, equity or partnership-based financing was encouraged. That shows how Islamic partnerships dominated the business world for centuries and also that the concept of interest found very little application in day-to-day transactions.

Endnotes

1 From a legal perspective, a contract in Islam could be either unilateral or bilateral. Unilateral contracts are usually of a gratuitous nature and may not require the consent of the recipient. Such contracts comprise of gifts (*Hadiah, Hibah*) or writing-off a debt (*Ibra*) or endowment (*Waqf*). Bilateral contracts, on the other hand, are more formal contracts and require the informed consent of both parties to the contract. Since bilateral contracts are formal contracts, these are subject to strict guidelines and rules when it comes to their documentation, rights and obligations. What is normally accepted or tolerated in unilateral contracts would not necessarily be accepted or tolerated in bilateral contracts. All commercial contracts are bilateral contracts and therefore are regulated by well-established legal rulings.

2 The general practice of Islamic banks is to wait for two consecutive defaults before taking any action.

3 In Sudan, Islamic banks do not authorize their clients to accept delivery of the product being financed. It is common practice among banks to take delivery and then at a later stage offer to sell the same to the client who has the right to accept or reject the offer.

4 It is common practice among Islamic banks to take a promise from the client before purchasing the product that the client will purchase the product from the bank.

5 In the early books of *Fiqh*, the partnership business has been discussed mainly under the caption of *Shirka*. However, contemporary scholars have preferred to use the term *Susharaka* to represent a broader concept combining features of *Shirka* and *Mudarabah*. Therefore, in case of *Musharakah*, a *Musharik* also provides capital in addition to the management skills. For further details, see Ayoub, M. (2002), *Islamic Banking and Finance: Theory and Practice.*

6 Yousuf De Larenzo, Yusuf Talah (2002), *The Religious Foundations of Islamic Finance.*

7 Abu-Lughod (1989).

8 Udovitch, Abraham L. (1970), "Commercial Techniques in Early Medieval Islamic Trade," *Islam and the Trade of Asia,* ed. D. Richards, pp. 37–62.
Udovitch, Abraham L. (1967), "Labor Partnership in Medieval Islamic Law," *Journal of Economic and Social History of the Orient,* Vol. 10, pp. 64–80.
Udovitch, Abraham L. (1967), "Credit as a Means of Investment in Medieval Islamic Trade," *Journal of the American Oriental Society,* Vol. 87, No. 3, (Jul.–Sept), pp. 260–264.

Udovitch, Abraham L. (1970), *Partnership and Profit in Medieval Islam*, Princeton University Press, Princeton, USA.

9   Udovitch, Abraham L. (1970), *Partnership and Profit in Medieval Islam*.

10   For further details see Goitein, S.D. (1964) "Commercial and Family Partnerships in the Countries of Medieval Islam", Gerber, H. (1981) "The Muslim Law of Partnerships in Ottoman Court Records", and Firestone, Y. (1975) "Production and Trade in an Islamic Context".

11   For further details see Goitein (1964), Gerber (1981) and Firestone (1975).

CHAPTER

5

Financial Intermediation

Financial systems are crucial for efficient allocation of resources in a modern economy. An efficient financial system is expected to perform several functions, including the vital function of facilitating efficient financial intermediation through financial markets and institutions such as banks. The landscape of any financial system is therefore dominated by the nature of financial intermediation, i.e., how the function of intermediation is performed, who intermediates between the suppliers and users of funds, and what role the intermediary plays in the saving-investment process and in corporate finance. Also at play are the issues in financial crises associated with financial intermediation, the kind of risk management tools being offered, and of the operation and the regulation of the intermediaries.

Financial intermediaries are special in comparison to other economic agents. The acquisition and processing of information about economic agents, the packaging and repackaging of financial claims, and financial contracting are among the activities that differentiate financial intermediation from other economic activities. Financial intermediaries not only channel resources from the capital-surplus agents (generally, households) to capital-deficit ones (the corporate sector); they also allow inter-temporal smoothing of households' consumption and businesses" expenditures and thus allow both firms and households to share risks. Since the early 1980s, the increased complexity and volatility of the financial markets have led financial intermediaries to innovate and offer products to mitigate, transfer, and share financial risks.

The primary functions of a financial intermediary are asset transformation, conducting of orderly payments, brokerage and risk transformation. Asset transformation takes place in the form of matching the demand and supply of financial assets and liabilities (e.g., deposits, equity, credit, loans and insurance) and entails the transformation of maturity, scale and place of the financial assets and liabilities of the ultimate borrowers and lenders. The administrative function of an accounting and payments system (e.g., check transfer, electronic funds transfer, settlement, clearing) is considered another important intermediation function. Typically, financial intermediaries have also offered brokerage or match-making between the borrowers and lenders, and facilitated the demand and supply of non-tangible and contingent assets and liabilities, such as collaterals, guarantees, financial advice, and custodial services.

The nature of intermediation has changed drastically over the last three decades due to the changes in macroeconomic policies, liberalization of capital accounts, de-regulation, advances in financial theory and, finally, breakthroughs in technology. Financial intermediation in the form of traditional banking has declined considerably in developed countries where market-based intermediation has become dominant. Traditional banking operations of lending are being replaced by more fee-based services that bring investors and borrowers directly in contact with each other. Some researchers even claim that some degree of disintermediation has taken place due to the reduced role of the traditional financial intermediary. However, irrespective of who performs the intermediation, i.e., bank or market, the basic function of intermediation itself has not changed.

Financial intermediation in Islamic history has an established historical record and has made significant contributions to economic development over time. Financiers in the early days of Islam were known as *sarrafs* who undertook many of the traditional and basic functions of a conventional financial institution such as intermediation between borrowers and lenders, operation of a secure and reliable domestic as well as cross-border payment system and offering services such as issuance of promissory notes and letters of credit. Commercial historians have equated the function of *sarrafs* with a bank. Historians like Udovitch considered them as "bankers without banks." *Sarrafs* operated through an organized network and well functioning markets, which established them as sophisticated intermediaries, given the tools and technology of their time. It is claimed that financial intermediaries in the early Islamic period also helped one another overcome liquidity shortages on the basis of a mutual help arrangement which was then called *ibda' or bidaah*. There is evidence that some of the concepts, contracts, practices, and institutions developed in the Islamic legal sources of the late eighth century provided the foundations for similar instruments in Europe several centuries later. Chapra and Khan (2001).

As mentioned in Chapter 4, the *Shariah* provides a set of contracts — **intermediation contracts** — which facilitate an efficient and transparent execution of transactional and financing contracts. This set of contracts is comprehensive enough to provide a wide range of typical intermediation services such as asset transformation, payment system, custodial services, and risk management. Intermediation contracts can be further sub-classified into three groups. (see Figure 5.1). The first group of intermediation contracts is the most significant one; it deals with intermediation through forming a partnership of capital and entrepreneurial skills. The second group, based on the concept of trust, deals with the placing of assets with intermediaries on the basis of trust for sake of protection or security. Finally, the third group facilitates explicit and implicit guarantees of financial performance between economic agents. These contracts play a critical role; they provide stability and mitigate risk in the financial system.

Intermediation contracts based on the principles of partnership include *Mudarabah* (a trustee finance contract) and *Musharakah* (equity partnership). In a *Mudarabah* contract, an economic agent with capital (*Rabb-ul-mal*) can develop a partnership with another agent (*mudarib*) with skills to form a partnership with the agreement to share the profits. Although losses are borne by the capital owner only, the *mudarib* may however be liable for a loss in case of misconduct or negligence on his part. *Musharakah* is a hybrid of *Shiraka* (partnership) and *Mudarabah*, combining the acts of investment and management. Details of *Musharakah* have been discussed in the previous chapter on financial contracts, while the contract of *Mudarabah* is discussed in detail in Section I of this chapter.

Both *Mudarabah* and *Musharakah* are cornerstones of financial intermediation for mobilization of resources, akin to an agent who, like a bank, develops expertise and knowledge of different markets acting as an

Figure 5.1 Intermediation Contracts Flow Chart

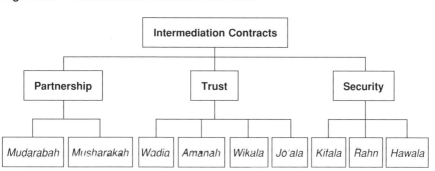

intermediary to screen and monitor investment opportunities for the deployment of funds placed with it. In this respect, the contracts of *mudarabah* and *musharakah* have existed as instruments of financial intermediation from the early periods of Islam. Both types of contracts were able to mobilize the entire reservoir of the monetary resources of the medieval Islamic world for financing agriculture, crafts, manufacturing and long-distance trade. These instruments were used not only by Muslims but were also acceptable and practiced by Jews and Christians to the extent that interest-bearing loans and other usurious practices were not in common use.

There is undeniable evidence that these two contracts spread rapidly throughout the Middle East and then to the other corners of the globe wherever Muslim traders were active in business and trade. In the Arabian Peninsula, the second caliph Omar is known to have invested the money of orphans with merchants who traded between Medina and Iraq. Similarly, as early as the seventh century AD, the tax revenues from Iraq were sent across the desert to Medina (Saudi Arabia) on the basis of *Mudarabah*. Based on the research on Geniza archives, it is documented that the trade between Egypt and Tunisia took place on the basis of *Mudarabah*. The practice of *Musharakah* is known to have existed in the north-south trade between Egypt and Syria as well as between Egypt and Saudi Arabia, during the eleventh century.

With the encouragement and blessings of early Muslim jurists, partnership-based intermediation contracts were promoted, which led to the evolution of *Mudarabah* and *Musharakah* contracts as standardized well-documented and well-established financial instruments. However, around the eleventh and twelfth century, further advancements in these contracts slowed down, with the result that further innovation of financial instruments became limited. For example, the same concept of *Mudarabah* and *Musharakah* was expanded further in Europe where the European business community constantly expanded its partnerships and invented larger and larger enterprises. The increasing size of European partnerships meant that the small savings of the small investors were effectively channeled into large investment projects. The concept of a joint stock company or a modern-day corporation grew out of the concept of partnership, but only on a larger scale.

Intermediation Contracts

Whereas *Mudarabah* and *Musharakah* contracts are critical in credit and capital creation, other contracts such as *Wikala*, *Jo'ala*, *Rahn*, etc. also play an important role in providing vital economic services that a conventional financial intermediary may offer. Intermediation contracts except *Musharakah* are discussed in these sections. The contract of *Musharakah* has been discussed in detail in the previous chapter.

Mudarabah

As mentioned earlier, in a *Mudarabah* contract, an economic agent with capital develops a partnership with another economic agent who has expertise in deploying capital into real economic activities with an agreement to share the profits. The earliest Islamic business partnerships can be traced back to the Prophet himself, who acted as an agent (*mudarib*) for his wife when he undertook several trade expeditions on her behalf. *Mudarabah* partnerships performed an important economic function by combining the three most important factors of production — capital, labor, and entrepreneurship. Typically, the contract of *Mudarabah* involved an arrangement in which the capital-owner entrusted his/her capital or merchandise to an agent (*mudarib*) to trade with it and then return to the investor the principal plus a previously-agreed-upon share of the profits. As a reward for the agent's labor and entrepreneurship, the agent (*mudarib*) received the remaining share of the profit. Any loss resulting from the exigencies of travel or from an unsuccessful business venture was borne exclusively by the investor.

More formally, a *Mudarabah* contract is a contract of partnership between the investor (principal) and the entrepreneur who acts as an agent of the investor to invest the money in a fashion deemed suitable by the agent with an agreement to share profits. This contract is usually limited to a certain period of time at the end of which the profits are shared as agreed. An example of *Mudarabah* in modern times would be of a contract between an investor and an Islamic bank where the investor deposits funds with the Islamic bank that has developed a certain expertise in the financial markets and in identifying profitable projects and uses its management skills to invest the investor's money on his/her behalf. After a certain period, both the bank and the investor share the profits according to their pre-determined profit-sharing ratios.

The contract of *Mudarabah* has the following distinct features:

Control
Although *Shariah* scholars have differences of opinion about the restrictions in a *Mudarabah* contract in regard to its activities, scope, and objectives, these difference do not have any significant impact on its function. In general, the investor designates the *mudarib* as an agent and therefore does not have any right to control, or participate in, the decision-making of the *mudarib* as to the placement of funds. In other words, the investor does not have any

management rights over the *mudarib*, who is free in selecting the projects in which to invest, or the manner in which to invest. However, in some cases, the investor may impose some upfront restrictions on the agent to participate in a particular project or in a particular fashion. In such cases, the contract becomes a restrictive one and is known as restrictive *Mudarabah*. If the *mudarib* acts contrary to such conditions or restrictions, they are deemed to have acted beyond their powers and, therefore, by virtue of the trust that was placed in them, they have to be liable for any resulting loss or damage.

Profit and Loss Sharing

One of the most significant features of *Mudarabah* is that while the profits are shared between the investor and the agent, any loss in the investment or business is borne solely by the capital-owner, unless such loss is caused by the misconduct or negligence of the *mudarib*. In the absence of misconduct or negligence, the *mudarib* is not responsible for any loss in the venture. In cases where the agent acts in good faith, and prudently, but still the investment results in a loss, the capital owner loses a portion of the capital, but the agent loses the time and effort deployed during the business venture. Therefore, both investor and agent suffer losses, but in different ways. The capital-owner suffers a financial loss due to the loss of capital, while the agent/entrepreneur does not make any financial gains, but instead loses the potential reward for their skills. The *mudarib* is not a guarantor of the capital, except where there is misconduct or negligence on his part.

Profit Distribution

In the *Mudarabah* agreement, the partners enjoy absolute freedom in the determination of the division of profit. The following are some of the rules applicable to the determination and distribution of profit and loss under a *Mudarabah*:

- The most critical requirement of a *Mudarabah* contract is that the division of profits between the investor and *mudarib* must be in the form of proportions and ratios rather than in absolute numbers.
- The profit-sharing formula itself must be made specific and certain beforehand and must be clearly indicated in the agreement for profit distribution. It cannot be made conditional in such a manner that one party shall have preferential right over part of the profit while the other party may or may not receive any share of the profit.
- The ratio of profit distribution may differ from that of capital contribution.

• The distribution of profits in a *Mudarabah* can only take place after the capital-owner has retrieved his capital. Any interim or periodic distribution before the closing of the accounts is considered tentative and subject to final review and revision and has to be made good on any loss of capital. In other words, if any periodic return was paid based on expected profits or interim proceeds, it shall be treated as partial return before the conclusion of the contract, when final profit or loss will be determined after adjusting any interim profits paid.

Multiple Tiers

Early *Shariah* scholars played an important role in the development of complex intermediation structures by granting the necessary freedom to the *mudarib* to form other partnerships with third parties. On the one hand, this freedom allowed the *mudarib* to expand the partnership to create a pool with a large number of capital providers as passive partners and, on the other hand, it allowed a *mudarib* to engage entrepreneurs on the basis of *Mudarabah* to invest the capital entrusted to the *mudarib*. This flexible structure of different tiers has become the basis of modern Islamic banks.

Credit Risk and Defaults

Since there may not be any tangible asset which can be used as collateral against potential losses, management of the credit risk and defaults often becomes an issue in the case of *Mudarabah*. In order to minimize such risk, the capital-owner or investor should perform due diligence in respect of the past performance and reputation of the *mudarib*. On the other hand, the *mudarib* who will be investing the funds should perform adequate screening and monitoring of potential projects worthy of good investment opportunities. In cases where an Islamic bank is acting as the *mudarib* and is investing in a business on the basis of *Mudarabah*, it may, in order to minimize its risk, ask for a guarantee, pledge or collateral of a property from the business.

Wikala (Representation)

The contract of *Wikala* means designating a person or legal entity to act on one's behalf or as one's representative. It has been a common practice to appoint an agent (*Wakil*) to facilitate trade operations. A *Wikala* contract gives a power of attorney or an agency assignment to a financial intermediary to perform a certain task. On the surface, there does not appear to be much difference between a *Mudarabah* and a *Wikala* contract, since both are principal-agent contracts. However, the main difference is that in case of

Mudarabah, the *mudarib* has full control and freedom to utilize funds according to their professional knowledge, as opposed to the case of *Wikala* where the agent (*Wakil*) does not have similar freedom. A *Wakil* (agent) acts only as a representative to execute a particular task according to the instructions given.

Amanah (Trust), *Ariya* (Gratuitous Lending) and *Wadia* (Deposits)

Amanah, *ariya*, and *wadia* contracts are all concerned with placing assets in trust with someone. These contracts are utilized in facilitating a custodial relationship between investors and the financial institutions.

Wadia (deposit) arises when a person keeps his/her property with another person for safe-keeping and also allows him/her to use it without the intention of receiving any return from it. The *Wadia* assets delivered for safe-keeping are a trust in the hands of the person who accepts them. Liability arising out of the *Wadia* contract depends on the nature of the agreement. For example, if the trustee does not charge any fee for the safe-keeping services, and losses to the property, if any, are not due to the negligence of the trustee, he/she are not liable for the losses. However, if a fee is involved as part of the contract, then the trustee is liable to compensate in the event of loss. The trustee has enough flexibility in utilizing the asset in various ways, with prior permission of the owner. For example, the trustee can let the asset on hire, or lend it for use, or pledge the asset or may use it him/herself. The trustee must return the asset upon demand.

The term *Amanah* (trust deposit) is a broad term where one party is entrusted with the custody or safekeeping of someone else's property. For example, when an employer hands over a property to an employee, it comes under the contract of trust. However, in the context of intermediation, *Amanah* refers to a contract where a party deposits its assets with another for the sole purpose of safekeeping. Unlike *Wadia*, where the keeper of the asset is allowed to use the asset, *Amanah* deposit is purely for safe-keeping and the keeper cannot use the asset. Demand deposits of an Islamic bank are offered through *Amanah* contracts. There are responsibilities that arise out of an *Amanah* contract and if a person who is keeping the property is found negligent or guilty of not taking proper care of the property, they are held liable for the losses.

Ariya or lending for gratuitous use, is a contract where the lending of an asset takes place between a lender and the borrower with the agreement that the former will not charge anything for the use of the asset he lent out. In other words, the borrower is entitled to enjoy the benefits yielding from the asset borrowed, without giving any payment or rent to the lender. The borrower is responsible for the maintenance and up-keep of the asset to the best of their capability. The borrower is to return the item immediately on demand by the lender. The lender may impose restrictions as to time, place, and the nature of use. The lender can discontinue the contract and withdraw the loan whenever they like.

Rahn (Pledge)

A financial institution reduces its credit risk of non-payment by the borrower by securing a financial obligation either through personal surety or through a pledge. In other words, the lender takes an asset as collateral against a financial liability to make sure that the borrower will repay the debt. The contract of *Rahn* (or pledge) is to make a property a security provided by the borrower against a loan, so that in case of the borrower's inability to make the payment, the liability may be recovered from the value of the pledged property. The main features of pledge are as follows:

- Only assets having a sale value can be offered in pledge.
- Two different creditors may take a common pledge from a single debtor, in which case the pledge will secure the whole of the two debts.
- Acceptance of the pledge does not cancel the demand for repayment of the debt by the creditor.
- If at the time for repaying the debt the borrower refuses to make payment, the lender may approach the court to force the borrower to sell the pledged asset in order to recover the debt. In case the borrower refuses to do so, the court has the authority to sell the pledged asset, if necessary, to repay the debt.

Kifala (Suretyship)

The contract of *Kifala* refers to an obligation in addition to an existing obligation in respect of a demand for something. This may relate to an individual, an act or a financial obligation. In the case of *Kifala* for an act or the performance of an act, it implies timely delivery/fulfillment of the obligation or timely action in respect of the task contracted by the principal. In the case of financial obligation, it refers to an obligation to be met in the event of the principal debtor's inability to honor their obligation. In financial transactions, under the contract of *Kifala*, a third party becomes a surety for the payment of a debt or obligation, if it is not paid or fulfilled by the person originally liable. It is similar to a pledge given to a creditor that the debtor will pay the debt, fine or any other liability. In this respect, the contract of *Kifala* can become the basis of a more sophisticated vehicle for a financial intermediary to undertake financial and performance guarantees and underwriting of financial claims, which are an integral part of modern banking and capital markets.

The following are some of the features of *Kifala*:

- It is important to understand that *Kifala* does not release the principal debtor from their liability since *Kifala* is only an obligation in addition to the existing obligation.
- More than one *Kifala* for a single obligation is acceptable.
- Persons jointly indebted may provide surety for each other, in which case both of them are jointly liable for the whole debt.
- If a delay is granted to the principal debtor for the payment of his debt, it implies that a delay is also granted to the *Kifala*.
- The discharge of the *Kifala* (surety) does not necessarily discharge the liability of the principal debtor.

Hawala (Transfer of Debt)

Hawala means transferring a debt or an obligation from one debtor to another. That means the first debtor is released from the debt or the obligation when *Hawala* takes place. The difference between *Kifala* and *Hawala* lies in the fact that in the former case the principal debtor is not released, but in the latter case the principal debtor is released.

Jo'ala (Service Fee)

The contract of *Jo'ala* deals with offering a service for a pre-determined fee or commission. A party undertakes to pay another party a specified amount of money as a fee for rendering a specified service in accordance with the terms of the contract stipulated between the two parties. *Jo'ala* allows contracting on an object not certain to exist or come under a party's control. It can be utilized to introduce innovative financing structures. In this respect, the scope of the *Jo'ala* contract is wide enough to open up several fee-earning opportunities and can be utilized to offer advisory, asset management, consulting and professional services, fund placements and trust services often offered by investment banks in the conventional system. In addition, by using this contract, a financial intermediary can offer custodial services for customers in the securities market as well, where securities exchange hands in a relatively short period of time, thus performing another important task of a modern financial intermediary.

Islamic Banking

This brief review of the contracts available under the Islamic economic system leads us to conclude that transactional and financial contracts (as discussed in Chapter 4), coupled with intermediation contracts, offer a comprehensive set of instruments with varying financing purposes, maturities and degrees of risk, to satisfy the needs of diverse groups of economic agents in the economy. This set of instruments can be used to design a formal model for an Islamic financial intermediary (IFI) or an Islamic bank that can perform the typical functions of resource mobilization and intermediation. By utilizing this set of intermediation contracts, an IFI will be able to offer a wide array of commercial- and investment-banking products and services. Figure 5.2 shows a simplified version of how a typical Islamic bank can be structured to mobilize funding from the deposits and how the funds are invested in different instruments. The bank's relationship with the depositors is based on *Mudarabah*, *Amanah*, *Wikala* or *Wadia* basis on its liabilities side. However, on the assets side, the bank has more freedom and choices to

Figure 5.2 Islamic Financial Intermediation

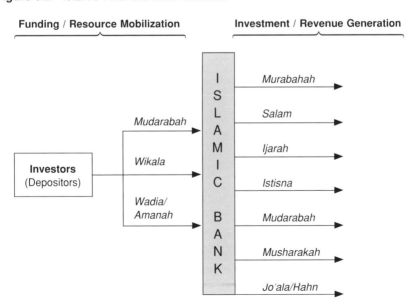

invest depositors' investments. Islamic banks carry *Murabahah*, *Ijarah*, *Istisna*, *Mudarabah* and *Musharakah* investments on their assets side.

Formally, two theoretical models have been suggested for the structure of an Islamic bank. The first model is based on *Mudarabah* and is commonly referred to as "*two-tier Mudarabah*" model, while the second model is known as "*two-windows*" model. A third but less known model for an Islamic bank has also been suggested. This model is based on the contract of *wakala* where an Islamic bank acts purely as *wakil* (agent/representative) of the investors and manages funds on their behalf on the basis of a fixed fee. The terms and conditions of the *wakala* contract are to be determined by mutual agreement between the bank and the clients.

Two-tier Mudarabah model

The first model, relying on the concept of profit-sharing, integrates the assets and liabilities sides on the basis of the principle called the "two-tier *Mudarabah*." This model envisages depositors entering into a contract with a banking firm to share the profits accruing to the bank's business. The basic concept of this model is that both funds mobilization and funds utilization are on the same basis of profit-sharing among the investor (depositor), the bank and the entrepreneur. The first tier of *Mudarabah* contract is between the investor analogous to a depositor and the bank, where investors act as suppliers of funds to be invested by the bank as *mudarib* on their behalf. The investors share in the profits and losses earned by the bank's business related to the investors' investments. Funds are placed with the bank in an investment account.

The liabilities and equity side of the bank's balance sheet thus shows the deposits accepted on a *Mudarabah* basis. Such profit-sharing investment deposits are not liabilities (the capital is not guaranteed and they incur losses if the bank does so), but are a form of limited-term, non-voting equity. In this model, in addition to investment deposits, banks accept demand deposits that yield no returns and are repayable on demand at par and are treated as liabilities. This model, though requiring that current deposits must be paid at the demand of the depositors, has no specific reserve requirement. It further stipulates that the bank is obligated to grant very short-term interest-free loans (*Qard-Hasan*) to the extent of a part of the total current deposits.

The second tier represents the *Mudarabah* contract between the bank as supplier of funds and the entrepreneurs who are seeking funds and agree to share profits with the bank according to a certain percentage stipulated in the contract. The bank's earnings from all its activities are pooled and are then shared with its depositors and shareholders according to the terms of their contract. Thus the profit earned by the depositors is then a percentage of the total banking profits. A distinguishing feature of the "two-tier" model is that, by design, the assets and liabilities sides of a bank's balance sheet are fully integrated, which minimizes the need for active asset/liability management, which, in turn, provides stability against economic shocks. The model does not feature any specific reserve requirements on either the investments or the demand deposits.

Two-windows model

The second model is referred to as the *"two-windows"* model, which also features demand and investment accounts but takes a different view from the "two-tier" model on reserve requirements. The two-windows model divides the liabilities side of the bank balance sheet into two windows, one for demand deposits (transactions balances) and the other for investment balances. The choice of the window is left to the depositors. This model requires a 100% reserve for the demand deposits but stipulates no reserve requirement for the second window. This is based on the assumption that the money deposited as demand deposits is placed as *Amanna* (safe keeping) and must be backed by 100% reserve, because these balances belonging to the depositors do not carry with them the innate right for the bank to use them as the basis for money creation through fractional reserves. Money deposited in investment accounts, on the other hand, is placed with the depositors' full knowledge that their deposits will be invested in risk-bearing projects, therefore no guarantee is justified. In this model, too, the depositors may be charged a service fee for the the safekeeping services rendered by the bank. Provisions of interest-free loans to those who may need them, according to this model, are limited to the funds deposited in such accounts by the depositors who think that the bank may to better equipped for this purpose. No portion of the deposits in the current account or investment accounts will be required to be used for this purpose.

The second model corresponds closely to the understanding that the early Muslims had of banking and investment practices, which by the mid-eighth century had developed a variety of credit institutions and instruments such as checks (*Ruqa*), document of debt transfer (*Hawala*), and bills of exchange (*Suftaja*). Banking services, including currency exchange transactions, were performed by the merchant bankers and investment activities through profit-sharing were accomplished through direct finance. As was understood by Muslim scholars and merchant bankers alike, a contract based on Islamic Law severely restricted the use to which "the depositary could put the deposited property." This is in contradistinction to the concept of deposits in the West, where the depositary not only kept the goods but also had a right to use them for a variety of commercial purposes. The Islamic conception of property rights imposes severe restrictions on the use of someone's property placed in another's safe keeping.[1]

Comparison of the two models

Both models treat the losses incurred as a result of investment activities by the banks as being reflected in the depreciation of the value of the depositor's wealth. However, both models see the probability of losses minimized through a diversification of banks' investment portfolios and careful project selection, monitoring, and control. Clearly, the risk to depositors is less in the second model than in the first and is only applicable to investment deposits. Even so, the proponents of the first model have suggested loss-compensating balances built up by the bank out of its earnings in good times and deposit insurance schemes launched in cooperation with the central banks as a means by which such risks can be reduced. Additionally, and perhaps more importantly, what will mitigate risks under the Islamic system is the fact that banks have both direct and indirect control on the behavior of the agent-entrepreneur through both explicit and implicit contracts. Banks can exert control through both the formal terms of their contract and through an implicit reward-punishment system in the sense of refusing further credit or the blacklisting of the agent-entrepreneur. To the extent that the reputation of firms and that of its managers is important, this is a strong deterrent to irresponsible behavior. The nature of the contract permits the banks to focus their attention on the probability of default and the expected rate of return, as also on the promotion and control of the firms in which they invest.

Distinct Features of the Islamic Mode of Intermediation

Profit/Loss Sharing

The profit-and-loss-sharing concept implies a direct concern for the profitability of the physical investment on the part of the creditor (the Islamic bank). The conventional bank is also concerned about the profitability of the project, because of concerns about potential default on the loan. However, the conventional bank puts the emphasis on receiving the interest payments according to set time intervals, and so long as this condition is met, the bank's own profitability is not directly affected by whether the project has a particularly high or a rather low rate of return. In contrast, the Islamic bank has to focus on the return on the physical investment, because its own profitability is directly linked to the real rate of return.

The direct links between the payment to the creditor and the profitability of the investment project is of considerable importance to the entrepreneur.

Most importantly, profit-sharing contracts have superior properties in the area of risk management, because the payment the entrepreneur has to make to the creditor is reduced in periods of economic downturn. Also, if the entrepreneur experiences temporary debt-servicing difficulties in the interest-based system, for example, on account of a short-term adverse demand shock, there is the risk of a magnification effect, that is, credit channels might dry up because of lenders overreacting to the bad news. This is due to the fact that the bank's own profitability is not affected by the fluctuating fortunes of the client's investment, except only when there is a regime change from regular interest payments to a default problem. In other words, interest payments are due irrespective of the profitability of the physical investment, and the conventional bank experiences a change in its fortunes only when there are debt-servicing difficulties. However a temporary cash-flow problem of the entrepreneur, and just a few delayed payments might be seen to be a regime change, which could blow up into a "sudden stop" in lending. In the Islamic model, these temporary shocks would generate a different response from the bank, because the lenders receive information on the ups and downs of the client's business regularly in order to calculate their share of the profits, which provides the important advantage that the flow of information, as indeed the payment from the borrower to the lender, is more or less on an on-going basis.

Enhanced Monitoring
Islamic financial contracting encourages banks to focus on the long term in their relationships with their clients. However, this focus on long-term relationships in profit-and-loss sharing arrangements means that there might be higher costs in some areas, particularly with regard to the need for monitoring the performance of the entrepreneur. Conventional banks are not obliged to oversee projects as closely as Islamic banks, because the former do not act as if they were partners in the physical investment. To the extent that Islamic banks provide something akin to equity financing as against debt financing, they need to invest relatively more in managerial skills and expertise in overseeing different investment projects. This is one reason why there is a tendency amongst Islamic banks to rely on financial instruments that are acceptable under Islamic principles, but are not the best in terms of risk-sharing properties, because in some respects they are closer to debt than to equity.

Principal–Agent Relationship
The agency theory has generated considerable interest in financial economics, including Islamic banking. In an agency relationship, one party (the principal)

contracts with another party (the agent) to perform some actions on the principal's behalf, and the agent has the decision-making authority. Agency relationships are ubiquitous: for example, agency relationships exist among firms and their employees, banks and borrowers, and shareholders and managers. Jensen and Meckling (1976) developed the agency model of the firm to demonstrate that a principal-agent problem (or agency conflict) is embedded in the modern corporation because the decision-making and risk-bearing functions of the firm are carried out by different individuals. They noted that managers have a tendency to engage in excessive perquisite consumption and other opportunistic behavior because they receive the full benefit from these acts but bear less than the full share of the costs to the firm. The authors termed this the agency cost of equity, and pointed out that it could be mitigated by increasing the manager's stake in the ownership of the firm. In the principal-agent approach, this is modeled as the incentive-compatibility constraint for the agent, and an important insight from this literature is that forcing managers to bear more of the wealth consequences of their actions is a better contract for the shareholders.

Application of the agency theory to profit-and-loss-sharing instruments such as *Mudarabah* has been modeled by Haque and Mirakhor (1989) and Presley and Session (1994). These models found that under a *Mudarabah* profit-and-loss-sharing contract, it is the managerial effort which picks up the role of policing the contract. A standard incentive-compatible interest based contract creates an explicit mapping between the input and remuneration of capital, so that the manager is left free to choose the individually optimal level of effort in each state contingent on the specified level of investment. However, in the case of a *Mudarabah*, an explicit mapping between the remuneration of capital and the outcome of the project is created. *Mudarabah*, therefore, allows the contract to control directly the manager's incentive to exert effort, since this effort affects the relationship between capital investment and the outcome of the project. Under a *Mudarabah* contract, the manager is free to choose the individually optimal level of investment in each state of the economy contingent on his contractually specified level of effort. Presley and Session's model concludes that these individually optimal levels correspond to the full information, productively efficient levels such that a mean-variance improvement in capital investment is obtained — average investment is increased whilst inefficiently large fluctuations around this level are reduced.

Asset/Liability Management

One of the most critical and distinguishing features of financial intermediation by Islamic banks as compared to that by conventional banks is the inherent design by which the assets and liabilities sides of the Islamic bank's balance sheet are matched.[2] In case of a conventional bank, deposits are accepted at a pre-determined rate irrespective of the rate of return earned on the assets side of the bank. This instantaneously creates a fixed liability for the bank without any certainty that the bank would be able to earn more than it promised or was committed to paying to the depositors. Since the return on the asset depends on the bank's ability to invest the funds at a higher rate than the one promised on the liability side and this rate is unknown, it can lead to the classical problem of mismatch between assets and liabilities.

In contrast, there is no pre-determined rate on the deposits/investments and the depositors' share in the profits and losses on the assets side of the Islamic bank; therefore, the problem of asset-liability mismatch does not arise. It has been argued that because of this pass-through nature of the business and the closely matched assets and liabilities, financial intermediation by Islamic banks contributes to the stability of the financial system.

Shariah Boards

One of the distinct features of Islamic banking is the existence of a *Shariah* board that comprises religious scholars and the influence this board exerts on the operations of an Islamic bank. Islamic banks cannot introduce a new product without the prior permission and approval of their *Shariah* board, and depending on the affiliation of the religious scholars on the board to any particular school of jurisprudential thought, this can determine the success or failure of a product with its target clients. Due to a shortage of *Shariah* scholars well versed in *Shariah* matters as well as in modern banking, many *Shariah* scholars sit on a number of boards, so that each institution may claim strong endorsement to enhance the credibility of the institution's practices. The existence of *Shariah* boards provides satisfaction to the depositors that the board is monitoring the adherence and compliance by the institution with *Shariah* principles.

Understanding the Balance Sheet of an Islamic Bank

In terms of activities, an Islamic bank is typically a hybrid between a conventional commercial bank and an investment bank, and thus resembles a universal bank. Figure 5.3 constructs a conceptual balance sheet of an Islamic bank based on different functions and services to give us an overview of its structure, operations and capabilities of intermediation.

This balance sheet may not be representative of each and every Islamic bank in existence, but gives us a general structure of intermediation using Islamic contracts. Unlike conventional commercial banks that accept deposits with the assumption of capital preservation and a promised return, an Islamic

Figure 5.3   A Stylized Balance Sheet of an Islamic Bank

Assets		Liabilities
Trade Financing		Demand Deposits
Salam	*Murabahah*	
Ijarah / Istisna		Investment Accounts
Mudarabah **(Profit/Loss Sharing Investments)**		
Musharakah **(Equity Partnership)**		Special Investment Accounts
Services (*Jo'ala, Wikala, Kifala*)		Capital Equity Reserves

financial intermediary does not offer such explicit guarantee but has to assure the depositors that the intermediary will select the best opportunities that will minimize the risk for the depositors. Using the techniques of portfolio management and diversification, a portfolio of trade-related, asset-backed securities is designed. By deploying the funds in this fashion, the intermediary will not only be able to offer short-term time deposits with minimized financial risk and sufficient liquidity for the depositors, but will also facilitate a system-wide payment system that is backed by real assets. This function is the closest substitute for the typical deposit-accepting function of conventional commercial banks.

On its liabilities side, an Islamic bank offers current, savings, investment, and special investment accounts to the depositors. Current accounts are demand accounts and are kept with the bank on custodial arrangements and are repayable in full on demand. Current accounts are based on the principle of *wadia* (trust or safekeeping), creating an agency contract for the purpose of protecting and safekeeping the depositor's assets. The major portion of the bank's financial liabilities would consist of investment accounts that are, strictly speaking, not liabilities but a form of equity investment, generally based on the principle of *Mudarabah*. Investment accounts are offered in different forms, often linked to a pre-agreed period of maturity, which may be from one month upwards and could be withdrawn if advance notice is given to the bank. The profits and returns are distributed between the depositors and the bank, according to a pre-determined ratio. A distribution of 80% to the investors (depositors) and 20% to the bank is typical, but this ratio may vary considerably from bank to bank.

A bank may offer special investment accounts customized for high net-worth individuals or institutional clients. These accounts also operate on the principle of *Mudarabah*, but the modes of investment of the funds and the distribution of profits are customized to suit the needs of the clients. In general, special investment accounts are linked to special investment opportunities identified by the bank. These opportunities have a specific size and maturity and result from the bank's participation in a pool of investment, private equity, joint venture or a fund. To some extent these special investment accounts resemble specialized funds to finance different asset classes. The maturity and the distribution of profits for special investment accounts are negotiated separately for each account, with the yield directly related to the success of the particular investment project. Special investment accounts have considerable potential for designing and developing funds with specific risk-return profiles to offer high net-worth and corporate clients opportunities to manage portfolios and to perform risk management. In addition to deposits, an Islamic bank offers basic banking services such as fund transfers, letters of credit, foreign exchange transactions, and investment management and advice, for a fee, to retail and institutional clients.

While the liabilities side of the bank has limited modes of raising funds, the assets side can carry a more diversified portfolio of heterogeneous asset classes, representing a wider spectrum of risk and maturity profile. For *short-term maturity, limited-risk investments*, there is a choice of asset-backed securities that resemble debt securities in terms of the payoffs. Such securities originate from trade related activities, such as, *Murabahah, Bay' al-Muajjil*, or *Bay' salam*, and are arranged by the bank, which uses its skills, market knowledge as well as its customer base to finance the trading activity. In addition, the bank can provide short-term funds to its clients to meet their working capital needs. The short-term maturity of these instruments and the fact that they are backed by real assets minimize their level of risk. The bank considers these securities highly attractive and gives them preference over other investment vehicles.

For the *medium-term maturity investments*, the bank has several choices. The funds can be invested in *Ijarah* and *Istisna*-based assets. A benefit of these contracts is not only that they are backed by an asset, but also that they can have either a fixed or a floating rate feature that can facilitate portfolio management. The common features of Islamic (*Ijarah*) and conventional leasing provide additional investment opportunities for the bank since investing in conventional leases with appropriate modifications can be made consistent with *Shariah* principles. However, leasing has its own overheads, which a bank may not like to accept. For example, leasing requires a bank to deviate from its primary role as a financial intermediary, as it will require it to get involved in purchasing an asset and then keep its ownership until the asset is disposed of, with the responsibility of maintenance and associated costs over the life of the contract (at least for operating lease). Disposing of the asset requires not only bearing all risks resulting from price fluctuations, but also some marketing expertise. All this will require the bank to engage in activities beyond financial intermediation.

In addition, an Islamic bank can set up special purpose (customized) portfolios to invest in a particular asset class and sector and can finance these portfolios by issuing special purpose *Mudarabahs* in the form of special investment accounts. In some way, this segment of the assets side represents a "fund of funds" where each fund is financed by matching *Mudarabah* contracts on the liabilities side through special investment accounts. For *longer-term maturity investments*, an IFI can engage in venture capital or private equity activities in the form of *Musharakah*.

Figure 5.4 shows the actual balance sheet of Bahrain Islamic Bank as of June 2005. More than 50% of the assets are invested in *Murabahah* transactions followed by non-trading investments. The rest of the assets are invested in leasing and partnership-based investments. A similar pattern of assets can be found in the assets sides of majority of Islamic banks which tend to rely heavily on short-term trade financing instruments. On the liabilities side, the main source of funding is unrestricted investment accounts. There are sizeable current account holders and equity capital. Equity capital, including reserves, amounts to more than 20% of total liabilities, which exceeds the percentage of equity capital of an average conventional bank.

Other Forms of Intermediation

Whereas early forms of Islamic financial institutions were focused on commercial banking activities, more diverse forms have emerged in the last two decades to cater to the demands of different segments of the market. Although the Islamic mode of banking is mandated and adopted by the Islamic Republics of Iran, Pakistan and Sudan, the supply of *Shariah*-compliant products has been primarily led by the private-sector, with the exception of the Islamic

Figure 5.4 Sample Balance Sheet

Bahrain Islamic Bank B.S.C.

CONSOLIDATED BALANCE SHEET
30 June 2005 (Unaudited)

	30 June 2005 BD '000	*Audited* 30 June 2004 BD '000
ASSETS		
Cash and balances with the BMA and other banks	12,146	9,407
Murabaha receivables	144,943	155,477
Mudaraba Investments	14,496	11,819
Musharaka Investments	5,537	2,721
Non-trading investments	69,661	55,770
Investments in associates	2,995	2,951
Investments in *Ijarah* assets	5,262	4,959
Ijarah Muntahia Bittamleek	12,457	5,116
Investments in properties	8,484	4,209
Other Assets	3,028	2,346
TOTAL ASSETS	**279,009**	**254,775**
LIABILITIES, UNRESTRICTED INVESTMENT ACCOUNTS AND EQUITY		
LIABILITIES		
Customers' current accounts	40,558	30,368
Other liabilities	4,739	2,828
TOTAL LIABILITIES	45,297	33,196
UNRESTRICTED INVESTMENT ACCOUNTS	172,503	168,829
EQUITY		
Share Capital	25,300	23,000
Share Premium	5,762	5,762
Reserves	30,147	18,928
Proposed appropriations	–	5,060
TOTAL EQUITY	61,209	52,750
TOTAL LIABILITIES, UNRESTRICTED INVESTMENT ACCOUNTS AND EQUITY	**279,009**	**254,775**
CONTINGENCIES (Note 3)	11,861	5,560

Source: IHS

Republic of Sudan, where the State has actively promoted the introduction of new modes of financing. In fact, private Islamic banks as a group are becoming some of the largest private sector financial institutions, with growing networks through branches and/or subsidiaries, within the Islamic world. There is no standard way of grouping Islamic financial institutions, but in terms of the services rendered, today's Islamic financial institutions can be divided into the following broad categories:

- Islamic Windows
- Islamic Investment Banks and Funds
- Islamic Mortgage Companies
- *Takaful* Companies (Islamic Insurance Institutions)
- *Mudarabah* Companies

Islamic Windows

Islamic windows are not independent financial institutions, but are specialized set-ups within conventional financial institutions that offer *Shariah*-compliant products for their clients. During the early stages of the Islamic financial market growth in the 1980s, Islamic banks faced a dearth of quality investment opportunities, which created business opportunities for conventional Western banks to act as intermediaries to deploy Islamic banks' funds according to guidelines defined by the Islamic banks. Western banks helped Islamic banks place funds in commerce and trade-related activities, by arranging for a trader to buy goods on behalf of the Islamic bank and to resell them at a mark-up. Gradually, Western banks realized the importance of the emerging Islamic financial markets and started offering Islamic products in an attempt to attract the clients directly without having an Islamic bank as intermediary. Meanwhile, due to the growing demand for *Shariah*-compliant products and fear of losing depositors, non-Western conventional banks also started offering Islamic sindows. In general, Islamic windows are targeted at high net-worth individuals who represent the wealthiest segment of investors — approximately 1–2% of the world Muslim population — who want to practice Islamic banking.

Most institutions that maintain Islamic windows also retain trained and respected *Shariah* scholars as *Shariah* advisors, whose input and approval is sought before introducing new products or entering into new transactions, to ensure that the product or the transaction does not violate any of the *Shariah* principles.

Islamic Investment Banks and Funds

The emergence of Islamic investment banks and investment funds is a development of Islamic financial markets during the 1990s, when large-sized transactions and investment banking became attractive. Whereas a typical Islamic bank's services are retail and consumer centered, Islamic investment banks are emerging and are aiming to capitalize on large investment syndication, market-making and underwriting opportunities. Islamic investment banks have been successful in developing innovative large-scale transactions for infrastructure financing, in conjunction with conventional project finance, for infrastructure projects such as the Hub Power Project in Pakistan. Another notable project financing with an Islamic component was the petrochemical project (EQUATE) in Kuwait, involving a US$1.2 billion joint venture between Kuwait's Petrochemicals Industries Corp. and Union Carbide of the United States. This project featured a US$200 million tranche raised by the Kuwait Finance House (KFH) for two leasing (*Ijara*) transactions, with maturities of 8 and 10 years respectively, for capital equipment. In late 1996, the then Bahrain-based Islamic Investment Company of the Gulf (GIIF) launched OIC Infrastructure Fund of US$1 billion in conjunction with the Islamic Development Bank (IDB), to finance parts of infrastructure projects using Islamic *Istisna* and *Murabahah* techniques. The Fund is targeted at governments and private investors to participate in a diversified group of profitable infrastructure projects in OIC (Organization of Islamic Countries) countries — a group of 56 Islamic countries. The objectives are to mobilize and redirect investment capital to Muslim countries, increase foreign direct investment, and to facilitate the development of national and regional capital markets through public listing of companies in which the fund invests.

Islamic investment funds are not new, but are making a comeback after the initial experimentation in which many of them did not survive.[3] The 1990s witnessed a real growth in Islamic funds, and by the start of the new millennium there were more than 150 Islamic funds of various types, including equity (of which there was in excess of 85), commodity, leasing and trade-related funds. Equity and other funds are discussed in detail in Chapter 8.

Islamic Mortgage Companies

Islamic mortgage companies are another recent development and are targeted at the housing market for Muslim communities in Western countries (Canada, the UK and the US), where there are developed conventional mortgage markets. There are four different models of Islamic mortgages currently in practice. The first model is based on the *Ijarah* (lease) contract, and is the closest to the structure of a conventional mortgage. The second model is based on equity partnership (*Musharakah*), where the mortgagee (lender) and the mortgagor (borrower) jointly share ownership, which, over a period of time, is transferred to the mortgagor who buys shares of ownership by contributing each month toward buying out the mortgagee's share in the property. Return to the lender is generated out of the fair rental value of the property. The third model is based on *Murabahah* and is practiced in the UK, where property transfer tax (stamp duty) discriminates against the *Ijarah-* or *Musharakah*-based mortgage. The fourth model is designed on the lines of cooperative societies, where members buy equity (*Musharakah*) membership and help one another in purchasing property from the pool of the society's funds. In the US, agencies like Fannie Mae and Freddie Mac have recognized the importance of Islamic mortgages, and underwrite and securitize Islamic mortgages. The chances of success for Islamic mortgages are bright in Western markets, where capital markets are liquid, transparent and regulated. In particular, there is great potential for Islamic mortgages in the Northern American markets, where there is a sizeable Muslim community in the middle and upper income brackets.

Islamic Insurance (*Takaful*) Companies

The closest Islamic instrument to the contemporary system of insurance is the instrument of *Takaful*, which literally means "mutual or joint guarantee." Typically, implementation of *Takaful* is carried out in the form of solidarity *Mudarabah*, where the participants agree mutually to share their losses by contributing periodic premiums in the form of investments. They are then entitled to to redeem the residual value of profits after fulfilling the claims and premiums.[4] One of the critical differences between contemporary insurance models and *Takaful* is the participant's right to receive surplus profits. The participants in a given solidarity (i.e., *Takaful*) *Mudarabah* have the right to share the surplus profits generated, but at the same time they are liable, in addition to the premiums, for amounts they have already distributed, if the initial premiums paid during a period are not sufficient to meet all the losses and risks incurred during that period. *Takaful* companies can constitute reserves (like conventional mutual insurance companies), which allow the need for the insured to make supplemental contributions if claims exceed premiums. At present, there is limited application of *Takaful* in Islamic financial markets, as there are few institutions which offer insurance services on a large scale. The current application of *Takaful* is for the most part indemnity-based and limited to the loss of physical property. According to some estimates, the global *takaful* industry currently stands at US$550 million, with around US$1.5 billion of assets under its management, which is significantly below its true potential.

Mudarabah Companies

The concept of a *Mudarabah* company is similar to that of a closed-end fund managed by a specialized professional investment management company. Like a mutual fund, a *Mudarabah* company is incorporated as a separate legal entity with a fund management company responsible for its operations.[5] Unlike an Islamic bank, a *Mudarabah* company is not permitted to accept deposits, but its source of funds is in the form of equity capital, provided by the sponsor's own subscribed capital and by *Mudarabah* investment certificates which are open to general investors through a public offering. Profits on investments made out of *Mudarabah* funds are distributed among the subscribers on the basis of their contribution, with the manager of the funds earning a proportion of the profits for his services. Commercial banks can serve either as managers or as subscribers. There can be two types of *Madurabah*: multi-purpose, that is, a *Mudarabah* having more than one investment purpose or objective, and specific-purpose. All *Mudarabah*, however, are independent of each other and none is liable for the liabilities of, or is entitled to benefit from the assets of, any other *Mudarabah* or *Mudarabah* company.

Considering that the *Mudarabah* contract is the corner-stone of Islamic finance, the concept of the *Mudarabah* company especially small- and medium size enterprises, can play a critical role and can become the backbone of the financial landscape of a developing economy. What is required is that the financial sector be designed to strengthen investor confidence and to facilitate making the operations of *Mudarabah* companies transparent and efficient.

Endnotes

1   The notion of property rights is crucial to an understanding of the economic system of Islam and many of its rules about economic behavior can be explained in light of this notion. In fact, the strong position that the early Muslim scholars took on such questions as the stability of the value of the currency, stability of prices and debasement of currency can be explained as a result of their understanding of the Islamic concepts of property rights and of economic justice. Whenever an action leads to the creation of instantaneous property rights claims for some members of the community, on the property of the rest without commensurate additional property being created to legitimize these claims, such an action is prohibited by Islam.

2   Failure of Savings and Loans companies in United States during 1980s is a classic example of bank failures due to assets-liabilities mismatch.

3   Kleinwort Benson was the first investment bank to introduce an Islamic unit trust in 1986 targeted at the market in the Gulf. The fund was not successful initially due to investors' reservations about the absence of a *Shariah* committee.

4   For instance, under the Malaysian *Takaful* Act 1984, the legal definition of a *Takaful* scheme is based on the concept of solidarity and brotherhood, which provides mutual financial aid and assistance to the participants in case of need, whereby the participants agree mutually to contribute for that purpose.

5   In 1980, a law was promulgated in Pakistan under which commercial banks and other financial institutions could register themselves as *Mudarabah* companies and mobilize funds through the issuance of *Mudarabah* certificates. Funds obtained through a *Mudarabah* can only be used in *Shariah*-sanctioned businesses.

6

The Islamic
Financial System

The primary role of a financial system is to create incentives for an efficient allocation of financial and real resources for competing aims and objectives across time and space. A well-functioning financial system promotes investment by identifying and funding good business opportunities, mobilizes savings, monitors the performance of managers, enables the trading, hedging and diversification of risks, and facilitates the exchange of goods and services. These functions ultimately lead to the efficient allocation of resources, rapid accumulation of physical and human capital and faster technological progress, which, in turn, feed economic growth.

Within a financial system, financial markets and banks perform the vital functions of capital formation, monitoring, information gathering, and facilitation of risk sharing. An efficient financial system is expected to perform several functions. First, the system should facilitate efficient financial intermediation to reduce information and allocation costs. Second, it must be based on a stable payment system. Third, with increasing globalization and demands for financial integration, it is essential that the financial system offers efficient and liquid money and capital markets. And, finally, it has to have a well-developed market for risk trading, where economic agents can buy and sell protection against event risks as well as financial risks.

Research on financial intermediation and financial systems in the past two decades has enhanced our understanding of the significance of the financial system and the crucial role it plays in economic development. For example, studies have shown that countries with higher levels of financial development grow faster by about 0.7% a year. Between 1980 and 1995, thirty-five countries experienced financial crises. These were, essentially, periods during which their financial systems stopped functioning and, consequently, these economies entered recessions. Although strong evidence points to the existence of a relationship between economic development and a well-developed financial system promoting efficient financial intermediation through a reduction in information, transaction and monitoring costs, this linkage is not as simple and straightforward as it may seem. The form of financial intermediation, the level of economic development, macroeconomic policies, and the regulatory and legal framework are some of the factors that can complicate the design of an efficient financial system.

Components of the Islamic Financial System

A financial system comprises different sub-systems such as the banking system, financial markets, capital markets, and the legal system. This section examines the roles of banking and financial markets when operating under the *Shariah* legal system.

Banking System

As discussed in the previous chapter, there are several contracts or instruments which facilitate financial intermediation and banking in the Islamic economic system. Although committed to carrying out their transactions in accordance with the rules of the *Shariah*, Islamic banks perform the same essential functions as banks do in the conventional system. That is, they act as the administrators of the economy's payments system and as financial intermediaries. The need for them in the Islamic system arises precisely for the same reason as that in the conventional system. That is, generally, their *raison d'etre* is the exploitation of the imperfections in the financial markets. These imperfections include imperfect divisibility of financial claims, transaction costs of search, acquisition, and diversification by the surplus and deficit units and existence of expertise and economies of scale in monitoring transactions.

Financial intermediaries in the Islamic system can reasonably be expected to exploit economies of scale with respect to these costs as their counterparts do in the conventional system. Through their ability to take advantage of these imperfections, they alter the yield relationships between the surplus and deficit financial units and thus provide lower costs to the deficit units and higher returns to the surplus units than would be possible with direct finance. Just as in the conventional financial system, the Islamic depository enables financial intermediaries to transform the liabilities of business into a variety of obligations to suit the preferences and circumstances of the surplus units. Their liabilities consist of investments/deposits and their assets consist mainly of instruments of varying risk/return profile. These banks are concerned with decisions relating to such issues as the nature of their objective functions, portfolio choice among risky assets, liability and capital management, reserve management, the interaction between the assets and liability liabilities sides of their balance sheets and the management of off-balance sheet items — such as revolving lines of credit, standby and commercial letters of credit and bankers' acceptances.

Moreover, as asset transformers, these institutions become risk evaluators and serve as filters to evaluate signals in a financial environment with limited information. Their deposit liabilities serve as a medium of exchange and they have the ability to minimize the cost of transactions that convert current income into an optimal consumption bundle. One major difference between the two systems is that, due to the prohibition against taking interest and the fact that they have to rely primarily on profit-sharing, the Islamic banks have to offer their asset portfolios of primary securities in the form of risky open-ended "mutual fund" type packages for sale to the investors/depositors. In contradistinction to the Islamic system, banks in the conventional system keep title to the portfolios they originate. These assets are funded by the banks through issuing deposit contracts, a practice that results in solvency and liquidity risks, since their asset portfolios and loans entail risky payoffs and/or costs of liquidation prior to maturity while their deposit contracts are liabilities that are often payable instantly at par. In contrast, Islamic banks act as agents of investors/depositors and therefore create a pass-through intermediation between savers and entrepreneurs.

Further, in the Islamic system, there will also be, by necessity, greater inter-dependence and closer relationship between investment and deposit yields, since Islamic banks can primarily accept investment deposits on the basis of profit-sharing and can provide funds to enterprises on the same basis. Due to the fact that the return on the liabilities has a direct correlation with the return on the asset portfolios and also because assets are created in response to investment opportunities in the real sector, the return on financing is removed from the cost side and transferred to the profit side, thus allowing the rate of return on financing to be determined by the productivity in the real sector. Thus, in the Islamic financial system, it is the real sector that determines the rate of return to the financial sector rather than the other way round.

It is also interesting to note that the structure of a hypothetical Islamic bank or financial intermediary combines the activities of commercial banking and investment banking as shown by the boxes on either side of the balance sheet in Figure 6.1. In this balance sheet, each box on the assets and liabilities sides represents a specialized function or financial service, whereas the arrows across liabilities and assets indicate how assets and liabilities can be matched. Each box can also help us understand the separation of assets and liabilities based on their function, risk profile, maturity structure and the targeted market. Similar to a conventional commercial bank, such a financial intermediary can raise funds as deposits and invest them in low risk and high quality investment grade trade financing or asset-backed securities. Like an investment bank, it can offer underwriting services, asset management through specialized *Mudarabah* funds and other advisory services such as research about financial markets, maintenance of benchmarks, portfolio management, and risk management.

Figure 6.1   Conceptual Balance Sheet of an IFI

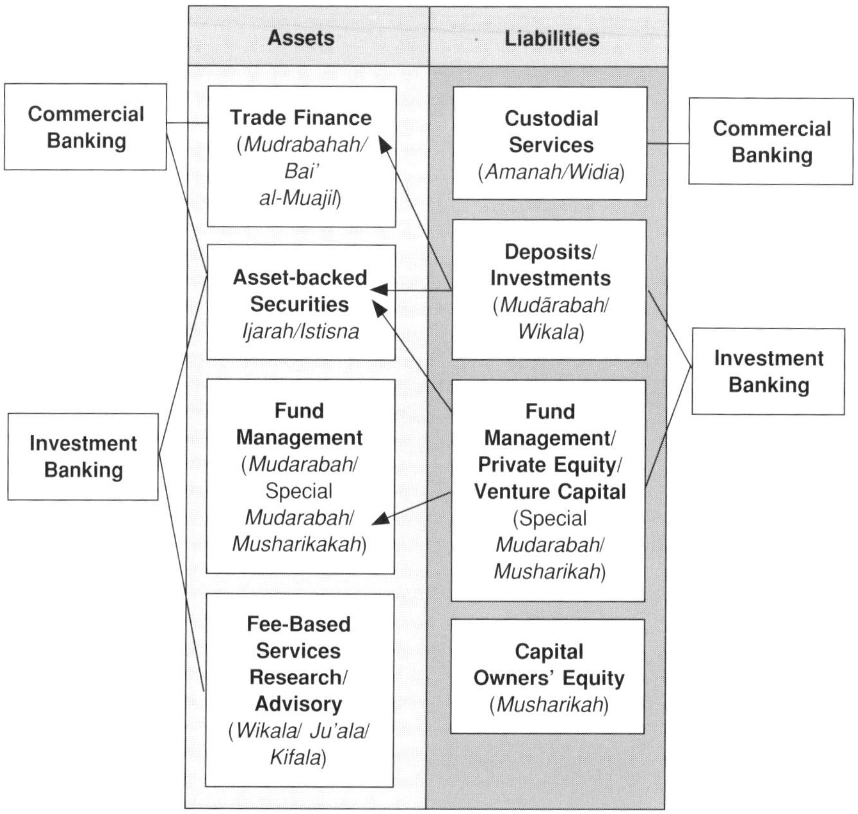

Primary, secondary, and money markets

With the division of the liability side of the balance sheet of the banking system into investment and demand deposits, wealth owners channel only part of their savings into an accumulation of physical capital and the remainder is allocated to the accumulation of idle balances. This argument requires assumptions regarding the responsiveness of the wealth owners to the rate of return as well as the assumption that money and physical capital are viewed as competing assets. Although the validity of the first assumption is an empirical question, the second assumption is not consistent with the Islamic exhortation against hoarding and accumulation of money (i.e., keeping money idle without corresponding transactions demand for it). Moreover, these balances not only cannot earn any return, and in this sense are barren, but also, if kept for a full year, they become subject to a compulsory levy of 2.5%, thus imposing relatively high opportunity costs on the idle balances. There is, however, a possibility that since the alternative to idle balances is risk-bearing deposits, it may make it worthwhile for the depositors to maintain a considerable portion of their savings in the form of either money or demand deposit balances, particularly if the conditions are conducive to the existence of a strong precautionary motive for liquidity purposes. There would, therefore, be an incentive in an Islamic financial system to develop short and long-term assets that would assure the depositors of a sufficient degree of liquidity and security, so as to reduce their reliance on money and demand deposits.

With the prohibition on interest and the preference for partnerships to share profits and losses, equity markets hold a significant place. Therefore, Islamic scholars have pointed out the necessity, desirability and permissibility of the existence of a stock market in the financial system of Islam in which transactions in primary capital instruments such as corporate stocks can take place. The conditions of the operations of these markets, in accordance with the rules of the *Shariah*, are much like those that must prevail in markets for goods and services. For example, in such markets the rules are intended to remove all factors inimical to justice in exchange and to yield prices that are considered fair and just. Prices are just or equitable not on any independent criterion of justice, but because they are the result of bargaining between equal, informed, free and responsible economic agents. To ensure justice in exchange, the *Shariah* has provided a network of ethical and moral rules of behavior for all participants in the market and requires that these norms and rules be internalized and adhered to by all. Given that a proper securities underwriting function is performed by some institutions in the system, e.g., the banks, the firms could then directly raise the necessary funds for their investment projects within the stock market, which would provide them a second source of funding other than the banks.

A stock market operating strictly in accordance with Islamic rules is envisioned to be one in which the disposal of investible funds is based on the profit prospects of the enterprises, in which relative profit rates reflect the efficiencies between firms and in which profit rates (as signals coming from the goods market) are not distorted by market imperfections. Such a market might be expected to allocate investible funds strictly in accordance with expected investment yields, i.e., resources would be allocated in order to finance higher return projects. Stock markets would also be capable of improving allocation of savings by accumulating and disseminating vital information in order to facilitate comparisons between all available opportunities, thus reflecting the general efficiency in resource allocation expected from a system that operates primarily on the basis of productivity of investment.

In addition to the stock market, another capital market can also exist, which provides a platform to trade asset-backed securities. The notion in Islamic economics of binding capital closely and tightly to a real asset encourages the issuance of securities against an asset. For example, an asset financed through *Ijarah* (lease) or *Istisna* can be used as collateral to issue securities linked to the pay-offs and cash flows of underlying assets. Once the assets are securitized and a financial security is created, such securities can be traded on an organized capital market either in the primary or the secondary segment.

The development of a secondary market is important and essential to the development of a primary market. All savers, to some degree or another, have a liquidity preference. This liquidity preference, although perhaps to a different extent and magnitude, can as much exist in an Islamic system as in any other system. To the extent that savers can, if necessary, sell securities quickly and at low cost, they will be more willing to devote a higher portion of their savings to long-term instruments than they would otherwise. Since the probability is high that primary securities in the Islamic system would be tied to the projects and management of particular enterprises, there are various risks that must enter into the portfolio decisions of the savers. The risks regarding the earning power of the firm and of its default are examples of these types of risks.

There is another type of risk that is closely tied to the secondary market for a given security issued by firms. If two securities are identical in all respects except that one has a well-organized secondary market while the other has a poor one, an investor in the latter runs the risk of liquidating their securities holdings at depressed prices as compared to the prices offered for the security with the well-organized market. Moreover, the degree of this marketability risk is directly related to factors such as the extent of the knowledge of the participants as well as the number of traders in the market, which determine the depth and the resilience of the secondary markets.

In an Islamic system, perhaps more than in any other, both the primary and secondary markets require the active support of the government and the central bank, not only in their initial development and promotion but also in their supervision and control, in order to ensure their compliance with the rules of the *Shariah*. Particularly in the case of the secondary markets, the traders and the market makers need the support and supervision of the central bank if these markets are to operate efficiently. For secondary markets to be able to transform an asset into a reliable source of cash for an economic unit whenever the latter needs it, they must be dealer markets, in which there is a set of position users who trade significant amounts of assets. In the traditional interest-based system, these position takers are financed by borrowings from banks, financial intermediaries, and other private cash sources. Since in the Islamic system refinancing on the basis of debt is not permitted, reliable and adequate sources of funds must be provided by the central bank. There will have to be arrangements through which the central bank can, at least partially, finance secondary markets and supervise them fully.

In a conventional interest-based system, the money market becomes a means by which financial institutions can adjust their balance sheet and finance positions in these markets. Short-term cash positions, which exist as a result of imperfect synchronization in the payment period, become the essential ingrediant for the presence of the money markets. The money market, in this case, becomes a source of temporary financing and an abode of excess liquidity in which transactions are mainly portfolio adjustments and no planned or recently achieved savings need be involved.

In an Islamic financial system, the liabilities that an economic unit generates are, by necessity, closely geared to the characteristics of its investment. On the other hand, the liabilities that financial intermediaries generate are expected to have nearly the same distribution of possible values as the assets they acquire. Hence, given that debt instruments cannot exist, money market activities will have different characteristics from their counterparts in the conventional system. As stated earlier, the existence of a poorly organized money market combined with a poor structure of financial intermediation leads to a situation where money becomes more important as a repository of wealth than in a situation with more active financial intermediation.

The existence of broad, deep, and resilient markets in which the assets and liabilities of the financial intermediary can be negotiated is a necessary ingredient. Additionally, to the extent that money markets help lower the income elasticity of demand for cash and help investment projects to be financed, their importance in the Islamic financial system cannot be overlooked. Even in this system, money markets will enable financial units to be safely illiquid, provided they have assets that are eligible for this market. In this system, too, the basic source of the money in the market is the existence of pools of excess liquidity. One main activity of money markets in this system is to make arrangements by which the surplus funds of one financial institution are channeled into profit-sharing projects of another. It is conceivable that, at times, excess funds may be available with some banks, but no assets, or at least assets attractive enough in terms of their risk–return characteristics, on which they can take a position. On the other hand, there may be banks with financial resources insufficient to allow them to fund all available opportunities or with investment opportunities requiring commitments of what the banks may consider excessive funds in order for them to take a position and for which they may prefer risk-sharing with the surplus banks. In such a case, the development of an inter-bank funds market is a distinct possibility. It may also be possible for some banks to refinance a certain position that they have taken by agreeing to share their prospective profits in these positions with other banks in the inter-bank funds market. Finally, since most of the investment portfolios of banks will contain equity positions of various terms and maturities, it is also possible that a subset of their asset portfolios comprising equity shares can be offered in the money market in exchange for liquidity.

Here too, effective and viable money markets in the Islamic system will require active support and participation by the central bank, particularly at times when the investment opportunities and/or the risk–return composition of projects and shortages of liquidity in the banking system may require a lender of last resort. Such money markets must be flexible enough to handle cash shortage periods for individual banks, based on some form of profit-sharing arrangement. The challenge for money markets, as well as for the secondary markets, in an Islamic financial system is the development of instruments that satisfy the liquidity, security and profitability needs of the markets while, at the same time, ensuring compliance with the rules of the *Shariah*, i.e., provision of uncertain and variable rates of return on instruments with corresponding real asset backing.

The Stability of the Financial System

Proponents of the Islamic system claim that a financial system based on the Islamic framework of profit-sharing would be more efficient in allocating resources compared to a conventional interest-based system. This claim can be defended on the basis of the general proposition that any financial development that causes investment alternatives to be compared to one another, strictly based on their productivity and rates of return, is bound to produce improved allocations. Such a proposition is the cornerstone of the Islamic financial system. But will such a system also improve stability?

The general argument underlying the proposition that the Islamic financial system is more stable than the conventional interest-based system is based on the constrained debt-carrying power of economic units in the Islamic system and on the argument that the inability to refinance positions in assets by creating additional debt along with the non-existence of interest rates renders the system more stable.

In a conventional interest-based system, financing of investments and ownership of capital assets, as well as of consumer spending, is carried out primarily through borrowing and lending, whereby a structure of expected money receipts embodies the various commitments to make payments on existing debt. The liabilities on the books of an economic unit at any time are the result of past financing positions that are taken on the basis of various margins of safety, one of which is an excess of anticipated receipts over payment commitments. Based on this relationship, an economic unit in such a system can assume one of three financial postures.

One is that a given economic unit in every period of its operation will have cash flows from its participation in income generation, which are expected to exceed contractual payments on outstanding debt. Another posture may place an economic unit in a position in which in the short-term, payment commitments exceed their corresponding cash flows, even though the total expected cash flows (totaled over the foreseeable future) exceed the total payments on outstanding debt and the net income position of the short-term cash flows exceeds the short-term interest payments on debts.

Finally, a third situation may arise in which not only do the short-term payment commitments exceed the expected cash flows, but the short-term interest payments on outstanding debt also exceed the income components of the short-term cash flows. It has been argued that, in such an interest-based system, there is a tendency on the part of the economic units, i.e., consumers, firms, banks, and governments to increasingly assume the last two types of financial postures, in which economic units can fulfill their payment commitments on debt only by borrowing or selling of assets. Since appreciation of an asset constitutes a portion of returns on that asset, the tendency is to refinance rather than sell assets. In terms of refinancing, the amount that the second type of unit needs to borrow is less than the maturing debt of the third-type of units, and the latter will only be able to meet its payment commitments by increasing its outstanding debt.

The last two types of units engage in speculative financing in the sense that they have to exchange short-term liabilities for long-term assets, thus speculating that, when the need arises to refinance and roll-over, refinancing of their maturing debts will be available at non-punitive interest rates. The viability of the third type of unit will rest on the assumption that some assets will be sold at high enough prices some time in the future. Both the second and third types of units are vulnerable to interest rate fluctuations, since these units finance a long position in assets by issuing short-term liabilities, hence their viability depends on the price and the extent of the availability of refinancing. Their commitments provide for the repayment of debt at a faster rate than their net income will allow for the recapturing of the money costs of capital assets. Besides, there is high probability of present value reversal for these units at higher interest rates, since higher interest rates lower the value of all cash receipts but this decrease is proportionately greater for more distant receipts. That is to say, a dated set of cash flows which yield a positive net present value (excess of asset values over the value of debts) at a lower interest rate, may yield a negative excess at higher interest rates.

High and rapidly rising interest rates increases financing activities in which investment undertakings depend on an increase in total short-term debt outstanding. This is because the interest payments that are due on earlier borrowings exceed the income earned by the assets. As the short-term debt that leads to a capitalization of interest increases relative to the gross capital income, there is an increase in demand for short-term financing because of the need to refinance debt. This increased need to rely on maturing debt not only shifts the demand curve for short-term debt to the right but also makes the curve less elastic. If, in addition, the supply of short-term refinancing is also inelastic, the short-term interest rates can increase rapidly, which, in turn, leads to higher long-term rates leading to a lower value of capital assets.

Moreover, rising short-term interest rates, in conjunction with increasing long-term interest rates, not only reduce the demand for capital assets but also increase the cost of production of the output with longer gestation period, thus leading to a decrease in investment. If the process of falling asset values, rising carrying costs for asset holdings, and decreasing profits increases the probability of illiquidity and insolvency for a significant number of firms and financial institutions, the participants in the market may not be willing to roll-over or refinance the maturing debts of these institutions and a crisis will develop. It follows that for any given regime of financial institutions, the lesser the weight of refinancing of debt discussed above, the greater the stability of the system.

An Islamic financial system can be expected to be more stable than an interest-based system, for at least four major reasons. First, in the Islamic financial system, the term and the structure of the assets and liabilities of the economic units are closely matched through profit-sharing arrangements. Second, the liabilities of each economic unit comprise equities and/or are fully amortized with an underlying future income flow. Third, payment commitments of firms and financial institutions are, mostly, dividends that will have to be paid only if profits are received. Finally, no debt refinancing can take place on an interest basis; if there is any refinancing it must be on the basis of sharing of future income expected from assets. In an Islamic system, the danger of insolvency arises for economic units only if their revenues fall short of their out-of-pocket costs and commitments. Such a situation can only occur either due to poor management or extraneous economic factors, but is not inherent in the financial system.

Similar reasoning can be applied to the banking firms in an interest-based system, where there is a tendency for the banks to become illiquid, in the sense that their liabilities mature faster than their assets. To handle illiquidity the banks have three options. One is to rely on the argument that the problem of liquidity is not so much a problem of maturity structure as a problem of shifting assets to other banks in exchange for cash. That is, if one bank can receive help from another bank when needed, there is no necessity of reliance on maturing loans to provide liquidity; assets can be shifted to other banks before maturity as the need arises. The second option is for a bank to increase interest rates in order to attract greater deposits or maintain existing ones in times of difficulty, thus engaging in liability management to solve the problem of liquidity. If the short-term stock of total deposits is fixed within the banking system, these two alternatives can quickly spread the problem of illiquidity throughout the system. The danger that all banks can become illiquid, in the sense that their liabilities mature faster than their assets, cannot be met except via the third option, which is debt monetization i.e., the banks must sell their slowly maturing assets to the central bank in order to raise cash with which to meet fast maturing liabilities. This option is not necessarily costless. For one thing, once the banks resort to monetization, they may set in motion a vicious circle with its own momentum of acceleration. It is argued that equity-based financing and unavailability of debt in the Islamic system would mitigate this source of instability.

The stability of the Islamic banking system has recently been investigated using a formal-mathematical approach by Khan (1987), who demonstrates that the Islamic system may well turn out to be better suited for adjusting to shocks that result in banking crises and disruption of the payments mechanism of the country. Khan's model assumes an Islamic banking system structured in accordance with the second principal model of Islamic banking discussed earlier. In the model, the banks accept deposits as if they were equity where the shares, nominal value is not guaranteed and the rate of return on which is variable. The model is shown to have stability in response to certain types of shocks. A major policy recommendation emanating from this study is that a two-window Islamic banking system, in which demand deposits have a 100% reserve requirement and investment deposits carry no guarantees, has desirable and inherent safety benefits.

It is clear that if demand deposits are backed by a 100% reserve requirement, the run-associated features of the fractional reserve banking would be eliminated. By not imposing any reserve requirements for investment deposits and replacing the par conversion privilege with a net asset liquidation rule (for example, the rule that depositors bear the asset value risks on a pro-rata basis), the incentive for runs on investment deposits would also be removed. The doctrinal justification for a 100% reserve requirement based on the property rights argument was advanced earlier; the stability argument proposed by Khan is a further support for this view. Not all Muslim scholars, however, are convinced of the necessity of a 100% reserve requirement. The proponents of the "two-tier *Mudarabah*" model of Islamic banking argue that a fractional reserve system fully guaranteed by a debt issuance scheme coupled with careful project selection is sufficient to head off any potential run on the banks.

Effect on Savings and Intermediation

It can be argued that in an Islamic economic system, particularly with its emphasis on work and moderation in consumption, saving would be enhanced. Moreover, it seems intuitively plausible that since, in normal circumstances, the rate of return on an investment must, generally, be higher than the rate of interest paid to depositors, replacement of interest rates with a rate of return should increase the reward on savings. Consequently, insofar as saving is responsive to reward, incentives would be created for increasing savings (it should be noted that an increase in return to depositors is a function of the share parameter negotiated between the banks and their depositors on the one hand and that negotiated between the banks and their customers, i.e., agent–entrepreneurs, on the other).

Concerns have been expressed, however, that the adoption of the Islamic financial system may lead to a reduction in savings and retardation of financial intermediation and development. This assertion is based on three different arguments. One argument suggests that since, in the Islamic system, the individual's income is subject to ordained levies, their savings will be lowered. The second argument asserts that since savings receive no reward (i.e., interest rate is zero), there is no incentive for individuals to save. The third argument maintains that savings will decrease because of increased uncertainly of future prospects for the Islamic systems. For the first argument to hold, it must be assumed that the ordained levies in the Islamic system are, in fact, larger than the numerous taxes that income and wealth are subjected to in other systems; this assumption ultimately requires empirical validation, but *prima facie* appears to be a strong assumption. But even if such an assumption were to be made, the next point to consider is the fact that these levies are transfers from groups with a low marginal propensity to consume to those with a higher marginal propensity. The question is whether or not, as a result of this transfer, aggregate demand will get sufficient impetus so as to increase investment, employment and income, so that aggregate saving is also enhanced, particularly in a demand-constrained economy.

The second argument stems from a misunderstanding about Islam's prohibition against interest. It is thought that this prohibition is tantamount to an imposition of a zero rate of return on investment and capital. This view clearly reflects confusion between rate of return and rate of interest. While the latter is forbidden in Islam, the former is not only permitted but is, in fact, encouraged.

The third argument is based on the proposition that increased uncertainty in the rate of return affects savings adversely. This view, however, is neither unique to the Islamic system nor unknown in the conventional economic literature. Alfred Marshall, for example, maintained, on the basis of casual observation, that uncertainty tends to reduce savings. Only recently has this question been subjected to rigorous theoretical analysis, with conflicting results. The few studies that have analytically or otherwise considered this question within the context of the Islamic framework have tended to neglect the risk–return tradeoff aspects of the questioning. That is, the effects on savings of a fixed and certain rate of return are compared with effects on saving when only uncertainty is taken into account. The result shows a reduction in savings. It should be obvious that if the expected value of return is kept constant while its variance is increased, i.e., when increased risk is not compensated by higher returns, savings will be adversely affected. This conclusion is, however, far from obvious when both risk and return are allowed to vary. The theoretical conclusion of an analysis in which risk and return variability have both been taken into account depends on assumptions regarding the form of the utility function and its risk properties, e.g., the degree and the extent of risk aversion, the presence future discount and the degree to which the future is discounted, whether or not increased risk is compensated by higher return and, finally, the income and substitution effects of increased uncertainty. It has been shown, for example, that when future non-capital income is subjected to risk, decreasing temporal risk aversion is a sufficient condition for increased uncertainty about future income to decrease consumption and increase savings. With respect to capital income, the combined substitution and income effects of increased uncertainty are indeterminable. Other studies have shown that under reasonable assumptions, in face of uncertainty, there does exist a precautionary demand for savings. The theoretical analysis has not, thus far, provided a clear-cut hypothesis in this regard and it becomes an empirical question whether savings will increase or decrease in an Islamic system. It can, however, be reasonably expected that "a rational planner may make more provision for the future when the future becomes more uncertain"; an expectation which, *prima facie*, cannot be contradicted by any of the features underlying the Islamic economic system.

It has already been indicated that incentives exist in the Islamic system for efficient intermediation and the system characteristics, most importantly the prohibition against interest, create an important opportunity for the integration of financial markets. Due to legislative action that would make charging of interest illegal and the society's value-orientation that would create a stigma for those charging interest, unorganized markets cannot operate on the basis of interest. They must allocate their resources on the basis of profit-sharing and it will be their relative ability and efficiency in exploiting market imperfection, vis-à-vis that of organized markets, which will determine how much of financial activities will be carried out by the unorganized markets.

The productivity of small-scale investment, the extent of the familiarity with agent-entrepreneurs and their ability to closely monitor projects, may still allow unorganized financial markets to exist, but it can be reasonably expected that the spread between the rates of return in the organized and unorganized market would not be as wide as that which exists in the two markets in an interest-based developing economy in which the organized financial sector is regulated and interest rates are kept artificially low.

It can be stated, however, that the other problems plaguing the financial development of most developing countries, such as discrimination against small and indigenous entrepreneurs, shallowness of financial markets and limited availability of asset choices for savers will not be automatically eliminated by the introduction of an Islamic financial system. In fact, the introduction of an attractive and varied menu of asset choices will, perhaps, be far more important in the mobilization of savings in the Islamic system, than in a conventional interest-based system. Moreover, effective financial intermediation requires more efficient resource allocation by the Islamic financial system. It can be expected that the monitoring costs would be higher, and the need for specialization and expert portfolio diversification and management far greater, at least in the initial phases of operation after the adoption of the Islamic system, than in a conventional interest-based system. While the integration of financial markets should present no difficulties in the Islamic system, the provision of a positive high rate of return, although not requiring any arbitrary decision by authorities to increase the nominal yield, would necessitate mobilization of indigenous entrepreneurial ability through efficient project selection and allocation of financial resources based on relative expected profitability of projects, rather the solvency credit-worthiness or the collateral strength of the agent-entrepreneurs. If the bias against indigenous and small entrepreneurs persists and financial resources continue to flow to well-established and large entrepreneurs and/or the financial markets remain weak and shallow and asset choices limited, adoption of an Islamic financial system will not achieve its full potential in promoting economic development.

Style of Financial System

The positive contribution a financial system can make to the process of economic development depends, among other things, on the style of the system and how it is influenced by surrounding factors such as the type of financial intermediation institutions, the legal system, the regulatory and supervisory system, the role of government policies related to stabilizing and controlling the financial system and, finally the degree of economic development.

Historically, two different styles of financial systems have evolved over a period of time, with an on-going, undecided debate about the superiority of one over the other. A centralized or "bank-centered" financial system has been developed in countries like Germany and Japan, whereas a decentralized and "market-centered" financial system has emerged in Anglo-Saxon countries like the United Kingdom and the USA. Economists are debating the question whether and if a financial architecture anchored on markets works better or worse than the one centered on the banks, and if so, under what conditions. Opinions range from the position that financial architecture has no real consequences, to arguments emphasizing the inherent superiority of either the market-based system or the bank-based system, without reaching any conclusion.

By historical accident, much of the academic research on financial systems has been undertaken in the US and UK, which has perhaps led to some bias toward the market system, but there is no cross-country empirical evidence in support of either the market-based or the bank-based views. However, there is empirical evidence that the level of financial development is more critical than the relative dominance of banks or stock markets. Studies show that while market-based systems outperform bank-based systems among countries with developed financial sectors, bank-based systems fare better among countries with underdeveloped financial sectors. Countries dominated by small firms grow faster in bank-based systems and those dominated by larger firms, in market-based systems.

The next question is will a bank-based or market-based system emerge in the Islamic economic system? Is there an inherent bias toward either of the two system. Major securities markets in the modern day financial system include currencies, debt, equity, and the respective derivative markets. The market for debt securities is the largest market in conventional financial markets. Over time, it has become an integral and critical part of all securities markets, which have become dependent on debt markets for efficient benchmarks and reference indices to represent the cost of capital in the economy. Absence of debt markets will entail a total change of landscape of all other financial markets. Prohibition of *Riba* (interest) immediately rules out the existence of debt security and therefore its markets in any Islamic economic system. Majority of the *Shariah* scholars maintain that debt instruments like bonds whose nominal value is guaranteed by the issuer cannot be traded in an Islamic market even though the element of interest is not apparently there.

The assets of an Islamic financial intermediary, excluding partnership-based contracts, are linked to another asset. This asset's portfolio has interesting features. First, it provides a wide-range of maturity structure, i.e., from short-term trade financing to medium-term lease-based assets. The second and equally important feature is that the risk profiles of such assets carry relatively low risk because the pay-offs are directly linked to the pre-determined cash flows. Finally, pre-determined cash flows and fixed maturities make these securities a close substitute for conventional fixed-income securities. Due to this resemblance, these securities may be attractive to investors in the conventional system. Recent developments in mortgage-backed securities (MBS) in conventional financial markets are clear empirical evidence that a vibrant and efficient market can be developed based on a pool of real assets. It is fair to assert that in an Islamic financial system, the market for debt securities will be replaced with the market for asset-backed securities. This market will perform the critical function of extending liquidity to financial intermediaries and to the financial system.

The next market worth exploring is that of derivatives. Research on the scope of derivative securities and trading of risk in Islamic financial system is in its early stages. *Shariah* scholars are working on assessing the permissibility of derivatives such as forwards, futures, options and swaps. So far, the general thinking is that derivative products as practiced in today's conventional markets incorporate an element of *gharar* and therefore are not permissible. This, however, does not preclude a financial intermediary from designing a risk-sharing or risk mitigating scheme. This can be achieved through the creation of a risk-mitigating instrument synthetically using existing instruments. For example, the famous Black and Scholes (1973) paper on option pricing theory demonstrated the creation and replication of an option by using an equity stock and a fixed income security.

Although the general rules of markets, i.e., fairness and justice in pricing, are equally applicable to the markets for financial securities, the operations of the markets for financial securities conforming to the principles of the *Shariah* will be somewhat different from those in the conventional markets. The main differences identified are due to various issues under debate regarding the negotiability and tradability of financial securities, the practice of maintaining margins and short selling. Negotiability and tradability are vital for the development of secondary markets. Actual implementation and internalization of the *Shariah* principles will, of course, raise market-specific issues and, therefore, will call for an in-depth understanding of each market, the products it exchanges, and its participants. Research on the structure and operations of securities markets in the Islamic economic system is very limited and such research has mainly focused on identifying the features of conventional securities markets that are not compatible with Islamic principles, rather than envisioning a market incorporating all aspects of the principles of Islamic economics. Unless efficient primary and secondary capital markets are developed, financial intermediaries will continue to dominate the financial system.

In light of the above observations, it is clear that the role of a financial intermediary is critical and consequently, the style of the Islamic financial system would be dependent on bank-like financial institutions — at least in the near future, unless further progress is made in developing markets. This conclusion is further supported by empirical evidence linking the strong role of intermediary institutions wherever capital markets are underdeveloped. To summarize, the style of the Islamic financial system would be similar to a bank-centered system, for the following reasons:

- Due to the prohibition of *Riba* and debt securities, debt-based capital market will not exist and therefore the role of the intermediary in providing direct capital through *Mudārabah* and *Mushārakah* will become vital.
- There are certain operational issues relating to equities markets (discussed in the next section), which need resolution by *Shariah* scholars. Meanwhile, the dependence on the intermediary for capital formation increases.
- The absence of a debt market demands development of a market for asset-backed securities to make a bank's assets liquid. The financial intermediary will play a critical role in the development of such a market through pooling and structuring through securitization and to provide credit enhancements throughout the life of the asset.
- Non-availability or limited application of derivative markets increases the burden on the financial intermediaries to perform the function of risk sharing and mitigation.

A financial system dominated by strong financial intermediaries is not necessarily an inefficient one. It is often quoted that Japan has sophisticated financial markets, but for most of the past fifty years, a concentrated banking system has played the dominant role in allocating resources and has contributed to economic development. A bank-centered financial system "where banks dominate the intermediation function" offers superior information processing because the banks form long-term relationships with firms to ease asymmetric information distortions, ameliorate the moral hazard through effective monitoring, and thereby boost economic growth. Banks acting as delegated monitors well-known economics term acquire information about firms and managers and thereby improve capital allocation and corporate governance. Further positive contributions to development are made by inter-temporal risk management as articulated by Allen and Gale (1999) and through utilization of economies of scale. Since the nineteenth century, many economists have argued that bank-based systems are better at mobilizing savings, identifying good investments, and exerting sound corporate governance, particularly during the early stages of economic development and in a weak institutional environment.[1]

The emerging "financial services view" argues that it does not matter if the system is bank-based or market-based, but the important issue is which institutions perform a particular function.[2] The financial services view stresses that financial arrangements — contracts, markets and intermediaries — arise to ameliorate market imperfections and provide financial services.

Another view expressed is one which is influenced by the significance of the legal system. This view argues that finance is a set of contracts that are defined by legal rights and are effective because of enforcement mechanisms. It is the overall level and quality of financial services — as determined by the legal system — that improves the efficient allocation of resources and economic growth. The strengthening of the legal system, which determines the overall level of financial services, is more critical for economic performance than distinguishing the financial system as bank-based or market-based.

When a financial system is viewed as a set of contracts, it can function optimally only if there exists a supporting legal and institutional infrastructure, free of any distortions, to execute and enforce the contracts. The functioning of the system can be further enhanced if contracts are standardized and institutionalized to perform specialized functions within the economic system. For example, a financial intermediary, whose primary function is financial intermediation, does not wish to engage in non-intermediary functions such as operating a leasing business. However, with the availability of well-established specialists who specialize in running and operating a leasing enterprise and in the case where there is an organized market for such specialists, a financial intermediary can focus on providing funds at competitive cost by issuing non-guaranteed securities to its investors. As a result, this division of labor will lead to a more efficient financial system. This can only be achieved if financial instruments are institutionalized on solid legal foundations.

Whereas there is theoretical support for a financial intermediary-centered financial system, there are other considerations in support of such architecture. As discussed earlier, the real consequences of financial architecture depend on a host of country-specific factors, including the contractual, legal, and institutional environment of the country and the associated degree of agency and informational problems in the economy. Studies have shown that a financial system in its infancy will be bank-dominated and increased financial market sophistication diminishes bank lending. Furthermore, the bank-based architecture suitably complements weak legal and institutional environments, as markets require a stronger legal and institutional environment to flourish. Several Muslim countries are developing countries where legal, institutional and governance structures are under-developed and as a result the financial development is not very sophisticated. While lawmakers and regulators are in the process of developing and strengthening the weak legal system, poor property rights and fragile regulatory institutions — ingredients for a sound financial system — financial intermediaries will dominate the financial system.

While the critical role a financial intermediary plays is recognized, the significance of financial and capital markets cannot be ignored. Competitive capital markets play a positive role in aggregating information signals and effectively transmitting this information to investors, with beneficial implications for firms seeking financing and ultimately overall economic performance. Competition between the financial intermediary and the market in providing financial services may not be desirable, but both can perform complementary functions. For a financial intermediary, the absence of efficient and liquid financial markets can greatly hamper portfolio and risk management on its assets side. An organized market for financial securities co-existing with strong financial intermediaries will offer diversification opportunities, lower transaction costs, and improved liquidity, leading to enhanced efficiency in the financial system.

Implementation Challenges

Operational challenges for setting up an Islamic financial system can be better understood when analyzed separately, both at the micro level, i.e., setting-up the financial institution on a profit-loss sharing principle, and the macro level, i.e., economy-wide implementation. While it has been relatively easy to create an Islamic bank where deposits do not bear interest, in reality, the asset portfolios do not contain sufficiently strong components based on profit sharing. The main reasons for this are the informational asymmetry due to inefficient markets resulting in costly delegated monitoring and the preference for short-term trade related transactions. Also, there is the fact that legal and institutional frameworks that facilitate appropriate contracts, as well as mechanisms to enforce them, do not exist.

The most important operational challenge of Islamic banking is in its system-wide implementation. At present, many Islamic countries suffer from financial disequilibria that frustrate attempts at wholesale adoption of Islamic banking. Financial imbalances in fiscal, monetary and external sectors of these economies cannot provide a fertile ground for the efficient operation of Islamic banking. Major structural adjustments, particularly in the fiscal and monetary areas, are needed to provide Islamic banking with a level playing field. Additionally, a legal framework of property ownership and contracts is needed, to specify the domains of private and public property rights and stipulate the legally enforceable rights of parties to contracts, in accordance with the *Shariah*.

An Islamic financial system can be said to operate efficiently if, as a result of its adoption, rates of return in the financial sector correspond to those in the real sector. In many Islamic countries fiscal deficits are financed through the banking system. To lower the costs of this financing, the financial system is repressed by artificially maintaining limits on bank rates. Thus, financial repression is a form of taxation that provides governments with substantial revenues. To remove this burden, government expenditures have to be lowered and/or revenues raised. Efficiency can be promoted by requiring that governments compete with the private sector when accessing the credit market, i.e., allowing the unification of rates of return on borrowings by the government and the private sector.

Massive involvement of governments in the economy makes it difficult for them to reduce their expenditures. Raising taxes is politically difficult. Thus, imposing controls on domestic financial markets becomes a relatively easy form of raising revenues. Under these circumstances, it is understandable why governments impose severe constraints on private financial institutions that can provide higher returns to their shareholders and/or depositors. However, these constraints make it very difficult for Islamic banks and other financial institutions to realize their full potential. For example, *Mudarabah* companies that can provide higher returns than the banking system would end up in direct competition with the banking system for deposits that are used for bank financing of fiscal deficits, thus leading to sizable disintermediation from the banking system that is often state-owned.

Efficient operation of system-wide Islamic banking is presently severely constrained by distortions in the economy. There are several factors that impede the efficient operation of an Islamic financial system. These include pervasive government intervention and controls, inefficient and weak tax systems, financial repression, lack of capital markets, unavailability of a well-targeted and efficient social safety net, lack of a strong supervisory and prudential regulatory framework in the financial system, and, finally, the deficiencies of the legal and institutional framework that provide *Shariah*-based definitions of property rights as well as the rights of the parties to contracts. These distortions need to be eliminated to minimize waste and promote efficient resource allocation in any case. Their removal prior to, or in conjunction with, the adoption of Islamic banking can be expected to create the dynamics necessary for sustainable and non-inflationary economic growth.

State-wide Implementation — Lessons Learnt

The process of making the economic and financial system compatible with Islam was undertaken in Islamic Republics of Iran, Pakistan and Sudan but under different political, economic, and cultural circumstances. In each case, this process did not take place in a carefully thought out manner and with the understanding of Islamic principles and jurisprudence, but rather in an ad-hoc fashion. A thorough examination and evaluation of the experience in each country can take a separate volume but some of the reasons for the lack of success can be summarized below:

- Implementing a banking system merely by removing interest from the system without preparing the ground work in terms of financial liberalization and strengthening the necessary institutions required by Islam (such as those that protect property rights and enforce contracts), is not realistic. Modern banking and financial systems require a sound legal infrastructure to support the system. Full implementation of the Islamic system demands conformity of the legal environment with the *Shariah*. The task of introducing changes in the common and civil law, regulations and investors' rights is a massive task, which often does not get priority due to social and political instability in the country.
- The institutional infrastructure for development of an efficient financial system does not exist. Institutions to promote transparency, to protect the rights of creditors and to encourage good governance are either non-existent or too weak to be effective.
- The economies of these countries are still developing. There are significant budget deficits and government involvement in borrowing leads to inefficiencies in the economy, putting strain on the banking and financial sectors.
- In some cases, there is lack of political will. Transforming the financial system is not an easy task and therefore requires commitment and support of the political forces in the country. For example in Pakistan, the process of Islamization was started by a military regime but was not taken seriously by the following political governments.
- There is a great shortage of expertise and skills in the financial sector. These shortages hamper the development of new products. In addition, it is hard to find knowledgeable people trained in *Shariah* as well as in other domains such as economics and finance.

Economy-wide benefits from the operation of an Islamic financial system may include the following:

- government expenditures that are fully rationalized,
- revenues from taxation, and those derived from property legitimately placed within the government domain by the *Shariah*, can be raised to meet the expenditure needs of the government,
- the financial sector can be liberalized to allow the returns in this sector to reflect returns in the real economy,
- equity markets can be developed to allow the financing of investment projects outside banking institutions, and, finally
- the structure of the banking system could be such as to allow strong banking supervision and prudential regulation commensurate with the risks involved in various transactions.

To accomplish the last objective, the banking structure can be tiered in accordance with the principal Islamic financial transactions.[3]

Endnotes

1   In contrast, the market-based or market-dominated view highlights the growth–enhancing role of well functioning markets through (i) fostering greater incentives to research new firms and to profit from this information by trading in large and liquid markets, (ii) facilitating corporate control by easing takeovers and linking managerial compensation to firm performance, and (iii) facilitating risk trading.

2   Merton, Robert C. and Bodie Zvi (1995), "A conceptual framework for analyzing the financial environment," in Dwight B. Crane et al., Eds., The Global Financial System: A Functional Perspective, and Levine, Ross (1997), "Financial Development and Economic Growth: Views and Agenda," *Journal of Economic Literature*, Vol. 35, No. 2, pp. 688–726.

3   It is not an accident that Islamic banking is making its most promising progress in Malaysia. This country has one of the least repressive financial systems, no fiscal deficits, low inflation, low interest rates, and a dynamic and vibrant equity market as well as a strong private sector. With the recent intense efforts of the monetary authorities, it can be expected that greater dynamism will be injected in the process of the growth of Islamic banking in the country.

7

Islamic Financial Services Industry

There is no doubt that Islamic financial markets have recorded significant growth in the last two decades, but researchers are contemplating how this rapid growth can be sustained given the structure of the institutions and the markets. Challenges imposed by globalization, the fast-changing financial landscape, and increasing demands of investors and entrepreneurs for wider and customized services should be taken seriously by providers of Islamic financial services. For years, Islamic banks have been offering *Shariah*-compliant products without much institutional support. The majority of the activities have been commercial banking activities and there are clear gaps in the areas of investment banking and insurance. In addition, supporting institutions such as standard setting bodies, rating agencies, clearing houses, etc. are also either non-existent or under-developed.

More recently, several positive developments have been taking place with the establishment of new institutions and agencies to support the financial system, but still there are several areas worthy of attention, with a view to achieving sustainable high growth, improving the level of service, and enhancing the stability of the system. These areas of improvement should be looked at by the players and the stakeholders of the market offering Islamic financial services. The major areas that call for improvement and recommendations in regard to further development are discussed in this chapter.

Islamic Banking: Theory versus Practice

The structure and current practices of Islamic banks differ from the theoretical models discussed in the previous chapter on several aspects. Some of these differences are the obstacles faced in the full implementation of an Islamic financial system. These factors not only affect the further evolution of the industry, but also pose challenges to the regulators. The following are the highlights of the main divergences between the theory and the practice:

Under-utilization of Partnership-based Contracts

The first difference is the significant deviation of the structure of assets from what the theory prescribes. On the assets side of the balance sheet, as expected, a clear preference for asset-backed securities (based on trade finance) is evident, as opposed to partnership-based instruments requiring sharing of profits and losses. This preference is due to the fact that sale-related securities are considered low risk and resemble familiar conventional fixed-income securities in terms of risk-return profile.

On average, as a mode of financing, *Murabahah* (41%) has been the first choice of Islamic banks, followed by *Musharakah* (11%), *Mudarabah* (12%), *Ijarah* (10%) and others (26%), add Archer and Ahmed (2003). The bulk of the financing is undertaken in the form of trade-financing activities and contrary to what the system promotes, i.e., partnership-based financing, equity-based assets are seriously lagging behind. In addition to trade-based instruments, Islamic banks prefer leasing, considered to have less uncertain returns than the partnership-based instruments of *Musharakah* or *Mudarabah*.

Predominantly, the transactions on the assets side consist of customized or tailor-made transactions between the bank and its client. There is no organized market to securitize the bank's assets and to trade the securities in the market, severely limiting the liquidity of the financial institutions. As a result, Islamic banks have limited themselves to a small set of asset classes, which constrain their opportunities for portfolio diversification and its benefits. Although this practice is conservative in its nature as assets are collateralized, it has associated costs in terms of additional exposure to credit and operational risk. This limited set of asset choices is a major impediment to the further growth of the Islamic financial services industry.

Islamic banks have not utilized partnership-based instruments like *Mudarabah* and *Musharakah*, on their assets side due to the high monitoring costs associated with these instruments, resulting from asymmetrical information and moral hazard. Islamic banks are not willing to allocate resources for monitoring due to their own limited resources. In addition, the market for partnership-based financing requires a well-functioning infrastructure where information about potential entrepreneurs and their projects is readily available and the majority of markets where Islamic banks are correctly operating lack such sophisticated infrastructure.

Limited Maturity Structure

Islamic banks' over-dependence on trade and commodity financing instruments has limited their choice of maturity structure, since a major portion of such financing is of short-term maturity. Whereas the theoretical models expect the financial intermediaries to participate in the full range of maturity structures to get the benefits of portfolio diversification, in reality, Islamic banks shy away from instruments requiring a medium- and long-term commitment. A cursory look at the data on the asset maturities collected from six Islamic banks as of 2003 makes it clear that 54% of their assets had a maturity of less than one year and 39%, of less than 6 months.[1] IFIs tend not to invest in longer maturities due to the lack of liquidity of the medium- to long-term assets. Due to this reliance on short-term maturity, Islamic banks are unable to offer investment opportunities to investors who are interested in long-term investments.

Separation of Investor Classes

Another aspect of the divergence between the practice and the theory is the choice and application of accounting policies that affect the allocation of income between shareholders and account holders or between different classes of account holders. In theory, Islamic finance has clear barriers in the deployment of assets between those funded by demand deposits, general investment accounts, special investment accounts and equity. However, current practice does not include such barriers, with the asset side treated as one large bucket with all stakeholders' funds mixed together. In terms of its functions, an Islamic bank is a hybrid of both a commercial and an investment bank, more akin to a universal bank. However, unlike conventional universal banks, Islamic banks do not erect firewalls to separate, legally, financially and managerially, their investment and commercial banking services. As a result, funds in investment accounts are not "ring-fenced" from the funds from others, including the equity holders. This is one of the most critical deviations in the practice of Islamic banks and one that poses a tough challenge to regulators, because different stakeholders of the Islamic banks need to be regulated under different regulating principles and therefore taking the one-solution-for-all approach becomes restrictive and may defeat the whole objective of regulation in this case. This is further elaborated and discussed in the chapter on the regulation of Islamic financial institutions.

Investors' Rights and Governance

The fourth divergence between principle and practice, related somewhat to the foregoing issues, is the status of the investment accounts. Although they are supposed to be operating on profit and loss principles, actual practice differs. IFIs have faced criticism when they write down the value of assets, because they do not in practice write down the value of deposits. This implies that losses on the asset side are absorbed by either other deposit holders or by the equity holders. This practice raises a question on their degree of transparency and information disclosure. It also raises the issue of the need to separate asset types to match them closely to liabilities, either through firewalling or through segmentation.

This deviation leads to the question of the governance rights of the investment account holders. Large size investment accounts serve as sources of capital to finance pools of investments and assets of the financial institution, but their holders are not granted any participation in the governance or monitoring process. The majority of investment account holders are individuals who may not organize themselves collectively to perform the necessary monitoring. Under such circumstances, the responsibility of the regulators and the *Shariah* boards increases further, to make sure that adequate monitoring mechanisms are in place to protect the rights of the investment account holders.

Efficiency of Islamic Banks

Before raising the question of improvement, it is worth surveying the studies conducted to examine the performance and efficiency of Islamic banks. A typical measure of efficiency is the ability to convert inputs (staff costs, fixed assets and total deposits) into outputs (total loans, liquid assets and other income). Several studies have been undertaken to evaluate the cost and production efficiency of Islamic financial institutions in different countries where Islamic finance is practiced. The majority of such studies have measured efficiency using accounting ratios and comparing them with the ratios of conventional banks of similar size and location. Metwally (1997) compared the performance of 15 interest-free banks with 15 conventional banks for structural differences between the two groups of banks in terms of liquidity, leverage, credit risk, profit, and efficiency. The study found that although profitability and efficiency differences are not statistically significant between the two types of banks, Islamic banks tend to be more conservative in utilizing funds for lending and were disadvantaged in terms of investment opportunities. Similar findings of constrained investment opportunities were observed by Samad and Hassan (1999) who looked at the inter-bank performance of Bank Islam Malaysia Berhad (BIMB) in terms of profitability, liquidity, risk, and solvency as well as community involvement for the period 1984–1997 and concluded that the average profit of an Islamic bank was significantly lower than that of the conventional banks, mainly due to the limited investment opportunities set for the Islamic bank.

Based on data from 1993 to 2000, Majid, Nor, and Said (2003) concluded that there was no statistically significant difference in the level of efficiency between Islamic and conventional banks operating in Malaysia. This study does, however, find a linkage between inefficiency and bank size. The bank size not only influenced inefficiency, it also did so in a non-linear fashion. Increasing size initially provides some economies of scale; however, diseconomies of scale set in once a critical size was reached, thus suggesting a U-shaped average cost function. In a comparative study of conventional and Islamic banking, Iqbal (2000) measured the efficiency of 12 Islamic banks by comparing their trends and profitability ratios with a "control group" of 12 conventional banks of similar size from the same countries. Islamic banks included in the sample accounted for more than 75% of the total assets as well as total capital of the whole Islamic banking industry and were accordingly a reasonable proxy representative of the entire sector. The study finds that during the period 1990–1997, Islamic banks achieved higher rates of growth of total investments, total assets, total equity, and total deposits than their conventional counterparts. More importantly, the study finds that Islamic banks also turned out to be more cost effective and made a better use of their resources than the banks in the control group, as indicated by their significantly higher deployment ratios.

Hussein (2003) estimated the operational efficiency of 17 Sudanese Islamic banks from 1990–2000 and found that these Islamic banks did not create inefficiency per se, but that there were wide efficiency differences across domestic Islamic banks. However, foreign banks were found to be more efficient, despite their small size, than the state-owned and joint-ownership banks. Finally, a more recent study by Yudistira (2004) analyzed the size efficiency relationship by grouping 18 Islamic banks by total assets. Banks with more than $600 million of assets were categorized as large size and banks below this level were categorized as small-to-medium size. The overall efficiency results for the period 1997–2000 suggested that low levels of inefficiency (around 10%) were observed across all banks, but the results were defended by arguing that such inefficiencies were within the industry norms when compared to many conventional banks. Interestingly, the study found that the largest degrees of scale inefficiencies were observed in large size Islamic banks.

In general, studies have found Islamic banks to be performing efficiently when compared with similar conventional financial institutions in similar market conditions. By international standards, the average size of an Islamic bank is relatively small but despite this fact, it is surprising that no study has been able to provide convincing evidence of inefficiencies in Islamic banks. There could be two possible explanations as to why Islamic banks are found to be efficient irrespective of their small size. First, most of the studies have been performed as a relative comparison with conventional banks in the same geographical region; thus ignoring the impact of systemic inefficiencies. A more realistic analysis should include comparison of efficiencies against international benchmarks, comparison with foreign banks, controlling for any protection against competition, and should take into account the quality of standards, and other macro-economic variables such as capital movement. Further, most of the studies were conducted during a period of high growth resulting from high demand for Islamic financial services. During the periods of high growth and demand, institutions are often subject to low levels of market pressures and competition. When institutions are entering into a niche market like Islamic finance, some level of inefficiency is compensated by the abnormal initial profit margins. These margins erode fast as more players enter the market and it becomes more competitive.

Another reason could be that undertaking an empirical study to review the performance of Islamic banks or to understand the efficiency of financial services is itself a challenge because of the low degree of transparency and quality of information disclosure of Islamic banks. For instance, many Islamic banks do not provide sufficient details as to the division of equity and deposits. Further, access to transaction level data is extremely difficult. When it comes to deposits, it is hard to get any reliable and detailed breakdown of the deposit types offered by these institutions because of the common practice of "clubbing" different types of deposits together. Similarly, details on the assets side are often not very transparent. The above factors imply that the results of these efficiency studies are to be taken with caution and one cannot conclude that there is no need to improve efficiency.

Islamic Banking: Areas of Improvement

Size and Fragmentation

Although Islamic financial institutions (IFIs) have grown in numbers, the average size of their assets is still small as compared to the average size of the assets of a bank in the conventional system. Table 7.1 shows the number of IFIs and their respective sizes of assets and capital by region as of the end of 1990s. It clearly indicates a wide dispersion of financial institutions with relatively small sizes of assets.

It is worth noting that as of 2001, not a single Islamic bank was on the list of the top 100 banks in the world. According to the same estimates, more than 60% of the Islamic banks were below the minimum assets size of US$500 million considered for an efficient conventional bank, and aggregate assets of all Islamic banks were less than those of any bank on the list of the top 60 banks in the world. Finally, the size of assets of the largest Islamic bank amounted to a meager 1% of the assets of the largest bank in the world.

Due to their small size, Islamic banks are unable to reap the benefits of the economies of scale and scope. Larger sized institutions have significant potential for efficiency gains through cost savings due to the economies of scale and scope, organizational efficiency, reduced cost of funding, and economizing of capital.

Table 7.1 Islamic Financial Institutions (IFIs)

Region	No. of IFIs	Average Capital (US$ Million)	Average Assets (US$ Million)
South Asia	51	17	770
Africa	35	6	45
South East Asia	31	5	75
Middle East	47	116	2204
Europe and Americas	9	70	101
Pacific and Australia	3	3	6
Total	176	42	839

Source: Kahf (1999)

Illiquidity

As mentioned earlier, Islamic financial institutions operate on a limited set of short-term traditional instruments and there is a shortage of products for medium- to long-term maturities. One reason for these shortcomings is the lack of markets to sell, trade, and negotiate financial assets of the bank. There are no avenues for securitizing dormant assets and taking them off the balance sheet. In other words, the secondary markets lack depth and breadth. An effective portfolio management strategy cannot be implemented in the absence of liquid markets, as opportunities for diversification become limited. Since the needs of the market in terms of liquidity and risk and portfolio management are not being met, a serious effect of this under-development is that the system is not functioning at its full potential. The realization is growing that sustainable long-term growth of Islamic financial markets largely depends on well-functioning secondary markets and on the introduction of liquidity-enhancing and risk-sharing products.

Limited Scope

In the absence of debt markets, coupled with the under-development of equities markets and lack of derivatives markets, the role of the financial intermediary providing Islamic financial services becomes critical. The financial intermediary not only becomes the main source of capital and risk mitigation, but it is also expected to undertake other activities with a wider scope. The changing global financial landscape expects Islamic banks to go beyond their traditional core commercial banking role and develop other areas of financial industry dealing with securities, risk management, and insurance businesses, which are currently either lacking or are on a limited scale.

The distinction between traditional commercial banking and investment banking is getting blurred and there is a global trend of mixing financial services with non-banking services in an efficient fashion. Although this trend is prevalent in major industrial economies, it has not been embraced by many of emerging markets where Islamic finance is practiced. For example, a recent study, which ranked several countries in the Middle East region (where Islamic finance is dominant) according to their level of financial development, finds that throughout the region, countries fared poorly on indicators for a strong institutional environment and for the development of the non-bank financial sector. (Creane, Goyal, Mobarak, and Sab (2003))

Concentrated Banking

Islamic banks tend to be concentrated in their deposit base or asset base. Due to the small size, Islamic financial institutions often concentrate on a few select sectors and avoid direct competition. For example, one IFI may specialize in agriculture sector financing, whereas another might do the same in the construction sector without attempting to diversify into other sectors. This practice makes IFIs vulnerable to cyclical shocks in a particular sector. Dependence on a few select sectors, or lack of diversification, increases an IFI's exposure to new entrants in the same sector, especially by foreign conventional banks who are better equipped to meet these challenges.

This concentration of the deposit or asset base of an Islamic financial institution can also be viewed as lack of diversification, which increases their exposure to risk. The data in Table 7.1, which show the assets composition of IFIs, clearly indicate that IFIs' asset side is concentrated in a handful of products and is definitely not diversified. In terms of sector allocation, the average financing activities of IFIs have been primarily trade oriented (32%) followed by sectors like industry (17%), real estate (16%), services (12%), agriculture (6%) and others (17%) (Kahf (1999)). Islamic banks are not fully exploiting the benefits of diversification, which come from both geographical and product diversification. At present, IFIs heavily rely on maintaining good relationships with the depositors to earn the depositors' loyalty. However, this relationship can be put to a test during distress or changing market conditions, when the depositors tend to change loyalties and shift to large financial institutions that are perceived to be safer.

This risk of losing depositors raises a more serious exposure, termed as "displacement risk." Displacement risk refers to a situation where, in order to remain competitive, an IFI pays its investment depositors a rate of return higher than what should be payable under the "actual" terms of the investment contract, by foregoing part or all of its equity-holders' profits which may adversely affect its own capital. An IFI engages in such practice to encourage its investment account holders not to withdraw their funds. Through a geographical diversification of the deposit base, an IFI can reduce its exposure to displacement or withdrawal risks. With the changing face of the banking business and introduction of Internet-based banking, achieving a high degree of geographical diversity on the liabilities side is conceivable and should be encouraged.

Scope of Consolidation

The financial services industry in major industrial countries has experienced a trend toward consolidation through mergers and acquisitions in the last two decades. This move toward consolidation started in the 1980s in the US, but at a much later stage in Europe where the trend developed at a relatively slow pace until 1996. The consolidation trend in both the US and Europe reached its peak during the last three years of the 1990s. Over this period, acquisitions of banking firms accounted for 60% of all financial consolidations and 70% of the total value of consolidated institutions. The clean-up was concentrated among the smallest institutions and as a result in this period the number of large banks (with total assets in excess of US$100 billion) actually increased from three to six while the number of medium-sized banks (with total assets in the range US$100 million to US$100 billion) remained relatively stable, falling from 2,446 to 2,284. Small banks (with total assets below US$100 million) were the target and their number fell from 10,014 to 5,636.

Many factors are cited as stimulants for this wave of consolidation. Among the critical forces encouraging consolidation are financial deregulation, globalization of financial and real markets, advances in technology, excess capacity or financial distress in the market, and increased shareholder pressure for financial performance. The barriers to entry decreased with the deregulation and globalization of financial markets, resulting in increased competition for financial firms. Deregulation in the US resulted in the end of the ban on inter-state banking and of the separation between commercial and investment banking. This changed the rules of the game.[2] In the case of Europe, economic, financial and monetary union and the introduction of the euro accelerated the pace of financial market integration and encouraged cross-border activity, partly through consolidation. The 1980s and 1990s also brought on the technology revolution, especially in the area of telecommunications and computing, which put further pressure on the financial industry to compete globally. Increased competition among banks forced them to seek ways to cut costs and to increase market share, which ultimately led to a trend of consolidation: either through mergers to create synergies, or through acquisitions of inefficiently small, poorly managed and insufficiently diversified financial institutions.

One of the earlier and more conventional arguments for consolidation has been the potential for efficiency gains through cost savings due to the economies of scale, organizational efficiency, enhanced risk management through diversifications, reduced cost of funding, and economizing of capital. It is also argued that large financial institutions are able to enjoy revenue enhancements through economies of scope offering a larger menu of products to the same customer base.

Researchers have argued that Islamic financial institutions which are characterized by small size and limited resources are prime candidates for consolidation which can help these institutions overcome several obstacles to their further growth. IFIs can benefit from consolidation in following ways:

- Expanding the scale of operations is not sufficient and it is essential that IFIs expand the scope of their products and services to meet the challenges of domestic and international markets and to sustain current levels of growth. An increase in scale and scope through consolidation could provide IFIs with the necessary threshold to justify building a solid infrastructure for new services on both sides of the balance sheet. In addition, with increased size, the institutions will be able to afford the resources required to undertake financial engineering.
- Consolidation of IFIs can lead to better risk management through diversification, enhanced quality of management, reduced operational risk, and lower systemic risk. There is no question that consolidation can bring benefits to IFIs through diversification and through enhanced management quality, as well as efficiency gains from prudent risk taking, monitoring and management. Efficiency in managing risk can also be achieved through improved technology and risk monitoring models and systems necessary to stay competitive in the market.
- Consolidation can also enhance the management quality of IFIs.[3] After consolidation, the managerial efficiency of IFIs can improve; as with increased scale, they will be able to afford and implement formal management training programs. Different financial instruments require different skills and training. Professionals trained in conventional banking are available in abundance, a professional with a deep understanding of the principles of Islamic finance and, to some extent, of the *Shariah*, is scarce. This shortage of professionals exposes IFIs to management and operational risks. According to a study using a survey methodology, 40 to 70% of bankers surveyed indicated that the lack of knowledgeable bankers for selecting, evaluating and managing profitable projects is a significant reason for Islamic banks in Malaysia not to engage in equity-financing projects.[4]
- There are several indirect benefits that an IFI may enjoy as a result of a well-diversified portfolio, and the perception of a well-managed

institution. An institution can lower its costs of funding because markets tend to view such institutions as less risky due to better risk diversification.

Empirical studies on assessing the effects of consolidation have yielded mixed results. Empirical analysis has fallen short of finding comprehensive evidence of gains in profitability.[5] Consolidation has also been unable to deliver the claims of increased efficiency due to economies of scale. However, there are several other arguments in favor of consolidation, which are applicable to emerging or developing markets such as Islamic financial services. The restructuring of the financial services industry is a challenge for the financial service providers and for the regulators. These challenges have direct implications for the decision- and policy-making — not only of the management of the financial service providers, but also of the regulators and the supervisors.

The management of any IFI interested in pursuing a policy of expansion through consolidation needs to avoid certain pitfalls and to factor in the following issues in its ultimate decision-making process:

- A policy of consolidation should be part of a strategic plan and not just for the sake of empire building. Management should have a clear vision of the objectives to be achieved through consolidation. The decision to consolidate should take into account the changing legal, economic and financial environment and consider how it will impact the future of the consolidated institution.
- The benefits of consolidation are directly related to the overall market size. Management should carefully review the target market size and the economy size to make an assessment of available capacity. It is conceivable that due to the small size of the economy, large banks may not be able to create enough business to optimally utilize their resources and minimize costs.
- IFIs should be aware of potential difficulties that may arise in consolidating different systems and management styles and cultures. The increased number of decision-making centers and the structural differences may affect the efficiency of the internal control systems. Many conventional banks experienced difficulties in integrating technology and systems after consolidation, which resulted in an increased level of operational risk for them after consolidation.
- If IFIs' main motive in consolidating is to benefit from diversification, IFIs will need to invest in developing state-of-the-art risk monitoring and management systems. Some of IFIs' products carry high credit

risk and monitoring costs, which will require robust internal systems to monitor and manage such risks. Special attention must be paid to prudent management of credit risk, in order to avoid undue concentrations of risks to individual entities, associates, industries, geographical areas, sectors or financial products and services. Management should be ready to bear the cost of sophisticated risk models and technology.

- IFIs' management should be aware that diversification gains can be easily offset by an increase in risk appetite in the post-consolidation period. Institutions tend to pursue the policies of undertaking additional risks to enhance expected returns, which can lead to an increase in the overall risk profile of the institution. Management should try to restrain the incentive for taking risks and follow a policy of manageable risk.
- IFIs should ensure that they have skillful managers who have the experience of managing of large-scale institutions. Otherwise, the potential benefits of consolidation cannot be realized and, on the contrary, the level of operational risk may increase.

From the regulators' point of view, the typical areas of concern associated with consolidation are (i) the possibility that increased moral hazard may lead large financial institutions to become "too big to fail," and to liquidate, or discipline effectively; (ii) reduction in competition that may provide a disincentive to the consolidated entities to improve efficiency; and (iii) an increase in systemic risk due to a highly concentrated industry (De Nicoló (2003)). These concerns would be equally relevant to any consolidation movement in the Islamic financial services industry. Regulation and supervision of IFIs that pose a diverse set of challenges for the policy-makers can also raise more specific concerns. Consolidating banking and non-banking financial services by an IFI without any well-defined segregation makes the task of regulation and supervision more complex. While policy makers may like to encourage consolidation of IFIs to derive the benefits from economies of scale and scope, and from diversification, they should also be watchful of the issues which may be applicable to IFIs, such as following:

- Systemic risk is defined as the possibility that credit or liquidity problems of one or more financial market participants may create substantial credit or liquidity problems for participants elsewhere in the financial system. Systemic risks may increase after consolidation as a result of a higher level of interdependence, or through excessive concentration of risk, or due to the enhanced risk-taking incentive for individual financial institutions. Consolidation of IFIs can lead to interdependencies, as the consolidated financial institutions become large and complex. On the assets' side, IFIs may change their portfolio composition by investing in other financial or non-financial institutions (such as leasing companies) through *Musharakah* (equity) and *Mudarabah* (trust financing), which can lead to a complex network of interdependencies. A high level of interdependencies would suggest the potential for higher systemic risks.[6] Supervisors should have a system to monitor and detect any such high levels of interdependencies.

- Low degree of disclosure and transparency in the Islamic financial services industry can make supervision less effective. Any prudent supervision would be incomplete without reliable data on the key financial services and products at the institutional level. A reduction in the number of financial institutions through consolidation can have a positive impact on bank supervision of IFIs, as dealing with a reduced number of institutions will streamline the collection and analysis of data, including the institution's interdependencies. Enhanced monitoring and evaluation of an individual service provider's data, in combination with the data on the financial markets as well as on the domestic and international macroeconomic variables, might yield valuable insights into the risks posed by interdependencies and possibly improve the early warning systems for any potential financial crisis.

- Financial innovation in pursuit of the expansion of the scope of services may bring additional challenges for regulators, such as ensuring that the process of introducing new products is transparent and that proper procedures are being followed in terms of product compliance with *Shariah* principles. With the reduced number of institutions, the regulators' interaction with an individual bank's *Shariah* board may be at a more manageable level, which could enhance the effectiveness of compliance and may facilitate development and establishment of standards.

- Policy makers may like to encourage consolidation of IFIs to compete internationally, but it may have an effect on the competition in the domestic financial services. Regulators will have to strike a balance between reduction in competition and the change in the balance of market power as a result of consolidation. Excessive concentration in financial services can lead to exertion of market power and extraction of higher margins and fees, especially in the case of the emerging markets. Regulators will have to make a judgement on how to maintain distortion-free competition in the market, to ensure that the consumers receive the highest quality service at the lowest possible costs. What may be the maximum desirable market share for a single IFI will largely depend on the regulator's capacity to manage, the size of the economy and the potential market size for financial services.

- Policy makers in emerging markets should pay attention to the financing needs of small firms, who are often neglected when financial institutions grow in size. Advocates of Islamic finance claim that it encourages entrepreneurship and thus contributes to economic development. An increase in size may have a negative impact on the availability of credit to small businesses and thus may impact the development aspect of Islamic finance.

- In order that the market and the consumers may benefit from diversification, regulators should consider reducing the obstacles in the mobility of customers across geographical regions and across financial service providers. For instance, in the case of the Middle East, which has a large number of IFIs, regulators of different countries will need to collaborate and cooperate to reduce the obstacles in the mobility of customers and capital.

- In order to avoid any excessive risk concentration by IFIs, supervisors should ensure that the risks of a merged entity are not more than the risks of the two stand-alone entities and should carefully make assessments of the credit and operational exposures of the merged entity. To prevent any situation of excessive risk, policy makers will need to closely monitor IFIs' post-consolidation risk-taking behavior to detect any potential effect on the systemic risk. This may call for establishing a comprehensive monitoring of IFIs' sector selection, geographic allocation and diversity of financial services at the firm as well as system level.

Looking Forward: Some Recommendations

There are several areas where improvement can be made to promote and to enhance the functioning of the institutions providing Islamic financial services. However, there are certain areas that deserve immediate attention and these areas are discussed further in this section.

Financial Engineering

For Islamic financial institutions, a financial engineering challenge is to introduce new *Shariah*-compatible products to enhance liquidity in the market and to offer tools to manage risk and to diversify portfolios. The significance of financial engineering is discussed in detail in Chapter 9. One primary reason for the lack of financial engineering is the non-availability of resources, because as mentioned earlier, the average size of an Islamic bank is relatively small and that prevents the banks from allocating resources for research and development required for financial engineering. Introduction of new products and services is resource-intensive and requires a solid infrastructure for successful completion at each stage, starting with solid market research, product design, development, placement and finally proper accounting. The investment needed to develop the supporting infrastructure entails significant cost.

Related to the challenge of financial engineering is another operational challenge for Islamic banks, which demands standardization of the process of introducing new products in the market. Currently, each Islamic bank has its own *Shariah* board examining and evaluating each new product, without coordinating the efforts with other banks. Each *Shariah* board may have its preferences or may adhere to a particular school of thought. This process should be streamlined and standardized to minimize time, effort and confusion.[7]

Risk Management and Diversification

Financial markets are becoming more integrated and interdependent, increasing the probability of expeditious contagion effects without leaving much room for swift measures against unexpected risk. Insufficient understanding of the new environment can create a sense of greater risk even if the objective level of the risk in the system is unchanged or reduced. The current wave of capital market liberalization and globalization is prompting the need for enhanced risk management measures, especially for the developing economies and the emerging markets, such as Islamic financial markets. Whereas risk management is widely practiced in the conventional financial markets, it is under-developed in the Islamic financial markets. Due to limited resources, Islamic banks are often unable to afford high cost management information systems or the technology to assess and monitor risk in timely fashion. With weak management and a lack of proper risk monitoring systems, Islamic banks' exposure is definitely high.

Benefits from managing risks come through the expanded set of diversification opportunities and through the value created by effectively managing financial risks. A more diverse mix of financial services provided, or an increased geographical spread of risks, usually implies the potential for improved diversification, so the same protection against financial distress can be attained with fewer resources.[8] For Islamic financial institutions, geographical expansion of the depositor-base can achieve diversification on the liabilities side. Diversification on the asset side can reduce the variance in the returns that accrue to claimholders of the financial intermediary. Also, geographical and sectoral diversification on the asset side can break the financial institutions' concentration in a region or a sector and reduce its exposures by benefiting from less perfectly correlated risks. Geographical spread of products can further help the financial intermediary improve its credit risk by selecting borrowers of the best credit quality and avoiding weak credit quality. It is also expected that with the diversification, Islamic banks will be able to extend the maturity frontier.

Islamic financial intermediaries need to adopt appropriate risk management measures not only for their own portfolios, but also to provide innovative risk management services to their clients. Diversification and risk management are also closely associated with the degree of market incompleteness. In case of high market incompleteness, financial intermediaries are in a better position to provide diversification and risk management for clients, because the responsibility of risk diversification shifts from the investors to the financial intermediary. Financial intermediaries are also considered to be better in providing inter-temporal risk management.

Keeping in view the nature of financial intermediation in the Islamic financial system, it is time for IFIs to pay due attention to the risk management aspect of intermediation. Islamic financial institutions need to take immediate steps to devise an infrastructure for implementing proper risk measurement, controls and management, and to innovate instruments to share, transfer and mitigate financial risk so that entrepreneurs can concentrate on what they do best — managing exposure to the business risk in which they have a competitive advantage.

Exposure can also be reduced by developing a close relationship with the entrepreneurs to promote close monitoring and by collaborating with the entrepreneurs to develop a risk culture for reducing their exposure, which will ultimately reduce the intermediary's exposure. In other words, if the debtor of the bank has a reduced financial risk, it will result in better quality credit for the bank. Furthermore, monitoring becomes vital in cases where Islamic banks invest in equity-based instruments, because an institution with limited resources may not be equipped to conduct thorough monitoring. An institution with adequate resources may develop processes, systems, and proper training to undertake effective monitoring. There is clearly a need for a financial institution that can, for a fee, offer guarantees, enhance liquidity, underwrite insurance against risks, and finally, develop hedging tools.

Finally, Islamic financial institutions need to realize the importance not only of financial risk and its management but also of operational risk — risk due to the failure of controls and processes. Currently, there is a serious lack of a risk culture and of enterprise level sponsorship of active risk management. Formulating a strategy for risk management in Islamic financial markets will require the following:

- comprehensive and detailed discussion of the scope and role of derivatives within the framework of the *Shariah*;
- an expanded role of financial intermediaries with special emphasis on facilitating risk sharing;
- the applicability of *Takaful* (*Shariah*-compliant mutual insurance) to insure against financial risk and, finally;
- the application of financial engineering to develop synthetic derivatives and off-balance sheet instruments.

Non-Bank Financial Services

For further growth, it is essential that the role of intermediation in the Islamic financial services industry is extended beyond its traditional set-up and there is a need to broaden the scope and range of financial services offered, establishing something that may well be called a "financial products-supermarket." Such a supermarket will act like an "all-in-bank," covering all sorts of financial services. In this role, an IFI needs to cater to different types of customers and clients ranging from private individuals to institutions, high-net-worth individuals and corporations for their investment, borrowing, risk management, and wealth management needs. For example, such an institution will serve retail customers, manage portfolios for individuals and provide various services for corporate customers. At the same time, like a broker, the financial products supermarket will be a retail firm that handles asset management together with payments and settlement services.

With increased sophistication of the financial system, institutional investors have grown significantly and have become an integral part of the modern financial system. For instance, contractual savings with defined benefits like insurance and pension funds' share of the market in assets management business have increased considerably. In a financial system where the securities markets are under-developed, as is the case with Islamic financial markets, the financial intermediary needs to provide a broader set of services including non-bank financial services. In addition, the majority of

IFIs are not adequately equipped for providing typical investment banking services such as facilitating the development of capital markets, underwriting, guarantees, market research, and fee-based advisory services. Refinement and development of fee-based services will certainly enhance the functionality of the financial services. It is critical that contracts like *Jo'ala*, *Wikala*, *and Kifala* which can expand investment banking functionality are further developed, recognized, and operationalized in order to fully exploit the capabilities of IFIs.

Performance Benchmarks

The practice of measuring the performance of an asset by comparing its return and risk relative to a well-defined benchmark is well-established in a market-centered financial system. Markets are good at offering an efficient, measurable, and consistent benchmark for different asset classes and securities. In contrast, a financial system concentrated around financial intermediaries does not offer this vital function. It is critical that such benchmarks be developed to equip investors with tools to measure the relative performance of different asset classes and ultimately to measure the performance of the financial intermediary. The current practice of using interest-based benchmarks such as London Inter Bank Offer Rate (LIBOR) has been accepted only on an ad-hoc basis, due to the lack of better benchmarks, but several researchers have raised the issue of developing benchmarks based on the rate of return reflecting Islamic modes of financing.

The absence of benchmarks also creates difficulty in evaluating the performance of Islamic financial institutions. There are no transparent benchmarks that can be used to perform a relative comparison of returns after adjustments for the risk. Due to non-availability of Islamic benchmarks, the task of evaluating the efficiency of the financial institutions becomes harder.

Payment System

The absence of risk-free or high grade investment securities and the dominance of trade financed asset-backed securities on the assets side of an IFI's balance sheet is of concern to regulators, as it poses threats to the payment system and increases its vulnerability due to the riskiness and illiquidity of the trade financed securities. In this context, it has been suggested that the concept of "narrow banking" be applied to Islamic banks. The concept of narrow banking was originally presented by Fischer and is broadly referred to as one specializing in deposit-taking/payment activities but does not provide lending services. Stability and safety is achieved if deposits are invested only in short-term treasury or their close equivalents. In the context of the Islamic financial system, the problem is that IFIs do not have access to highly secured risk-free securities such as government bonds. One alternative suggested by El-Hawary, Grais and Iqbal (2004) is to segment the balance sheet of IFIs in such a way that at call and short-term deposits are invested only in high grade, liquid asset-backed securities. In this way, the systemic risk to the payment system can be reduced. This concept needs to be refined further to develop a secondary market to enhance the liquidity of asset-backed securities and through standardization of contracts to reduce the riskiness of the securities.

Institutionalization of Instruments

One cannot overemphasize the need for the development of institutions for the further growth of the Islamic financial services industry. Institutions to support equity-style financing and investment are the most critical. Due to the nature of trade and asset-related financing instruments, Islamic banks tend to act more than like a financier. The responsibility extra of this non-financing aspect of banking can be minimized through the establishment of institutions supporting such instruments. For example, in order to promote leasing without increasing overhead capital costs, there is a need to develop specialized institutions to administer, maintain and facilitate lease-related operations and these need to work closely with the banks to provide funding. Standardizing the operations and the instruments will pave the way for pooling heterogeneous assets for securitization purposes — a much needed function for enhancing the liquidity in the market.

Universal Banking

The nature of financial intermediation and the style of financial products and services offered by an IFI make it a hybrid between commercial and investment banking similar to a universal bank. Universal banks are known to benefit from the economies of scope due to information of close relationships with their clients, and access to private information gained through these relationships. Combining different product lines (such as banking and insurance products or combining commercial and investment banking lines) may increase the relationship value of banking at a much lower average marketing cost. IFIs can strengthen this aspect of the financial services to fully utilize the benefits of universal banking.

For example, by expanding the scope of services, IFIs can spread the fixed costs of managing a client relationship, in terms of both physical and human capital, over a wider set of products leading to more efficient use of resources. Through expansion, IFIs can use their branch networks and all their other existing delivery channels to distribute additional products at low marginal cost. As universal banks, IFIs can also capitalize on the good reputation established in one product or service to market other products and services with relatively less effort. Finally, expanded scope of IFIs can benefit consumers as well, since they may save on searching and monitoring costs by purchasing a bundle of financial services from a single provider, instead of acquiring them separately from different providers.

While universal banking has several advantages, there are several inefficiencies as well, which should be avoided. For example, universal banks tend to suffer from a size syndrome because of their powerfulness and large size. Empirical evidence suggests that powerful banks can stymie innovation by extracting informational rents and protecting from competition established firms having close ties with themselves.

Endnotes

1 Data was collected from the 2003 annual reports of the following banks: Kuwait Finance House, AlBaraka, Al-Tawfeek, Dubai Islamic Bank, Al Rajhi, and National Bank of Sharjah.

2 In the US, *Glass-Steagall Act* of 1934 which prohibited the combination of banking, securities and insurance business was repealed by *Financial Services Modernization Act* of 1999.

3 It is not surprising that Hassan, K. and Abdel-Hameed Bashir (2004), *Determinants of Islamic Banking Profitability*, found a negative correlation between big size and level of profitability in select Islamic banks. This counter-intuitive finding can be attributed to deteriorating capacity, ability, and quality in managing large scale institutions, ultimately introducing inefficiencies and lower profitability.

4 Samad, H. and Hassan, M. K. (1999), *Consultative Document-Overview of the New Basel Capital Accord*, April, Bank for International Settlements, Basel, Switzerland.

5 Marcus, G. (2000) "Issues for Consideration in Mergers and Takeovers from A Regulatory Perspective," *BIS Review 60*, pp. 1–12, points out that bank profitability has fallen in 12 countries despite a wave of consolidation. A study by the US Federal Reserve concluded that 50% of mergers by big banks in the United States of America eroded returns, whereas only 17% produced positive returns.

6 Group of Ten (2001) observes increased interdependencies between large and complex banking organizations in the US, Japan, and Europe subsequent to consolidations. These interdependencies include inter-bank loans, market activities such as OTC derivatives, and payment and settlement systems.

7   Informal discussion with practitioners reveals that religious boards sometimes become extremely rigid on minor technical matters and make the process of introducing new products difficult and lengthy, resulting in missed business opportunities.

8   A study which looked directly at the diversification gains from improvements in the risk/expected return tradeoff by examining the tradeoffs among expected profit, variability of profit, profit inefficiency, and insolvency risk for large US banking organizations in the early 1990s, found that when organizations are larger in a way that geographically diversifies, especially via interstate banking that diversifies macroeconomic risk, efficiency tends to be higher and insolvency risk tends to be lower. Hughes et al., (1999).

CHAPTER 8

Capital Markets

The role of capital markets in promoting an efficient financial system cannot be overemphasized. Given that a developed financial system can make positive contributions to economic development, the existence of vibrant capital markets becomes a necessity for any economy. Capital markets facilitate long-term financing for businesses and entrepreneurs by attracting savings from a large pool of investors. These markets provide long-term capital to entrepreneurs through a series of short-term contracts (securities) with investors who may enter and exit the market at will. An efficient capital market is expected to perform the following functions:

- To provide a resource mobilization mechanism leading to an efficient allocation of financial resources in the economy.
- To provide liquidity in the market at the cheapest price, i.e., the lowest transaction cost or low bid–ask spread on the securities being traded in the market.
- To ensure transparency in the pricing of securities by determining the price of the risk premia, reflecting the riskiness of the security.
- To provide opportunities for constructing well-diversified portfolios and to reduce the level of risk through diversification across geographic regions and across time.

Capital markets consist of primary and secondary markets. Whereas primary markets are important to raise new capital and depend on the supply of funds, secondary markets make a significant contribution by facilitating the trading of existing securities. In some ways, secondary markets play an equally critical role by ensuring liquidity and fair pricing in the market and by giving valuable signals about the security. In other words, secondary markets not only provide liquidity and low transaction costs, they also determine the prices of the securities and their associated risk on a continuous basis, incorporating relevant new information as it arrives.

Just as capital markets play a critical role in the conventional financial system, their role in the Islamic financial system is also equally important. Whereas conventional capital markets have an established and long-running track record, Islamic capital markets are at a rather early stage of development. Conventional capital markets have two main streams: the securities markets for debt trading and the stock markets for equity trading. As we have already discussed, raising capital through debt is not possible in the Islamic system due to the prohibition of interest. Although borrowing and lending on the basis of debt is a common practice in modern conventional markets, Muslims cannot participate in any debt markets. The concept of stock markets is in consonance with the *Shariah*'s principles of profit-and-loss sharing, but not every business listed on the stock market is fully compatible with the *Shariah*. These issues pose challenges for the development of Islamic capital markets.

The need for capital markets was realized at the early stages of development of the Islamic financial industry, but not much progress was made. During the 1980s and 1990s, IFIs mobilized funds successfully through growing deposits, which were invested in a few financial instruments, mostly dominated by commodities or trade-financing. Due to the limited investment opportunities, lack of liquid assets and other constraints, the composition of IFIs' assets side remained fairly static and heavily focused on short-term instruments. The main areas of concern were the lack of portfolio and risk management tools and the absence of derivative instruments. With continuing demand for *Shariah*-compliant financing, there was a pressing need to develop capital markets to facilitate long-term, *Shariah*-compliant financing for businesses and to create portfolio diversification opportunities for investors and financial intermediaries.

By the late 1990s, Islamic financial markets had realized that the development of capital markets was essential for their survival and further growth. Meanwhile, the wave of deregulation and liberalization of capital markets in several countries led to close cooperation between IFIs and conventional financial institutions to find solutions for liquidity and portfolio management. Since then, several efforts have been made in this respect, especially in two areas. The first is the development of a debt-like security in the form of an asset-backed security, and the second is the development of Islamic funds comprising of portfolios of securities such as, but not limited to, equity stocks or commodities. Islamic equity funds became popular with investors who had a risk appetite for equity investment, IFIs kept demanding a fixed-income like security, which could behave like the conventional fixed-income debt security at a low level of risk but which also complied with the *Shariah*. In addition, IFIs wanted to extend the maturity structure of their assets to go beyond the typical short-term maturity given by trade-finance instruments. This led to experimentation with creating *Shariah*-compliant, asset-backed securities, namely the *Sukuk*, which have risk/return characteristics similar to a conventional debt security.

Development of Equity Markets

The Islamic economic system relies upon vibrant markets for equity-based securities. A formal model for a stock market according to principles of Islam has yet to be formulated, but there have been a few attempts to identify issues distinguishing an Islamic stock market from a conventional stock market. There are at least three major structural issues that need to be resolved.

Limited Liability

First and the foremost is the question of what is the best contractual agreement representing a share in a joint stock company with limited liability. Limited liability raises the issue of how to deal with a legal entity such as a corporation, which has a legal "personality" and needs to be treated as a "juridical person." Some argue that limited liability conflicts with a basic Islamic moral and legal principle, that obligations are, as it were, indestructible without agreed release of forgiveness from the creditor.[1] In this respect, Islamic *Fiqh* scholars need to address several critical issues such as the acceptance of a corporation as a partnership (on basis of *Musharakah*) or some other similar contract. In addition, what happens to the liability in case of the insolvency of the judicial person (i.e., company)? Some *Shariah* scholars are of the view that there are certain precedents wherefrom the basic concept of a juridical person may be derived by inference in Islamic *Fiqh*.[2]

Contractual Structure of an Equity Stock

The second issue is related to the type of contract most appropriate to represent a common share as a partnership in a joint stock company. The

Shariah identifies two broad categories of *musharakah* contracts, *Musharakah Mulk* giving the partner ownership rights to a specific real asset and *Musharakah Aqed*, granting the partner ownership rights to the value of assets without any specific linkage to any real asset. It is important to understand this distinction. For example, if a stock is represented as *Musharakah Mulk*, then buying and selling of stock will be equivalent to buying and selling an identifiable real asset and hence becomes subject to the rules applicable for *bay'* (trade/sale). On the other hand, if a stock is treated as *Musharakah Aqed*, then it is not subject to *bay'* rules but this raises other issues such as trading, valuation, and possession. A review of current rulings indicates that the joint stock company has been treated as a new form of *Musharakah* which is neither a *Musharakah Mulk* or *Musharakah Aqed*, but a combination of the two, in that the rulings regarding buying and selling stocks are largely treated under the former, while shareholder rights and basic investment operations are treated under the latter. This adds to the confusion surrounding the issue. Shabsigh (2002) argues that classifying the joint stock company as *Musharakah Mulk* renders most transactions in a stock market illegal from the *Shariah*'s point of view.

Negotiability and Tradability

The third structural issue to be resolved is the most critical of all and is related to the negotiability, transferability and tradability of stocks in primary and secondary markets. While Islamic law encourages trading and markets in all tangible goods and properties, it restrains, if not prohibits, the trading of financial interests under the suspicion of trading leading, through a back-door, to the prohibited element of *Riba*. The law blocks trading in monetary obligations (such as *Dayn* (debt), currency, or equivalents of currency), obligations demarcated in generic goods (e.g., so many bushels of a particular grade of wheat), and even contingent or future rights generally. For example, the *Shariah* ruling being followed at present is that the stocks of a company are negotiable only if the company owns some non-liquid assets. If all the assets of a company are in liquid form, i.e., in the form of money, then the stock cannot be purchased or sold, except at par value, because it is argued that in this case the stock represents money only and money cannot be traded except at par. With the changing economic structure where there is a large number of economic entities engaging in providing services and holding illiquid assets, this poses serious problems. Consequently, a financial intermediary cannot exist in the form of a public company.

In addition to these structural issues requiring serious analysis and debate, there are several operational aspects of conventional stock markets which are in direct conflict with the principles of Islamic markets. The following three operational differences are noteworthy.

Practice of Margin Accounts

First, the widely accepted practice of maintaining a margin account to purchase stocks can be questioned. Since margin accounts allow a buyer to purchase stocks using leverage and borrowed funds at the prevailing interest rate, this arrangement cannot exist in the Islamic economy where the instrument of debt is prohibited. The usage of leverage in stock trading will eliminate a large number of buyers from the market. A reduction in the number of market participants will directly hamper the liquidity in the market and result in a higher transaction cost and thus lead to operational inefficiency in the markets.

Speculative Trading

Second, it is argued that trading in the stock markets opens the door to speculation and leads to practices amounting to gambling — another element strictly prohibited in Islam. The practice of day trading which has become popular in the conventional markets raises the question of speculation. Earlier researchers in Islamic economics raised the concern that trading in stock markets is speculative and may contain the element of gambling, and therefore measures need to be taken to eliminate or discourage speculative behavior. Recent scholars have distinguished between speculation and calculated risk taking based on information available in the market. Several measures have been suggested to reduce unwanted speculation and to eliminate the element of gambling. These measures include design of a tax structure linked to the holding period of investment, introduction of transparency, regulation of institutional investors who influence the market and imposition of restrictions on price changes, so that no dealer is allowed to push prices upwards or downwards rapidly.

In the Islamic framework, although speculation is not unlawful per se, professional speculators cannot exist, because most speculation is made possible only with funds borrowed on the basis of interest, which is prohibited in Islam. However, this counter-argument does not address the contribution of speculators to price discovery, liquidity and the efficiency of the markets.

On a related matter, it has been argued that the presence of *Ghabun*, the difference between the price at which a transaction is executed and the fair price (as per the opinion of valuation experts), makes a transaction unethical. The consensus view seems to be that marginal over-pricing is permissible, but gross over-pricing should be curbed. The issue of fair prices is also a tricky one, as pricing is a function of the information available in the market and expectations of investors about the market and the security. Any measure, other than the forces of demand and supply, introduced to enforce prices, will introduce unwanted distortions and inefficiencies.

Practice of Short-Selling

Third, the practice of short-selling a stock is not compatible with the principles of Islam. According to Islam, an exchange contract is void unless the intention of the buyer is to buy and of the seller to sell, and that no one sells what he does not have. This raises the question of trading a borrowed financial claim which does not appear to be compatible with *Shariah*. By eliminating the short-selling facility, markets will discourage speculative behavior but will also eliminate arbitrage opportunities, which may hamper price discovery of a security.

Equity contracts and markets for equity-based capital are so vital in the Islamic financial system that absence of such markets will hinder achievement of the full potential of the system. The structural and operational issues identified above are difficult but not insurmountable. Financial intermediaries cannot operate optimally without supporting markets and institutions in the financial system. Serious efforts should be made to encourage equity financing.

Islamic Bonds — *Sukuks*

Efforts to develop and launch a *Shariah*-compatible bond-like security were made as early as in 1978 in Jordan where the government allowed the Jordan Islamic Bank to issue Islamic bonds known as *Muqaradah* bonds. This was followed by the introduction of the *Muqaradah Bond Act* of 1981. Similar efforts were made in Pakistan where a special law called the *Mudarabah* Companies and *Mudarabah* Flotation and Control Ordinance of 1980 was introduced. Neither of these efforts resulted in any noteworthy activity, because of the lack of proper infrastructure and transparency in the market. The first successful introduction of Islamic bonds was by the Malaysian Government in 1983 with the issuance of the Government Investment Issues (GII) — formerly known as the Government Investment Certificates (GIC). The pace of innovation was very slow and IFIs were unable to develop an active market for such securities. Meanwhile, the success of securitization of assets in the conventional markets provided a framework which could work for Islamic assets as well. It was not till the late 1990s that a well-recognized structure of an asset-backed security in the form of a *Sukuk* was developed in Bahrain and Malaysia. This structure is attracting the attention of borrowers and investors and is considered a potential vehicle to develop Islamic capital markets.

There are several advantages offered by a market for Islamic bonds or *Sukuk*, which are introduced in the market to meet the demands of the users of funds, i.e., businesses, corporate sector, sovereigns, etc. and all kinds of investors ranging from retail investors, institutional investors and financial institutions. Users of funds gain direct access to the funds through the *Sukuk* market and at the same time bypass intermediaries. The users of funds expect that an efficient *Sukuk* market will ultimately lower their cost of funding. Investors prefer *Sukuk* as it widens their opportunity set with more choices on maturity and portfolio selection. A well-functioning primary and secondary *Sukuk* market can provide much needed liquidity to institutional investors and financial intermediaries, who become better equipped with portfolio and risk management. Finally, in many cases, payoffs of *Sukuk* resemble a conventional fixed-income debt security, which is popular among conventional investors. In this respect, *Sukuk* can also serve as an integrating tool between Islamic and conventional markets.

What is a *Sukuk*?

The word *Sukuk* (plural of the Arabic word *Sakk* meaning certificate) reflects participation rights in the underlying assets. The term *Sukuk* is not new and is recognized in the traditional Islamic jurisprudence. The idea behind *Sukuk* is simple. The prohibition of interest virtually closes the door for a pure debt security, but an obligation that is linked to the performance of a real asset is acceptable. In order words, the *Shariah* accepts the validity of a financial asset that derives its return from the performance of an underlying real asset. The design of *Sukuk* is very similar to the process of securitization of assets in conventional markets where a wide range of asset types are securitized. These asset types include mortgages, auto loans, accounts receivable, credit card payoffs, and home equity loans. Just as in conventional securitization, a pool of assets is built and securities are issued against this pool. *Sukuks* are participation certificates against a single asset or a pool of assets.

Formally, *Sukuk* represent proportionate beneficial ownership of an asset for a defined period when the risk and the return associated with cash flows generated by underlying assets in a pool are passed to the *Sukuk* holders (investors). *Sukuk* is similar to a conventional bond as it is also a security instrument that provides a predictable level of return. However, a fundamental difference between the two is that a bond represents pure debt of the issuer but a *Sukuk* represents, in addition to the risk on the creditworthiness of the issuer, an ownership stake in an existing or well-defined asset or project. Also, while a bond creates a lender/borrower relationship, the relationship in *Sukuk* depends on the nature of the contract underlying the *Sukuk*. For example, if a lease (*Ijarah*) contract underlies a *Sukuk*, then it creates a lessee/lessor relationship, which is different from the typical lender/borrower relationship.

The core contract utilized in the process of securitization to create *Sukuk* is the *Mudarabah* (trust financing), which allows one party to act as an agent (manager) on behalf of a principal (capital owner) on the basis of a pre-agreed profit-sharing arrangement. The contract of *Mudarabah* is used to create a Special Purpose *Mudarabah* (SPM) entity similar to the conventional Special Purpose Vehicle (SPV) to play a well-defined role in acquiring certain assets and issuing certificates against the assets. The underlying assets acquired by the SPM need to be *Shariah*-compliant and can vary in nature. The tradability and negotiability of issued certificates is determined on the basis of the nature of the underlying assets.

Figure 8.1 shows the process and linkage among the different players involved in structuring a *Sukuk*. This process is a generic process and there will be differences depending on the type of underlying instrument used to acquire the assets. The process of structuring a *Sukuk* involves the following steps:

Step I: An asset is identified, which is currently held by the entity wishing to mobilize resources and raise funds. In simple cases, this asset needs to be a tangible asset such as an office building, land, highway, or an airport. But in other cases, a pool could be made from a set of heterogeneous assets combining tangible and non-tangible assets, i.e., financial assets. Once the assets to be securitized are identified, these assets are transferred to a special purpose *Mudarabah* (SPM) for a pre-determined purchase price. SPM is established only for this particular purpose and is a separate legal entity that may or may not be affiliated to the issuer. By establishing an independent SPM, the certificates carry their own credit ratings, instead of carrying the credit ratings of its original owner. Also, by transferring the asset to this special entity, the asset is taken off the issuer's balance sheet and is therefore immune to any financial distress the issuer may face in the future. Thus, the existence of an SPM provides confidence to the investors (*Sukuk* holders) about the certainty of cash flows on the certificates and therefore enhances the credit quality of the certificates. SPM also

Figure 8.1   Anatomy of a Sukuk

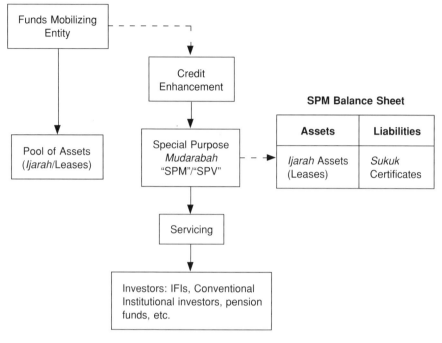

Source: Iqbal (1999)

enjoys special tax status and benefits. SPM is considered a bankruptcy-remote entity.

Step II: The underlying asset is brought on the asset side of the SPM by issuing participation certificates or *Sukuk* on its liability side to investors in an amount equal to the purchase price. These certificates are of equal value representing undivided shares in the ownership of the asset. The proceeds from the sale of certificates are used to purchase the assets. The holders of the *Sukuk* participate in the equity interest of the SPM's assets, which are jointly owned.

Step III: The SPM either sells or leases the assets back to a lessee — an affiliate of the seller, or directly back to the seller itself — in exchange for a future payment or periodic lease payments. For example, in case of a lease, the asset will be leased to a lessee or to the issuer who will be responsible for making future rental payment on the lease. These future cash flows in the form of rental income are passed through to the holders of the *Sukuk*. The cash flows are subject to deduction of minor administrative, insurance, and debt servicing fees.

Step IV: In order to make the certificates investment-quality and to enhance their marketability, an investment bank may also provide some form of a guarantee. This guarantee may be in the form of a guarantee of performance regarding the future payments or it may be a guarantee to buy or replace the asset in the event of default. The investment bank or guarantor charges a few basis points as premium for the guarantee. This credit enhancement makes the certificates investment grade securities and therefore makes them attractive to institutional investors.

Step V: During the course of the life of the *Sukuk*, periodic payments are made by the benefactor of the asset, i.e., lessee, which are transferred to the investors. These periodic payments are similar to coupon payments on a conventional bond. The difference between bond coupon payment and *Sukuk* payments is that whereas bond coupon accrues irrespective of the outcome of the project for which the bond was issued, *Sukuk* payments accrue only if there is any income out of the securitized asset. However, the interesting point is that in the case of lease-based *Sukuk*, since the coupon payments are based on rental income and there is a low probability of default on rental income, investors consider these coupons with high expectations and low risk. Anyone who purchases *Sukuk* in the secondary market replaces the seller in the pro rata ownership of the relevant assets and all the rights and obligations of the original subscriber are passed on to him/her. The price of *Sukuk* is subject to the forces of the market and depends on the expected profitability. However, there are certain limitations to the sale of *Sukuk* in the secondary market, which are discussed later in this chapter.

Step VI: At maturity, or on a dissolution event, the SPM starts winding up, first by selling the assets back to the original seller/owner at a pre-determined price and then paying back to the certificate holders or investors. The price is pre-determined to protect capital loss to investors. Otherwise, the sale of the underlying asset at the market value may result in capital loss for the investor, which may not be acceptable to the investor. It is a common practice that the *Sukuk* contract embeds a put option to the *Sukuk*-holders by which the issuer agrees to buy the asset back at pre-determined price, so that at maturity the investors can sell the *Sukuk* back to the issuer at the face value. At the completion of the *Sukuk*, the SPM is dissolved and it ceases to exist, since the purpose for which it was created is achieved.

The above-mentioned process is a general process to issue *Sukuk*, but there are different variations depending on the type of contract used to create the underlying asset. Due to this diversity in contracts, the Accounting and Auditing Organization of Islamic Financial Institutions (AAOIFI) recognizes the following different types of *Sukuk*:

1. Certificates of ownership of leased assets (*Ijarah Sukuk*)
2. Certificates of ownership of right to use: (i) of existing assets, (ii) of described future assets, (iii) of services of specified party, and (iv) of described future services
3. *Salam* certificates
4. *Istisna* certificates
5. *Murabahah* certificates
6. *Musharakah* certificates
7. *Mudarabah* certificates
8. *Muzaraah* (share cropping) certificates
9. *Musaqah* (irrigation) certificates
10. *Mugharasa* (agricultural/seed planting) certificates

Most of these are *Shariah*-compatible for trading in the secondary market, except the *Salam*, *Istisna*, and *Murabahah* certificates; and some particular cases of *Muzaraah* and *Musaqah* certificates when the certificate holder does not own the land. This restriction on the tradability in the secondary market comes from a *Shariah* ruling by the Organization of Islamic Countries (OIC) *Fiqh* council — a well-respected *Shariah* council — which states that "a bond or note can be sold at a market price provided that the composition of the group of assets, represented by the bond, consists of a majority of physical assets and financial rights, as compared to a minority of cash and interpersonal debts."

In other words, *Sukuk* issued against a pool consisting of cash or debt-like instruments cannot be traded in the secondary market. This restriction is imposed to avoid dealing with *Riba* while trading debt securities in the secondary markets. *Shariah* is of view that since *Salam* and *Murabahah* contracts create debt as the result of *Salam*- and *Murabahah*-based sale, *Sukuk* based on these contracts cannot be traded in the secondary market.

The following is a discussion on selected types of *Sukuk*:

Ijarah Sukuks

Ijarah Sukuk are based on the contract of *Ijarah* or lease and are subject to certain prerequisites to qualify for securitization. First, the underlying leasing contract must conform to the principles of the *Shariah*, which may differ from the terms and conditions used in the agreements of conventional financial leases. Secondly, the leased assets must have some beneficial usage to the users for which they are willing to pay a rent. Third, the leased assets must be of such a nature that their use is fully compliant with the *Shariah*. For example, leasing of a casino building would not be acceptable. Finally, necessary maintenance expenditure related to the underlying asset is the responsibility of the owner — *Sukuk* holders in this case.

The nature of the *Ijarah* contract offers several advantages, which make it a natural candidate for securitization. These advantages include:

Flexibility: *Ijarah* instrument is one of the instruments that is most similar to the conventional lease contract and offers flexibility of both fixed and floating-rate payoffs. The cash flows of the lease, including rental payments and principal repayment, are passed-through to the investors in the form of coupon and principal payments. Due to its resemblance to the conventional lease, *Ijarah*-based *Sukuk* are attractive to conventional investors as well. There is flexibility in the timing of inflows and outflows since it is not necessary that the cash flows to the certificate holders should coincide with the timing of the rental payments. Another element of flexibility is that in case of *Ijarah*, the *Shariah* does not require that the underlying asset to be leased and securitized should be in existence at the time of the contract.

Extended Maturity: The *Ijarah* contract can be of any length as long as the asset that is the subject of the *Ijarah* contract remains in existence and the user can draw benefit from it. Due to the extended term of *Ijarah*, *Sukuk* can be structured to provide an efficient mode of financing for medium-to long-term maturity.

Transferability: Since *Shariah* does not restrict the right of the lessor to sell the leased asset in the case of an *Ijarah* contract, persons who share the ownership of a leased asset through *Sukuk* can dispose of their property by selling it to new owners individually or collectively as they may desire. This feature is critical in developing a secondary market for *Ijarah*-based *Sukuk*.

Negotiability: The *Shariah* requires that a bond or note like *Sukuk* can be sold at a market price provided that the underlying assets consist of a majority of physical assets. This makes *Ijarah Sukuk* completely negotiable and therefore they can be traded in the secondary markets. This feature of

Ijarah Sukuk make them attractive to investors as it enhances their liquidity in the market.

The *Ijarah Sukuk* are also subject to risks other than the market risk. These risks are related to the ability and willingness of the lessee to pay the rental payments over the life of the *Sukuk*. In addition, return to the investors is not always pre-determined as the lease is subject to maintenance and insurance costs. Therefore, the amount of rent given in the contractual relationship represented by the *Sukuk* indicates a maximum possible return subject to the deduction for maintenance and insurance expenditures. However, given that in any event risk is protected through insurance and the financial risk may be protected through guarantees, return to the investors is fairly stable.

In the case where an asset that can be sold and leased back does not exist, another type of contract, *Istisna* can be utilized. *Istisna* contract is suitable for situations where a new asset is created through construction or manufacturing activity to a specified description and at a pre-determined price. For such cases, *Darrat Sukuk* have been suggested, which are *Sukuk* against assets which do not exist at the time of securitization. A combination of *Istisna* and then *Ijarah* is used in the structure of the contract to first create the asset and then to rent it back to the originator. In addition to the originator of the asset, a new party — the contractor — also gets involved; who is responsible for the construction of the asset before it can be handed over to the SPM for leasing.

Salam Sukuk

Salam-based *Sukuk* have proved to be a useful investment vehicle for short-term maturity since the underlying commodity financing tends to be for short-term tenor, ranging from 3 months to 1 year. *Salam Sukuk* can be based on either *Salam* (spot sale) and/or deferred-payment sale (*Bay' al-Muajjil*) or deferred-delivery sale (*Bay' al-Salam*) contracts, whereby the investor undertakes to supply specific goods or commodities, incorporating a mutually agreed contract for resale to the client and a mutually negotiated profit margin. Bahrain Monetary Agency (BMA) was one of the innovators and originators of early *Salam*-based *Sukuk*.

According to the structure promoted by BMA, an SPM is a set-up, which buys a commodity such as crude oil or aluminum on a *Salam* basis, whereby the purchase price is paid entirely up-front with the proceeds from the *Sukuk* certificates. The delivery of the purchased commodity is set at a specified future date and subsequently to the *Salam* contract, there is a promise by the beneficiary of the commodity to buy the commodity from the SPM on the date when it is due to be delivered. Return on *Sukuks* is determined by the pre-agreed cost of financing the purchase.

In addition to being short-term, *Salam Sukuk* have another special characteristic. Due to the fact that the *Sukuk* results in a pure financial claim and are somewhat de-linked from the risk/return of the underlying asset, the *Shariah* treats them as a pure debt security, which cannot be traded in the secondary market either at discount or at premium. Otherwise, it will introduce a mechanism to indulge in *Riba* or interest in the transaction. This feature adversely affects the transferability and negotiability of these certificates in the secondary market. As a result, investors have no option but to hold *Salam Sukuk* up to the maturity of the certificates.

Bai' Bithaman Ajil (BBA) Sukuk

Sukuk based on *Bai' Bithaman Ajil* (BBA) is an innovation of the Malaysian market. The contract is based on a sale of an asset to the investors, with a promise by the issuer to buy the asset back in the future at a pre-determined price which includes a margin of profit as well. Therefore, the issuer gets immediate cash against the promise to buy back at the purchase price, plus a pre-agreed profit, which creates an obligation to be released over an agreed period. The issuer issues securities (*Sukuk*) to the investors to reflect this financing arrangement. Investors expect to earn a return equal to the pre-agreed profit.

This structure is not very popular with the Middle Eastern investors because of a debatable *Shariah* issue, which does not accept the tradability of debt created through BBA arrangement. In addition, some BBA issuances in Malaysian markets are based on financial assets — an objectionable practice in the eyes of *Shariah* scholars in the Middle East.

Muqaradah bonds

Muqaradah bonds are based on the *Mudarabah* contract whereby the capital is provided by a pool of investors against certificates or bonds for a specific project undertaken by an entrepreneur (*mudarib*) with the agreement to share revenues. In this respect, they bear close resemblance to revenue bond financing in the conventional system, where bonds are generally backed only by the revenue generated by the project funded by the bond issue. These bonds are suitable for undertaking development projects to build networks of roads or other infrastructure projects. Investors have the right to share in the revenues generated by the project. Investors are solely dependent on the revenues generated by the project and they have no recourse to the *mudarib*. On the expiry of the specified time period of the subscription, the investor is given the right to transfer the ownership by sale or trade in the securities market at his/her discretion.

The concept of the *Muqaradah* bond was for raising capital for public finance projects, but due to several reasons such as lack of transparency in the public sector and lack of liquidity, these bonds did not gain much popularity with the investors.

Musharakah Bonds

Musharakah bonds are based on the partnership and profit-and-loss-sharing contract (*Musharakah*) and are relatively similar to *Muqaradah* bonds. The only major difference is that the intermediary or the entrepreneur is a partner with the investors (the group of subscribers) as well as acting like an agent (*mudarib*). Several *Musharakah*-based bonds have been issued by the Islamic Republic of Iran and Sudan. In the case of Iran, *Musharakah* certificates were devised and approved by the Money and Credit Council to finance the Tehran Municipality. Sudan has made considerable progress in the development of *Musharakah*-based certificates. With the help of the International Monetary Fund (IMF), the Ministry of Finance designed *Musharakah* bonds based on state ownership of key profitable and large public enterprises, which can be traded in the market. A similar arrangement was launched by the central bank, Bank of Sudan, to be used for the purposes of Treasury intervention and open market operations for monetary policy management. Another example of a successful launch of *Musharakah* bonds was in Turkey in 1984 to finance the construction of a toll bridge in Istanbul. The *Musharakah* bonds were well received by the investor community.

Both *Muqaradah* and *Musharakah* bonds are based on the profit-and-loss-sharing principle of Islam and are ideal for promotion of Islamic finance. Although the issuers of these bonds are public sector institutions, the low transparency that prevails in the affairs of governments of several Muslim countries keeps the investors away from this structure. One would expect that with enhanced monitoring and transparency, and with a reduction of asymmetrical information, these bonds can also contribute to the development of Islamic capital markets.

Sukuk Market

The market for the *Sukuk* was originated by government entities. Although the market is still dominated by the sovereign issues, gradually corporate issues are also emerging. In terms of total amount outstanding, the current ratio between sovereign and corporate *Sukuk* is 3.5 to 1. With a growing market for *Sukuk*, many conventional rating agencies including Standard & Poor's (S&P) and Fitch have started to rate select issues. For example, S&P has now designed a methodology to rate *Ijarah*-based *Sukuk*. In another positive development, Dow Jones has announced plans to constitute a *Sukuk* Index to monitor the performance of this market. Another particularly encouraging sign in the *Sukuk* market is that it is no longer the sole preserve of specialist Islamic issuers or investors. For example, 48% of a recent sovereign issue was subscribed for by conventional investors, including 24% by institutional investors, 11% by fund managers and 13% by central banks and government institutions.

Tables 8.1A and 8.1B show a list of recent *Sukuk* issues. Table 8.2 lists the top 20 investment banks that were active in underwriting these issues during 2005. A majority of top investment banks that managed *Sukuk* issues are based in Malaysia (ranking 1,3,4,5,6). This is not surprising, as it is a reflection of how Malaysia has developed the *Sukuk* market and how active these banks are in this market. Another notable performance is by the Hong Kong and Shanghai Banking Corporation's (HSBC) Islamic investment entity — *Amanah* — which has played an important role in the development of this market.

Figure 8.2 shows the term sheet of an innovative and successful *Sukuk* issue by the Jeddah-based multilateral development bank, the Islamic Development Bank (IsDB).

Challenges of *Sukuk* Market

The *Sukuk* market is in its embryonic phase, but holds great potential for further growth of the Islamic financial industry. The following are some of the issues currently faced by this market:

- The *Sukuk* issued so far, with the exception of those by the Islamic Development Bank (IsDB), have been linked to a particular real asset, rather than to a pool of assets. This model can work for sovereign, supranational or multilateral borrowers who have large scale assets to securitize, but poses difficulty for institutions that want to raise capital on a smaller scale. In addition, *Sukuk* issued against *Salam* or *Murabahah* contracts can not be traded in the secondary markets. The majority of Islamic banks hold a large portion of assets that can be securitized, but so far no Islamic commercial bank has issued a *Sukuk* mainly due to the lack of large-scale assets or due to

Issuer	Issue Date	Country	Arranger/Advisor	Issue Currency	Issue Size 'MM	Index	Spread	Tenor	Rating/Listing
Govt. of Bahrain — BMA (Issue#7)	May-03	Kingdom of Bahrain	LMC / BMA	USD	250	6m Libor	0.60%	5 Years	S&P: A- / Bahrain
Islamic Development Bank	Jun-05	International	HSBC, Deutsche, DIB, CIMB Bhd	USD	500	6m Libor	0.12%	5 Years	S&P: AAA Fitch: AA / Luxembourg, Lubuan & Bahrain
Pakistan International Sukuk Co. Ltd.	Jan-05	Pakistan	CitiGroup, HSBC, National Bank of Pakistan, DIB, Arab Bank, ABC Islamic	USD	600	6m Libor	2.20%	5 Years	S&P: B+ Luxembourg
Dubai Global Sukuk	Nov-04	United Arab Emirates	DIB, Standard Chartered, HSBC, GIB, KFH, Arab Bank	USD	1000	6m Libor	0.45%	5 Years	Govt. rating applicable
Saxony-Anhalt State Properties	Jun-04	Germany	CitiGroup / KFH	Euro	100	6m Euribor	1.00%	5 Years	S&P: AA Fitch: AAA
Government of Qatar	Sep-03	Qatar	QIIB / HSBC Amanah/ HSBC Bank Middle East	USD	700	6m Libor	0.40%	7 Years	S&P: A+ / Lubuan & Luxembourg
IDB Trust Services (ISDB)	Aug-03	International	CitiGroup	USD	400	6m Libor	0.12%	5 Years	S&P: AAA Fitch: AA / Lubuan & Luxembourg
Malaysia Global Sukuk	Jul-02	Malaysia	HSBC	USD	600	6m Libor	0.95%	5 Years	S&P: A- / Bahrain & Lubuan
The World Bank	Apr-05	International	CIMB, ABN Amro Bank Bhd	USD	760	–	–	5 Years	–

Source: Islamic Financial Information Service (IFIS)

Table 8.1B Corporate *Sukuks*

Issuer	Issue Date	Country	Arranger/Advisor	Issue Currency	Issue Size 'MM	Index	Spread	Tenor	Rating/Listing
Al Marfa'a Al Mali Sukuk	Jul–05	Kingdom of Bahrain	LMC	USD	134	3m Libor	2.50%	5 Years	–
Durrat Al Bahrain Sukuk	Jan–05	Kingdom of Bahrain	LMC / KFH	USD	152.5	3m Libor	1.25%	5 Years	–
The Commercial Real Estate Sukuk	May–05	Kuwait	LMC, KFH, Markaz / The Commercial Real Estate Company	USD	100	6m Libor	1.25%	5 Years	CI: A-
Rantau Abang Capital Sukuk	Mar–06	Malaysia	CIMB	USD	2,726	–	–	7 Years	–
WAPDA First Sukuk Company Limited	Jan–06	Pakistan	Citi Group / Muslim Commercial Bank / Jahangri Siddiqui and Company	USD	134	6m Kibor	0.35%	7 Years	–
PCFC Sukuk	Jan–06	United Arab Emirates	Dubai Islamic Bank	USD	3,500	–	7.125–10.125%	2 Years	–
Arcapita Multicurrency Sukuk	Oct–05	Kingdom of Bahrain	HVB Group Standard Bank Plc West LB AG	USD	210	3m Libor/ Euribor	1.75%	5 Years	–
Gold Sukuk dmcc	May–05	United Arab Emirates	Dubai Islamic Bank / Standard Bank	USD	200	6m Libor	0.60%	5 Years	CI: A-
Solidarity Trust Services Ltd	Aug–03	Region wide	Citigroup Global Markets Ltd / Abu Dhabi Islamic Bank / Kuwait Finance House	USD	400	Fixed	3.63%	–	S&P: AAA Fitch: AA

Source: Islamic Financial Information Service (IFIS)

Table 8.2 Islamic Bonds Managers League Table 2005

Rank	Manager	Amount (US$m)	No. of Issues	% Share
1	Commerce International Merchant Bankers Berhard (CIMB)	2670.13	11	22.94
2	HSBC Amanah	1304.59	10	11.21
3	AmMerchant Bank Berhad	1006.21	15	8.65
4	MIMB	666.12	7	5.72
5	RHB Sakura Merchant Bhd	657.90	11	5.65
6	United Overseas Bank Bhd	657.89	2	5.65
7	Citigroup	392.10	3	3.37
8	Dubai Islamic Bank	383.33	2	3.29
9	Bank Muamalat	319.98	5	2.75
10	Deutsche Bank	292.17	4	2.51
11	Standard Bank	270.00	2	2.32
12	ASEAM	263.15	1	2.26
13	Liquidity Management Centre	258.72	4	2.22
14	ABN-Amro Bank Bhd	234.86	2	2.02
15	Bumiputra Commerce Bank — BCB	208.87	1	1.79
15	Bank Islam Malaysia Berhard BIMB	208.87	1	1.79
16	Standard Chartered Bank	183.33	1	1.58
17	Aseambankers Malaysia	142.10	1	1.22
18	Kuwait Finance House	126.25	2	1.08
19	OCBC Bank	113.95	4	0.98
20	Affin Bank Berhad	110.52	3	0.95

Source: Islamic Financial Information Service (IFIS)

Figure 8.2   Case Study: Islamic Development Bank (IsDB) *Sukuk*

- *Sukuk* issued by the Jeddah-based multilateral development bank, the Islamic Development Bank (IsDB), are different from typical Sukuk, as the underlying asset is a pool of real and financial assets; comprising leased assets (*Ijarah*) and receivables from *Murabahah* and *Istisna* contracts. In order to make the *Sukuk* tradable in the secondary market, the portion of leased assets is kept at more than 50% in the total asset pool. The Sukuk issue of up to USD 500.00 million was given an AAA rating by Standard and Poors.
- *Sukuk* is linked to a floating rate (LIBOR plus a spread of +12 basis points) with a maturity of 5 years. The proceeds from the issue are to be used for the funding of development projects, trade financing transactions and other activities of the Bank.
- The issue was oversubscribed by 1.56 times by both conventional and Islamic investors. Far East investors accounted for 35% of the uptake; Middle East investors for 32%; European investors for 26%; and the remainder was taken up by supranational institutions.

Issuer	Islamic Development Bank
Issue Launch Date	2005-06-11
Amount — US$m	500.00
Bond Currency	USD
Price	100
Return	6 Months libor + 0.12%
Type of Issue	Corporate (Issued)
Maturity	5 Years (2010)
Bookrunner	Co-Bookrunner — HSBC Amanah Co-Bookrunner — Deutsche Bank
Manager	Co-Lead Manager — Dubai Islamic Bank Co-Lead Manager — HSBC Amanah Co-Lead Manager — Commerce International Merchant Bankers Berhard (CIMB) Co-Lead Manager — Deutsche Bank
Structuring Adviser	Clifford Chance (IDB); Linklater (to Dealer & Transaction Administrator as to Laws of England); Ogier & Le Masurier (Trustee as to Laws of Jersey)
Rating	S&P, FITC HAAA / AA
Global Shariah Compliance Endorsement	Hussein Hamed Hassan; Saleh Al Husayn; Abdul Sattar Abu Ghodda; Mohammad Ali Taskhiri; Mohamed Mokhtar Sellami; Mohamed Hashim Bin Yahaya
Listing	Luxembourg Stock Exchange & Labuan International Financial Exchange
Country	Saudi Arabia
Geographical Distribution	Far East; Middle East; Europe

Source: Islamic Financial Information Service (IFIS)

the holding of short-term *Salam* or *Murabahah*-based assets. Islamic banks should make serious efforts to utilize the securitization process to take the assets off their balance sheets in order to enhance liquidity of their existing portfolios. The challenge is to develop *Sukuk* based on pools of heterogeneous assets with varying maturities and different credit qualities. Islamic banks' participation in the market will further develop the *Sukuk* market.

- Issuers, investors as well as intermediaries need to nurture the market patiently. Islamic transactions often face a competitive disadvantage against conventional bond issues in terms of cost-efficiency. Each new issue incurs higher levels of legal and documentation expenses as well as distribution costs; and involves examining structural robustness in addition to evaluating the credit quality of the obligor. Standardization of contracts will reduce this problem.

- Floating-rate *Sukuk* are often linked to a conventional interest rate benchmark such as London Inter Bank Offer Rate (LIBOR). When it comes to pricing, *Sukuk* compete directly with the conventional bonds in terms of level of relative spreads. From the conventional borrowers' point of view, there is no inherent funding cost advantage by tapping into *Sukuk* markets, since the terms available are mostly derived from competitive pricing levels in the more liquid and cheaper conventional bond market. Borrowers, therefore, need to formulate a comprehensive, long-term and strategic view on how to reduce the overall funding cost by tapping into Islamic markets, rather than focusing on a single transaction.

- In principle, *Sukuk*-based funding should be relatively cheaper, since it is based on collateralized cash flows, but in reality this is not the case. It is expected that as the market matures and investors are more comfortable with the instrument, costs will decrease and the market will become more efficient.

- Due to the shortage of good quality bond issues in the market, the subscribers (investors) to *Sukuk*, which include institutional investors, central banks, and private sector Islamic banks, tend to hold the *Sukuk* till maturity. As a result, the level of activity in the secondary market is low, which, in turn, reduces liquidity and also increases transaction costs by the way of high bid–ask spreads. This problem can be overcome by increasing the supply of *Sukuk* and by developing a market for retail investors.

- There may be intermediation costs involved in issuing *Sukuk* when more than one layer of investment banks are involved. Conventional banks often co-lead a *Sukuk* issue with the Islamic banks and may be taking a larger share of fees. Also, a conventional investment bank may not be willing to invest time and effort to develop small scale *Sukuk* in the local market. This gap should be filled by a more active involvement of Islamic investment banks.

- It should also be noted that monitoring costs are not eliminated altogether in *Sukuk*. A potential problem of adverse selection exists with such a contract. Borrowers may be tempted to exaggerate competence, ability, or willingness to provide the effort required by the principal in order to obtain a contract or to obtain a contract with or on more favorable terms. In such cases, the principal, in order to protect its interests, often requires that borrowers present some evidence proving their competence, ability and willingness to put in the necessary effort. Such evidence may include past performance. In order to protect themselves from adverse selection, principals (investors) may enter into contracts with entrepreneurs who have the necessary credentials, with the assurance that these agents are competent, and trustworthy. Investment banks can play a critical role in reducing this adverse selection problem by conducting due diligence and providing a transparent execution of the deal.

Islamic Funds

Islamic funds are based on the *Mudarabah* contract and are structured very much like mutual funds in the conventional system. In the last decade, different kinds of funds have been introduced in the market, some of which are discussed below.

Equity Funds

Islamic equity funds are similar to the Socially Responsible Investment (SRI) equity mutual funds of the conventional market, which involves investment in stocks that meet certain criteria. Construction of equity funds is a two-step process — screening and filtering. Screening involves review of stocks to eliminate stocks of companies involved in businesses considered unlawful according to the *Shariah*. After the initial screening, a certain filtration process is applied by each fund manager according to their judgement regarding certain financial ratios such as existence of debt or income from debt securities.

Elimination of stocks of a business that is not *Shariah*-compatible is easy, but there are differences in practices with regard to other filtering criteria, because of the differences in jurisdictions and judgements of individual fund managers. The following are the general guidelines used for screening and filtering the stock of a company before it is included in an equity fund.

- *Shariah*-**compatibility of Business:** The main business of the company should be in conformity with the principles of the *Shariah*. This constraint eliminates all companies dealing with the financial services industry operating on interest, such as conventional banks and insurance companies, companies manufacturing, selling or offering liquor and pork products, and businesses involved in activities such as gambling, night clubs, casinos, pornography, etc.
- **Existence of Debt:** Stocks of companies that depend heavily on debt financing as determined by their debt ratio, are eliminated. Different funds set different levels of tolerance depending on how strictly they want to adhere to the *Shariah*. The typical level of tolerance is set at a maximum of 33% debt to equity ratio. This constraint is applied for ensuring that the company is capitalized in a *Shariah*-acceptable manner and with the expectation that debt may be eliminated in the future. Actually, some *Shariah* scholars encourage shareholders to raise their voices against the use of debt financing by the company and thus fulfilling their responsibility to make serious effort to eliminate debt all together.
- **Interest Income:** Fund managers also try to avoid those stocks where companies have substantial amounts of income derived from interest on securities. This could be the case of companies that invest excess liquidity in debt securities and therefore earn interest income that becomes part of the company's profits. However, if only a negligible portion of income is driven through interest, *Shariah* scholars have given permission to acquire the stock on two conditions. First, the shareholder must express his disapproval against such dealings, preferably by raising his voice against such activities in the annual general meeting of the company. Second, a cleansing of interest income should be done through contribution to charity. It is suggested that the proportion of interest income in the dividend paid to the shareholder must be given in charity, and must not be retained by the shareholder. For example, if 5% of the whole income of a company has come out of interest-bearing deposits, 5% of the dividend must be given in charity to purify the income derived from dividend.

- **Negotiability of Shares (Liquidity Test):** According to *Shariah* scholars, the shares of a company are negotiable only if the company owns some illiquid assets. Although there is no fixed tolerance level of illiquid assets, a ratio of 33% is typically used. The reasoning behind this constraint is that if all the assets of a company are in liquid form, i.e., in the form of money, they cannot be purchased or sold except at par value, because in this case the share represents money only and money cannot be traded except at par.
- **Ordinary versus Preferred Stock:** Although there is a general consensus among the *Shariah* scholars on the permissibility of ordinary shares, since they represent undivided ownership in the business of the company by the shareholders, other forms of shares such as preferred stock and warrants do not have the same permissibility. This is due to the fact that preferred stock and warrants promise a definite return to their holders, compared to the holders of other types of shares, who bear the same liability but are not entitled to any definite return.

The future of Islamic equity funds is bright, partly because of a new wave of privatization under way in Muslim countries, increasing demand for capital-intensive infrastructure projects in countries like Iran and Pakistan as well as in high-growth Islamic countries such as Indonesia and Malaysia, where the demand for Islamic financial products is also growing rapidly. Malaysia has taken an active role in the promotion of equity funds. For example, in terms of market capitalization, more than 50% of the stocks listed on the Kuala Lumpur Stock Exchange are *Shariah*-compliant. Malaysia is the only country where the screening of listed stocks is undertaken by a centralized body, which works closely with the regulators. Twice a year, The *Shariah* Advisory Council (SAC) recommends *Shariah*-compliant stocks, which are officially published by The Securities Commission.

The demand for Islamic equity funds and the successful application of the screening process have been supported by the introduction of several equity Indices. Dow Jones and Company launched the Dow Jones Islamic Market Index (DJIMI) in February 1999, which was followed by the introduction of the Kuala Lumpur *Shariah* Index (KLSI) by Bursa Malaysia in April 1999 and the FTSE Global Islamic Index Series (FTSE-GII) by the Financial Times Stock Exchange (FTSE) Group in October 1999. Market capitalization of Global DJIMI as of March 31, 2005 was estimated to be US$10.65 trillion, and the universe of *Shariah*-compliant stocks included 1942 stocks. The number of the stocks included is relatively low because DJIMI includes only those stocks that are open to an international investor who can repatriate the proceeds. As a result, several of the qualified local stocks are excluded. The screening process may also differ from index to index. For example, whereas the global DJIMI uses screening criteria by applying ratios derived from both the income statements and the balance sheet, Malaysian indices use only income statement ratios and do not use balance sheet ratios to determine debt or liquidity levels.

Figure 8.3 shows the screening process used to construct the Dow Jones Islamic Index. Figure 8.4 shows the performance of this index for a period of three years since 2003.

Challenges for Equity Funds

The following issues and challenges need to be addressed for further growth and development of Islamic equity funds:

- The shallow stock markets in many OIC countries do not offer opportunities for meaningful portfolio construction after applying

Figure 8.3 Dow Jones Islamic Index Screening

1. **Screens for *Shariah*-Compatible Businesses:**
    Based on revenue allocation, if any company has business activities in the *Shariah*-inconsistent group or sub-group of industries, it is excluded from the Islamic Index universe. The DJIMI *Shariah* Supervisory Board established that the following broad categories of industries are inconsistent with the precepts of the *Shariah*: Alcohol, Pork-related products, conventional financial services (banking, insurance, etc.), entertainment (hotels, casinos/gambling, cinema, pornography, music, etc.), tobacco, and weapons and defense industries.

2. **Financial Ratios Filter:**
    Stocks of companies passing the following filter for financial ratios are included as components of the Dow Jones Islamic Market Index.

    2.1. **Debt to Assets:**
          Exclude companies if Total Debt divided by Trailing 12-Month Average Market Capitalization is greater than or equal to 33%.(Note: Total Debt = Short-Term Debt + Current Portion of Long-Term Debt + Long-Term Debt)

    2.2. **Liquid Assets to Total Assets:**
          Exclude companies if the sum of Cash and Interest Bearing Securities divided by Trailing 12-Month Average Market Capitalization is greater than or equal to 33%.

    2.3. **Receiveables to Assets:**
          Exclude companies if Accounts Receivables divided by Total Assets is greater than or equal to 33%. (Note: Accounts Receivables = Current Receivables + Long-Term Receivables)

Source: Syed (2005) and Dow Jones (2006)

Figure 8.4   Performance of DJIMI — 2003–2006

RIC	.DJIMI
Security Name	DJ ISLAMIC NDX
Last Trade	1894.21
Last Trade Date	04 MAR 2006
Last Trade Time	21:46 GMT
Net Change	2.29
Percentage Change	0.12
Previous	1891.92
Previous Close Date	05 MAR 2006
Open	1891.92
Daily High	1895.17
Daily Low	1891.85
52 week high	1917.04
52 week high date	31 JAN 2006
52 week low	1599.55
52 week low date	28 APR 2005
Lifetime High	2309244.00
Lifetime High Date	14 JUL 2000
Lifetime Low	983.17
Currency	USD

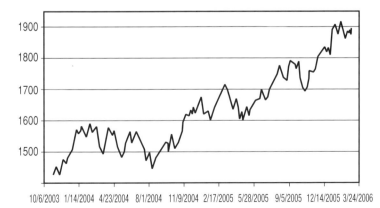

the screening criteria. Several of the listed stocks have weak financials and do not have depth in the market. In terms of market capitalization, Malaysia has the largest segment of the *Shariah*-compliant market (57.7%), followed by the Karachi Stock Exchange (KSE) (51.78% in 2004), Turkey (12%) and Bahrain (6.4%). The low proportion of *Shariah*-compatible markets is due to the high debt to equity ratio of a majority of the listed companies, which disqualifies them for inclusion in the equity funds.

• The screening criteria are not very stable as changing market conditions can change the financial ratios of a company, which means that it may or may not pass the filter set by the fund manager from one period to another. For example, depending upon the market price, a stock can be in and out of the fund during a relatively short period of time due to the fluctuating debt to equity ratios. This can adversely affect the diversification of the portfolio and may lead to additional transaction costs each time a portfolio is re-balanced.

• As a result of the screening and filtering process, the resultant universe of stock may not be large enough to offer good portfolio diversification opportunities. Effort should be made to expand the universe of *Shariah*-compliant stocks.

• On a more serious note, the main emphasis of fund managers has been on the screening mechanism, but little attention has been paid to certain market practices such as short-selling and margin account maintenance, which are not compatible with the *Shariah*. Practices followed by each fund manager should be clearly spelled out and should be cleared by *Shariah* scholars.

Commodity Funds

Commodity funds are another popular form of Islamic Funds. In this type of fund, the investors' contribution is used in purchasing different commodities for the purpose of their resale. The profits generated by the sales are the income of the fund, which is distributed pro rata among the subscribers. Commodity funds are subject to certain conditions such as (i) short sales are not allowed; (ii) forward sales are allowed only in the case of *Salam* and *Istisna*'; and (iii) dealing with commodities like pork or alcohol is prohibited. Many of the commodity funds are developed by financial intermediaries or by conventional Western banks to cater to high net worth individuals.

Challenges of Capital Market Development

Development of capital markets is not an overnight task. Today's conventional capital markets are the result of years of evolution, especially in the last couple of decades, during which the markets have seen innovation at an unprecedented pace. One of the positive externalities of this development and innovation in the conventional market is that the learning curve for developing any new market is not a steep one. New emerging markets such as Islamic capital markets can learn from the rich experience that conventional markets offer and can cut short the development time.

Today's capital markets do not operate in isolation but rather are part of a complex system. This system functions and operates subject to several different components, such as the state of the regulatory system, the quality of supporting institutions, the design of the incentive and corporate governance systems and market micro-structure and practices. In addition, other factors like the breadth of the market determined by the product range, the existence of reliable benchmarks for performance evaluation, the culture of market players and the degree of integration with external markets are also critical in the development of an efficient capital market.

Although there are several challenges facing the development of Islamic capital markets, the major ones are discussed here:

Legislative and Regulatory Framework

The existence of a strong legislative and regulatory framework is essential for capital markets. Laws to protect the rights of investors and mechanisms to resolve disputes in an efficient manner help in establishing the confidence of the investors. This issue has become more relevant these days, when there is increasing competition to attract cross-border investors.

In a majority of Muslim countries where there is a demand for Islamic products, a sound legal and regulatory system is not in place. In many cases, amendments are made to local laws and regulations on an ad-hoc basis to accommodate the needs of a transaction, but this style of operation is inefficient as well as frustrating for the players in the market. The framework should facilitate smooth execution of transactions in the market without creating any technical, legal or regulatory issues. The experience of recent *Sukuk* issues is some indicator of the extent of the problem. For example, for an *Ijarah Sukuk* transaction, the owner of the operating assets needs to enter into a leasing transaction. While the owners of operating assets are often the government itself or its related public-sector bodies, the relevant laws and regulations in the host country may not allow these public-sector bodies to pledge or lease assets needed to structure an *Ijarah* transaction. This is a fundamental point; the host country's policy actions to promote such Islamic finance will be a key prerequisite for the market to develop further.

The following suggestions are made in this respect:

- **Standardization of Legal Framework:** One major reason for this inefficiency is that the majority of the markets in Islamic countries operate in a legal system subject to conventional civil and common law which may not always be compatible with the *Shariah*. Different legal environments from country to country make the task of introducing new products very difficult and costly. Countries wishing to develop Islamic capital markets need to review the legal system as a whole and make serious efforts to make the legal framework comply with the *Shariah*. Countries should make coordinated efforts to ensure that their legal systems are standardized and harmonized. In this way, there would not be any ambiguity on the status of Islamic capital markets' transactions undertaken in a particular jurisdiction.

- **Dispute Resolution:** Dispute resolution is another critical area worthy of attention in the development of the Islamic capital markets. In the countries in which Islamic capital markets are being developed alongside conventional markets, the existence of different legal systems for addressing issues with Islamic instruments is not an ideal situation. Necessary amendments should be made to accommodate Islamic instruments within the framework of existing dispute resolution procedures, as opposed to setting up a dedicated system, in order to minimize any confusion. The approach to dispute resolution should aim to avoid duplication of resources and maintain the confidence in Islamic products.

- **Strengthening the Regulatory Framework:** Regulatory rules exist in a number of markets, but the enforcement is weak. The regulatory authorities should play a more active role in the development of Islamic capital markets by strengthening the regulatory framework and by establishing the credibility of the regulatory institutions. In many Islamic countries, regulatory institutions either do not exist or are very weak. Strong and independent regulatory and other supporting institutions should be established for further promotion of Islamic capital markets.

Market Structure and Practices

Capital markets in several Muslim countries do not have a good reputation among foreign investors. This low level of confidence stems from a number of practices that leave investors vulnerable to different forms of market abuses, such as price manipulation, front running, insider trading, and blank selling. Regulators should make sure that the credibility of the markets is restored and the execution and trading of securities take place in a transparent fashion.

Further, the operation of markets should be reviewed with a view to complying with *Shariah* requirements. For example, the practice of short selling and margin account maintenance is not considered acceptable by some *Shariah* scholars. A system-wide procedure should be established to standardize these practices. In order to encourage foreign borrowers and to access liquid markets in Muslim countries, regulators should promote the listing of Islamic securities issued by foreign member countries on their domestic exchanges.

Incentives to Promote Capital Markets

For further development of Islamic capital markets, policy makers should provide incentives for businesses and financial institutions to engage in Islamic instruments. These incentives can come in the form of tax breaks for the issuers and underwriters of Islamic securities. For example, a tax deduction of research and product development expenses to develop Islamic securities or a tax deduction on the payments made on *Sukuk* similar to the tax deduction of interest payments in the conventional system can serve as good incentives.

In the area of equity markets, policy makers should try to attract retail investors to participate in *Shariah*-compliant stocks. With the rapid development of Internet banking, policy makers can attract retail investors from different geographical areas, provided the markets are liberalized and there are no unnecessary restrictions on foreign investors.

Development of Supporting Institutions

Today's capital markets are supported by many institutions that perform critical functions for their smooth operation. These institutions include rating agencies, standard-setting agencies and industry associations. Some progress has been made in this respect in the form of establishment of institutions like International Islamic Financial Market (IIFM) and International

Islamic Rating Agency (IIRA). IIFM was established in 2002 in Bahrain to act as an industry association to promote cooperation among market players and with conventional financial institutions, to further enhance the growth of new Islamic products and financial instruments. IIRA was established to rate, evaluate and provide independent assessments and opinions on the likelihood of any future loss by Islamic financial institutions as well as their products and services. Both these institutions are based in Bahrain and are focused on that market. However, similar institutions should be established in domestic markets to support local markets.

Financial Engineering

Financial engineering has revolutionizeed the conventional capital markets. *Sukuk* is a good example of financial engineering and further application of financial engineering in the area of development of money markets and intra-bank markets should be encouraged. Existence of money markets provides liquidity in the short term and supports capital markets to focus on long-term capital needs. Another strong candidate for further growth is the development of Mortgage-Backed-Securities (MBS) and Asset-Backed-Securities (ABS), where a pool of homogeneous assets is securitized.

Role of *Shariah* Scholars

Shariah scholars can also play an important role. It is essential that multi-disciplinary expertise, covering topics ranging from theological interpretation to financial structuring, be developed through knowledge-sharing, cross-training and acquiring an understanding of the functioning of markets. To stimulate cross-border activities in the primary as well as secondary markets, the acceptance of contracts across regions and across schools of thought and markets will also be helpful.

Endnotes

1   Vogel, F. E. and Hayes, Samuel L. (1998), *Islamic Law and Finance: Religion, Risk and Return*.

2   Usmani, Taqi (1999), *An Introduction to Islamic Finance*.

CHAPTER

9

Financial Engineering

Financial engineering and financial innovations are the forces driving the global financial system toward the goal of greater economic efficiency. The 1980s witnessed the rapid introduction of financial innovations in the international financial markets. Financial innovations transformed the traditional financial and banking markets into highly sophisticated markets featuring a high degree of liquidity and a wide array of instruments to share and transfer various sources of risk. The trend occurred in both domestic and international financial markets. The demand for liquidity-enhancing and risk-managing instruments was prompted by the increased volatility in financial asset prices due to the breakdown of the fixed exchange rate system, the oil shocks, excessive government spending and inflationary policies. The innovation and growth in financial markets was further induced by advances in financial theory, breakthroughs in the information-processing and communication technology and deregulation of financial markets.

Financial engineering involves the design and development of innovative financial instruments and processes, as well as the search for creative solutions to problems in finance. Financial engineering may lead to a new consumer-customed financial instrument, or a new security, or a new process which ultimately results in the lowering of funding costs or in increasing return on investments or expanding opportunities for risk sharing. The following are three types of financial innovation activities that have the most significant impact on the markets:

- To enhance liquidity. Marketability, negotiability, and transferability of financial claims create liquidity by expanding the menu of options available to market participants.

- To transfer and share price and credit risk through the development of derivatives markets. Derivatives, apart from risk-sharing, make markets more complete and create important additional social benefits such as the dissemination of uniform prices upon which investment decisions can be made, and the lowering of transaction cost in the capital markets.
- To generate revenues from credit and equity.

In the long term, financial development and innovations exhibited a positive impact on the economic growth of various countries. One of the advantages of financial engineering is that it is for the common good and that there is no copyright on financial products. Once an instrument is launched, it can be copied by anyone, improved upon, combined with other instruments and re-launched.

Financial Engineering in the Islamic Financial System

Financial engineering is one of the most critical current needs of Islamic financial markets in general and of Islamic risk management practices in particular. Islamic financial institutions are still operating on traditional instruments, which do not satisfy the needs of the market fully in terms of liquidity as well as risk and portfolio management. Asset portfolios of Islamic financial institutions predominantly consist of trade-related short-term assets. There is a shortage of products for medium- to long-term maturities, as secondary markets lack depth and breadth.

The lack of efficient secondary markets and liquidity in the Islamic financial markets has indirectly limited the range of maturity structures available to the investor. Due to the absence of liquidity, Islamic financial institutions cannot easily expand portfolios across capital markets and are restricted in opportunities for portfolio diversification. This presents a challenging opportunity of developing highly liquid instruments to satisfy the demands of the investors and the users of funds seeking medium- and long-term maturity structures with the flexibility of adjusting portfolios at the lowest cost.

Derivatives markets are an integral part of the contemporary financial system. They play an increasingly important role in financial markets through three key economic functions:

(a) risk management by offering a mechanism through which investors, corporations and countries can efficiently hedge themselves against financial risks,

(b)   price discovery by providing information about expected market-clearing prices in the future as indicative of future demand and supply, since knowledge of prices in the spot and derivatives markets is essential for investors, consumers and producers to make informed decisions and, finally,

(c)   transactional efficiency, as derivatives typically involve lower transaction costs.

The absence of derivatives and risk management tools in Islamic finance has and will have a significant impact on the current and future growth of the market because of the following:

- a firm in the Islamic financial markets will lose its business competitiveness due to its inability to handle variability in its cost, revenues and profitability through managing financial risk,
- a firm without active risk management will be perceived as a high-risk firm and thus will be subject to higher funding costs,
- a firm will be subject to high risk of financial distress,
- a firm will be exposed to a higher risk during a system-wide financial crisis and, finally
- it will be difficult for Islamic financial institutions to integrate with the international financial markets.

The key to the rapid development of secondary markets and of liquidity-enhancing products for implementing effective risk management is the application of financial engineering.

Scope of Financial Engineering

The process of financial engineering can be viewed as a process of building complex instruments utilizing basic building blocks or unbundling and repackaging different components of existing financial instruments, e.g., return, price risk, credit risk, country risk, etc. Today's highly liquid instruments and derivatives are based on a simple and basic set of instruments. A close scrutiny of the instruments underlying the Islamic financial system reveals that these instruments have characteristics similar to many of today's basic building blocks and it is a matter of designing more complex instruments without violating any of the boundaries defined by the Islamic system.

The process of financial innovation is complex and sensitive, as it requires multi disciplinary considerations involving not only knowledge of economics, finance and banking, but also a deep understanding of Islamic jurisprudence. Throughout history, businesses and traders have worked closely with *Shariah* experts as pious Muslims are conscious of complying with the *Shariah*. Centuries of experience across several geographical regions have grown into a rich body of *Shariah* rulings and precedents in the area of business and economics. However, the process of innovative application of the *Shariah* through *Ijtihad* to resolve the problems of the time has been dormant for a long time and there is a need to revive the practice which was once alive and vibrant.

The process of determining the legitimacy of a new product involves approval by *Shariah* scholars who ensure that the new product does not violate any of principles of the *Shariah*. From a legal point of view, any instrument is acceptable as a legitimate financial instrument provided it does not incorporate certain elements considered unlawful in Islam. The scope of financial engineering can be explored further by developing further understanding of three aspects; (i) the freedom to contact given to economic agents, (ii) what are the basic building blocks, and (iii) spectrum of risk/return profile of instruments.

- **Freedom of Contract:** It is critical to understand the laws governing contracts in Islam. Individuals have wide freedom of contract and the contracting parties are free to engage in any transactions not prohibited by the *Shariah*. In other words, any transaction is permissible so long as it does not contain any of prohibited elements of *Riba*, *Gharar*, *Qimar*, and *Ikrah*. Historically, *Shariah* scholars would not dictate how a contract should be formulated, but it was a common practice by economic agents to bring a contract to the *Shariah* scholar who could only declare its legitimacy or non-compliance with the *Shariah* by testing for the prohibited elements. If the Shariah scholar did not find any of the prohibited elements, the contract was given the blessing of compliance. This practice implies that rather than imposing restrictions on the contracts, *Shariah* gives freedom of contract to the parties so that they can develop new tools and mechanisms of financing and lending, and the role of the *Shariah* scholar is limited to ensuring that the contract is valid according to the *Shariah*. Financial instruments and services should be viewed as sets of contracts, which identify the rights and obligations of each party. The *Shariah* scholar can examine the contract to verify that these rights and obligations of the parties are preserved according to the notions of contracts and property rights in Islam.
- **Basic Building Blocks:** No effort to introduce financial engineering can take place without understanding the basic building blocks of

the Islamic financial system. Contrary to common belief, the system provides basic building blocks that can be further used to construct more complex structures. Almost all of the complex financial instruments in today's conventional financial markets can be broken down to a set of basic instruments. For example, a floating rate bond with a cap and floor on its coupon is nothing but a set of plain-vanilla floating bond plus a call and a put option. Even call and put options can be replicated using cash and fixed income instruments. Therefore, a financial engineer not only needs to understand the principles of spanning in order to determine where and how a complex structure can be developed on top of the basic blocks, but also needs to understand what is the nature of such building blocks in the Islamic financial system and what are the principles which can be applied to build more sophisticated instruments.

- **Risk/Return Profile:** It is also critical to develop an understanding of the spectrum of the risk and return profiles of different financial instruments in the Islamic financial system. Often the Islamic financial system is equated with an all equity-based system, which ignores the fact that the system also has several other types of contracts, which are not based on profit-and-loss-sharing. Contracts like sales, trade financing and leasing constitute a large portion of the system, but these contracts are not based on equity. The existence of such non-equity-based instruments has an important implication. These instruments have a risk/return profile that is very similar to a conventional fixed-income security — a vital part of the more exotic financial instruments. While the instruments based on *Murabahah*, *Salam*, or *Ijarah* contracts may resemble an interest- bearing, fixed-income instrument, these are allowed and recognized by the *Shariah*. Further, the notion of cash flows collateralized against an underlying asset — another essential tool of financial engineering — is compatible with the principles of Islam, which promotes investment in real sector.

By understanding the process of formulating contracts, the functions of the basic building blocks and the risk/return profile of different instruments, especially the ones that resemble fixed-income securities, one can apply the principle of financial engineering to introduce advanced financial instruments. The following two approaches have been suggested:

Reverse Engineering: The first approach entails taking an existing instrument in the conventional system, and evaluating each of its components to find the closest substitute from the basic set of Islamic instruments. This means breaking down the instrument and then rebuilding it, using equivalent instruments from the set of *Shariah*-approved instruments. The major advantage of this approach is the instant recognition and understanding it gets from the practitioners of conventional finance; this paves the way for efficiency and the integration of Islamic financial markets into the conventional system. This approach may be used for determining the legitimacy of a product for approval purposes when such a product is introduced in a conventional market. This will make the instrument easy to understand for the regulatory authorities of the host country, which will facilitate speedy approval of the instrument. Extreme care is required in this approach, in order to avoid any misidentification of close substitutes. Any misidentification or use of a wrong substitute can not only break the trust of investors, but will also create a reputation risk for the industry. All efforts should be made to avoid any contamination, which may occur during the process where exact substitutes are replaced by close but not fully *Shariah*-compatible instruments. Contamination may occur when an Islamic instrument or contract is used where its intended usage is either doubtful or questionable, or some important features or conditions of the contract is compromised. This danger of contamination will increase as the level of complexity of the instrument increases.

Innovative Engineering: A second approach to financial engineering, preferable, in principle, to "reverse engineering," is to design instruments *de novo* from an established menu of Islamic instruments. The result will be a new array of instruments, each having a unique risk–return profile, bought and sold in specialized markets compatible with *Shariah* principles. Since this approach requires a deep understanding of the Islamic economic and financial system as well as the risk/return characteristics of each basic building block, it is a long-term solution and requires extensive research and commitment. Although this approach is better aligned with the essence of the *Shariah*, pioneering new frontiers in a different paradigm always poses new challenges and takes time. Some of the prerequisites of or for an Islamic financial system, such as efficient markets, information symmetry and *Shariah*-compatible property rights and regulatory and supervisory laws, are absent from most of the developing Islamic countries.

Although the second route of "innovation" is in principle the better approach, operational difficulties associated with this route impose constraints and force compromises. It is conceivable that due to the pressing need for innovation, the first approach will dominate in the short term, and an adoption of some combination of "reverse engineering" and "innovation" will take place in the medium term. However, the full potential of the system will only be achieved if serious efforts are made to introduce new instruments, which provide unique risk/return characteristics that are equally desirable for Islamic and non-Islamic financial markets.

Application of Financial Engineering

The following are a few examples demonstrating the application of financial engineering techniques in the area of risk management and benchmarking. These examples use the basic instruments to develop new instruments, which are currently not available in the market. It should be noted that the instruments discussed here are only examples and they should be taken with the qualification that the final approval and application rests with the *Shariah* experts.

Case I: Synthetic Currency Forward Contract

The concept of arbitrage pricing and the ability to replicate a security synthetically have played a critical role in the development of derivatives and risk management tools in conventional finance. The concept of arbitrage is extensively used to demonstrate that in an efficient market two instruments with identical risk-return characteristics cannot have different prices. The ability to construct and to replicate a security or portfolio synthetically helped in the development of derivative products, as it was demonstrated that two portfolios — one with a derivative security and the other with plain-vanilla securities — would have identical risk/return profiles in a world free of arbitage. Such arbitrage principles and the techniques of financial engineering can be applied, using the basic building blocks of the Islamic financial system, for devising derivative instruments that are not currently practiced.

A currency forward contract is an agreement to buy or sell a foreign currency at a pre-determined price at a pre-determined future date. Islamic instruments permit similar forward contracts (future delivery at pre-agreed price) but only in case of commodities, provided certain conditions stated by the *Shariah* are followed. The Islamic forward contract, *Bay' al-Salam* permits one party to purchase a commodity at a pre-determined price for a future delivery and the purchaser is required to make full payment at the time of contract. However, application of *Bay' al-Salam* to foreign currency is not permitted simply because Islam treats currency as a medium of exchange and not as commodity. There are no other instruments, that can be used to hedge against the volatility of the exchange rate.

The following section demonstrates how a currency forward contract may be constructed synthetically without a standard forward contract. The synthetic construction of a forward contract, means that the payoffs are identical to a forward contract, but they are achieved through a set of different transactions executed in a certain sequence. These products can make significant contributions to risk management in Islamic financial markets providing hedging against by currency risk.

Let us take an example of an importer in an Islamic country, who wants to hedge against the volatility of a foreign currency. In the absence of a currency forward contract, the importer will be exposed to risk due to any appreciation in the value of the foreign currency. Assuming that there are no market frictions such as taxes, capital controls and transaction costs and that financial intermediaries who have access to both local and foreign money markets exist, a forward contract can be constructed synthetically, using the Islamic contract of *Murabahah*. A *Murabahah* contract results in a financial claim as a result of the sale of a real asset. However, since the margin above cost (mark-up) is agreed upon in advance, the expected rate of return is pre-determined. The financial claim created in this fashion is similar to a zero-coupon fixed-income security or a certificate of deposit (CD) in conventional banking.

Suppose that the importer requires to hedge X amount of foreign currency obligation for a period of time (T) from today (T_0). Current market rates of return on a three-month *Murabahah* contract in domestic and foreign markets are R_d and R_f respectively. The importer can approach a financial intermediary or Islamic bank to arrange for the purchase of X amount of foreign currency in the future.

The following steps can be taken by the financial intermediary to provide a currency hedge to the importer by taking positions in assets in foreign markets in collaboration with a local investor:
On the date of contract (T_0):

Step 1: Importer requests the bank to arrange for a currency forward contract for maturity T. The banker enters into a *Joala'* contract with the importer to deliver X amount of foreign currency at the foreign exchange rate at time T. *Joala'* contract allows the importer to hire the bank to provide a service, i.e., to arrange or deliver currency at time T for a pre-determined fee.

Step 2: The banker finds an investor in the domestic market, who is willing to participate in arranging a currency forward contract for maturity T. Or, the bank may use funds from an existing depositor's investment account as well. Let us assume that the expected rate of return in the local market at time T_0 was R_d.

Step 3: The bank determines the amount in the foreign currency required today (at T_0) to hedge X amount of foreign currency at time T. In other words, what is the present value of X amount of foreign currency given the expected rate of return? That should be equal to the value of a *Murabahah* in foreign currency at time T_0, so that the cost plus the profit margin in the foreign market is equal to the required hedge amount of X in foreign currency at time T. Therefore, the amount required today to hedge X amount of foreign currency would be equal to x in foreign currency as shown below:

$$x = \frac{X}{(1 + R_f)}$$

Step 4: Local currency (L) required at time T_0 will be equal to $x \times$ spot exchange rate between the local and the foreign currency. The bank invests L amount of local currency in foreign *Murabahah* after converting L amount of local currency into x amount of foreign currency at the spot rate at T_0.

Step 5: The bank agrees with the importer to deliver X amount of foreign currency on maturity date T at rate F. The bank determines the rate F based on the rate of return differential between the domestic and foreign markets. In other words, the future rate F is a function of the expected rate of returns on local and foreign *Murabahah* for time T. The difference between domestic and foreign *Murabahah* mark-up rates determine the discount/premium on forward rate. This rate F can also be called the unbiased predictor of the future spot rate, because if this rate is not the equilibrium rate, there is opportunity for arbitrage where the arbitrageur can make risk-less profit by taking off-setting positions in the market creating the arbitrage. In other words, the forward exchange rate (F) will be determined in such a way that the forward discount/premium on the currency is equal to the differential of expected rates of return on *Murabahah* contracts of equal risk in domestic and foreign capital markets. This rate (F) is not only the best estimate of the future spot exchange rate, but is also an arbitrage-free forward rate for the currency.

At the date of delivery (T):

Step 6: The bank receives X amount of foreign currency against the *Murabahah* investment. The importer buys X amount of foreign currency by paying $X \times F$ amount of local currency to the bank. Since the bank initially invested L amount, the bank's or the investor's rate of return would be equal to R_d, or the same as the bank or the investor would have earned by investing in local *Murabahah*.

This synthetic forward contract is fully backed by an Islamic investment in form of a *Murabahah*. As a result, the bank or the investor earns R_d on the investment. The importer benefits from the exchange rate hedge in case the future exchange rate moves unfavorably.

The following illustrates the calculations involved in a synthetic forward contract and the profit made by the bank or the investor in our example:

Local currency:	Euro (€)
Foreign Currency:	US Dollar ($)
Period:	3 months
Rate of Return on 3 month *Murabahah* in domestic market ($R_€$):	10%
Rate of Return on 3 month *Murabahah* in foreign market ($R_$):	5%
Spot Rate:	€0.85/$1
Amount to hedge:	$1,000,000.00

Amount of investment required in foreign currency on settlement date (T_0):

$$\frac{Hedge\ Amount}{(1 + R_)} = \frac{1,000,000}{(1.05)} = \$952,381$$

Amount of investment required in local currency at settlement date (T_0):

$$Foreign\ Amount \times Spot\ Rate = \$952,381 \times 0.85 = €809,524$$

Convert €809,524 @ €0.85/$1 to $952,381 and invest the proceeds in *Murabahah* with expected rate of return = 5%.

Arbitrage free forward rate (*F*) quoted to importer:

$$F = Spot \times \frac{(1 + R_\text{€})}{(1 + R_\$)} = 0.85 \times \frac{1.1}{1.05} = 0.8905/\$$$

Value of *Murabahah* at maturity (*T*):

$$Investment\ amount \times (1 + Rate\ of\ Return) = \$952,381 \times (1.05)$$
$$= \$1,000,000$$

The bank receives \$1,000,000 from foreign *Murabahah* investment and sells \$1,000,000 to the importer at €0.8905/\$1 and receives €890,500.00 from the importer.

The bank or investor's rate of return:

$$\frac{Amount\ at\ Maturity}{Initial\ Investment} - 1 = \frac{890,500}{809,524} - 1 = 10\%$$

The importer is able to hedge his/her currency risk and the bank/investor has earned a 10% return, which is also equal to the rate of return on domestic *Murabahah*, indicating the bank/investor's opportunity cost.

The above example is a simple demonstration of the construction of a synthetic currency forward contract. In a capital market where there are large numbers of users and providers of capital, a financial intermediary can serve the purpose of matching the needs of both entrepreneurs and investors. The financial intermediary that has wider access to several money and capital markets can perform the function more efficiently by standardizing the products, enhancing credit through underwriting (*Kifala*) and offering clients risk management services for a reasonable fee (in the form of *Jo'ala*).

Figure 9.1 illustrates the construction of the synthetic forward contract in our example:

Case II: Currency Swap

Currency swaps are one of the most popular applications of financial engineering. The market for currency swaps has grown exponentially since its introduction in the early 1980s. The concept behind a currency swap is to exploit one's comparative advantage in a particular market by raising capital at favorable rates and then agreeing with another party to exchange

Figure 9.1   Illustration of Creating a Synthetic Forward Contract

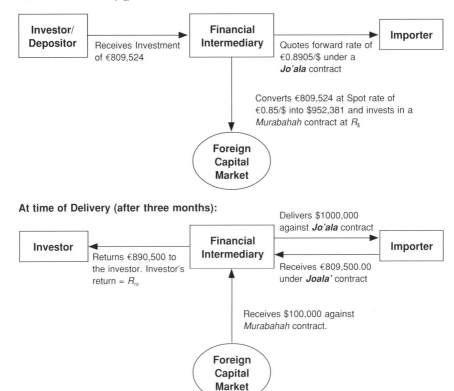

At time of contract (T_0):

Investor/Depositor → Receives Investment of €809,524 → Financial Intermediary → Quotes forward rate of €0.8905/$ under a *Jo'ala* contract → Importer

Converts €809,524 at Spot rate of €0.85/$ into $952,381 and invests in a *Murabahah* contract at $R_{\$}$

Foreign Capital Market

At time of Delivery (after three months):

Delivers $1000,000 against *Jo'ala* contract

Investor ← Returns €890,500 to the investor. Investor's return = R_{rs} ← Financial Intermediary ← Receives €809,500.00 under *Joala'* contract ← Importer

Receives $100,000 against *Murabahah* contract.

Foreign Capital Market

Note: The illustration does not take into account any transaction cost or the financial intermediary's fees.

cash flows according to a pre-determined schedule for cash flows in another currency. As an off-balance sheet instrument, a currency swap is frequently used to hedge against currency risks, to lower funding costs through arbitrage in different capital markets, and to gain access to emerging markets otherwise not accessible.

A currency swap can help an institution reduce its exposure to a particular currency by allowing it to swap existing assets or liabilities for more desirable ones. For example, an Islamic financial institution may develop a comparative advantage in the market for assets or liabilities in a particular currency and this advantage can lead to increased exposure in a particular currency. With the use of instruments like currency swaps, financial institutions can manage currency exposure and also achieve better asset/ liability management, which can ultimately reduce the overall financial risk.

Since a currency swap is an agreement to exchange cash flows according to a fixed schedule, a currency swap can also be viewed as a series of currency forward contracts for each period of the schedule. Currency swaps are currently not practiced in Islamic financial markets, mainly due to the prohibition of currency trading in the forward markets. However, there are other ways of creating currency swaps without using currency forward rates. Currency swaps were a by-product of a practice known as "parallel loans," which was followed by several corporations to avoid regulatory constraints. According to this practice, both a parent company and its foreign subsidiary borrow in their respective markets (foreign and local currencies) and then swap the proceeds internally between the parent and the subsidiary. In this way, one can view a currency swap as exchange of two bonds (loans) in different currencies.

The following two sections describe two different ways to construct a currency swap, which may be acceptable in the Islamic financial market. The first method involves a partnership with a financial intermediary and the second method is based on the exchange of *Sukuk* proceeds.

Partnership-based Currency Swap

Suppose that an Islamic financial institution (IFI) has accumulated a portfolio of *Ijarah* assets in a currency that is different from the currency of its liabilities (funding side). In order to reduce its exposure to a single currency on its assets side, the IFI would prefer to swap a portion of its portfolio into currency of liabilities in order to improve its asset/liability management. For the sake of simplicity, the example is reduced to a single *Ijarah* asset, but the principle can be extended to a pool of assets through securitization.

A financial intermediary can arrange such currency swaps through the following steps:

Step 1: The financial intermediary and the financial institution (A) agree to enter into a partnership where the financial intermediary will buy that portion of the portfolio which the financial institution would like to swap. In our case, the *Ijarah*-based asset denominated in Japanese yen (¥).

Step 2: The financial intermediary agrees to pay for the assets through equity participation certificates issued by the financial intermediary in a foreign currency, i.e., US dollars ($).

Step 3: In order to be fully hedged, the financial intermediary enters into an identical agreement with another financial institution (B), which is holding an *Ijarah* asset in the foreign currency ($) and desires to swap its assets to ¥. Party A and B exchange the principal amounts in the respective currencies equal to the respective asset values at the time of the settlement.

Step 4: All future cash flows of party (A) in ¥ will be passed on to the financial intermediary as part of the partnership agreement.

Step 5: All future cash flows of party (B) in $ will be passed on to the financial intermediary as part of the partnership agreement.

Step 6: At each future cash flow date, the financial intermediary will pass ¥ cash flows which it received from party (A) to party (B). At the same time, the financial intermediary will pass all $ cash flows which it received from party (B) to party (A). This will effectively convert each party's assets from one currency to the other. At maturity, the principal amounts equal to asset values will be exchanged back in the original currencies.

Figure 9.2 illustrates the flows and the role played by the financial intermediary, who earns fee income for arranging and servicing this agreement.

Figure 9.2   Illustration of the Setting Up of a Currency Swap

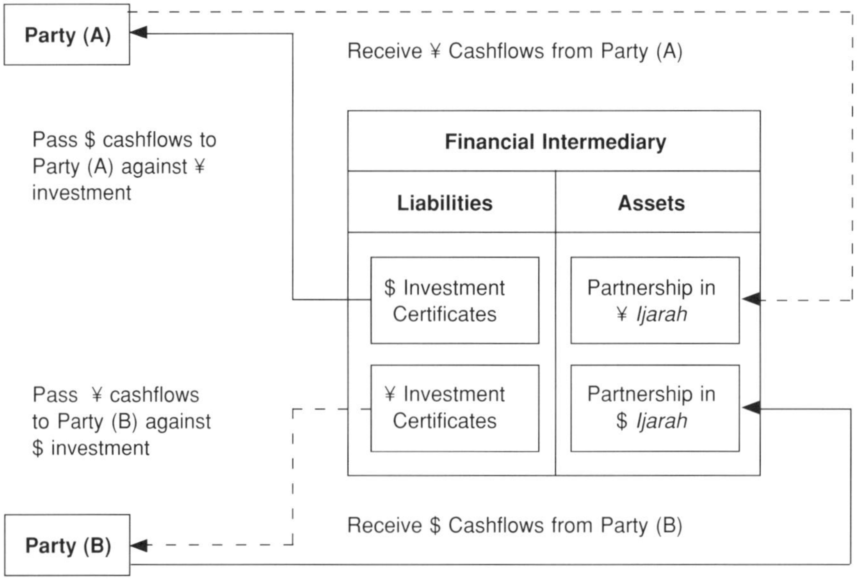

The main difference between this swap agreement and a conventional currency swap is that the financial intermediary becomes a partner in the assets of each financial institution and the cash flows are fully backed by the cash flows on each underlying asset. Whereas in the case of a conventional currency swap, the financial intermediary underwrites the credit risk only, in the Islamic version, the financial intermediary backs each agreement with a real asset in addition to underwriting the credit risk.

While the above example is a simple case to demonstrate the concept, there are practical issues with this approach. For example, finding assets of the same maturity is not easy. Also, finding assets that are of equivalent value and are of the same maturity is also difficult. One way to reduce this problem is to collect a pool of assets of similar maturity and to securitize the assets through a *Sukuk* issuance, which can be swapped as one security. This idea is further refined in the second method.

Sukuk-based Currency Swap

As mentioned earlier, a currency swap can be viewed as two parallel streams of cash flows from two bonds in two different currencies which the parties agree to swap. Since Islamic bonds, *Sukuk*, are similar to conventional bonds in terms of payoffs, a currency swap can be constructed by utilizing the structure of *Sukuk*.

For example, suppose party A is able to raise funds through *Sukuk* in ¥ at attractive rates, since it is well established and well-known in ¥ capital markets. However, its funding objectives are to borrow in $ to match its liabilities but its cost of funding in $ is relatively higher. At the same time, party B is able to raise funds through *Sukuk* in $ market at attractive rates due to its established track record and credit standing, but its funding objectives are to borrow in ¥. Following the theory of comparative advantage, both parties issue a *Sukuk* in the respective markets, where they have the comparative advantage and then agree to swap cash flows to achieve their respective funding objectives.

The following steps can be taken to create a currency swap using *Ijarah*-based *Sukuk*:

At the time of settlement (T_0):

Step 1: Party A issues an *Ijarah Sukuk* in ¥, and party B issues an *Ijarah Sukuk* in $. *Ijarah Sukuk* is selected in this case to benefit from the possibility of trading *Ijarah*-based *Sukuk* in the secondary market. Otherwise, if a *Salam*-base *Sukuk* is used, it is not permissible to trade it in the secondary market.

Step 2:   With the help of a financial intermediary, both parties agree to enter into a currency swap where party A promises to take party B's liability in $ and party B promises to take party A's liability in ¥. At the time of settlement, both parties exchange the proceeds from the *Sukuk* which each party received from the market, i.e., party A passes ¥ proceeds to party B and party B passes $ proceeds to party A.

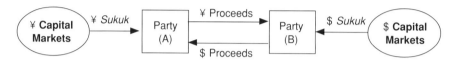

At each *Sukuk* coupon payment:

Step 3:   At each coupon period, party A pays $ coupons on party B's *Sukuk* and receives ¥ cash flows from party B, which are used to pay to the *Sukuk* investors. Similarly, party B pays ¥ to party A in exchange for $ coupon from party A, which are passed on to the *Sukuk* investors.

At the time of Maturity (*T*):

Step 4:   The principal amounts of *Sukuk* in respective currencies are exchanged. Party A receives ¥ principal from party B, which is used to pay off ¥ *Sukuk* issued by party B. Similarly, party B receives $ principal from party A which it used to pay back the $ *Sukuk*.

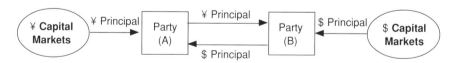

Case III: Rate of Return Swap

The interest rate swap market is the largest over-the-counter (OTC) derivative market, which indicates the importance and prevalence of this instrument. The idea behind an interest rate swap is to exchange cash flows in the same currency according to a pre-determined schedule. The main purposes of entering into an interest rate swap agreement are to lower the cost of funding, to enhance yield, or to manage the interest rate risk. The most common interest rate swap is a fixed-to-floating interest rate swap, where one party agrees to swap fixed rate coupon payments against receipt of floating rate coupon payments for a pre-determined notional amount.

The concept described in Case II to develop currency swaps using *Sukuk* can be applied to developing an instrument similar to the rate of return swap in Islamic finance with the main difference being that parties will agree to exchange the rate of return on one asset with another instead of exchanging interest rates. Rate of return swaps are different from currency swaps, in that there is no exchange of principal since the cash flows belong to the same currency. Note that *Ijarah*-based *Sukuk* are suitable for constructing a rate of return swap, since *Ijarah Sukuk* are available in the market in both fixed and floating return format.

A fixed-to-floating rate of return swap can be constructed as follows:

Step 1: Party (A) has a comparative advantage in raising funds through fixed rate *Sukuk*, but it would like to convert this fixed rate liability into a floating rate liability to match its assets. Similarly, party (B) has a comparative advantage in raising funds through floating rate *Sukuk*, but would prefer to have a fixed rate liability to match its assets.

Step 2: Party (A) decides to issue fixed rate *Sukuk* and party (B) issues a floating rate *Sukuk*. Both parties enter into an agreement to exchange cash flows on the coupon dates. This agreement to exchange cash flows could be an agreement to assume the other party's liability. Since both *Sukuk* have the same amount of proceeds in the same currency, there is no exchange of principal cash flows.

Step 3: On each coupon period, party (A) pays floating rate payments to party (B) against receipt of fixed rate coupons, which are ultimately passed on to pay the *Sukuk* holders. For party (A), the net effect is a floating rate liability. Similarly, party (B) pays fixed coupons against receipt of floating coupons from party (A), which are passed on to the holders of the floating rate *Sukuk*.

Step 4: At maturity, no principal exchange takes place between party (A) and party (B). Both parties make payments to their *Sukuk* holders.

Example: Cost saving through interest rate swap

Costs before Swap	Party (A)	Party (B)
Fixed Rate *Sukuk*:	5%	5.5%
Floating Rate *Sukuk*:	[Islamic Index] +25 bps	[Islamic Index] –25 bps

Based on the comparative advantage, party (A) decides to issue fixed rate *Sukuk* at 5% and party (B) decides to issue floating rate *Sukuk* at [Islamic Index]-25 bps.

Costs After Swap	Party (A)	Party (B)
Receives from counter party:	5.0%	[Islamic Index]–25 bps
Pay to counter party:	[Islamic Index] –25 bps	5.0%
Pay to *Sukuk* holders:	5%	[Islamic Index]–25 bps
Net Funding Cost:	[Islamic Index] –25 bps	5%
Net Savings (Difference in before and after swap cost):	50 basis points	50 basis points

In this example, both parties agree to exchange cash flows to match their obligations to the *Sukuk* holders. However, in reality, the party with the better credit quality tends to charge the other party with the lower credit rating an additional cost to reduce its own overall cost. Since the charging of an additional cost to assume the other party's liability may raise *Shariah* objections, no additional cost in the swap is incorporated. We leave this issue to be discussed by *Shariah* scholars.

Case IV: Development of an Islamic Benchmark

The availability of an efficient, frequently quoted and globally accessible reference rate for pricing assets and a benchmark for evaluating portfolio performance is vital to the success of today's financial markets. Islamic financial markets are no exception to this and their growth and development are similarly dependent on an efficient and stable benchmark. While Islamic financial markets have made considerable progress in the last few decades, the issue of benchmarks have received little attention and low priority so far. In the absence of a suitable equity-based benchmark compatible with the principles of the Islamic financial system, markets have often resorted to the use of interest-based benchmarks, e.g., LIBOR to determine mark-up rates in trade finance, to price assets and to evaluate portfolio performance. This practice is due to the lack of a suitable alternative.

A model developed by Haque and Mirakhor (1997) addressed the design of an equity-based index, which fully conforms to Islamic principles and can ultimately serve as a benchmark for issuing government paper.[1] Their approach is based on a simple argument, namely that government paper collateralized against its development and infrastructure projects which do qualify for equity-participation should not carry a return which is anyway less than the private sector projects of similar risk. Therefore, given an efficient index to measure the return on private sector security, governments can issue paper like the National Participation Paper (NPP) to finance its developmental projects. The return on such an index needs to be adjusted for a risk premium which would be negative for the government paper because governments are assumed to be insulated from credit and default risks.

The model argues that the principles of Islam dictate that the return on the financial sector in the economy should be determined by the return on the real sector of the economy. The return on the real sector could be derived from the expected growth of the dominant private sector productivity as it is the main contributor to a country's nominal GDP. A desirable index needs to be efficient in terms of its ability to eliminate any arbitrage opportunity, to discourage speculative behavior and to be allocationally and operationally efficient. Due to the fact that financial markets in the developing Islamic countries are not fully developed yet, an index based on a single indicator may not prove to be efficient. However, a weighted index of different indicators representing activity in domestic, international, private sector and public sector can be more robust, efficient and stable.

Figure 9.3 gives a summary of how a weighted composite index, which represents equity returns in an Islamic economy, can be constructed. The

Figure 9.3   Islamic Index representing equity returns

$$I = w_1 WI + w_2 LSI + w_3 PPI + w_4 ROG$$

where:

I = Index representing rate of return on the private sector.

w_1, w_2, w_3 and w_4 are weights for each indicator. Weights to be determined by each market to match individual market characteristics.

WI = An international stock market index such as the IFC emerging market index.

LSI = Domestic market performance index, e.g., stock market index, average q for the economy, return on equity (ROE), etc.

PPI = A weighted average of returns in commercial participation paper market as it develops.

ROG = measure of the rate of return on government investments in developmental and infrastructure projects against which government paper is issued.

inclusion of a local stock market index is natural, but not without certain reservations. Depending on the degree of the domestic stock market's depth, breadth and liquidity determining the competition and efficiency of the market, the domestic stock market index may or may not be included. In case of a shallow market, other factors influencing investment decisions such as the economy's q ratio, price earning (PE) ratio and dividend yield or return on equity (ROE), can be included.

Basing the index on the domestic stock market or local indicators alone is not recommended mainly due to the lower degree of development of domestic equity markets in Islamic countries. In order to broaden the index, it is advisable to include an external index representative of the regional or international financial environment. Given recent economic liberalization, globalization and integration of the international capital markets, it is reasonable to assume that the domestic rate of return will reflect the returns worldwide. It is desirable that the selected external index is easily monitorable, relatively stable and broadly in line with the domestic economy.

Challenges of Financial Engineering

The development of new instruments and financial engineering are not easy tasks. The success of financial engineering in conventional markets was not achieved overnight, but was the result of many years of gradual progress and preparation. Conventional markets had another advantage — the availability of a highly liquid fixed-income securities market. A steady supply of short- and long-term securities with minimal cost of entry and exit helped the development of new products in an arbitrage-free market. Innovation and product development were further boosted by advances in technology with more computing power enabling the analysts to build complex models to solve complex equations.

Islamic financial markets face several challenges in introducing the process of financial engineering. Some of these challenges are discussed below.

Theoretical Foundation

One of the major stimulants to rapid innovation in conventional financial markets was the breakthrough in the financial theory. The theories of capital structure, portfolio diversification and option pricing laid the foundation of more sophisticated solutions to complex problems. Although some theoretical work has been undertaken in Islamic finance, there are many areas such as asset pricing, risk pricing, derivatives, etc. which still need further research. Without solid theoretical work and without a full understanding of the risk/return profiles it becomes difficult to apply financial engineering.

An economist cannot solve all theoretical issues without understanding the principles of the *Shariah* or without working closely with a *Shariah* scholar. Therefore, it is essential that serious research efforts be made collectively to address the theoretical foundation of the system upon which a more sophisticated set of instruments can be built. This requires allocation of resources by all stakeholders, i.e., banks and governments, who are interested in the further growth of the industry.

Investment in Infrastructure

Development of new products and financial engineering are resource-intensive activities. All major conventional banks have dedicated departments to conduct background market research, product development, and analytical modeling. These activities demand financial and human resources, which are costly. Conventional financial institutions can justify these costs, because they are able to recover costs, in most cases, from the volume of business generated as a result of the innovative product. Costs associated with the development of new products are further increasing due to the increasing complexity of the business environment because of regulatory, accounting and reporting standards.

Islamic financial institutions are, in general, of small size and cannot afford to invest substantial funds in research and development. Due to their small size, they are unable to reap the benefits of the economies of scale. Considering the importance of financial engineering, Islamic financial institutions should seriously think about making joint efforts to develop the basic infrastructure for introducing new products. Although joint collaboration is counter intuitive since innovation leads to an institution's competitive edge, conducting basic research and development collectively may save some of the costs required to build this infrastructure individually. A good example of such collective effort could be to sponsor research in the areas of the development of analytical models, computer systems and tools to analyze the risk and return on different *Shariah*-compatible instruments.

Collaboration and Cooperation

Financial engineering is an area where Islamic financial institutions can benefit from more experienced western institutions to become more advanced and sophisticated in engineering and marketing the products to the right clients. Conventional investment banks, who have already made heavy investments in the infrastructure for developing new products, can work for, or with, Islamic financial institutions to develop products according to the requirements specified by Islamic financial institutions. Once a financial engineering shop is set, it can be used to develop different products of different risk and return profiles. In this respect, Islamic financial institutions should try to develop synergies and make collaborative efforts with conventional institutions. Islamic financial institutions can outsource the development part to conventional institutions and keep the marketing part to themselves. This division of labor can be beneficial to both the institutions.

Cross-Training

Shariah scholars play a critical role in approving new financial products. While they may be masters in *Shariah* matters, their knowledge of non-*Shariah* matters, especially of business practices, economics and finance may be limited. Today's financial institutions work in a complex business environment, with complex demands by investors and entrepreneurs. This puts the onus upon the *Shariah* scholars to be more vigilant and sympathetic to the needs of institutions and their customers. They need to assume an active role in understanding the nature of business and banking. Special training institutions can be set up to develop targeted training for *Shariah* experts in understanding non-*Shariah* issues and for non-*Shariah* experts, i.e., economists and bankers in *Shariah* matters. Such cross training will help each party to understand the other's point of view.

Standardization

Introduction of new products can benefit greatly from standardization of contracts and unification of standards across markets. *Shariah* scholars can play a positive role in the standardization of contracts and practices. Regulators can help in defining accounting, reporting and supervisory standards. This standardization can help in reducing the cost of introducing new products in different markets.

Judicial use of "Law of Necessity"

It is observed that *Shariah* scholars tend to invoke the law of necessity (*Dharoora*) to accommodate pressing demands from bankers or customers. Extreme caution should be observed in making sure that a practice allowed under the law of necessity does not become a rule. Frequent use of such exceptions may not only contaminate the essence of the system, it may also raise suspicions in the minds of those who have put their trust in the system.

Endnote

1   Nadeem ul Haque and Abbas Mirakhor, "The Design of Instruments for Government Finance in an Islamic Economy," IMF Staff Papers, October 1997.

10

Risk Management of Islamic Financial Institutions

As the banking business has changed significantly in the last two decades, the nature of the risks faced by a financial institution has also changed. Whereas two decades ago, a financial institution was primarily faced with credit and market risks only, today's financial institution is exposed to a whole array of new risks and this list is expanding. Several factors are responsible for this changed scenario. These factors are:

- **Increased Market Volatility:** Financial institutions first realized the importance of risk management after the breakdown of the Bretton Woods system of fixed exchange rates, which led to significant volatility in the foreign exchange and interest rate markets. Since then, volatility in the markets and therefore the demand for risk management products have become a permanent feature of the markets.
- **Financial Innovations:** Financial innovations and rapid developments in the derivatives market have increased the complexity of managing financial institutions. Innovative products have appeared on both sides of the balance sheet and each new product brings its own unique risk/return profile, which ultimately impacts the risk profile of the institution. The risk and return characteristics of some of the new instruments are complex and are subject to highly volatile markets, exposing banks to new or higher degrees of risks.

- **Shift in Banking Business:** There has been a permanent shift in traditional banking business, as a result of which the business has moved away from traditional lending business toward fee-earning activities. The expanded role of money and capital markets has changed the nature of intermediation by moving it away from formal institutions to direct access to the market. The emergence of institutional investors such as mutual funds has taken a significant share of the market from traditional banking business.
- **Increased Competition:** Competition in banking has increased, making the survival of small banks difficult. Small banks are unable to compete due to the increasing costs of doing business and the high costs associated with managing risks. A wave of consolidation of financial institutions was witnessed in industrial countries in the late 1990s and with larger-sized institutions, the need for risk management also became critical.
- **Regulatory Environment:** In the wake of a series of financial crises, from the Third World debt crisis of the 1980s to the East Asian crisis of the 1990s, there has been greater awareness of the need for coordinated regulation and supervision of financial institutions, with a special focus on risk measurement and management and prudential capital requirements. There is emphasis on coordinated efforts at the global level to harmonize standards, promote transparency in the system, and to combat money-laundering and financing of terrorism.

These developments have increased the need for risk measurement, management, and controls. A comprehensive framework of risk management is applicable equally to a conventional and an Islamic bank. Research and experience in the past two decades have resulted in a much deeper understanding of the issues relating to risk management and, consequently, well-established principles of risk management have emerged. The process of risk management is a two-step process. The first step is to identify the source of the risk, i.e., to identify the leading variables causing the risk. The second step is to devise methods to quantify the risk using mathematical models, in order to understand the risk profile of the instrument. Once a general framework of risk identification and management is developed, the techniques can be applied to different situations, products, instruments and institutions.

Similar to conventional banks, a robust risk management framework can also help Islamic banks reduce their exposure to risks, and enhance their ability to compete in the market. A reduction in each institution's exposure will reduce the systemic risk as well. Therefore, it is necessary that Islamic financial institutions have in place a comprehensive risk management and reporting process to identify, measure, monitor, manage, report and control different categories of risks. This process should also pay special attention to compliance with *Shariah* rules and principles.

Realizing the significance of risk management, the Islamic Financial Services Board (IFSB) — a regulatory authority for Islamic financial services — issued a comprehensive standards document on risk management in December 2005. This document identifies and discusses different risks and lists fifteen guiding principles of risk management for institutions offering Islamic financial services. Some of the key principles are provided in this chapter.

Figure 10.1 presents an overview of the risk profile of operating an Islamic Financial Institution (IFI). Risks are grouped into four broad categories: financial, business, treasury, and governance risks. While these categories are also applicable to conventional finance, there are risks specific to Islamic banks and financial institutions, arising from the different nature of the intermediation, products and constitution of the balance sheet. This list focuses on the major risks, while several lesser risks are also applicable but not discussed here.

Financial Risks

Financial risks are the exposures that result in a direct financial loss to the assets or the liabilities of a bank. In the evolution of the risk management discipline, financial risks were the first to appear in the discussion and policy making. Both conventional and Islamic financial institutions are exposed to credit and market risks, but Islamic financial institutions are also exposed to equity investment risk.

Credit Risk

Credit risk is commonly known as the potential risk that a counter party will fail to make payments on its obligations in accordance with the agreed terms. It also includes the risk arising in the settlement and clearing of the transactions. Credit risk is present in almost all of the instruments to varying degrees and there are many techniques to mitigate such risk. Traditional banking business based on lending operations is considered a credit risk business since the bank's ability to minimize credit risk is the source of its profitability. In the case of Islamic financial institutions where lending is replaced with investments

Figure 10.1   Overview of the Risk Profile of Operating an Islamic Financial Institution (IFI)

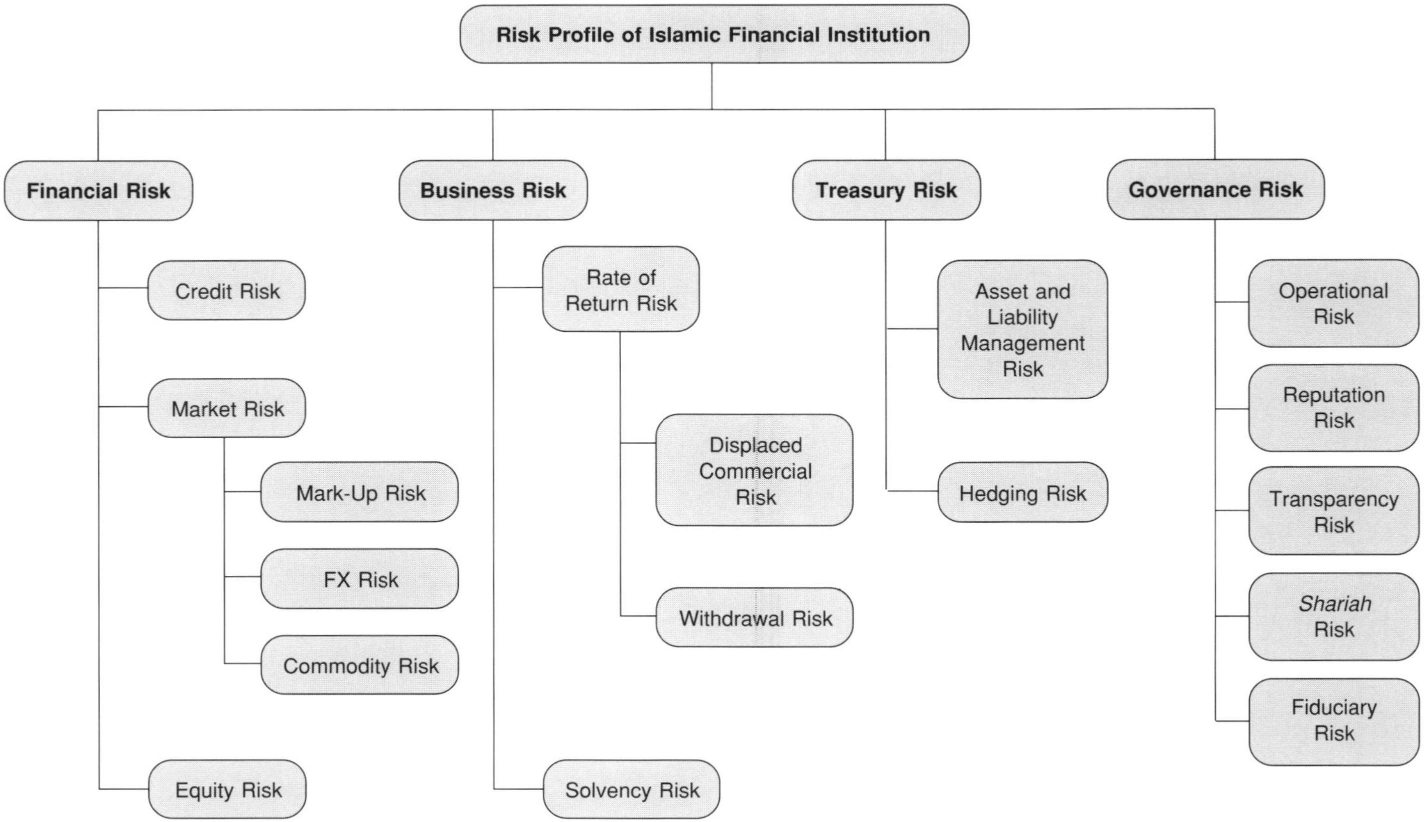

and partnerships, the importance of credit risk management becomes more critical. The unique characteristics of the financial instruments practiced by Islamic banks have special credit risks such as the following:

- In the case of *Murabahah* transactions, Islamic banks are exposed to credit risks when the bank delivers the asset to the client but does not receive payment from the client in time. In the case of a non-binding *Murabahah* where the client has a right to refuse the delivery of the product purchased by the bank, the bank is further exposed to price and market risks.
- In *Bay' al-Salam* or *Istisna* contracts, the bank is exposed to the risk of failure to supply on time or to supply at all, or failure to supply the quality of goods as contractually specified. Such failure could result in a delay or default in payment, or in delivery of the product, and can expose Islamic banks to financial losses of income as well as capital.
- In the case of *Mudarabah* investments, where the Islamic bank enters into the *Mudarabah* contract as *Rabbul-mal* (principal) with an external *mudarib* (agent), in addition to the typical principal-agent problems, the Islamic bank is exposed to an enhanced credit risk on the amounts advanced to the *mudarib*. The nature of the *Mudarabah* contract is such that it does not give the bank appropriate rights to monitor the *mudarib* (agent) or to participate in the management of the project, which makes assessment and management of the credit risk difficult. The bank is not in a position to know and decide how the activities of the *mudarib* can be monitored accurately, especially if claims of losses are made. This risk is especially present in markets where information asymmetry is high and there is low transparency in financial disclosure by the *mudarib*.

Credit risk management for Islamic banks is further complicated by some additional externalities. In case of default by the counterparty, Islamic banks are prohibited from charging any accrued interest or imposing any penalty, except in the case of deliberate procrastination. This can be misused by clients who may delay the payment, since they know that the bank will not charge any extra charge or payment. During the delay, the bank's capital is not productive and the bank's investors/depositors are not earning any income. Another example is where the bank's share in the capital invested through a *Mudarabah* or *Musharakah* contract is transformed into a debt obligation in the case of proven negligence or misconduct of the *mudarib* or the *Musharakah*'s managing partner. As a result, the rules to recover a debt

---

IFSB Principles of Credit Risk:

Principle 2.1: [Islamic Financial Institutions] shall have in place a **strategy** for financing, using the various Islamic instruments in compliance with *Shariah*, whereby it recognises the potential credit exposures that may arise at different stages of the various financing agreements.

Principle 2.2: [Islamic Financial Institutions] shall carry out a **due diligence review** in respect of counterparties prior to deciding on the choice of an appropriate Islamic financing instrument.

Principle 2.3: [Islamic Financial Institutions] shall have in place appropriate **methodologies for measuring and reporting the credit risk exposures arising** under each Islamic financing instrument.

Principle 2.4: [Islamic Financial Institutions] shall have in place *Shariah*-compliant **credit risk mitigating techniques** appropriate for each Islamic financing instrument.

---

are applied, which are different from the rules of *Mudarabah* and *Musharakah* investment.

Risk mitigation techniques used by Islamic banks for credit risk do not differ much from those used by conventional banks. Risk measurement can be achieved by maintaining good quality data on past performances of the counterparty and by determining the probability of default. In many developing countries where there are no formal institutions to maintain credit data, banks often rely on the client's track record with the bank. Often, information about the creditworthiness of the client is gathered through informal sources and through local community networks. However, in developed economies credit data is accessible through rating agencies and disclosures of public companies.

Using collateral and pledges as security against credit risk is a common practice among all Islamic banks. The bank might ask the client to post additional collateral before entering into a *Murabahah* transaction. In some cases, the subject matter of *Murabahah* is accepted as collateral. Posting collateral as security is not without difficulties, especially in the developing countries. Typical problems include the illiquidity of the collateral or the inability of the bank to sell the collateral, difficulties in determining the fair market value on a periodic basis, and most importantly is the legal hindrances and obstacles in taking possession of the collateral. Due to weak legal institutions and slow processing, it becomes difficult for the bank to claim the collateral. In addition to collateral, personal and institutional guarantees are also accepted to minimize credit risk.

Market Risk

Market risk for a financial institution arises in the form of unfavorable price movements such as yields (rate of return risk), benchmark rates (interest rate risk), foreign exchange rates (FX risk), equity and commodity prices (price risk) which has a potential impact on the financial value of an asset over the life of the contract. Islamic banks are further exposed to market risk due to the volatility in the values of tradable, marketable or leaseable assets. The risks relate to the current and future volatility of market values of specific assets due to different risk factors such as following:

Mark-up Risk: Islamic banks are exposed to mark-up risk as their mark-up rate used in *Murabahah* and other trade-financing instruments is fixed for the duration of the contract while the benchmark rate may change. This means that the prevailing mark-up rate in the market may increase beyond the rate the bank had fixed in a contract and therefore the bank is unable to benefit from increased rates. This is especially applicable to the *Murabahah* contract where the mark-up rate is fixed at the time of the contract. As previously mentioned, in the absence of any Islamic index of rate of return, Islamic banks often use LIBOR as the benchmark, which aligns their market risk closely with the movements in LIBOR rates.

Price Risk: In the case of *Bay' al-Salam*, Islamic banks are exposed to commodity price volatility during the period between the delivery of the commodity and the sale of the commodity at prevailing market price. This risk is similar to the market risk of a forward contract if it is not hedged properly. In order to hedge its position, the bank may enter into a parallel (off-setting) *Bay' al-Salam* contract. In such cases the bank is exposed to price risk if there is default on the first contract and the bank is obligated to deliver on the second contract.

Leased Asset Value Risk: In the case of an operating *Ijarah*, the bank is exposed to market risk due to a reduction in the residual value of the leased asset at the expiry of the lease term or in the case of early termination due to default, over the life of the contract.

FX Risk: Foreign exchange rate movement is another transaction risk arising from the deferred trading nature of some of contracts offered by Islamic banks, as the value of the currency in which receivables are due may depreciate or the currency in which payables are due may appreciate.

Securities Price Risk: With an increasing market for Islamic bonds (*Sukuk*), Islamic banks invest a portion of their assets in marketable securities (*Sukuk*). However, the prices of such marketable securities are exposed to current yields. Similar to a fixed-income security, the prices go down as yields go up and vice-versa. Islamic banks holding such securities will be exposed to volatility in yields, unless they hold the security till maturity. Furthermore, the secondary market for such securities may not be very liquid and therefore Islamic banks are exposed to distorted prices in an illiquid market.

IFSB Principle of Market Risk

Principle 4.1: [Islamic Financial Institutions] shall have in place an appropriate **framework for market risk management** (including reporting) in respect of all assets held, including those that do not have a ready market and/or are exposed to high price volatility.

Equity Investment Risk

Islamic financial institutions are exposed to equity investment risk in profit-and-loss sharing investments on the assets side. These include partnership-based *Mudarabah* and *Musharakah* investments. Typical examples of equity investments are holdings of shares in the stock market, private equity investments, equity participation in specific projects or syndication investment.

This risk is somewhat unique to Islamic financial institutions, considering that conventional commercial banks do not invest on the basis of equity-based assets. Equity investments can lead to volatility in the financial institution's earnings due to liquidity, credit, and market risks associated with equity holdings. Although there is credit risk in equity-based assets as discussed earlier, there is also considerable financial risk of losing capital invested due to business losses.

Some of the distinct features of equity investment risk are:

- The nature of equity investment requires enhanced monitoring measures to reduce informational asymmetries. These include proper financial disclosures, closer involvement with the project, transparency in reporting and supervision during all phases of the project from appraisals to completion. Therefore, Islamic banks need to play an active role in the process of monitoring, in order to mitigate equity investment risk.

- Both *Mudarabah* and *Musharakah* are profit-and-loss sharing contracts and are subject to loss of capital despite proper monitoring. The degree of risk in equity investments is relatively higher than in other investments and, therefore, Islamic banks should take extreme care in evaluating and selecting the projects, in order to minimize any potential losses.
- Equity investments other than stock market investments do not have secondary markets and therefore an early exit is costly. Illiquidity of such investments can cause financial losses to the bank.
- Equity investment may not generate a steady income, and capital gain might be the only source of return. This unscheduled nature of cash flows can pose difficulties for the Islamic banks in forecasting and managing the cash flows.

IFSB Principle of Equity Investment Risk

Principle 3.1: [Islamic Financial Institutions] shall have in place appropriate strategies, risk management and reporting processes in respect of the **risk characteristics of equity investments, including *Mudarabah* and *Musharakah* investments**.

Principle 3.2: [Islamic Financial Institutions] shall ensure that their **valuation methodologies** are appropriate and consistent, and shall assess the potential impacts of their methods on profit calculations and allocations. The methods shall be mutually agreed between the institution and the *mudarib* and/or *Musharakah* partners.

Principle 3.3: [Islamic Financial Institutions] shall define and establish the **exit strategies** in respect of their equity investment activities, including extension and redemption conditions for *Mudarabah* and *Musharakah* investments, subject to the approval of the institution's *Shariah* Board.

Business Risks

Business risks are associated with a bank's business environment, including macroeconomic and policy concerns, legal and regulatory factors and the overall financial sector infrastructure such as payment systems and the auditing profession. Business risk also includes the risk of becoming insolvent due to insufficient capital to continue operations. While Islamic financial institutions are exposed to the regular business environment, solvency, and financial sector infrastructure risks, they are particularly exposed to one specific business risk, i.e., the rate of return risk.

Rate of Return Risk

The rate of return risk stems from the uncertainty in the returns earned by Islamic banks on their assets. This uncertainty can cause a divergence from the expectations investment account holders have on the liabilities side. The larger the divergence, the bigger the rate of return risk. Another way of looking at this risk is the risk generally associated with overall balance sheet exposures where mismatches arise between assets and balances of the depositors. For example, an Islamic bank is expected to make 5% on its assets, which will be passed on to the investors/depositors. Meanwhile, current market rates rise to 6%, which is higher than what the bank may make on its investment, the investment account holders/depositors may also expect to earn 6% on their deposits.

The rate of return risk is different from the interest rate risk in two ways. Firstly, since conventional commercial banks operate on interest-based fixed income securities on the assets side, there is less uncertainty in the rate of return earned on their investments if investments are held till maturity. Since Islamic banks have a mix of mark-up based and equity-based investments, this uncertainty is higher. Secondly, the return on deposits in conventional banks is pre-determined; in contrast, the returns on deposits in Islamic banks are expected but not pre-agreed. In addition, returns on some of the investments, i.e., those based on equity partnership by Islamic banks, are not known accurately until the end of the investment period. Islamic banks have to wait for the results of their investment to determine the level of return their investment account holders/depositors will earn. If, during this period, the prevailing yield levels or expected rates of returns in the market change, then the investors may expect similar yields from the bank.

It therefore becomes the responsibility of Islamic banks to manage the expectations of their investment account holders/depositors, which makes the rate of return risk also a strategic risk issue as part of the business environment. Two sub-categories of rate of return risk have been identified which are discussed here:

Displaced Commercial Risk: This risk was first identified by the Accounting and Auditing Organization of Islamic Financial Institutions (AAOIFI) as the risk when an Islamic bank is under pressure for paying its investment depositors a rate of return higher than what should be payable under the "actual" terms of the investment contract. This may be due to the fact that the bank has underperformed during a period and was unable to generate adequate profits for distribution to the account holders.

To mitigate the displaced commercial risk, Islamic banks may decide to waive their portion of profits in order to retain their deposits and thus dissuade the depositors from withdrawing their funds. Islamic banks often engage in such *self-imposed* practice to induce their investment account holders not to withdraw their funds in the bank for investing them elsewhere. An extreme example is the International Islamic Bank for Investment & Development in Egypt, which distributed all of its profits to investment account holders while the shareholders received nothing from the mid to late 1980s (Warde (2000)). In 1988, the bank distributed to its depositors an amount exceeding its profits, and the difference appeared in the bank's accounts as "loss carried forward." The practice of foregoing part or all of its shareholders' profits may adversely affect its own capital, which can lead to insolvency risk in extreme cases.

The experience gained from the abovementioned self-imposed practices to mitigate the displaced risk has led to the development of two standard practices in the industry. The first practice is the maintenance of a Profit Equalization Reserve (PER) by the financial institution. This reserve is funded by setting aside a portion of the gross income before deducting the bank's own share (as *mudarib*). The objective of the reserve is to maintain a cushion to ensure smooth future returns and to increase the owners' equity for bearing future shocks. Similar to PER, an Investment Risk Reserve (IRR) is maintained out of the income of investment account holders/ depositors after allocating the bank's share, in order to dampen the effects of the risk of future investment losses. It has been suggested that the basis for computing the amounts to be appropriated should be pre-defined and fully disclosed.

IFSB Principles of Rate of Return Risk

Principle 6.1: [Islamic Financial Institution] shall establish a comprehensive risk management and reporting process to assess the potential impacts of market factors affecting **rates of return on assets in comparison with the expected rates of return for investment account holders (IAH)**.

Principle 6.2: [Islamic Financial Institution] shall have in place an appropriate framework for managing **displaced commercial risk**, where applicable.

The practice of maintaining reserves to ensure smooth income over a period of time is becoming a common practice, but this practice has attracted objections as well. While this practice is in alignment with prudent risk management, it raises a governance issue that needs attention. Firstly, limited disclosure of such reserves makes investment account holders uneasy. Secondly, investment account holders do not have the rights to influence the use of such reserves and verify the exposure of overall investments. Thirdly, investment account holders with long-term investment objectives may welcome this practice, but investors with a short-term view may feel that they are subsidizing the returns of the long-term investors. Finally, some banks require investment account holders to waive their rights on these reserves.

Islamic financial institutions should standardize the practice and the rights of investment account holders to these reserves should be clearly stated and explained to the depositors. One suggestion is that deduction from the profits belonging to investment account holders should apply only to long-term depositors who are more likely to be exposed and not to every depositor — including short-term depositors — who are not exposed to such risk.

Withdrawal Risk

Another type of business risk is "withdrawal risk." It mainly results from the competitive pressures an IFI faces from its existing Islamic or conventional counterparts. An Islamic bank could be exposed to the risk of withdrawals by its depositors as a result of a lower rate of return, compared to what its competitors may offer. Such competition may come from other Islamic banks or from conventional banks with Islamic windows. If an Islamic bank is run inefficiently and keeps producing lower returns, it will lead to withdrawals by the depositors, which could eventually erode the franchise value of the bank.

Treasury Risks

Treasury risks include risks arising from the management of the financial resources of the financial institutions in terms of cash management, equity management, short-term liquidity management, and finally, assets and liabilities management (ALM). Generally, the function of risk management is part of the treasury of the financial institution and therefore any inability to manage risks properly can be a risk itself. Typical treasury risks, which are critical for an Islamic financial institution, are liquidity, assets and liabilities management (ALM), and hedging risks as discussed below.

Liquidity Risk

The treasury management function of Islamic financial institutions becomes a challenging task affecting the performance of Islamic banks, since they are particularly vulnerable to liquidity risk, given their limited opportunities to access external funds to meet their obligations. Liquidity risk as it applies to Islamic banks can be of two types; the first type is of lack of liquidity where the financial institution is constrained by illiquid assets to meets its liabilities and financial obligations. The second type is where, unlike conventional banks, Islamic banks do not have access to borrow or raise funds at reasonable cost, when needed.

Liquidity risk also impairs the bank's ability to match the maturity of assets and liabilities, and to be able to perform active portfolio management. Such risk results from the mismatch between the maturities of the two sides of the balance sheet, creating either a surplus of cash that is required to be invested or a shortage of cash that is required to be funded. Lack of liquidity adversely affects the bank's ability to manage portfolios in a diversified fashion and its ability to enter or exit the market when needed. Due to the following reasons, liquidity risk can be considered as one of the most critical risks faced by Islamic banks.

- Limited availability of *Shariah*-compatible money market and intra-bank market is the leading cause of the liquidity risk. Prohibition by *Shariah* law from borrowing on the basis of interest and the absence of an active inter-bank money market have restricted Islamic banks' options to efficiently manage their liquidity positions. Conventional banks have access to borrowing from overnight to extended short-tem maturity through well-developed and efficient inter-bank markets. This access to short-term borrowing is vital for meeting a financial institution's short-term cash flow needs.
- Shallow secondary markets are another source of the liquidity risk. There are limited financial instruments that can be traded in the secondary market. There are certain limitations imposed by the *Shariah* on the trading of financial claims, unless such claims are linked to a real asset. Therefore, there is a need for the development of asset-backed tradable securities such as *Sukuk*. Even where there are instruments available, the number of market participants is limited.

- Typical avenues of liquidity management available to conventional banks, namely the inter-bank market, secondary market debt instruments, and discount windows from the lender of last resort (central bank) are all considered as *Riba* (interest) based and therefore, not acceptable.

- Certain characteristics of some Islamic instruments can also lead to liquidity risks for Islamic banks. For example, cancellation risks in *Murabahah*, or non-permissibility of trading of *Murabahah* or *Bay' al-Salam* based contracts since these are financial claims and therefore can be traded only at par, pose liquidity problems.

- Islamic banks have a considerable amount of funds in current accounts which are demand deposits and can be withdrawn at any time. Repayment of principal amounts deposited by current account holders is guaranteed by the bank without any rights to a share in the profits. Islamic banks may be investing only a small fraction of the current account holders' funds and may be maintaining high levels of liquidity in the form of idle cash in the absence of illiquid short-term instruments.

IFSB Principles of Liquidity Risk:

Principle 5.1: [Islamic Financial Institution] shall have in place a liquidity management framework (including reporting) taking into account separately and on an overall basis their **liquidity exposures in respect of each category** of current accounts, unrestricted and restricted investment accounts.

Principle 5.2: [Islamic Financial Institution] shall undertake liquidity risk commensurate with their ability to have sufficient **recourse to *Shariah-compliant* funds** to mitigate such risk.

The above factors have raised Islamic banks' exposure to liquidity risk, and have adversely affected their profitability by limiting their ability to invest their capital in long-term and illiquid but more profitable assets. Several developments have taken place with a view to meeting this challenge. First, the introduction of *Sukuk* can provide the foundation for the development of secondary markets. The Central bank of Sudan has also introduced *Shariah*-compatible securities to provide liquidity in the market. Second, progress has been made in establishing an institutional framework to address this problem. In this respect, the establishment of the International Islamic Financial Market (IIFM) and the Liquidity Management Center

(LMC) are vital steps toward a more efficient management of Islamic banks' liquidity needs.

Malaysia has also taken significant steps to promote Islamic banks and to provide solutions to reduce liquidity risk. The central bank, Bank Negara Malaysia, introduced the Islamic Inter-bank Money Market (IIMM) in early 1994. The activities of the IIMM included the purchase and sale of Islamic financial instruments among market participants (including the central bank), inter-bank investment activities through the *Mudarabah* Inter bank Investment (MII) Scheme and a check clearing and settlement system through an Islamic Inter-bank Check Clearing System (IICCS). The Islamic financial instruments that are currently being traded in the IIMM on the basis of *Bay' al-Dayn*, are the Green bankers acceptances, accepted Islamic bills, Islamic mortgage bonds and Islamic private debt securities. In addition, financial institutions can sell Government Investment Issues (GIIs) to the central bank, as and when required, to meet their liquidity needs. GIIs are government securities issued on an Islamic basis, which financial institutions can also buy from the central bank, depending on the availability.

It is important to note that whereas the contract of *Bay' al-Dayn* (sale of debt) is commonly accepted and practiced in the Malaysian financial markets, this practice is not accepted by a majority of *Shariah* scholars outside Malaysia who maintain that debt can be traded only at par. If trade is not at par, it opens the door for *Riba* (interest). *Shariah* scholars in other jurisdictions need to become proactive in finding solutions for reducing the liquidity risk.

Assets Liabilities Management (ALM) Risk

Assets and liabilities management (ALM) risk is a balance sheet mismatch risk resulting from the difference in maturity terms and the conditions of a bank's portfolio on its assets and liabilities sides.

According to theory, Islamic banks are less exposed to assets and liabilities mismatch, and therefore to instability, than their conventional counterparts. This comparative advantage is rooted in the "pass-through" nature of Islamic banks that act as agents for investors/depositors and all profits and losses are passed through to the investors/depositors. In addition, the risk-sharing feature where banks participate in the risks of their counter-parties and investment depositors share the risks of the banking business, plays a critical role. Direct market discipline, one of the three main pillars recently emphasized by the Basel Committee in enhancing the stability of the international financial market, is embedded in this risk-sharing principle.

Following the theoretical model, any negative shock to an Islamic bank's asset returns is absorbed by both shareholders and investors/depositors,

While depositors in the conventional system have a fixed claim on the returns to the bank's assets as they get paid a pre-determined interest rate in addition to their guaranteed principal irrespective of the bank's profitability on its assets side, holders of profit-sharing investment accounts in the Islamic system share in the bank's profits and losses alongside the shareholders, and hence are exposed to the risk of losing all or part of their initial investment. Therefore, the assets and liabilities are matched as a result of the "pass-through" structure.

In the prevailing practice, however, the risk-sharing and pass-through features are not fully followed, which in turn creates unwanted assets and liabilities mismatch risks. For example, rather than strictly sharing profits and losses with depositors, the practice of distributions of profits even if there are no or low profits creates distortions and puts strains on the equity shareholders (capital providers). Further mismatches of assets and liabilities arise from the heavy dependence on short-term trade financing and limited use of partnership based agreements such as *Mudarabah* and *Musharakah*. The outcome is the dominance in the asset portfolios of short-term, low-profit and fixed-income-like assets, i.e., mark-up based trade financing which limit the funds that can be invested in longer-term, more profitable but riskier assets. In short, although in theory there should not be any mismatch in assets and liabilities of an Islamic bank, current practices have introduced distortions which are exposing the banks to assets and liabilities mismatch risk, especially when the banks do not have any liquid assets to hedge such risks.

Hedging Risk

Hedging risk is the risk of failure to mitigate and manage different types of risks. This increases the bank's overall risk exposure. In addition to non-availability of derivative products to hedge risks, illiquid, non-existent and shallow secondary markets are other sources of the increasing hedging risk of the Islamic banks.

Governance Risks

The importance of governance and the risks associated with poor governance have recently attracted the attention of researchers and policy-makers. Governance risk refers to the risk arising from a failure in governing the institution, negligence in conducting business and meeting contractual obligations, and from a weak internal and external institutional environment, including legal risk, whereby banks are unable to enforce their contracts.

Operational Risk

A related type of governance risk is operational risk, defined as the risk of loss resulting from the inadequacy or failure of internal processes, as related to people and systems or from external risks. Operational risk also includes the risk of failure of technology, systems and analytical models. It is argued that operational risks are likely to be significant in the case of Islamic banks due to their specific contractual features and the general legal environment. Specific aspects that could increase operational risks in Islamic banks include the following:

- Cancellation risks in the non-binding *Murabahah* and *Istisna* contracts,
- Failure of the internal control systems to detect and manage potential problems in the operational processes and back office functions, and technical risks of various sorts,
- Difficulties in enforcing Islamic contracts in a broader legal environment,
- Need to maintain and manage commodity inventories often in illiquid markets, and
- Costs and risks in monitoring equity type contracts and the associated legal risks.

People risk is another type of operational risk arising from incompetence or fraud, which exposes Islamic banks to potential losses. For instance, an internal control problem cost the Dubai Islamic Bank US$50 million in 1998 when a bank official did not conform to the bank's credit terms. This also resulted in a run on its deposits of US$138 million, representing 7% of the bank's total deposits, in just one day. Warde (2000)

Operational risk is considered high on the list of exposures of Islamic banks. A survey conducted by Khan and Ahmed (2001) shows that the managers of Islamic banks perceived operational risk as the most critical risk after mark-up risk. The survey finds that operational risk is lower in fixed income assets of *Murabahah* and *Ijarah* and one of the highest in deferred sale contracts of *Salam* and *Istisna*. The relatively higher rankings of the instruments indicate that banks find these contracts complex and difficult to implement.

Fiduciary Risk

Fiduciary risk is the risk that arises from an institution's failure to perform in accordance with explicit and implicit standards applicable to its fiduciary responsibilities. Fiduciary risk leads to the risk of facing legal recourse action in a situation where the bank breaches its fiduciary responsibility toward depositors and shareholders. As fiduciary agents, Islamic banks are expected to act in the best interests of investors/depositors and shareholders. If and when there is divergence in the objectives of investors and shareholders, and the actions of the bank, the bank is exposed to fiduciary risk.

The following are some examples of fiduciary risk:

- In the case of a partnership based investment in the form of *Mudarabah* and *Musharakah* on the assets side, the bank is expected to perform adequate screening and monitoring of projects and any deliberate or even non-deliberate negligence in evaluating and monitoring the project can lead to fiduciary risk. It becomes incumbent upon management to perform due diligence before committing the investors/depositors' funds.
- Mismanagement of funds of current account holders, which are accepted on trust (*Amanah*) basis, can expose the bank to fiduciary risk as well. It is a common practice of Islamic banks to utilize current account holders' funds without any obligation to share the profits with them. However, in a case of heavy losses on the investments financed by current account holders' funds, the depositors can lose confidence in the bank and this can lead to their taking legal recourse.
- Mismanagement in governing the business, incurring unnecessary expenses, or allocation of excessive expenses to investment account holders is a breach of the implicit contract to act in a transparent fashion.

Fiduciary risk can lead to dire consequences for a bank. First, it can cause reputation risk creating panic among depositors, who may decide to withdraw their funds. Secondly, legal recourse may lead to charging the bank a penalty or compensation which can result in a financial loss. Thirdly, it can impact negatively on the market price of shareholders' equity. Fourthly, it can impact the bank's cost and access to liquidity. Finally, it may lead to insolvency if the bank is unable to meet the demands of the current and investment account holders.

Transparency Risk

Transparency is defined as "the public disclosure of reliable and timely information that enables users of that information to make an accurate assessment of a bank's financial condition and performance, business activities, risk profile and risk management practices." Accordingly, lack of transparency creates the risk of incurring losses due to bad decisions based on incomplete or inaccurate information. Islamic banks are exposed to transparency risk due to the practice of non-standard accounting and financial reporting of Islamic financial instruments, which are different from conventional instruments and therefore require different conventions of reporting to truly reflect the financial picture. Transparency also demands that all banks in the system use a uniform set of standards, which is not the current practice.

Shariah Risk

Shariah risk is related to the structure and functioning of the *Shariah* boards at the institutional and systemic level. This risk is of two types; the first is due to non-standard practices in respect of different contracts in different jurisdictions and the second is due to failure to comply with *Shariah* rules. Different adoption of *Shariah* rules sometimes results in differences in financial reporting, auditing and accounting treatments by Islamic banks. For instance, while some *Shariah* scholars consider the terms of a *Murabahah* or *Istisna* contract to be binding on the buyer, others argue that the buyer has the option to decline even after placing an order and paying the commitment fee. While each practice is acceptable by different schools of thought, the bank's risk is higher in non-binding cases and it may lead to potential litigation problems in case of unsettled transactions.

Similar to fiduciary risk, banks are exposed to the risk of non-compliance with the *Shariah* rules and principles determined by the *Shariah* board or the relevant body in the jurisdiction. The nature of the relationship between the bank and the investors/depositors is not only of an agent and principal, but it is also based on an implicit trust between the two that the agent will respect the desires of the principal to fully comply with the *Shariah*. This relationship distinguishes Islamic banking from conventional banking and is the sole justification for the existence of the Islamic banks. In case the bank is unable to maintain this trust and the bank's actions lead to non-compliance with the *Shariah*, the bank is exposed to the risk of breaking the confidence of the investors/depositors. Breaching the trust and confidence of investors/depositors can lead to dire consequences, including the withdrawal and insolvency risk. Therefore, the bank should give high priority to ensuring transparency in compliance with the *Shariah* and take necessary actions to avoid any non-compliance.

It has been suggested by some *Shariah* scholars that if a bank fails to act in accordance with the *Shariah* rules, the transaction should be considered null and void from the *Shariah*'s point of view and any income derived from it should not be included in the profits to be distributed to the investors/ depositors.

Reputation Risk

Reputation risk or "headline risk" is the risk that the trust of the clients of Islamic bank is damaged due to irresponsible actions or behavior of management. Although the fiduciary and *Shariah* risks also stem from negligence and non-compliance, reputation risk is also a risk because irresponsible behavior by a single institution can taint the reputation of other Islamic banks in the industry. Negative publicity can have a significant impact on an institution's market share, profitability and liquidity. The Islamic financial services industry is a relatively young industry and a single case of failed institution can give a bad name to all others who may not be engaged in any such irresponsible behavior. Nevertheless, all Islamic banks in a given market are exposed to such risk. Close collaboration among financial institutions, standardization of contracts and practices, self-examination, and establishment of industry associations are some of the steps to mitigate reputation risk.

Risk Management Framework

The complex nature of risks faced by Islamic banks requires a comprehensive risk management, risk reporting and risk control framework. A survey of Islamic financial institutions inquiring into their perception of different types of risks for different modes of financing shows that the risk level is considered elevated in most of the cases. Results of a survey of several Islamic banks are given in Table 10.1. High perception of risks may also be an indication of the low degree of active risk management as also absence of risk control through internal processes and controls, especially in the case of operational risk.

There is a need for the development of an organization-wide risk management framework, which is comprehensive enough to cover measurement, reporting, management and control of all risks and all instruments. Efficient risk management is essential for reducing the overall risk exposure. Adequate resources need to be devoted to risk identification and measurement as well as the development of risk management techniques. The Islamic Financial Services Board (IFSB) has formulated a set of principles for sound risk management. This set of principles should be followed by

Table 10.1 Risk perception: Risks in different modes of financing (scale 1-5)

Instrument	Credit Risk	Mark-up Risk	Liquidity Risk	Operational Risk
Murabahah	2.56	2.87	2.67	2.93
Mudarabah	3.25	3.00	2.46	3.08
Musharakah	3.69	3.40	2.92	3.18
Ijarah	2.64	3.92	3.10	2.90
Istisna	3.13	3.57	3.00	3.29
Bay' al-Salam	3.20	3.50	3.20	3.25
Diminishing *Musharakah*	3.33	3.40	3.33	3.40

Source: Khan and Ahmed (2001)

Islamic banks to mitigate various risks they are exposed to. There are several areas where there is room for improvement. These are discussed below.

IFSB Principles of Risk Management

- [Islamic Financial Institution] shall have a **sound process for executing all elements of risk management**, including risk identification, measurement, mitigation, monitoring, reporting and control. This process requires the implementation of appropriate policies, limits, procedures and effective management information systems (MIS) for internal risk reporting and decision making that are commensurate with the scope, complexity and nature of the activities.
- [Islamic Financial Institution] shall ensure an **adequate system of controls with appropriate checks and balances** are in place. The controls shall (a) comply with the *Shariah* rules and principles; (b) comply with applicable regulatory and internal policies and procedures; and (c) take into account the integrity of risk management processes.
- [Islamic Financial Institution] shall ensure the **quality and timeliness of risk reporting available to regulatory authorities**. In addition to a formal standardized reporting system, [Islamic Financial Institution] shall be prepared to provide additional and voluntary information needed to identify emerging problems possibly giving rise to systemic risk issues. Where appropriate, the information contained in the report shall remain confidential and shall not be used for public disclosure.

- [Islamic Financial Institution] shall make **appropriate and timely disclosure of information** to Investment Account Holders (IAH) so that the investors are able to assess the potential risks and rewards of their investments and to protect their own interests in their decision making process. Applicable international financial reporting and auditing standards shall be used for this purpose.

Use of Quantitative Methods of Risk Measurement

Risk assessment and measurement is an art as well as a science. Increased complexity of financial instruments calls for more sophisticated risk assessment tools for all sorts of risks including credit, market and operational risk. Identification of the sources of risks associated with Islamic banking has made good progress. However, there is need to apply risk measurement techniques and models to quantify risks. Sundararajan (2004) has suggested several quantitative methods for risk measurement. For example, similar to the idea of Value-at-Risk (VaR), the risk of the investors/depositors can be quantified by a measure of Profit-at-Risk (PaR) based on the historical profits and the volatility of returns. PaR model assumes normal distribution and can be calculated as equal to $Z\alpha \times \sigma p \times \sqrt{T}$; Where $Z\alpha =$ is the constant that gives the appropriate one-tailed confidence interval with a probability of *1-α* for the standard normal distribution (e.g., $Z_{..01} = 2.33$ for 99% confidence interval), *T* holding period or maturity of investment account as a fraction of month and σp as the standard deviation of the monthly profit as a percentage of assets.

The PaR measure can have multiple uses. First, PaR measure can provide an indication of the level of volatility in expected profits of investors/depositors. Secondly, it can determine the level of income smoothing reserves — Profit Equalization Reserves (PER) maintained by some of the Islamic financial institutions to mitigate displaced commercial risk. The correlation between PER and the asset's return could, therefore, be an indicator of "displaced commercial risk." Thirdly, the PaR model can also be applied to individual business lines within the bank, such as the case of specific portfolios linked to restricted investment deposits to determine the level of risk. Application of quantitative models like PaR can help management with their decision making regarding the level of PER and it can offer transparency to investors about the volatility of profits.

Trade financing and lease-based financial instruments on the assets side of IFIs resemble fixed-income asset-based securities and thus some of the standard risk measurement techniques such as duration, gap analysis, bucketing, DV01, and Value-at-Risk (VaR) can be computed to monitor the level of the risks. Baldwin (2002) provides a discussion on duration and VaR measures Islamic instruments. Use of such monitoring tools becomes more important for IFIs due to lack of risk-mitigating derivative products and due to low liquidity of the assets. Also, there could be issues in the use of parametric VaR for instruments based on *Mudarabah* and *Musharakah* contracts and therefore alternative measures of risks should be designed.

On the credit risk side, valuation of collaterals needs special attention. Although collaterals are recognized as one of the risk mitigating tools, in practice, many supervisory authorities tend to underestimate the existence of collaterals for several reasons. Valuation and determination of fair market value of collaterals is not an easy task, especially in the case of under-developed markets. Therefore, advanced models based on simulations and other analytical techniques should be developed to measure the extent of exposure due to credit risk.

Implementation Challenges

Implementation of the risk management framework requires close collaboration between the management of Islamic financial institutions, regulators and the supervisors. Implementation of risk management at the institutional level is the responsibility of management, which it can discharge by clearly identifying the objectives and strategies of the institution and by establishing internal systems that can identify, measure, monitor, and manage various risk exposures. Although the general principles of risk management are common between conventional and Islamic financial institutions, there are specific challenges in the risk management of Islamic financial institutions such as the following:

- Establishment of supporting institutions such as a lender of last resort, deposit insurance system, liquidity management system, secondary markets, and a legal infrastructure favorable to Islamic instruments, and for efficient dispute resolution.
- Achievement of uniformity and harmonization in *Shariah* standards across markets and borders. The current practice of maintaining individual *Shariah* boards by individual institutions is inefficient and should be replaced by a centralized *Shariah* board for a jurisdiction.
- Development of risk management systems is costly, which many of Islamic financial institutions cannot afford due to their small size. Efforts should be made to collaborate with other institutions to

develop systems that are customized to the needs of Islamic financial institutions and which address instrument, specific modeling needs.

- Effective risk management will assist Islamic financial institutions to integrate with global financial markets. Efforts should be made to enhance transparency in financial reporting and developments of accounting and reporting standards across markets.
- Risk management requires highly skilled human resources, which are currently in short supply. Efforts should be made to develop customized research and training programs to spread the knowledge and awareness of the significance of risk management. Such training programs should provide certifications to the participants after successful completion of the program.

Regulation of Islamic Financial Institutions

Firms in the financial services industry, especially banks and insurance companies, are subject to various forms of regulation. As the financial services industry has advanced, the regulation of the industry has also become more experienced, complex and dynamic. The nature of regulation of any industry can be understood by asking the questions; why is regulation required?, what needs to be regulated?, and finally how to regulate? The rationale for regulation (i.e., "Why") is the same for Islamic Financial Institutions (IFIs) as for conventional financial institutions but there are visible differences in the "what" and "how" questions.

Diverse views on the need for regulation in conventional finance range from positions of almost total opposition to any regulation, to the justification of broad, intrusive regulation. The arguments for the regulation of conventional financial services include the public good, mitigation of systemic risk, the protection of depositors, and the integrity of fiduciary contracts.

- **Public Good View.** One view of regulation is that it provides a public good that the market cannot supply on its own. This perspective proceeds from two premises. The first is that the objective of prudential regulation is the mitigation of risks taken by the stakeholders (e.g., depositors) unable to undertake on their own the necessary due diligence to assess these risks. Some stakeholders have sufficient investment savvy to develop these assessments on their own and would not, in principle, need, in the same degree, the support of public regulation, except for transparency and disclosure requirements necessary to conduct their due diligence. Consequently, from the public good perspective, the design of prudential regulation would call for a clear sense of the type, quality and quantity of the public good to be delivered, as well as the nature of the risk and risk exposure or values at risk involved.

- *Mitigation of Systemic Risk.* Another rationale for regulation, which is also indirectly related to the first rationale of public good, is that it is a pre-emptive measure to avoid or mitigate any systemic risk, which can cause a series of failures following a single failure and lead to a contagious collapse of the financial system. Such mitigation of the systemic risk can reduce the financial distress costs as well as social costs associated with the failures. Banks are particularly vulnerable to such collapse because of the nature of their business, i.e., illiquid assets financed by liquid liabilities. Therefore, the objective of prudential regulation is the mitigation of the risk of disruption of the normal business performed by the financial system in terms of payments or the provision of liquidity. Such systemic risks could be the outcome of a spillover from distress in one institution unable to honor its commitments, undermining confidence in the system. It could also be the result of a failure in the payments system itself — either failure of its material infrastructure or of the mechanisms and instruments to exchange liquidity.

- *Protection of Public Resources View.* Another view of financial regulation is that the existence of an explicit or implicit safety net, notably in the form of deposit insurance, creates a contingent government liability. The existence of such a commitment of public resources entails not only the right, but also the duty of the public authority to regulate activities that may endanger these resources. This view is not unrelated to the public good view, as the existence of deposit insurance is itself a public service. Existence of any safety net or deposit insurance also creates a moral hazard, as it reduces the incentive for depositors to impose market discipline on banks with regard to their risk-taking. Regulation is one of the means to check such moral hazard.

- *Integrity of Fiduciary Contracts.* Another perspective on regulation is provided by a focus on the fiduciary nature of the business of finance. The role of regulation is seen here as the provision of sufficient checks and balances to mitigate the risk of the intermediary failing the trust of its stakeholders. These are generally seen as the depositors, but also include small shareholders, raising the importance of sound corporate governance.

Chapra and Khan (2000) suggest four reasons for the regulation of IFIs, considered now in the light of the aforesaid rationale for regulation:

(i) *Systemic considerations.* Particularly the need to maintain an orderly payments system and ensure the development of the economy.
- Maintaining orderly payments is clearly in the nature of a public good whose supply stability needs to be protected. Whether IFIs operate according to core principles or follow prevailing practices, regulation to mitigate the risks of disruption in payments can be justified.
- In contrast, the promotion of economic development may be beyond the role that should be assigned to financial regulation. Activity expansion and growth is promoted by increased trust in the financial system that regulation can provide. However, its design to explicitly promote development may distort its objectives of ensuring soundness and stability and pose difficult challenges for regulators having to choose between promoting economic development and ensuring the stability of the financial system.

(ii) *Protecting the interests of demand depositors.* The protection of demand depositors is envisaged in the "two-windows" model of an Islamic financial intermediary. The model asks for the maintenance of 100% reserves against demand deposits.

(iii) *Ensuring compliance with the Shariah.* The relationship between civil and religious law varies across national jurisdictions. In the case where there is an orientation toward a strong separation, it is difficult to justify assigning to public authorities the role of ensuring that financial intermediation activities comply with the *Shariah.* This is considered a private religious matter that does not call for public intervention. The issue of truth in disclosure and in advertisement, however, remains and allows stakeholders to have recourse. This is not, however, a matter of financial regulation, but one of broad institutional infrastructure for business. In jurisdictions where the distinction between civil and religious law is less pronounced, one can well see a public policy choice for assigning to a public regulator the role of ensuring that banking activity complies with the *Shariah.*

(iv) *Supporting the integration of IFIs in the international financial system.* Integration would develop from the participation of IFIs in the financing of international trade and international payments. Counterparts of IFIs would want to be satisfied with the ability and commitment of IFIs to fulfill the contracts they enter into. In this respect, national and international regulation can be grounded in the public good and needs to ensure orderly participation in international payments and the integrity of fiduciary contracts.

Distinct Features of Regulating IFIs

The aforesaid rationale addresses the question "why" financial regulation for IFIs. The "what to regulate" and "how to do it" questions are now considered. It has been often argued that the case for introducing regulation to protect the value of deposits of IFIs fully abiding with risk-sharing principles is less compelling than for conventional finance. IFIs are different from conventional banks in several respects, which makes their regulation somewhat different. The following are the areas of differences:

Nature of Intermediation

The financial intermediation undertaken by IFIs is based on the principal-agent model and the contractual relationship is based on the profit-and-loss-sharing principle, which is different to the intermediation relationship between depositors and conventional banks. Due to the partnership-based relationship, the "two-tier *Mudarabah*" model of Islamic banking does not require banks to have reserves. It is argued that in the presence of symmetrical risk as well as profit-and-loss-sharing of Islamic financial intermediation, introducing a guarantee on the downside would run counter to the essence and the core objective of the system. Investment depositors should, however, expect to be informed on the features of the contract they enter into and have recourse if it is breached. Therefore, the focus of regulation will shift from protection of investment account holders to ensuring the integrity of the fiduciary contracts.

Depositors versus Investors

Depositors in the conventional banking system create a debt claim on the financial institution, whereas the depositors in the Islamic banking system are investors and therefore do not create a debt claim, but act like pseudo-equity holders. Due to the pass-through nature of intermediation, where all profits and losses are passed through to the investors, investors in the case of Islamic banks theoretically do not have a claim on the capital of the bank except in case of misconduct or negligence. This pass-through feature has a major impact on the capital requirements of Islamic banks. Requiring a certain minimum level of capital is the cornerstone of the regulation of conventional banks.

Systemic Risk

Similar to conventional banks, Islamic banks are not immune from "bank runs" when depositors/investors lose confidence in the bank and withdraw funds in panic. Large volumes of "panic" withdrawals of investment account holders could result in financial distress to an Islamic bank. Archer (2004) argues that whereas in the case of conventional banks, which maintain liquid assets on their liabilities, Islamic banks' assets are illiquid, which makes such risk primarily a liquidity risk. In the event of a liquidity crisis, a conventional investment firm faced by such problems will generally be able to wind down its business in an orderly manner by meeting its obligations through prompt disposals of marketable securities at the market price. In contrast, Islamic banks' asset portfolio is dominated by less liquid trade financed or rental-generating assets, which enhance the problem of illiquidity and therefore the systemic risk.

IFIs as Universal Banks

As mentioned in earlier chapters, financial intermediation performed by IFIs combines commercial and investment banking activities similar to a universal bank in the conventional system. This combination of banking with securities (underwriting) operations demands that a different regulatory framework, including capital adequacy requirements, be applied to banking and securities operations. Differences in commercial and investment banking activities have led to the adoption of a banking book/trading book approach in the EU Capital Adequacy Directive of 1993. The securities activities grouped as "trading book" are subject to a capital adequacy regime that is separate from the banking business as defined by the "banking book" (Archer 2004). One marked difference in the case of IFIs is that the trading operations are not confined to securities business only, but also include positions in commodities and other non-financial assets, for example by means of *Salam* and *Istisnah* contracts. Due to the universal banking nature of Islamic financial intermediation, it is important that well-defined rules and standards are designed to clearly demarcate the boundaries of banking and trading books with respective allocations of capital, depending upon the nature of business.

Regulators have traditionally governed their jurisdictions through direct rules, mostly on capital, assets, and income allocations. At the same time, regulatory changes often lag behind financial developments and may consequently either constrain the ability of financial institutions to flexibly manage their portfolios, or provide them with opportunities to take unchecked risks implicitly comforted by the existence of the safety net. In adapting to these developments, the industry is now moving toward letting the regulated institutions assess and manage their risks within a framework agreed on with the regulator. In this context, there is a call for the introduction of mechanisms to let the market impose the needed discipline on the financial intermediaries. The essence of market discipline is to induce market investors to penalize excessive risk-taking by raising the cost of funding and limiting its availability. This can happen directly, with depositors demanding higher returns or withdrawing their deposits. It can also happen indirectly if there is an asset traded in the market whose price reflects the investors' assessments of the risks that the institution that has issued it is taking.

In light of the discussion on risks and the rationale for regulation, capital, transparency, and licensing requirements are primary candidates for the question what to regulate. The method of regulation can rely, to various degrees, on a combination of direct "command and control" rules, market discipline (direct and/or indirect), or organization-specific home-developed risk assessments. The type and method of regulation chosen depends on the adopted view on the rationale for regulation, on the extent to which IFIs follow core principles, and on the assessment of their practices.

For IFIs fully following risk-sharing principles, one can envisage minimal regulation. It would emphasize less capital requirements, more transparency and disclosure, more screening of management, more licensing of business lines, that is, regulation equivalent to conventional banking. Larger reliance on direct market discipline and less on "command and control regulation" can also be features of their regulation.

The "*two-tier Mudarabah*" or "*two-window*" frameworks use mostly profit-and-loss-sharing (PLS) accounts on both sides of the balance sheet. They would provide trade finance or facilitation as well as payments services. They would take demand deposits as part of these services. The PLS intermediation has direct market discipline embedded in it and, hence, should not require significant capital. Some minimal capital may be needed for protecting the reputation of the institution, which is its legitimacy as a partner for all its stakeholders. But one could argue that sufficient transparency and disclosure should allow markets to judge this legitimacy and induce the institution on its own volition to maintain the needed level of capital. The case for a capital requirement to protect orderly payments and demand deposits would be stronger. It is not likely to lead to the same level of capital requirement, but suggests the need to consider the appropriateness of bundling the intermediation and payments services in the same balance sheet. Consequently, the regulation of an IFI, compliant with risk-sharing principles, would need to put a heavy emphasis on transparency and disclosure as well as licensing requirements, but de-emphasize capital requirements.

In existing IFIs, prevailing intermediation practices point to the need for equivalent emphasis on capital requirements, supervision and licensing, but more emphasis on transparency and disclosure, compared to conventional banks. Competitive pressure is encouraging the established IFIs to provide sufficient safety and return to depositors in unrestricted investment accounts. They consequently face the risk of "displacing" shareholders in their returns and capital to accommodate these depositors. As a result, they face an intermediation risk similar to the one conventional banks face and should therefore be subject to similar capital and supervision requirements.

To summarize, keeping in view the rationale for regulation, it is reasonable to propose minimal regulation for IFIs operating fully in accordance with the core principle of risk sharing. However, as prevailing practices of IFIs are not fully compliant with profit-and-loss-sharing principles, the situation presents risks akin to those in conventional banking. Therefore, a similar regulatory framework can be justified. Such specific regulation for IFIs should be supplemental to the existing regulatory framework and not a whole new separate framework. This is the view notably taken by the Accounting and Auditing Organization of Islamic Financial Institutions (AAOIFI) and the Islamic Financial Services Board (IFSB).

Capital Adequacy Requirement (CAR) for IFIs

Capital plays an important role in any business but is critically important in case of financial institutions such as banks. The role of capital is vital for a banking institution because of the following reasons:

- Capital is one of the key determinants and indicators of the safety and soundness of a bank, since an adequate capital base serves as a safety net for a variety of exposures.
- Capital provides a safety net against losses and absorbs possible losses. A well-capitalized bank can boost the confidence of the depositors and creditors.
- Capital also is the ultimate determinant of a bank's lending and investment capacity.

Due to the above reasons, it is argued that the capital of a bank should have three important characteristics — (i) it must be permanent; (ii) it must not impose mandatory fixed charges against earnings; and (iii) it must allow for legal subordination to the rights of depositors and other creditors. The nature of a financial intermediary like a bank is such that its capital-to-liabilities ratio is lower than other types of businesses. This low ratio is a reflection of the nature of the intermediation business and acceptance of large-sized liabilities in the form of deposits. To encourage prudent management of the risks associated with this unique balance sheet structure, the regulatory authorities require that the banks maintain a certain level of capital, which is considered adequate to meet the risks of the assets. The idea behind such a requirement is that a bank's balance sheet should not be expanded beyond the level determined by the ratio of the level of the capital and the risks of the assets, so that the level of capital determines the maximum level of assets.

The Basel Committee on Banking Supervision (BCBS) under the auspices of the Bank for International Settlement (BIS) took the initiative in the 1980s to develop a framework to determine standards for capital adequacy of banks with the objectives of promoting soundness and stability in the international banking system and to set standards across the globe to ensure uniformity in assessing the financial health of a bank. This initiative resulted in the Basel Capital Accord of 1988 (commonly referred to as "Basel I"), which laid the framework for a "regulatory capital" and defined the guidelines to measure the risk exposures of different asset classes. The Basel Accord introduced the concept of assigning risk weights to different asset classes based on the riskiness of the asset and defined the minimum levels of capital and reserves that a bank should maintain in order to meet the risk-weighted exposures.

According to Basel I, the determination of capital adequacy is a two-step process. The first step involves measurement of risk exposures of the assets based on the risk weights. For example, an investment in a government security is assigned a lower risk weight than the lendings to a corporation or private business, which carries a significant credit risk. In the second step, the regulatory capital available to support the risk is measured. For the sake of regulatory capital, it was divided into Tier 1 and Tier 2 capital. The ratio of regulatory capital to the amount of risk-weighted assets is the Capital Adequacy Ratio (CAR). The aim of the 1988 Capital Accord (Basel I) was to indicate a *minimum* recommended level of regulatory capital, with a CAR of 8%.

The Capital Accord standard has been accepted and adopted by more than 100 countries. Although the initial standard was mainly focused on credit risk, a refined standard in 2004 ("Basel II") included provisions for market and operational risks but the desired CAR level was kept at 8%. The notion of a minimum capital requirement should not be confused with the optimal economic capital. The minimum capital is a guideline and requirement by regulatory authorities, but well-capitalized banks tend to carry more than the minimum level of 8%. In addition, the minimum level of 8% is recommended, but the regulator of a particular country may decide to increase this level based on the level of risk in the system.

With the growth of Islamic banks, the issues of regulation and capital requirements are being raised and addressed. The framework for capital adequacy designed by BCBS provided impetus to dealing with similar issues for the Islamic banks. Although the need for a minimum capital ratio was recognized, at the same time it was argued that the nature of intermediation by Islamic banks is different to that of conventional banks and therefore the same capital requirements may not apply. Two main features of Islamic banks were highlighted: the nature of intermediation and the risk weights of assets held by Islamic banks.

CAR and the Nature of Intermediation

Unlike depositors of conventional banks, the contractual agreement between the Islamic bank and the investment account holders (IAHs) is based on the concept of sharing profit and loss. The arrangements to share profits and losses make IAH a unique class of liability holders — they are neither depositors nor equity holders. Although IAHs are not part of the bank's capital, they are expected to absorb all losses on the investments made through their funds, unless there is an element of negligence or misconduct on part of the bank. The nature of intermediation and liabilities has serious implications for the determination of adequate capital for Islamic banks. Some of the implications are as follows:

- Deposits taken on the basis of profit-and-loss-sharing agreements should not be subject to any capital requirements other than to cover negligence and misconduct liability, and winding-down expenses.
- Investments funded by current accounts carry commercial banking risks and should be subject to adequate risk weights and capital allocation accordingly.
- Existence of restricted investment accounts on the liabilities side form a collection of heterogeneous investment funds resembling a fund of funds and therefore such financial institutions should be

subject to the same capital requirements as are applicable to a fund manager.

- Presence of displaced commercial risk and the practice of income smoothing have indirect implications for the Islamic bank's capital adequacy, which a regulator may take into account while determining the CAR.
- Islamic banks acting as an intermediary (*mudarib*) can face a moral hazard issue. Since, as *mudarib*, the bank is not liable for losses but shares the profits with IAH, it may have an incentive to maximize the investments funded by IAH and by attracting more IAH than it may have the capacity to handle. This in turn can lead to risky investment decisions whereas the IAH's level of risk acceptance may be lower. Such incentive misalignment may lead to an increased displaced commercial risk, which necessitates higher capital requirements.

Determination of Risk Weights

Assigning risk weights to different asset classes depends on the contractual relationship between the bank and the borrower. For conventional banks, a majority of assets are debt-based, whereas for Islamic banks, the assets range from trade financing to equity partnerships; this fact changes the nature of risks. In some instruments there are additional risks, which are not present in conventional lending instruments. Therefore, the calculation of risk weights for the assets of Islamic banks differs from the conventional banks because:

- Assets based on trade are not truly financial assets and carry risks other than credit and market risks;
- There are non-financial assets such as real estate, commodities, and *Ijarah* and *Istisna*-based contracts that have special risk characteristics;
- Islamic banks carry partnership and profit-and-loss-sharing assets, which have a higher risk profile;
- Finally, Islamic banks do not have well defined risk mitigation and hedging instruments such as derivatives to hedge some of the risks on the assets side, which raises the overall risk level of assets.

In the case of partnership-based contracts such as *Mudarabah* and *Musharakah*, the bank is exposed to both credit and market risks which need to be analyzed within the credit and market risk methodology of the Basel Accords. When such partnership-based assets are acquired in the form of tangible assets, i.e., commodities, and are held for trading, the only exposure is to the market risk because the credit risk is minimized by direct ownership of the assets. However, there is significant risk in the form of the risk of capital impairment when direct investment takes place in partnership-based contracts and the investments are intended to hold for maturity. Treatment of this risk within the Basel framework is not straightforward and therefore requires special attention.

CAR for IFIs — IFSB Methodology

In the early 1990s, the Accounting and Auditing Organization of Islamic Financial Institutions (AAOIFI) drafted a basic standard on capital adequacy of Islamic financial institutions. In December 2005, the working group on Capital Adequacy of Islamic Financial Services Board (IFSB) issued the first exposure draft on Capital Adequacy Standards for Institutions (other than insurance institutions) offering only Islamic Financial Services (IIFS). This standard comprehensively discusses the nature of risks and the appropriate risk weights to be used for different assets. The standard deals with the minimum capital adequacy requirements for both credit and market risks for seven of the *Shariah*-compliant financing and investment instruments; (i) *Murabahah* and *Murabahah*; (ii) *Salam*; (iii) *Istisna*; (iv) *Ijarah*; (v) *Musharakah* and diminishing *Musahrakah*; (vi) *Mudarabah*; and (vii) *Sukuk*. Discussion of each contract includes risk weights to be assigned to each for market and credit risks.

IFSB Principles for Minimum Capital Adequacy Requirements:

- The minimum capital adequacy requirements for IFIs shall be a CAR of not lower than 8% for total capital. Tier 2 capital is limited to 100% of Tier 1 capital.
- In calculating the CAR, the regulatory capital as the numerator shall be calculated in relation to the total risk-weighted assets as the denominator. The total of RWA is determined by multiplying the capital requirements for market risk and operational risk by 12.5 (which is the reciprocal of the minimum CAR of 8%) to convert into risk-weighted equivalent assets, and adding that resulting figures to the sum of RWA computed for credit risk.
- The *Shariah* rules and principles whereby IAH provide funds to the IFI on the basis of profit-sharing and loss-bearing *Mudarabah* contracts instead of debt-based deposits, i.e., lending money to the IFI, would mean that the IAH would share in the profits of a successful operation, but could also lose

all or part of their investments. The liability of the IAH is exclusively limited to the provided capital and the potential loss of the IIFS is restricted solely to the value or opportunity cost of its work.

- However, if negligence, mismanagement or fraud can be proven, the IFI will be financially liable for the capital of the IAH. Therefore, credit and market risks of the investment made by the IAH shall normally be borne by themselves, while the operational risk is borne solely by the IFI.

The IFSB standard requires that an IFI maintain a minimum capital of 8% of total risk-weighted assets. The assets financed by IAH are excluded, considering that the IAH directly share in profits and losses of those assets and the loss to the bank (as *mudarib*) is limited to the time and resources spent on the investments, except in the case of negligence and misconduct. Therefore, it is argued that the risks on the assets financed on the basis of profit and loss sharing agreement by investment account holders do not represent risks for the IFIs' shareholders' capital and thus should not entail a regulatory capital requirement for the IFIs. This implies that assets funded by either an unrestricted or a restricted investment account holder are to be excluded from the calculation of the capital ratio.

The IFSB standard is defined in two forms; standard and discretionary. In the standard formula, capital is divided by risk-weighted assets excluding the assets financed by IAH, based on the rationale given earlier. The size of the Risk-Weighted Assets (RWA) is determined for the credit risk first and then an adjustment is made to accommodate for the market and operational risks. To determine the adjustment to RWA for the market and the operational risk, the capital requirements for market risk and operational risk is multiplied by 12.5 which is the reciprocal ratio (1/0.08) of the minimum CAR of 8%. For example if an asset has a market risk capital charge of 10, RWA will be increased by $10 \times 12.5 = 125$. Similarly, if operational risk capital requirement is 5, then weight for operational risk would be $5 \times 12.5 = 62.5$.

Determination of Risk Weights — An Example:

Risk weights are assigned depending on the nature of the asset and the kind of collateral. For example, if an Islamic bank provides *Murabahah* financing to a client, and there is no pledged collateral, a risk weight of 100% is applied to the value of the asset. On the other hand, if the client pledges collateral with market value of X, then the asset value is reduced by 75% of X before applying risk weight of 100% to the asset. An asset valuing $500,000 will get risk weight worth $500,000 if there is no collateral and risk weight of $425,000 if collateral worth $100,000 is pledged as following:

$$\$425,000 = (\$500,000 - \$100,000 \times 75\%) \times 100\%.$$

In case of *Musharakah* (equity) investment, when there is no third party guarantee, the credit risk weight of 400% is assigned. However, this weight is reduced considerably when there is a third party bank guarantee and risk weight of only 20% (for AAA rated bank guarantees) is assigned. For detailed methodology of how to determine risk weights for different assets, consult IFSB standard on capital adequacy at www.ifsb.org.

IFSB CAR Standard Formula

Eligible Capital		
(Total Risk-Weighted Assets) PLUS (Operational Risk Capital Requirement)	MINUS	Total Risk-Weighted Assets Funded by PSIA

Notes:

- Risk-weighting includes weights for market and credit risk.
- PSIA stands for Profit Sharing Investment Accounts.
- PSIA balances include Profit Equalization Reserves (PER) and Investment Risk Reserve (IRR).

In the second formula referred to as the Supervisory Discretion formula, the formula is modified to make appropriate adjustments to accommodate the existence of reserves maintained by IFIs to minimize commercial displaced, withdrawal and systemic risks. In markets where IFIs are maintaining Profit Equalization Reserves (PER) and Investment Income Reserves (IIR), the supervisory authorities are given discretion to adjust the denominator of the CAR formula for such reserves. Supervisors may adjust the formula according to their judgement of the systemic risk and prevalent practices.

IFSB CAR Supervisory Discretion Formula

Eligible Capital		
(Total Risk-Weighted Assets) PLUS (Operational Risk Capital Requirement)	MINUS	$(1-\alpha) \times$ Total Risk-Weighted Assets Funded by PSIA MINUS $\alpha \times$ Risk Weighted Assets Funded by PER and IRR

Notes:

- Risk-weighting includes weights for market and credit risk.
- PSIA stands for Profit Sharing Investment Accounts.
- PSIA balances include Profit Equalization Reserves (PER) and Investment Risk Reserve (IRR).
- α Refers to the proportion of assets funded by PSIAs which is to be determined by the supervisory authorities. The value of would not normally be expected to exceed 30%.

In the discretionary formula, the supervisory authority has the discretion to include a specified percentage (represented by α in the formula) of assets financed by investment account holders in the denominator of the CAR. The percentage set by the supervisory authority is applied to assets financed by both unrestricted and restricted investment account holders. Further adjustment is made for PER and IRR reserves in such a manner that a certain fraction of the risk-weighted assets funded by the reserves is deducted from the denominator. The rationale given for this adjustment is that these reserves have the effect of reducing the displaced commercial risk.

As Basel II takes into account the capital requirements for operational risk, IFSB's exposure draft also deals with the issue in detail. Due to difficulties in quantifying the exposures from operational risk, determination of how much capital should be allocated for such risks also becomes complex. An IFSB exposure draft recommends that the proposed measurement of capital to allocate for the operational risk may be based on either the Basic Indicator Approach or the Standardized Approach. It is further recommended that due to the different structure of Lines of Business (LOBs) for IFIs, at the present stage, IFIs may use the Basic Indicator Approach.

IFI CAR Computation: An Example

Liabilities:	
Demand Deposits	$200M
Unrestricted Investment Account Deposits	$500M
Restricted Investment Account Deposits	$250M
PER and IRR	$ 50M
Shareholders' Capital	$ 20M

Assets:	
Trade Financing (*Murabahah*)	$550M
Salam/Ijarah/Istisnah	$250M
Mudarabah and *Musharakah* Investments	$220M
Total Risk Weighted Assets for credit risk	$250M
Risk Adjusted Assets Financed by Investment Account Holders	$100M
Risk Adjusted Assets Financed by PER and IRR	$10M
Supervisory Authority's discretion (α)	30%
Adjustment for Market and Operational Risk (12.5 × $5M)	$62.5M

CAR According to Standard Formula:

$$\frac{\$20}{(\$250M + 62.5M) - (\$100M + \$10M)} = 9.88\%$$

CAR According to Supervisory Discretion Formula:

$$\frac{\$20}{(\$250M + 62.5M) - (0.7 \times \$100M - 0.3 \times \$10M)} = 8.35\%$$

Bank Supervision and Market Discipline

Basel I was an early attempt to define the framework for ensuring financial stability, but it was a simplistic approach mainly focused on capital requirements. Increased volatility in the market, rapid development of the financial markets, introduction of innovative products, and a series of financial crises spreading from one continent to another soon exposed the weakness of Basel I. The financial crisis in East Asian countries in 1997 and that in Eastern Europe in 1998 were evidence of the increased complexity of risks faced by international banks and it also highlighted the need for transparency, governance, and supervision of financial institutions.

In light of the aforesaid factors, the BCBS issued in June 2004 a Revised Framework (Basel II), which covered more than the capital adequacy requirements. In addition to capital adequacy (Pillar I), the new Accord deals with the principles of the enhanced supervisory review process (Pillar II) and effective use of market discipline (Pillar III). While the new framework aims to provide a comprehensive approach to measuring banking risks, its fundamental objectives remain the same as those of the 1988 Accord: to promote safety and soundness of the banking system and to enhance the competitive equality of banks. All three pillars are mutually reinforcing and no one pillar should be viewed as more important than another.

The message of Basel II is that a robust financial system infrastructure and adequate macro prudential surveillance are the prerequisites for effective supervision and risk management. Several recent studies by the World Bank and the IMF have highlighted the significance of the appropriate balance of prudential supervision and market discipline in Islamic finance, and the related implications for the organization of the industry and further linking it to the financial stability. These studies stress the importance of disclosure and market discipline in Islamic finance, because it is observed that the different nature of the risks of IFIs and their limited capacity for risk mitigation expose them more than the conventional financial institutions. This exposure is further enhanced due to the inadequate financial infrastructure, such as low level of transparency, absence of derivative instruments and markets, and a weak insolvency and creditor rights regime. Weak disclosure and low market discipline also call for active supervision.

While understanding the risks and the allocation of capital under Pillar I is a critical step, the core elements of supervision (Pillar II) and market discipline (Pillar III) are equally or more important. A well-designed capital requirement standard cannot be made effective in the absence of strong and prudent supervision. Therefore, the strengthening of the existing supervisory framework to achieve full compliance with Basel Core Principles of Banking Supervision is highly desirable in case of IFIs. In many countries with Islamic banks, available information on compliance with Basel Core Principles seems to suggest that the disclosure requirements for banks relating to risk management processes and detailed risk exposures need strengthening.

The disclosure practices of IFIs are not standardized and are highly varied. Although the AAOIFI Financial Accounting Standards provide a sound basis for further developing prudential disclosures, it has been suggested that further development should have two key purposes: (i) to develop *consumer-friendly disclosures* to inform investment account holders on the inherent overall risks that they face, and the related policies about investment risks exposures and mitigations; and (ii) to develop *market-oriented disclosures* to inform the public at large, particularly other professional counterparties, including regulators (who will require more details, not publicly disclosed) on capital, risk exposures and capital adequacy, along the lines of Pillar III of Basel II. The true risks borne by the investment account holders can be made transparent by enhancing the reporting and disclosure requirements. For example, disclosure of the definition of *Mudarabah* profits and of the level and variations in these profits and in profit equalization reserves can not only help the investor in determining the level of their exposure, it can also provide valuable insights to the supervisors.

The following issues, which are relevant to the implementation of Basel II in case of IFIs, are worth discussing:

- *Risk Reporting:* The significance of risk reporting cannot be underestimated and therefore it is necessary that IFIs work together and with the supervisory authorities to implement a comprehensive risk reporting framework. The IFBS recently issued an exposure draft for risk reporting of IFIs which emphasises the need to have in place a comprehensive risk reporting process, including appropriate board and senior management supervision to identify, measure, monitor, report and control relevant categories of risks and to ensure the adequacy of relevant risk reporting to the supervisory authority. Supervisory authorities need to allocate resources to ensure timely implementation of the proposed risk reporting framework.
- *Information Infrastructure:* There is a need to establish an information gathering infrastructure to provide reliable information about the credit-worthiness of borrowers, fair value of collaterals and independent valuation of assets. This requires a systematic effort of data collection and analysis and establishment of credit registries that can track the credit history of potential borrowers, and well-functioning rating agencies. There is now increasing recognition that credit registries with appropriate modifications in data content could facilitate systematic credit risk measurement.
- *Liquidity Enhancement:* IFIs have limited choices for maintaining liquidity, especially in times of stress. Availability of liquidity is critical for risk management and therefore it is essential that IFIs allocate resources to introduce liquidity-enhancing financial instruments through securitization and the development of capital markets.

- *Fragmentation and Concentration:* IFIs are often fragmented, highly concentrated, and are of relatively small size as compared to average conventional banks. As a result, IFIs do not have enough opportunities to gain from the benefits of diversification. Supervisors need to monitor IFIs that have significant exposure to a particular industry or deposit base. Supervisory authorities should also encourage IFIs to seek diversification. Through geographical diversification of the deposit base, an IFI can reduce its exposure to displacement or withdrawal risks. Diversification on the asset side can reduce the variance in the returns that accrue to the claimholders of the financial intermediary. Geographical spread of products can further help an IFI mitigate its credit risk by selecting borrowers of the best credit quality and avoiding those with weak credit quality. Further diversification benefits can come from economies of scope by extending the line of products and services.
- *Investment in Risk Management Infrastructure*: Establishment of risk assessment and measurement systems often becomes an expensive proposition as it requires sophisticated models, software, technologies and skilled human resources who can understand the nature of the risks and prepare models accordingly. Measurement and control of the operational risk are still evolving. Given the small size of the Islamic financial institution, establishing such a framework at the organization level may not be possible. IFIs and supervisory authorities should work together to find a reasonable solution to this problem.

Regulation of IFIs: Looking Forward

The legal and regulatory practice governing IFIs varies across countries. Indonesia, Iran, Lebanon, Malaysia, Pakistan, Sudan, Turkey, U.A.E., and Yemen have enacted Islamic banking laws. However, these laws may not always fully take into account the unique characteristics of Islamic banking. For example, the *Malaysian Islamic Banking Act* (1993) refers to banking as a "lending business" and investment accounts are considered to be liabilities. In Iran, IFIs accept customer investments on the basis of the *Wikala*, agency contract, not the *Mudarabah* contract, as is the case in other countries. In other countries, such as Saudi Arabia and Egypt, no laws have been enacted to regulate IFIs. They operate under the same laws governing conventional banks. Kuwait's sole IFI was licensed as a finance house, not a bank, and supervised by the Ministry of Commerce, rather than the Central Bank, until 2004, when it came under the latter's supervision.

Table 11.1 Diversity in the Legal, Regulatory, and Supervisory Arrangements

Country	Banking System	AAOIFI Standards	Islamic Banking Law	Existence of *Shariah* Boards	Supervision
Iran	Islamic	No	Yes	No	No
Jordan	Dual	IAS	Yes	Yes	Consolidated
Kuwait	Dual	IAS	Considered	Yes	Consolidated
Sudan	Islamic	Yes	Yes	Yes	–
Yemen	Dual	No	Yes	Yes	No
Malaysia	Dual	IAS	Yes	Yes	Consolidated

Source: Compiled from Zaher and Hassan (2001), Chapra and Khan (2000), El-Hawary, Grais, and Iqbal (2004)

Effective regulation requires readable, reliable signals of the risks that a financial institution faces resulting from its own behavior or from events external to it, as well as risks that may affect the financial system through contagion or infrastructure failure. It also requires an ability to process these readable signals and to introduce appropriate corrective actions as needed. In this respect the role of the broader institutional infrastructure is the most important. Of particular importance is the clarity and enforceability of property rights, the quality of the contract law and the feasibility of quick action in case of breaches, the efficiency of judicial recourse and other dispute resolution mechanisms. The majority of existing IFIs, however, operate in jurisdictions where these matters leave much to be desired, which adversely affect their performance.

More closely related to finance, the quality and transparency of accounting and auditing play a crucial role. Measurement and comparison of risk exposure should underlie regulation. The efforts at establishing accounting and auditing standards for IFIs have made a significant contribution in this respect. However, disclosures of accounting results may not be an adequate instrument for risk assessment because, as a structure, accounting is directed toward value, not risk allocation. This situation gives additional importance to other services, such as the collection and dissemination of financially relevant information and credit rating. In addition, it would call for renewed efforts at enhancing the relevance of accounting and auditing for risk assessment.

El-Hawary, Grais and Iqbal (2004) suggest that under the circumstances, regulators dealing with IFIs may want to consider a two-pronged strategy: managing current practices and a transition toward stable and efficient intermediation. In managing current practices, regulators need to promote the stability of existing IFIs that conduct financial intermediation, reflecting the market pressures they face, their stakeholders' demands and their institutional environment. A long-term perspective of the industry calls for the development of a consensus on a vision on its nature, the role it would play in the development of the communities it serves, and how it would play it. A significant intellectual effort, geared at providing practical ways of achieving consistency between the demands of the market place and the underlying principles, needs to be made. This effort needs to include debates that remain substantive, consultative, and evidence-based. In particular, it is important to be clear on the type of Islamic financial intermediation being considered, with special attention given to the core principles and how practice can develop consistent with them.

The combination of the services offered by IFIs and the prevailing practices they follow compound the difficulties of designing a regulatory framework to govern them. Specially, the problem of co-mingled funds from different classes of deposit holders needs to be addressed. IFIs are often criticized for not maintaining proper firewalls between the funds of different investor classes and equity shareholders. This creates difficulties in regulating and supervising an IFI. One approach for better regulation could be to encourage IFIs to structure their operations in clearly defined and separated segments catering to different classes of depositors, depending on their respective investment objectives. For example, one class of depositors may be looking for custodial services only, while the others may need to place funds for performing day-to-day transactions and therefore do not exhibit much risk appetite. Similarly, there may be a class of depositors that is less risk-averse and therefore would like the IFI to deploy its savings for a longer term.

A visionary design consistent with the founding principles of Islamic finance could see an IFI structured as a group of fairly independent entities, each designed to optimize the functional demands of its clients. This view is presented by El-Hawary, Grais and Iqbal (2004), who argue that institutions offering Islamic financial services can be viewed as three distinct segments (Figure 11.1), which can then be regulated individually for greater stability and transparency.

Segment A is designed to handle funds for depositors who are highly risk-averse and require a high level of liquidity and would use the funds for daily transactions or would prefer to keep savings in safe assets where

Figure 11.1   A Segmented View of an IFI

Assets	Liabilities
Asset-based/Trade Financing **Minimal Risk**	**Segment (A) Depositors** (Risk-Averse Investors)
Ijarah, Istisna, Mudarabah **Low-Medium Risk**	**Segment (B) Depositors** (Low Risk Takers)
Partnership/Profit and Loss Sharing *Musharakah,Mudarabah* *Venture Capital* *Private Equity* **Medium-High Risk**	**Segment (C) Depositors** (Investors with Risk Appetite)

Source: El-Hawary, Grais, and Iqbal (2004)

their capital (principal) is preserved. This segment will invest funds in asset-based securities with fixed-income characteristics and the IFI will intermediate by screening and monitoring such opportunities and making sure that credit and operational risks are contained. The concept is similar to narrow banking and would require a similar approach in its regulation.

Segment B is designed to cater to depositors with the next level of risk appetite who are willing to take some risk in the expectation of a higher return, with capital preservation and liquidity less high on their agenda. The IFI would deploy these funds in medium- to long-term instruments, such as *Ijarah* or *Istisna*, or may prefer to invest on *Mudarabah* basis directly with the entrepreneur or through *Mudarabah* certificates. If there is a well-developed secondary market for *Mudarabah*-based funding, then the form of intermediation taken by the IFI will be very similar to mutual funds where the IFI will manage and invest the depositors' money in different *Mudarabah* funds. Since the contractual agreement with the depositors would be similar to the fiduciary responsibility of a mutual fund in a conventional system, the same regulatory principles would apply.

Segment C is designed for investors who are willing to take additional risk and are prepared to participate in riskier investments, like private equity or venture capital. IFIs could deploy these funds on the basis of *Musharakah* or *Mudarabah* instruments. When funds are invested on *Musharakah* basis, the IFI also gets rights to participate in the governance of the enterprise, which raises another issue for the regulators. The IFI's relationship with *Musharakah* enterprises would be of long-term nature with active involvement in governance in contrast to a short-term, transactional relationship.

To summarize, an IFI structured to provide financial intermediation through clearly segmented windows or even separate institutions would make the task of the regulators easier. Each entity could then be subject to a regulating principle most suited to its nature. Such a separation could promote greater transparency of the risks faced by depositors, shareholders and regulators. The outlined framework would also bring to bear the market discipline through the risk-sharing feature of Islamic financial intermediation, and contribute to the stability of the system. An Islamic financial industry incorporating such segmentation would likely require lighter and more focused regulation.

Endnotes

1   See Basel Committee On Banking Supervision (BCBS) (2003), *Consultative Document-Overview of the New Basel Capital Accord*, April, Bank for International Settlements, Basel, Switzerland.

2   See Calomiris, C. (1999), "Building An Incentive — Compatible Safety Net," *Journal of Banking and Finance*, Vol. 23 (1999), pp. 1499–1519, and Evanoff, D. and L. Wall (2000), "Subordinated Debt and Bank Capital Reform," *Federal Reserve Bank of Chicago*. WP 2000–07, Chicago, US.

3   Under the Basic Indicator Approach, a fixed percentage, namely 15%, of the annual average gross income, averaged over the previous three years, is set aside. Under the Standardized Approach, this percentage varies according to the line of business (LOB), from 12% to 18%; it is 18% for corporate finance, trading and sales, and payment and settlement, 15% for commercial banking and agency services, and 12% for retail banking, asset management and retail brokerage.

4   See El-Hawary, Dahlia, Wafik Grais, Zamir Iqbal (2004), *Regulating Islamic Financial Institutions-The Nature Of The Regulated*, Policy Research Working Paper No. 3227, The World Bank, Washington, D.C. US., Sundararajan, V. and Luca Errico (2002), "Islamic Financial Institutions and Products; the Global Financial System; Key Issues in Risk Management and Challenges Ahead," IMF working paper WP/02/192, IMF, November; Marston, David and V. Sundararajan (2003), "Unique Risks of Islamic Banks and Implications for Systemic Stability," paper presented at international conference on Islamic banking, Jakarta, September 30–October 2, 2003.

5   For a detailed discussion of banking risks and risk reporting, see van Greuning, Hennie and Sonja Brajovic Bratanovic (2003), *Analyzing and Managing Banking Risk: A Framework for Assessing Corporate Governance and Financial Risk*, 2nd ed., The World Bank, Washington, D.C., US.

6   The *Wikala* contract operates on the basis of the agent receiving a fixed fee, not a share of profits like in the *Mudarabah*.

12

Corporate Governance

The issue of corporate governance and the search for an optimal governance structure have received considerable attention in conventional economic literature and public policy debates. This increased attention can be attributed to several factors such as:

- The growth of institutional investors, i.e., pension funds, insurance companies, mutual funds and highly leveraged institutions, and the role that these institutional investors play in the financial sector, especially in the major industrial economies;
- Widely articulated concerns and criticism that the contemporary monitoring and control of publicly held corporations in Anglo-Saxon countries, especially the UK and the US, is seriously defective, leading to sub-optimal economic and social development;
- A shift away from the traditional "shareholder value-centered" view of corporate governance, toward a corporate governance structure extended to a wide circle of stakeholders; and
- The impact of increased globalization of financial markets, the global trend of deregulation, and liberalization of institutional investors' activities, which have raised concerns abot corporate governance.

The concept of corporate governance is diverse and, over a period of time, the definition of the term "corporate governance" has oscillated between two extremes — from a narrow concept of a mechanism of safeguarding investors' interests to a broad concept advocating protection of all internal and external stakeholders' rights. This wide spectrum of the concept stems from two divergent views: (i) how the entity of a "firm" should be perceived in an economic system, and (ii) the form of the incentive system to protect the rights and preserve the obligations of the economic agents in the environment in which the firm operates. Whether one views the firm as a bundle of assets and liabilities, a legal entity, an economic or social organization, a nexus of contracts, or as a combination of these elements, will influence the way in which the evolution of the concept of corporate governance is analyzed.

Role of Stakeholders in Corporate Governance — Islamic Perspective

The basic agency problem suggests a possible definition of corporate governance as that which constitutes an efficient monitoring structure solving both the adverse selection and the moral hazard problems. A corporate governance structure focused on the investor-manager contract and relationship is often referred to as the shareholder model of corporate governance. It can be characterized as a model where (i) shareholders ought to have control, (ii) managers have a fiduciary duty to serve shareholder interests alone, and (iii) the objective of the firm ought to be the maximization of the shareholders' wealth.

This traditional definition of corporate governance, propounded by economists and legal scholars, is based on the agency relationship between the investor and the manager and is concerned with the protection of shareholders' or investors' interests only.

The neo-institutional economists rely on the agency theory to define the firm as a "nexus of contracts" and consider agents and transactions, institutionally, socially, legally, and culturally, as contingent (incomplete) constructs. They argue that the firm's claimants go beyond shareholders and bondholders to include others with whom the firm has any explicit and/or implicit contractual interaction. In this "nexus-of-contracts" view, each corporate constituency, including employees, customers, suppliers and investors, provide some asset in return for some gain. Contracts result from bargaining by these constituencies over the terms of their compensation, as well as the institutional arrangements that protect this compensation from post-contractual expropriation.[1] According to this view, there is nothing unique to corporate governance; it is simply a more complex version of the standard contractual governance.[2] All stakeholders are regarded as contractors with the firm, with their rights determined through bargaining.

Stakeholder theorists reject the three main propositions of the shareholder system and argue that all stakeholders have a right to participate in corporate decisions that affect them, managers have a fiduciary duty to serve the interests of all stakeholders groups, and the objective of the firm is the promotion of all interests and not only those of shareholders. This view is commonly referred to as the "stakeholder model" of corporate governance, where "stakeholders" include customers, suppliers, providers of complementary services and products, distributors, and employees. Therefore, this theory holds that corporations ought to be managed for the benefit of all who have some stake in the firm.[3]

The stakeholder model is largely normative and is still evolving; it is yet to find a sound theoretical foundation in conventional economic literature. In this respect, the distinction between explicit (or formal) and implicit (or relational or self-enforcing) contracts and claims is the key to understanding the basis of the stakeholder model. When it is difficult to write complete state-contingent contracts, people often rely on "unwritten codes of conduct," that is, on implicit contracts, which implies that, in addition to the obligations on explicit contracts, obligations arising out of implicit contracts have to be incorporated into the "nexus of contracts" theory with convincing arguments. This can only be articulated by expanding the scope of analysis to encompass ethics, morals and the social order. Hart (2001) forcefully argues that many economic transactions are sustained by self-enforcing ("implicit") contracts or norms of behavior, such as honesty or trust; concepts which so far have proved difficult to formalize in economic theory.

The second issue is how to draw a line of distinction between a stakeholder and a non-stakeholder. Existence of a stakeholder entity and its rights are easy to recognize, but questions still remain as to who really qualifies as an actual stakeholder. The third issue deals with the stakeholders' right to influence management decision-making or to participate in the governance of the firm. Questions arise as to why stakeholders should be given such a right and why managers should have a fiduciary duty to protect the rights of non-investor or non-owner stakeholders if such stakeholders have protected their rights, through bargaining, within the terms of the contracts. Whereas there appears to be a consensus on identifying the rights of non-owner stakeholders and an implicit agreement to protect these rights, there is still a debate on why such stakeholders should participate in the control and management processes of a firm. So far, discussions of the stakeholder model have not been able to articulate a convincing argument on either theoretical, moral, or legal grounds to recognize an active role for the stakeholders in the management and control of a firm.

In considering the Islamic view of the role of stakeholders, it is noted that two fundamental concepts of the Islamic economic system pertaining to property rights and contracts govern the economic and social behavior of individuals, society and state. These two principles also dictate the objective function of the economic agents, including legal entities like firms. A firm in the Islamic economic system can be viewed as a "nexus-of-contracts" whose objective is to minimize transaction costs with a view to maximizing profits and returns to investors, subject to the condition that these objectives do not violate the property rights of any party, whether it interacts with the firm directly or indirectly. In pursuit of these goals, the firm honors its obligations on explicit and implicit contracts without impinging on the social order. This definition incorporates the stakeholders' role in its view of the firm and supports recognition and protection of their rights.

Property Rights and Governance

The design of the governance system in Islam can be best understood in light of the principles governing the rights of the individual, society, and State, the laws governing property ownership, and the framework of contracts. Islam's recognition and protection of rights is not limited to human beings only, but encompasses all forms of life as well as the environment. Each element of *Allah* (swt)'s creation has been endowed with certain rights and each is obligated to respect and honor the rights of others. These rights are bundled with the responsibilities for which humans are held accountable.[4] The *Shariah* offers a comprehensive framework to identify, recognize, respect and protect the rights of every individual in creation, community, society, and the state. Islamic scholars and *Fuqha* have defined and codified detailed principles identifying these rights.[5] The importance of being conscious and mindful of the rights of others (including stakeholders — human or non-human) and the significance of discharging the responsibilities associated with such rights is reflected by the following saying of the Prophet (*pbuh*):

> **"So give to everyone who possesses a right (*kull dhi haqq*) his right."**

The term "right" (*haq*) denotes something that can be justly claimed, or the interests and claims that people may have been granted by the *Shariah*. The majority of *Shariah* scholars and jurists hold that similar to a physical property, rights are also property (*al mal*) because, like physical property, which has beneficial uses and can be possessed, rights also have beneficial uses and can be possessed.[6] Rules defining the property rights in Islam deal with the rights of ownership, acquisition, usage and disposal of the property. Any violation of these rules is considered a transgression and leads to disruption in the social order.

The notion of ownership in Islam is two-tiered: (i) real and absolute, and (ii) delegated and restricted through time-bound possession. The former belongs to *Allah* (swt) only, because He is the ultimate creator, while the latter is reserved for man in order that he may be materially able to perform his duties and obligations. Therefore, the first axiom of the property rights in Islam is that *Allah* (swt) — the real owner, creator, and benefactor — reserves the right to prescribe for man — His vicegerent, recipient and possessor-owner — rules governing the property while it is in the temporal possession of man.[7] Ownership rights in Islam originate from the concept of *Khilafah* (stewardship) as the *Quran* and *Sunnah* clearly and explicitly state that *Allah* (swt) is the sole owner of property and that man as vicegerent of *Allah* (swt) is merely trustee and custodian.[8] This relationship implies that man has the right to use and manage his private property in a manner similar to that of a custodian and trustee. Property is not an end itself, but a means to discharge effectively man's responsibilities as the vicegerent of *Allah* (swt).

The second axiom of property rights in Islam is that this right of possession is a collective right and individuals can only earn a priority in the use of these resources.[9] While a part of these resources is reserved for the exclusive possession of the collectivity, the remaining part is allowed to become the possession of an individual without the collectivity losing its initial right of possession to these resources. However, when individuals apply their creative labor to these resources, they get or acquire a right of priority in the use and enjoyment of the resulting product, without the rights of others being nullified. Individuals are to use these resources with the full understanding that *Allah* (swt)'s ultimate ownership, and the collectivity's prior right, remain intact. This notion is the result of the permanence, constant, and invariant ownership of *Allah* (swt) of all the resources, and by implication, that of a prior right to these resources by the collectivity. This proposition becomes a legislative basis for requiring preservation of society's well-being and interests.

Social interest and the collective dimension of human life demand that individual freedom is kept within certain limits and a balance is created in such a way that the individual, the society, and the State each has a claim on property rights in respect of the roles assigned to them. Property rights of these three agents should not conflict with one another, nor should the exercise of those rights by any one of these agents jeopardize the exercise of rights by the others. Ibn Taimiyah was one of the earliest scholars to recognize and advocate the rights of the society and the State along with private ownership.[10] If as a result of the growth of the society, division of labor, or increasing complexities of markets, either the obligation to share is shirked or the rights of the society and the cohesion of the community are undermined, or a harmonious social order is at stake, intervention by the legitimate authority to take corrective measures is justified.

The second axiom of property rights implies that while the individuals' possession of these resources and their share in the outcome is allowed, sanctioned and protected by the *Shariah*, it is so as long as it does not come into conflict with society's interests and well being. Hence, private initiative and choice are recognized, but such recognition is not allowed to subvert the principle of sharing or to lead to a violation of the rights of the society and the State. However, once the individuals have discharged the duties to the society and the State, in accordance with prescribed manner and to the extent of the prescribed amount, and are not in violation of the rules of the *Shariah*, their rights to their possessions is held inviolate and no one has a right to force appropriation (or expropriation) of that person's property to anyone else.[11] This is further endorsed by the hadith stating that "*Muslims' blood, property and dignity are protected against each other.*"

Ibn Taimiyah views property as a right granted by the *Shariah* to utilize an object but a right of varying kinds and degrees. Sometimes the right is an extended one so that the proprietor can sell or give away the object, lend it or make a gift of it, bequeath it or use it for productive purposes; but sometimes the right is incomplete, and therefore the proprietor's rights are limited or restricted.[12] Rules concerning property acquisition, possession, usage and disposal should be looked at as regulations rather than restrictions. Basic conditions to maintain lawful rights to property are as follows:

- property should not have been acquired by unlawful means (i.e., means repugnant to the *Shariah*),
- the acquisition and its continuity should not result in any damage or harm to others; and
- the acquisition of property should neither invalidate any valid claim nor establish a non-valid one. Islam places great emphasis on acquiring and maintaining rights to property through lawful means, but does not impose any limits, or cap, on the amount of the property owned, or on the amount of wealth an individual can accumulate, as long as the individual conforms to the obligations set by the *Shariah*.

Islam recognizes two ways in which individuals can obtain rights to property:

(i)   through their own creative labor and/or
(ii)   through transfer — via exchange, contract, grants or inheritance — of property rights from another individual who has gained title to the property or asset through their own labor. Property acquired through non-permissible and unjustifiable means like gambling (*maysir*), bribing, stealing, cheating, forgery, coercion, or illegal trading does not qualify as *al-mal* as defined by the *Shariah* and therefore is proscribed and forbidden. Consequently, any property, which is considered counter-productive or non-beneficial, loses its legitimacy and its associated rights. Hoarding with the intention of creating artificial scarcity and profiteering are considered unacceptable means of building wealth and property. Similarly, property acquired through breach of trust, adulteration, non-compliance with weights and measures, or unethical means does not satisfy the definition of property (*al-mal*) and therefore its ownership is not considered legitimate.

Concomitant with property rights, the *Shariah* imposes responsibilities, among which are obligations — severely incumbent upon the individual — not to waste, destroy, squander, or to use the property for purposes not permitted by the *Shariah*.[13] To do so is to transgress the limits set on one's rights and an encroachment on the rights of the others. The right of the collectivity to property is further protected by the *Shariah* through the limitations imposed on the right of disposal of the property by the person who has gained priority in the use and enjoyment of that property. Hence, while the right of use and enjoyment of property is affirmed by the *Shariah*, the exclusive and absolute right of disposal of property is rejected.[14] The prohibition of *israf* and *tabdhir* (wasting and squandering) in all areas applies to property as well. An individual may not make an alteration in his property that may harm even his neighbor. If the property owner proves unable to use the property properly (within the boundaries defined by the *Shariah*), he forfeits his ownership rights. Under such conditions, the legitimate authority is fully justified in withdrawing the rights of usage of that property in order to protect it from misuse by the owner.[15] This position of the *Shariah* is in conformity with the Islamic conception of justice (*al-adl* and *al-ihsan*) and the rights and responsibilities of the individual and the community.

Islam's concept of property rights differs in many aspects from the concept of property rights in conventional economic systems. At one extreme, proponents of the market-based system argue in favor of individual-centered private property rights as fundamental rights, while at the other extreme, a small minority believes that private property right is fundamentally immoral.

In contrast, Islam promotes a balance among the rights of individuals, society and the State. This concept sharply contrasts with the self-centered utility maximizer economic agent idealized in neoclassical economics in an unbounded, insatiable, quest for acquisition and accumulation. Before the full market society came to prevail in the West, a great deal of the property rights in land and other assets was a right to use and enjoy the asset but not a right to dispose of it. The development of full market society required revision of this notion of property, since the right not to be excluded from the use or enjoyment of something came to be considered as not marketable. It was thought that it was impossible to reconcile this particular right with a full market economy. Hence, of the two earlier kinds of property rights — the right to exclude others and the right not to be excluded by others — the second was all but abandoned and the conception of property rights was narrowed to cover only the right to exclude others. In Islam, however, this right is preserved without in any way diminishing the role of the market as a resource-allocating and an impulse-transmitting mechanism. Islam does not endorse the notion under the conventional system that a person does no harm to members of his group if as a result of his effort he is better off and others are no worse off than they would otherwise be.

Several conclusions can be drawn from the preceding discussion. Firstly, Islam's concept of property rights is different, inasmuch as the individual has a delegated right to the property whose acquisition, usage and disposal are subject to rules including the principle of sharing as dictated by the *Shariah*. Secondly, while Islam fully recognizes the individual's private property rights, these rights are governed by rules designed to protect the rights of society and the State. Thirdly, by virtue of the first and second axiom of property rights, every individual, group, community, society and the State become a stakeholder whose rights are granted and preserved by the *Shariah* in order to promote social order and economic development. Fourthly, whereas it is difficult to recognize or justify some rights of others in a formal economic theory in the conventional system without drawing any reference to ethics and morality, such a problem does not exist in Islam where everyone's rights are recognized and protected by Law (*Shariah*). Finally, inclusion (or exclusion) and recognition (or denial) of rights of stakeholders in the Islamic economic system are based on rules and laws that need no justification on the grounds of morality alone, but are derived from principles aimed at creating justice and balance in the economic and social system.

Whereas the *Shariah* guarantees some basic property rights to individuals by virtue of their being members of the society, rights of a firm or a legal entity like a corporation are earned and acquired. It is not the firm that acquires property rights, but it is the property acquired in the course of the firm's economic activity that has property rights and claims. Once a property is earned or acquired by the firm, it is subject to the same rules of sharing and prohibition of wasting which apply to the property of individuals. The firm's property rights also come with the same claims and responsibilities as do those of individuals. This implies that the firm is expected to preserve the property rights of not only the local community or society, but also of those who have participated in the process of acquiring or earning the firm's property. No action of the firm that violates the basic set of property rights of those with whom the firm interacts is acceptable.

The principles of property rights in Islam clearly justify the inclusion of stakeholders into the decision-making and accountability of an economic agent's activities. This inclusion is based on the principles that

- the collectivity (community, society, State) has sharing rights with the property acquired by either individuals or firms,
- exercise of property rights should not lead to any harm or damage to the property of others (including stakeholders),
- rights of others are considered as property and therefore are subject to rules regarding violation of property rights,
- any property leading to the denial of any valid claim or right is not recognized as *al mal* and therefore is considered unlawful according to the *Shariah*.

Contracts and Governance

The significance of contractual obligations in economic and social relations cannot be over-emphasized. The whole fabric of Divine Law is contractual in its conception, content, and application. Islam forcefully places all economic relations on the firm footing of "contractus."[16] It recognizes only one status, i.e., moral consciousness and virtue, all other status on any basis is obliterated. The very foundation of the *Shariah* is the covenant between *Allah* (swt) and man; this imposes on man the duty of being faithful to his word. On *Allah*'s (swt) side, the *Quran* often states: "*Allah will not fail in His Promise.*" On man's side, his commitment to the contractual obligations is considered the best form of honoring his acceptance of *Allah* (swt) as his Lord.

A contract in Islam is a time-bound instrument, which stipulates the obligations that each party is expected to fulfill in order to achieve the objective(s) of the contract. Contracts are considered binding and their terms are protected by the *Shariah* no less securely than the institution of property. The freedom to enter into contracts and the obligation to remain faithful to their stipulations has been so emphasized in Islam that a characteristic that distinguishes a Muslim is considered to be his faithfulness to the terms of his contracts. In the *Shariah*, the concept of justice, faithfulness (called *Amanah*, whose antonym is *Khiyanah* meaning betrayal, faithlessness and treachery), reward and punishment are linked with the fulfillment of obligations incurred under the stipulation of the contract.

The contractual foundation of the *Shariah* judges the virtue of justice of individuals not only for their material performance but also by the essential attribute of their forthright intention (*Niyya*) with which they enters into every contract. This intention consists of sincerity, truthfulness, and insistence on rigorous and loyal fulfillment of what they have consented to do (or not to do). This faithfulness to one's contractual obligations is so central to Islamic belief that when the Prophet (*pbuh*) was asked "who is the believer?" He replied that "*a believer is a person in whom the people can trust their person and possessions.*"[17] In a very terse, direct and forceful verse, the *Quran* exhorts "*O you who believe, fulfill contracts.*" So basic is the notion of contracts in Islam that every public office is regarded primarily as a contract or agreement that defines the rights and obligations of the parties.

The emphasis placed on contracts in Islam, by implication, makes the members of the society and economic agents aware of the obligations arising from their contractual agreements — verbal or written, explicit or implicit. In the case of explicit contracts, parties to the contract clearly stipulate the expected behavior and duties with respect to the terms of the contract. This contract is to be free of information asymmetry; parties intend to comply with the terms of the contract and are fully aware of their rights and obligations. Importantly, the State ensures enforceability of the contract in case of violations by either party. On the other hand, implicit contracts are not formal contracts with clearly defined terms but are claims and obligations that come with the rights to be part of a society. The principles of sharing and the rights of the collectivity to property are types of implicit contracts to preserve and protect the rights of others and thus establish a wide spectrum of implicit obligations. Within the property rights framework, one has contractual obligations to others, including the community and the society, according to the rules of the *Shariah*, and honoring these obligations is considered a sacred duty. This sacred duty to preserve the property rights of others is the moral, social and legal foundation for recognizing and enforcing the obligations arising from implicit contracts.

Islam's framework of contracts places equal emphasis on obligations arising from both explicit and implicit contracts. Individuals as well as public and private entities are expected to be aware of this. Therefore, just as it is incumbent upon economic agents to honor explicit contracts, it is obligatory for them to preserve the sanctity of implicit contracts by recognizing and protecting property rights of stakeholders, community, society and the State. Whereas conventional stakeholders' theory is searching for sound arguments to incorporate implicit contracts in the theory of the firm, in the Islamic economic system, rights of and obligations to stakeholders are taken for granted.

Islam's framework of property rights and contracts also establishes guidelines regarding who can qualify as a stakeholder and whether such a stakeholder has any right to influence the firm's decision-making and governance. In a broad sense, any group or individuals with whom a firm has any explicit or implicit contractual obligations qualifies as a stakeholder, even though the firm may have formal contracts with them through mutual bargaining. In Islam, a stakeholder is the one whose property rights are *at stake* or *at risk* due to the voluntary or involuntary actions of the firm. In case someone's rights are encroached upon or threatened as a result of the firm's operations, that individual, group, community or society becomes a stakeholder.[18] This risk-based definition of a stakeholder is supported by a saying of the Prophet (*pbuh*): "*a Muslim is the one from whose hand others are safe.*"

Stakeholder Oriented Governance Structure

In Islam, the behavior expected of a firm is not any different from the behavior of any other member of the society. Since the firm itself does not have a conscience, the behavior of its managers becomes the behavior of the firm and their actions are subject to the same high standards of moral and ethical commitment expected from a Muslim. In other words, the firm's economic and moral behavior is shaped by its managers acting on behalf of the owners and it becomes their fiduciary duty to manage the firm as a trust for all the stakeholders and not for the owners alone. Consequently, it is incumbent upon the managers to ensure that the behavior of the firm conforms to the principles and rules of the *Shariah*. If there is any deviation, institutional arrangements discourage it. In an ideal situation where all agents are true believers *Mo'meneen*, those among Muslims whose behavior corresponds fully to the requirements of the *Shariah*, their faithfulness to the terms of contracts and accountability for respecting others' property rights will lead to the elimination of the problems due to asymmetric information, moral hazard and adverse selection and thus guarantee optimal governance. In a less perfect world where commitment to contracts may be influenced by personal interests at the expense of the interests of the collectivity, to induce deviation from the terms of contract, the design of the structure of governance has to ensure faithfulness to the agent's contractual agreements and protection of everyone's rights.

The design of a corporate governance system in the Islamic economic system, therefore, entails implementation of a rule-based incentive system in which compliance with the rules ensures an efficient governance system to preserve social justice and order among all members of society. This implies institutions and rules that designed should be to compel managers to internalize the welfare of all stakeholders. The rights that are claimed for stakeholders are not ends in themselves — which ought to be recognized in any form of economic organization — but means of protecting constituency rights.[19] In an Islamic system, the observance of the rules of behavior guarantees internalization of stakeholder rights (including those of the society at large). No other institutional structure is needed. It is the Islamic government that specifies the appropriate corporate governance structure, "incorporating all stakeholders' rights into fiduciary duties of managers" of the firm on behalf of none — investors or stakeholders. So no other institutional arrangement that would allow individual non-investor stakeholders to negotiate directly with the firm is necessary. Incorporating all stakeholders' rights into the fiduciary duties of managers is counter-productive and leads to sub-optimal results. The important point is that each stakeholder is given the freedom of bargaining to protect their rights and there are systematic institutional arrangements in place to provide protection and to mediate where disputes and disagreements arise.

Institutional arrangements can be part of system-wide infrastructure surrounding the governance structure of the firm. For example, because contracts are invariably incomplete, judicial interpretations can fill in the gaps. It is permissible to regard employment law, consumer law, tort law, as well as judicial rulings and administrative regulations, as part of the contracts that various stakeholders have with the firm. Similarly, the concept of the *Shariah* boards is unique to Islamic financial system. A *Shariah* board, consisting of *Fuqah* (scholars in *Shariah* matters) has been used to oversee the operation of a financial institution, with a view to ensuring that the operations and code of conduct of the Islamic bank is in accordance with the rules of the *Shariah*. A *Shariah* board for every firm, which is seen in the present architecture of Islamic banking, is not efficient, as only one set of rules is needed for all firms for appropriate corporate governance based on the *Shariah*. The same idea of *Shariah* board can be extended to a system-level board consisting of scholars from different disciplines including *Shariah*, economics, finance, and commercial law, to ensure that rules are so framed and enforced that economic agents fully comply with their contractual obligations to all the stakeholders.

To summarize, the Islamic economic system fully endorses a stakeholder view of governance based on Islam's principles of preservation of property rights and the sanctity of contracts. The corporate governance model in an Islamic financial system can be derived from a comprehensive understanding of three principles of Islam:

- Recognition of property rights of individuals, legal entities, i.e., firm, and the society;
- Significance of contractual obligations, explicit as well as implicit, among economic agents;
- An incentive system to enforce *Shariah* rules for preserving the social order; and
- Stakeholders' right to participate in the decision-making process.

Corporate Governance of IFIs[20]

Corporate governance relates to the manner in which the business of the bank is conducted, including setting corporate objectives, the bank's risk profile, aligning corporate activities and behavior with the expectation that management will operate in a safe and sound manner, running day-to-day operations within an established risk profile, while protecting the interests of depositors and other stakeholders. It is defined by a set of relationships between the bank's management, its board, its shareholders, and other stakeholders.

The key elements of sound corporate governance in a bank include:

- A well articulated corporate strategy against which the overall success and the contribution of individuals can be measured.
- Setting and enforcing clear assignment of responsibilities, decision making authority and accountabilities that are appropriate for the bank's risk profile.
- A strong financial risk management function (independent of business lines), adequate internal control systems (including internal and external audit functions), and functional process design with the necessary checks and balances.
- Adequate corporate values, codes of conduct and other standards of appropriate behavior and effective systems used for ensuring compliance. This includes special monitoring of the bank's risk exposures where conflicts of interest are expected to appear (e.g., relationships with affiliated parties).

- Financial and managerial incentives for acting in an appropriate manner offered to the board, management and employees, including compensation, promotion and penalties. (i.e., compensation should be consistent with the bank's objectives, performance and ethical values).

Due to the fiduciary nature of the financial industry and the scope of asymmetry in access to information, corporate governance arrangements may matter more for financial businesses than other firms. In its essence, a financial business organization is a fiduciary trustee that is entrusted with the intangible assets of another party, specifically depositors and other investors. Therefore, it carries a special obligation to act in the best interests of that other party when holding, investing, or otherwise using the principal's property. This is crucial in the context of banking, where informational asymmetries are likely to be higher than in other firms.

The distinct nature of financial intermediation conducted by IFIs raises certain governance issues worth discussing. These issues relate to

- financial interests of IFIs' account holders,
- IAH as stakeholders,
- IFIs as stakeholders,
- the governance of reserves,
- *Shariah* boards as stakeholders,
- the degree of transparency.

Financial Interests of Account Holders

Investors or depositors are among the most important stakeholders and protecting their financial interests is critical. In the case of current accounts, IFIs obtain an explicit or implicit authorization to use the deposit money for whatever purpose permitted by *Shariah*, but pay no return or profit to the depositors. Any negligence or misconduct of IFIs can result in financial losses to the current account holders. There should be proper procedures to ensure that the IFI's management does not go for risky investments or excessive use of current account holders' funds to enhance the performance of overall investments to benefit other unrestricted investment account holders.

In the case of restricted investment accounts (RIA), the bank acts only as fund manager — agent or non-participating *mudarib* — and is not authorized to mix its own funds with those of the investors without their prior permission. It is in the interests of RIAH that all relevant information about the returns and risks is disclosed to the account holders. In addition, it is the responsibility of the management of IFIs to ensure that investments funded by RIAH are ring-fenced from the rest of the investments and there is full transparency in the identification and distribution of profits and losses. Similarly, unrestricted investment accounts, which constitute the majority of deposits, pose specific corporate governance problems. It is a common practice of IFIs to place shareholders' and investment funds in common pools without any mechanism to separate the two. Consequently, there is the concern that shareholder-controlled management and boards may favor and protect shareholders' investments at the expense of those of investment account holders.

IAH as Stakeholders

Investment account holders (IAH) are like quasi-equity holders, but without any participation in the governance of the financial institutions. As a result, IAHs do not have any direct means to protect their rights. Since they do not have any participation in the governance mechanism they are at the mercy of public policy makers, regulators and *Shariah* boards. A transparent and efficient governance arrangement should be devised to include and protect the rights of IAHs.

IFIs as Stakeholders

A considerable portion of IFIs' assets side includes profit-and-loss-sharing instruments, akin to those of *Mudarabah* and *Musharakah*. Due to the high degree of asymmetry of information in equity and profit-and-loss-sharing contracts, there is greater need for close monitoring by IFIs. In order to minimize the cost of monitoring, there is also a need for institutional arrangements to facilitate monitoring and governance. Absence of such a governance mechanism is one of the reasons why the share of profit-and-loss-sharing instruments is small on the assets side of the IFIs.

Furthermore, the presence of profit-and-loss-sharing instruments creates a situation where financial institutions themselves become stakeholders in the businesses to whom they provide finance This is similar to the "insider" system of governance like the German model of banking where bankers may also be represented on the board of directors or may participate in the management of the business. Although not much attention is paid to this aspect at present, it does impose additional governance burden on the financial institutions.

Governance of Reserves

Maintaining reserves to smooth income over a period of time is becoming a common practice. The objective of the "Profit Equalization Reserve (PER)" is to hedge against future losses or low income by keeping a portion of current profits to pay off investment account holders in the future. Whereas this practice is in alignment with prudent risk management, it raises a governance issue that needs attention. Firstly, limited disclosure of such reserves makes investment account holders uneasy. Secondly, investment account holders have no rights either to influence the use of such reserves or to verify the exposure of overall investments. Thirdly, an investment account holder with long-term investment objectives may welcome this practice, but an investor with a short-term view may feel that they are subsidizing the returns of the long-term investors. Finally, some banks require investment account holders to waive their rights on these reserves, For example, the terms and conditions of the Islamic Bank of Britain state:

> "you (the investment account holders) authorize us to deduct from the net income your profit stabilization reserve contribution for payment into the profit stabilization reserve account. Upon such deduction you agree that you relinquish any right you may have to the monies in the profit stabilization reserve account."[21]

Islamic financial institutions should standardize the practice and the rights of investment account holders to these reserves should be clearly stated and explained to the depositors. One suggestion is that deduction from the profits belonging to investment account holders should apply only to long-term depositors who are more likely to be exposed and not to every depositor, including short-term depositors, who are not exposed to such risk.

Role of *Shariah* Boards as Stakeholders

The concept of the *Shariah* boards is unique to Islamic financial institutions. This board consists of *Shariah* scholars who oversee and monitor the activities of a financial institution to ensure compliance with the principles of the *Shariah*. *Shariah* boards take on a major responsibility and serve as stakeholders as they are the protectors of the rights of investors and entrepreneurs who have put their faith and trust in the financial institution to perform economic activities according to their belief.

IFIs have created corporate governance structures and processes that reassure stakeholders on the conformity of all transactions and ensure compliance. A widely adopted approach is to have internal or independent bodies certify IFIs' compliance with the *Shariah*. Each IFI has in-house religious advisers, collectively known as the *Shariah* Supervisory Board (SSB).[22] In principle, the prerogatives of the SSBs lie in five main areas:

(i) certification of permissible financial instruments through *fatwas*[23] (ex-ante *Shariah* audit), verification of transactions' compliance with issued *fatwas* (ex-post *Shariah* audit),

(ii) the calculation and payment of *Zakat*,

(iii) disposal of non-*Shariah* compliant earnings, and

(v) advice on the distribution of income or expenses among the bank's shareholders and investment account holders. SSBs issue a report to certify the conformity of all financial transactions with the aforesaid principles. It is usually an integral part of the IFI annual report.

The role of Shariah boards in sound governance is critical — especially in regard to consistent application. It is common practice in the current governance structure of Islamic financial institutions to maintain a *Shariah* board or a *Shariah* advisor for each institution. This practice, however, leads to inefficient decision-making due to duplication of effort, lack of standardization and lack of competent *Shariah* experts. Instead, a system-wide board of knowledgeable religious scholars, who are also specially trained in Islamic economic and financial principles, is a more efficient way and facilitates an optimal governance structure. A group of scholars and experts in finance, banking, economics, accounting and finance may constitute an ideal *Shariah* board. Such a system-wide *Shariah* board can work closely with the regulators and supervisors to make sure that effective monitoring and supervisory controls are devised to protect the rights of all stakeholders according to the spirit of Islam. It is the board's responsibility to ensure that compliance with the monitoring system protects the rights of those stakeholders with whom the financial institution has "explicit" or "implicit" contracts. This structure of governance with a system-wide religious board will be more efficient and cost-effective because:

- stakeholders will not require duplicate monitoring,
- institutions will not need to maintain their own boards,
- the board will consist of knowledgeable experts in the *Shariah* as well as finance, and

- there will be uniformity in expected behavior which will set the standards to be followed by individual institutions.

The functioning of internal SSBs raises five corporate governance issues: independence, confidentiality, competence, consistency, and disclosure. The first issue concerns the **independence** of the SSB from management. Generally, members of SSBs are appointed by the shareholders of the bank, represented by the board of directors. SSBs report to the board. As such, they are employed by the bank, and their remuneration is proposed by the management and approved by the board. The SSB members' dual relationship with the IFIs as providers of remunerated services and as assessors of the nature of operations may create a conflict of interest. In principle, SSBs are required to submit an unbiased opinion in all matters pertaining to their assignment. However, their employment status generates an economic stake in the bank, which may have a negative impact on their independence.

Confidentiality issues may be intertwined with those of independence. Often, *Shariah* scholars sit on SSBs of various IFIs. This multiple membership may be seen as a strength as it may enhance independence vis-à-vis a particular IFI. However, it entails access to proprietary information about different and possibly competing IFIs. Thus SSBs' members may find themselves in the midst of another type of potential conflict of interest. SSBs' members are required to combine a diverse set of competencies. Due to the unique role that they are called upon to play, SSB members should be knowledgeable in both Islamic law and commercial and accounting practices. In practice, it would appear that very few scholars are well-versed in both disciplines.

The fourth issue concerns **consistency** of judgement across IFIs, over time or across jurisdictions within the same IFI. In essence, the SSBs' activities are in the nature of creating jurisprudence by interpreting legal sources. As such, there may be conflicting opinions on the admissibility of specific financial instruments or transactions. However, the diversity of opinions is seemingly less widespread than would be expected. The Council for Islamic Banks and Financial Institutions (CIBAFI) sampled about 6000 *fatwas*, and found that 90% were consistent across IFIs. The fact that over one hundred *Shariah* scholars around the world issued these *fatwas* suggests an overall consistency in the interpretation of the sources.[24] Nevertheless, as the industry expands, the number of conflicting *fatwas* or rulings on the permissibility of an instrument is also likely to soar if no efforts are made to harmonize the standards. This may undermine the customer's confidence in the industry and have repercussions on the enforceability of contracts.

The last and overarching issue relates to ***disclosure*** of all the information relating to *Shariah* advisory. An objective of a stable Islamic corporate governance system is to enhance the soundness of *Shariah* governance. The framework is enhanced by arrangements put in place by regulators and the presence of providers of financial information services external to the firms. In addition, public rating agencies aid prudent disclosure by filtering out permissible investments and IFIs. They are meant to create a positive climate for *Shariah*-compliant investments. However, private mechanisms for the external governance of *Shariah*-compliance are equally limited. Private rating agencies have not yet developed the necessary skills or found enough incentives to monitor IFIs' *Shariah*-compliance.

Transparency

Transparency refers to the principle of creating an environment where information on existing conditions, decisions, and actions is made accessible, visible, and understandable to all market participants. Disclosure refers more specifically to the process and methodology of providing the information and of making policy decisions known through timely dissemination and openness. Accountability refers to the need for market participants, including the relevant authorities, to justify their actions and policies and accept responsibility for both decisions and results. Islamic financial institutions have made considerable efforts to improve the level of transparency and the quality of information disclosure in the market in the last couple of years. However, there are still several areas that demand attention in order to enhance the level of transparency, such as the following:

- Analysts often have difficulty in collecting useful information regarding Islamic financial institutions. One of the factors contributing to this problem is the lack of uniform reporting standards followed by the financial institutions. For example, a study was recently conducted on the basis of a cursory survey of a sample of nine Islamic banks for which balance sheet data was easily available. It showed that one bank did not provide sufficient details as to the division of equity and deposits, while the remaining eight banks provided a satisfactory division of equity and deposits. However, when it came to deposits, only five of them provided a detailed division of the deposit types that they offered, with the remaining three combining different types of deposits together. Out of these latter three, two made no specific reference to special investment accounts, while the other one maked no distinction between demand

and saving deposits.[25] The disclosure practices of Islamic banks are thus highly dispersed, and the supervisor's authority to impose disclosure norms is also highly varied.

- The collection and dissemination of financially relevant information and credit ratings need significant improvement. However, this requires an institutional infrastructure that facilitates the production of accurate financial information, the development of agents that can interpret and disseminate it, as well as arrangements to protect its integrity. Considering that reliable and timely information is more critical for a system like the Islamic financial system, the current level of financial information infrastructure is not satisfactory. The existing limited infrastructure reduces the role that information flows may play in promoting competition and market activities that would induce managers to adopt sound corporate governance practices.

- A transparent Islamic financial institution would ideally reveal the duties, decision-making, competence and composition of the *Shariah* board, as well as publish all *Fatwas* issued by the board. This would strengthen stakeholders' confidence in the credibility of *Shariah* board assessments. In addition, public disclosure would provide a venue for educating the public, thus paving the way for a larger role to market discipline with respect to *Shariah* compliance. Again, this aspect of transparency is missing from the market. Often, annual reports of the *Shariah* boards are not easily available to the public and other relevant information regarding *Fatwas* by a *Shariah* board are not made available.[26]

- The application of financial modeling to the measuring of assets/ liabilities risks is very limited. Use of quantitative methods (discussed in the previous Chapter), such as Value-at-Rik (VaR) or Profits-at-Risk (PaR), can enhance the financial disclosures due to enhanced measurements of risk exposures, especially in the area of credit and equity risk. Risk exposures can provide disclosure to the investors about their expected profits and losses.

Endnotes

1   Boatright, J. (2002), "Contractors as Shareholders: Reconciling Stakeholder Theory with Mexus-of-Contractors Firm," *Journal of Banking and Finance*, Vol. 26, pp. 1837–1852.

2   Zingales, L. (1997), "Corporate Governance," Working Paper No. 6309, National Bureau of Economic Research (NBER), Cambridge, US.

3   Donaldson, T. and Preston, L. E. (1995), "The Stakeholder Theory of the Corporation: Concepts, Evidence, and Implications," *Academy of Management Review*, Vol. 20, No. 1, pp. 65–91; Freeman, R. E. (1984), *Strategic Management: A Stakeholder Approach*, Boatright, J. (2002), "Contractors as Shareholders: Reconciling Stakeholder Theory with Nexus-of-Contracts Firm," *Journal of Banking and Finance*, Vol. 26, pp. 1837–1852.

4   *Shariah* scholars consider that the human self or soul (*nafs*) has "rights" as well as many duties and responsibilities.

5   Imam Zayn al-Abidin's treatise on the rights, "*Risalat Al-Huquq*" covers a full spectrum of rights in Islam. For example, the right to one's property (*al-mal*) means that one takes it only from what is lawful and spends it only on what is proper. The right of the associate (*khalit*) is that one neither misleads him, nor acts dishonestly toward him, nor deceives him. The right of the adversary (*Khasm*) who has a claim against one is that, if his claim is valid, one gives witness to it against oneself. Ali ibn al-Husayn (1990).

6   Islam, Muhammad W. (1999), "Al-Mal: The Concept of Property in Islamic Legal Thought," *Arab Law Quarterly*, pp. 361–368. The term *mal* or its derivatives have been mentioned in the Quran in more than 90 verses and in numerous sayings of the Prophet (*pbuh*).

7   See Mirakhor, Abbas (1989), "General Characteristics of An Islamic Economic System," *in* Baqir Al-Hasani and Abbas Mirakhor, *(ed.) Essays on Iqtisad: The Islamic Approach to Economic Problems*, (Nur Corp., MD, USA), pp. 45–80, and Ahmed (1995), *Business Ethnics in Islam*.

8   *Allah* (swt) explicitly states that "*Believe in Allah and His messenger, and spend of that whereof He made you **trustee**.*" Quran (57:7). By implication, the ownership of property (*al-mal*) is understood to be a trust and is considered to be a test of faith. Bashir (1999).

9   Mirakhor, Abbas (1995), "Outline of an Islamic Economic System," *Zahid Husain Memorial Lecture Series No. 11*, State Bank of Pakistan, Islamabad, March 1995, makes reference to a number of verses to support this axiom. For example:

هُوَ ٱلَّذِى خَلَقَ لَكُم مَّا فِى ٱلْأَرْضِ جَمِيعًا

"*He it is who has created for **you all** that is on earth*" Quran (2:29)

Both لَكُم and جَمِيعًا refer to collectivity for whom the plurality of resources have been created by *Allah* (SWT). In another verse, *Allah* (SWT) says:

وَلَا تُؤْتُوا ٱلسُّفَهَآءَ أَمْوَالَكُمُ ٱلَّتِى جَعَلَ ٱللَّهُ لَكُمْ قِيَـٰمًا

"*Do not give your **resources** that Allah has made you its preservers on to the foolish*" Quran (4:5)

Again, جَعَلَ ٱللَّهُ لَكُمْ قِيَـٰمًا and أَمْوَالَكُمُ indicate the right of collectivity.

10   Islahi, Abdul Azim (1988), *Economic Concepts of Ibn Taimiyah*, claims that this distinguishing characteristic of his economic views is not found in any of scholastic scholars.

11   The Prophet (*pbuh*), during his last sermon at Arafat declared the inviolability of property to be at par with that of life and honour: "Like this day of this month in this territory, sacred and inviolable, *Allah* (swt) has made the life and property and honor of each of you onto the other until you meet your Lord."

12   Islahi, Abdul Azim (1988), *Economic Concepts of the Ibn Taimiyah*.

13   These rules are supported by various verses in Quran as following:

"And do not eat up your property among yourselves for vanities, not use it as bait for the judges, with intent that ye may eat up wrongfully and knowingly a little of (other) people's property." Quran (2:188).

"Those who when they spend are not extravagant and not niggardly, but hold a just (balance) between those (extremes)." Quran (25:67).

"Behold, the squanderers are, indeed, of the ilk of the satans...." Quran (17:27).

14   The concept that man has an unrestricted handling authority over his wealth is unacceptable. *Allah* (swt) has condemned the people of Shuayb for adopting such an attitude. See Quran (11:87). Ahmed (1995).

15   Bashir, Abdel-Hameed M. (1999), "Property Rights in Islam," Conference Proceedings of the Third Harvard University Forum on Islamic Finance, Harvard University, October 1999, pp. 71–82, argues that Islam attaches great importance on protecting people from harm caused by others. The Prophet is reported to have said *"to cause harm to others is not allowed in Islam."*

16   Relationship between *Allah* (swt) and human beings initiated as a contract. A covenant was made when *Allah* (swt) asked *"**Am I not your Lord**?"* to which human being replied *"**Yes, we testify**."* Quran (7:172).

17   The Prophet (*pbuh*) is also reported as having said *"a person without trustworthiness is a person without religion."*

18   The classical definition of stakeholders is given by Freeman (1984) as any group or individual who may affect or be affected by the attainment of the firm's goals. Clarkson's (1995) offers a refined view of a stakeholder based on the stakeholder's exposure to the risk (a hazard, a danger, or the possibility of suffering harm or loss) as result of the firm's activities.

19   Boatright (2002).

20   See Grais, Wafik and Zamir Iqbal (2006), *"Corporate Governance Challenges of Islamic Financial Institutions,"* 7th Harvard Forum on Islamic Finance, Boston, US, April 22–23, and Iqbal (2006) and Greuning and Iqbal (2006) for further details.

21   Grais, Wafik. and M. Pellegrini (2005), "Corporate Governance of Business Offering Islamic Financial Services: Issues and Options," Working paper, The World Bank Group, Washington DC, US.

22   They exist in all Islamic countries with the exception of Iran, where compliance of the whole banking system with the *Shariah* is guaranteed and monitored by the central bank.

23   A *Fatwa* is a religious edict or proclamation. It is a legal opinion issued by a qualified Muslim scholar on matters of religious belief and practice.

24   Grais and Pellegrini (2005).

25   Grais and Pellegrini (2005).

26   Grais and Pellegrini (2005) A survey of thirteen IFIs shows the level of transparency to be low. Out of thirteen IFIs reviewed, all declared the existence of the SSB within the organization and disclosed information on its composition. However, only seven made the annual report of the SSB easily accessible and seven did not provide detailed information on the professional background of the SSB members. Moreover, only two IFIs disclosed the *Fatwas* authorizing the provision of financial services and products. Only one disclosed provisions for decision-making and interaction with other bodies of the firm. Finally, only one IFI disclosed on its website the duties and obligations of the SSB. IFIs' practice of limited disclosure would not inspire confidence in *Shariah* compliance.

Globalization and Challenges for Islamic Finance

The last few decades have witnessed dramatic and rapid changes in the structure of financial markets and institutions across the world. Advances in financial theory, the rapid pace of financial innovation, the revolution in information technology, deregulation, and institutional reforms have irreversibly changed the nature of financial relations and a "new finance" has emerged. As a result:

> "people can borrow greater amounts at cheaper rates than ever before; invest in a multitude of instruments catering to every possible profile of risk and return, and share risks with strangers from across the globe. These changes have altered the nature of the typical transaction in the financial sector, making it more arm's length and allowing broader participation. Financial markets have expanded and have become deeper. The broad participation has allowed risks to be more widely spread throughout the economy."[1]

The new finance has an important role in leveling economic playing fields, thus becoming the great equalizer of our time: it requires no passport, and does not discriminate on the basis of color, creed, race, or national origin. It unwinds and un-bundles, dissects, analyses, and prices risk, and searches for the highest return. It explores all opportunities for risk-return sharing, in order to exploit the wedge between the real rate of return to assets and the real rate of interest, leading to greater reliance on risk sharing.

Globalization is a multifaceted and multidimensional process of growing interconnectedness among nations and peoples of the world. Its main dimensions are cultural, socio-political, and economic. Its economic dimensions include growing trade flows, unhindered movements of finance, investment and production, accompanied by standardization of processes, regulations, and institutions — all facilitated by the free flow of information and ideas. Globalization is the result of reduced information and transportation costs, and liberalization of trade, finance, investment, capital flows, and factor movements.

As globalization gathers momentum and becomes pervasive, and as more economies liberalize in order to integrate into the global economy, the new finance will grow and so will the risk-sharing and asset-based securitization: both are the core of Islamic finance. The present globalization is considered unfair because the risks and rewards of the process are not shared equitably. However, as equity-based and asset-backed financing grows, the fruits of globalization can be distributed more widely and more equitably among the participants than has been the case thus far, at least in terms of the financial linkages. There remains the question of protectionism in industrial countries, segmented labor markets and impediments to the transfer of technology, which require full international cooperation to be addressed and mitigated.

If the present globalization process is characterized as the free flow of trade, investment, and production, then it is possible to identify a similar episode of globalization — that of the Middle Ages. During the period referred to as "the age of the commercial revolution," from the middle of the eighth century to the latter part of the sixteenth century, trade flowed freely across the then-known world, supported by risk-sharing methods of finance, which were developed in the Muslim countries consistent with the *Shariah*. Information regarding the basic features of these methods was transmitted via the intermediation of Jewish scholars and merchants, and importantly also Spain, from the Muslim world to Egypt, Europe, India, and North Africa. These new financial techniques were also transmitted by Muslim merchants to Eurasia, Russia, China as well as to East Asia.

As globalization proceeds, its main engines — the new finance and advances in information technology — will shift the methods and instruments of financing trade, investment, and production in favor of more risk-spreading-and-sharing rather than risk-shifting via fixed-price debt contracts. This is the result of financial innovations that are dissecting, analyzing, and pricing risk better, so that — combined with efficient availability of information and adoption of best international standards of transparency, accountability, and good governance in public and private sectors — the *raison d'être* of fixed-price debt contracts will erode.

The current wave of globalization is here to stay and will change the financial landscape. As the new financial landscape emerges, risk-sharing and ultimately profit-and-loss-sharing contracts will become standardized which will create opportunities for new financial systems to develop. Globalization and consequently the expansion of equity and risk-sharing modes of financing should pave the way for further growth of Islamic finance. However, Islamic finance has to overcome several challenges that have been discussed in previous chapters and are summarized below.

Challenges for Islamic Finance

There are challenges on several fronts; theoretical, operational, and implementational. On the theoretical side, further work needs to be done on developing core principles of Islamic economics, and understanding the functioning of a financial system operating on a profit-and-loss-sharing basis. On the operational side, issues relating to innovation, intermediation, and risk management are worthy of attention. Finally, special attention should be given to efforts required on a system-wide implementation. Each of these challenges can take a volume itself, but some of these challenges are briefly discussed below.

Refining Islamic Economics

Whether Islamic economics is considered to be an entirely different discipline from traditional economics — a position justified by its world view, its view of rationality, its view on man's nature, its emphasis on the need for correspondence between behavior and prescribed rules as well as its other specific dimensions — or as a special subfield within that discipline, it has made considerable progress since its revival a little over three decades ago. This is remarkable, given that there is virtually no organized support for this effort, in sharp contrast to the multitude of private and public foundations providing financial support to research traditional economics. Despite the wealth of resources available in many Muslim societies, there is lamentably little support for scholarship in Islamic economics. Moreover, even the academic recognition of research activities in this field is, by and large, lacking and there is a lack of incentives for scholars to pursue their interest in furthering contemporary thinking in the discipline. Nevertheless, the personal dedication of scholars has produced a credible body of work that provides a sense of optimism regarding the future of Islamic economics.

There is no reason to doubt that scholarly activities in this field will continue, nor to think that, at some point in the future, it will develop a rigorous analytic foundation for policy analysis and prescription to achieve the objectives of Islam for the economy. Learning from the history of development of traditional economics — both its successes and failures — research in Islamic economics should anchor its progress on an interdisciplinary approach, paying due attention to historical, philosophical, psychological, and sociological dimensions of what Islam intends for individual and collective economic behavior. The immense scholarly works of Muslim philosophers, *Fuqaha*, historians, and social critics provide a valuable legacy that will be extremely helpful in this process. Developments in traditional economics are also a fertile field for researchers in Islamic economics to harvest as a source of ideas. While the economic history of Muslim societies and thoughts can serve as a major source of ideas, special attention should also be directed at developing a proper language of discourse in Islamic economics, with the hope of the emergence of a consensus-based, analytical, and operational definitions, and descriptions of major concepts that scholars need to further refine ideas and generate new insights. A common language, with its own "grammar," of Islamic economics is fundamentally important. For this reason, a plea is made for the development of a coherent, comprehensive, and systematic economic hermeneutics as a foundational structure that supports research, dialogue, and debate in Islamic economics, as well as in building the future edifice of theoretical, empirical, and policy structure of this discipline. The present generation of researchers is in a position to make an important contribution by focusing on activities that can draw economic meanings and inferences from terms, ideas, and concepts expounded in the sources of Islam. The hope is that at some point in time a collection similar to Palgrave's Dictionary of Economics is developed for Islamic economics. The momentum of these efforts will be much accelerated if financial resources, similar to those provided to investigations in traditional economics by major foundations, could be mobilized in Muslim societies to support such activities.

Trust, Institutions and Economic Development

Recent cross-country research indicates that the best performing countries are those with relatively high trust levels and strong institutions. In poor performing economies the level of trust is low, and institutions are either absent or weak. If trust is low, strong institutions should be established to protect property and investors' rights as well as to enforce contracts. While current Muslim societies have low levels of trust, they are adopting best practice and international standards of policy formulation and implementation as well as legal institutions and practices that compensate for this weakness. Therefore, it is expected that risk-sharing methods of Islamic finance will expand rapidly in these countries.

As mentioned earlier, an important reason for the dominance of risk-sharing finance during the Middle Ages was mutual trust. It is possible that the breakdown in the general level of trust relationships may have led to the dominance of debt contracts beginning at the end of the Middle Ages. Economists, however, have been empirically investigating trust only recently after Fukuyama raised the possibility that it may be an important factor in explaining cross-country economic performance.[2] Specifically, he asserted that the general level of trust, an important component of social capital, was a strong explanatory factor in the economic performance of industrial countries. Moreover, he indicated that a high level of general trust was reinforced in these societies by strong institutions. The last decade of the twentieth century had already witnessed a large volume of empirical research that focused on the existence (or the lack) of strong institutions explaining cross-country differences in economic performance. This literature isolated two specific institutions — those that protect property rights and those that enforce contracts — as the most important in explaining why some economies performed well and others did not.

The last decade has witnessed a growing literature on the importance of trust to, inter alia, the development of the financial system. This body of research has demonstrated that since finance, particularly risk-sharing instruments like equity, is trust-intensive, high-trust societies exhibit more developed and deeper financial systems. In particular, this literature indicates that there is a high correlation between trust and development of the financial sector. If the level of trust is high, people rely more on risky assets, such as equity, invest a larger share of their wealth in stocks, use more checks, and have access to a greater amount of credit than in low-trust countries. Importantly also, since the second half of the 1990s, a number of researchers, using a variety of techniques, have attempted to demonstrate the impact of trust on economic performance.

There is growing evidence suggesting that low trust is a crucial factor in explaining the low level of stock market participation. If such research proves robust, trust may well become the long awaited solution to the Equity Premium Puzzle. Trust is defined as "the subjective probability that individuals attribute to the possibility of being cheated." Based on the analysis of cross-country data, where the level of trust is high, investment in equities, in general, and in the stock market, in particular, is also high. In low-trust countries, equity participation depends on observance of the rule of law and the existence of legal institutions that protect property and investor rights and those that enforce contracts. It suggests that in low-performing economies not only is the level of trust low, but property and investor rights are poorly protected, and legal contract enforcement weak. Consequently, in these countries, corporations either do not form and if they do, they resort to debt financing. The policy implications for these economies is to strengthen legal institutions, improve transparency, accountability, and governance — both in private and public sectors — and to provide the public with a greater amount of information and education on risk-reward-sharing finance, in general, and equity markets, in particular.

If low trust is a crucial factor in explaining poor economic performance, then the results of recent research is a wake-up call for Muslim countries, since trust is considered the most important element of social capital in Islam, and the cornerstone of the relationship of individuals with the Supreme Creator and with others in the society. Islam places a strong emphasis on trust and considers being trustworthy as an obligatory command. The root of the word belief — *Iman* — is the same as that of trust — *Amanah*. Moreover, abiding by one's contracts and remaining faithful to promises with other members of society derives from the need to remain faithful to the original, primordial covenant between human beings and the Supreme Creator (*Quran*, Chapter 7, Verse 172). Accordingly, the *Quran*, in a number of verses, insists that a strong signal of true belief is faithfulness to contracts and promises made. Moreover, the *Quran* makes clear that performing the obligations one has contracted or promised is mandatory for a believer. Indeed, fidelity to one's promises and to the terms of contracts one enters into as well as maintaining trust are considered important characteristics of a true believer.

In the chapter of the "Faithful" the *Quran* — Chapter 23, Verses 1-8 — keeping trust and promises are two of the major characteristics of the faithful. In the first verse of Chapter 5 of the *Quran*, the faithful are ordered to abide by the terms of contracts they have entered into. Similarly, in Verse 34 of Chapter 17, the faithful are commanded to keep their promises, for they will be asked about their faithfulness to promises. There are other verses of the *Quran* that emphasize the duty of the faithful to remain fully conscious of *Allah* (swt) while entering into a contract or making promises, or being trustworthy when they are entrusted with objects for safekeeping (see, for example, Verse 283 of Chapter 2 and Verse 58 of Chapter 2). The *Quran* also identifies a chief characteristic of prophets and messengers of *Allah* (swt) as trustworthiness (for example, see Chapter 42, Verses 107, 125, 143, 162, 178, 193) and chastises betrayal of trust (see Chapter 8, Verse 58 and Chapter 12, Verse 52). In short, Islam has made trust and trustworthiness obligatory

— as well as keeping faith with contracts and promises — and has rendered them inviolable without explicitly permissible justification.

The reason for poor economic performance of some countries is a low level of trust, combined with weak legal institutions protecting property and investor rights and poor contract enforcement. In the case of Muslim countries, it is argued that weak adherence to the rules, norms, and values demanded by Islam, which constitute its social capital, is the explanation of poor economic performance (Chapra, 2000). There is hope that as Muslim societies continue the process of strengthening legal institutions, which some have already begun, their economic performance will improve. Efforts at reforming education with concentration on adherence to Islamic values, norms and rules should strengthen the social capital — including, importantly, the level of trust — in these countries. One result of strengthening institutions and enhancing the general level of trust will be adoption of Islamic financial techniques of risk- and-reward-sharing. Consequently, a global convergence process may be already at work toward risk-sharing in the West and in the Islamic world. As the risks of globalization are shared more equitably, so will its rewards, at least in terms of financial transactions and investment.

Given the strong heritage of trust and trustworthiness in Islam, the low level of trust within and among Muslim societies is inexplicable unless one considers the historical erosion and loss of values, norms, and rules critical to Islam. While the present low economic performance in Muslim societies, attributable to the low level of trust, is discouraging, signs are emerging that the future is more hopeful. The governments of these countries are implementing policies to strengthen the institutional structure of society, even if it is clear that the required level of trust will take a prolonged and sustained effort to achieve the strength commensurate with Islamic teachings. These policies include:

- those intended to strengthen transparency, accountability, and good governance for public and private sectors
- enactment of fiscal responsibility laws; capital market laws
- instituting legal structures that protect property and investor rights and enforce contracts
- financial sector reforms that create a level playing field for all participants and deepen these markets
- liberalization of trade and foreign direct investment.

Reform is also required in public education in Muslim societies with an emphasis on Islamic values and behavioral norms and rules, including the importance of trust and trustworthiness. Depending on the speed of reforms, it is possible for Muslim countries to "leap frog" in achieving higher growth rates for their economies.

Emergence of a Risk-Sharing Financial System

The question is why greater use is not made of equity finance with its risk-sharing characteristics. Prescott and Mehra (1985) demonstrated that over many decades, a large differential existed between the real rate of return to equity and the real rate of return to a safe asset, i.e., US Treasury bills. Furthermore, the differential was too large to be explained by existing theories of rational investor behavior. This result became known as the "Equity Premium Puzzle." It is a puzzle why rational investors, noting the differential, would not invest in equities until the point where the remaining differential could be explained as the risk premium on equities. Subsequent research demonstrated that the puzzle existed in other countries as well. Since the publication of the paper, a large body of literature has attempted to explain the puzzle, but Mehra (2004) argued that all explanations failed, for one reason or another, to provide a satisfactory resolution.[3]

A major economic-historical puzzle is why, after dominating the world of finance for eight centuries, risk-sharing methods lost their supremacy to debt-based financing. One important reason may be that, since risk sharing is trust-intensive, a systemic breakdown of trust in Europe led to the emergence of debt-based financing. It is likely that the breakdown of trust in Europe and elsewhere was a major factor for the loss of dominance of risk-sharing finance by the end of the Middle Ages. Risk-sharing finance is trust-intensive, and trade financing during the Middle Ages was based on risk-sharing which, in turn, was based on mutual trust.

While risk-sharing techniques continued to be used in Europe until mid-seventeenth century, beginning in mid-sixteenth century, the institution of interest-based debt financing began to be used more widely and extensively throughout Europe. The explanation for the initial utilization of this method of financing and its dominance over risk-sharing methods has been a combination of several factors, including:

- the demise of the scholastic prohibition of usury;
- the appearance and rapid growth of fractional reserve banking that led to specialization of finance by intermediaries who preferred to provide financing to agent-entrepreneurs at fixed interest rates based on contracts enforceable by law and the State in order to reduce monitoring and transaction costs;

- inflow of vast amounts of gold and other riches into Europe from the European colonies in the Americas and elsewhere. This immense inflow reduced the incentive for the elite classes to continue financing trade on the basis of risk sharing. Instead, they preferred to turn their wealth over to intermediaries, or to loan directly to merchant-entrepreneurs on the basis of fixed interest debt contracts;
- the emergence of nation-states whose governments were in need of finance for wars or other state activities, but could not raise resources except by means of fixed interest rate contracts according to which an annuity was paid in perpetuity without the need for governments to repay the principal.

However, the full-scale adoption of a fixed-interest-based financial system with a fractional reserve banking sector at its core had a major deficiency. The system was considered inherently fragile.[4] Toward the end of the 1970s and the early 1980s, the existence of financial intermediaries, in general, and banks, in particular, was justified due to their ability to reduce transaction and monitoring costs as well as to manage risk. However, little attention was paid to reasons why banks operated on the basis of fixed, pre-determined interest rate-based contracts, i.e., on a fixed interest system that rendered the system fragile and unstable requiring a lender of last resort to regulate it. The traditional model of intermediaries existing to lower transaction/monitoring costs does not explain why their liability structure is not all equity. With the development and growth of information economics and agency literature, another explanation was added to the list of reasons for the existence of intermediaries. They served as delegated monitoring as well as signaling agents to solve the informational problems, including asymmetric information existing between principals and agents.

Based on the findings of the developing field of information economics, it is argued that adverse selection and moral hazard effects in a banking system operating on the basis of fixed interest contracts in the presence of asymmetric information — particularly in cases where this problem is acute — mean that some groups will be excluded from the credit market even when the expected rate of return for these groups may be higher than for those with access to credit. Furthermore, it is argued that in the case of risk-return-sharing, contracts — e.g., equity — are not subject to adverse selection and moral hazard effects, "the expected return to an equity investor would be exactly the same as the expected return of the project itself."

The fragility of a financial system operating on the basis of a fixed, pre-determined interest rate was underlined by Stiglitz (1988) who argued:

"interest rate is not like a conventional price. It is a promise to pay an amount in the future. Promises are often broken. If they were not, there would be no issue in determining creditworthiness. Raising interest rates may not increase the expected return to a loan; at higher interest rates one obtains a lower quality set of applicants (adverse selection effect) and each one's applicants undertakes greater risks (the adverse incentive effect). These effects are sufficiently strong that the net return may be lowered as banks increase the interest rates charged: it does not pay to charge higher interest rates."

The findings of the new field of information economics strengthened the arguments that a debt-based financial system with fractional reserve banking operating with a fixed, pre-determined interest rate mechanism at its core is inherently fragile and prone to periodic instability. Stiglitz's findings underlined Minsky's argument that, as returns to banks declined, unable to raise interest rates on their loans, they enter a liability-management mode by increasing interest rates on their deposits. As this vicious circle continues to pick up momentum, the liability management transforms into Ponzi financing and eventually runs on banks. The last two decades of the twentieth century witnessed a number of global bouts of financial instability and debt crises, with devastating consequences for a large segment of humanity, thus raising consciousness regarding the vulnerabilities and fragilities of the financial system which originate, at their core, from fixed-price debt contracts. The risks of country-specific debt crises with potential risks of contagion have not diminished, particularly for a number of emerging economies, including some Muslim countries.

Risk-sharing finance of trade, investment, and production — based on Islamic modes of finance — dominated interest-based modes of financing throughout the then-known world based on mutual trust between agents and principals. The breakdown of trust may have been crucial among the factors that explain the decline in risk-sharing finance as well as the growth, and eventual dominance, of fixed-price debt contracting modes of finance. The rapid progress in development of risk-sharing techniques and asset-backed instruments is evidence of this shift; in particular, there is already a perceptible shift of household portfolios toward equity and share holding in a number of industrial countries. As risk-sharing financial instruments gain wide acceptance and confidence of investors, one can envisage a financial system founded on risk-sharing as promoted by Islamic finance.

System-wide Implementation

The most important challenge is system-wide implementation of Islamic financial system. At present, many Islamic countries suffer from financial disequilibria that frustrate attempts at wholesale adoption of Islamic finance. Financial imbalances in the fiscal, monetary, and external sectors of these economies cannot provide a fertile ground for the efficient operation of Islamic finance. Major structural adjustments particularly in fiscal and monetary areas are needed to provide a level playing field for Islamic finance. The efficient operation of system-wide Islamic banking is presently severely constrained by distortions in the economy, such as:

- pervasive government intervention and controls,
- inefficient and weak tax systems,
- financial repression,
- lack of capital markets,
- unavailability of a well-targeted and efficient social safety net,
- lack of a strong supervisory and prudential regulatory framework in the financial system
- deficiency of legal and institutional frameworks that provide *Shariah*-based definitions of property rights as well as the rights of the parties to contracts

These distortions need to be eliminated to minimize waste and promote efficient resource allocation. Their removal prior to, or in conjunction with, the adoption of Islamic banking should create the dynamics necessary for non-inflationary and sustainable economic growth.

These distortions not only increase price instability but also aggravate the risk and uncertainty surrounding contracts that do not promise a fixed nominal return. Since Islamic modes of transaction shift more risks to the investor, the investor needs credible government policies to maintain stable prices. The choice of a monetary and fiscal policy regime determines the types of risks and uncertainty that the society bears. Individuals reduce the costs of risks and uncertainty associated with a given monetary or fiscal regime by refusing to share in risks of projects and opt for safe, rather than risky, assets with fixed nominal payoffs, rather than returns that are outcome-dependent.

An Islamic financial system can be said to operate efficiently if, as a result of its adoption, rates of return in the financial sector correspond to those in the real sector. In many Islamic countries, fiscal deficits are financed through the banking system. To lower the costs of this financing, the financial system is repressed by artificially maintaining limits on bank rates. Thus, financial repression is a form of taxation that provides governments with substantial revenues. To remove this burden, government expenditures have to be lowered and/or revenues raised. Massive involvement of governments in the economy makes it difficult for them to reduce their expenditures. Raising taxes are politically difficult. Thus, imposing controls on domestic financial markets becomes a relatively easy form of raising revenues. Under these circumstances, governments impose severe constraints on private financial operations that can provide higher returns to their shareholders and/or depositors. This makes it very difficult for Islamic banks and other financial institutions to fully realize their potential. For example, *Mudarabah* companies that can provide higher returns than the banking system end up in direct competition with the banking system for deposits that are used for bank financing of fiscal deficits.

While it has been relatively easy to create a system in which deposits do not pay interest, the asset portfolios of Islamic banks do not contain sufficiently strong components that are based on profit sharing. The main reasons for this are:

- The lack of legal and institutional frameworks that facilitate appropriate contracts as well as mechanisms to enforce them. The banking system is a direct function of the returns to asset portfolios and since assets are created in response to investment opportunities in the real economy, it is the real sector that determines the rate of return to the financial sector rather than the reverse; and/or
- The lack of range and variety of maturity structures of financial instruments.

Consequently, there is a perception that profit-sharing methods in particular and Islamic finance in general are high risk. This, in turn, has led to a concentration of asset portfolios of the Islamic banks in short-term and trade-related assets. The problem is exacerbated by the fact that Muslim countries, as is the case in much of the developing world, suffer from the lack of deep and efficient capital and money markets that can provide the needed liquidity and safety for existing assets. The absence of suitable long-term instruments to support capital formation is mirrored in a lack of short-term financial instruments to provide liquidity.

Whereas theoretical developments have demonstrated the viability and practicality of an Islamic financial system, its system–wide implementation faces several challenges. It is critical to identify and meet the challenges if current growth is to be maintained and sustained for the long term.

Considerable efforts have been made recently to address issues of regulation and supervision of Islamic financial institutions and as a result, a solid regulatory framework for Islamic financial institutions is emerging. Excluding the regulatory and supervisory challenges, the major and the most immediate challenges are:

- to develop risk-sharing financial instruments and benchmarks;
- to develop liquid secondary and money markets;
- to develop instruments for effective monetary and fiscal policy;
- to standardize accounting and auditing standards as well as the process of religious approval of new instruments and techniques.

These challenges can be classified into two groups:

(i)   financial engineering challenges to apply principles of Islamic finance for further innovation and

(ii) challenges to make the operation of the system more efficient, stable, and well integrated with international capital markets.

A **financial engineering** challenge is to introduce new *Shariah*-compatible products to enhance liquidity in the market and to offer tools to manage risk and to diversify portfolios. Applications of financial engineering techniques to Islamic banking requires commitment of resources to understand the risk-return characteristics of each building block of the Islamic financial system and to offer new products with different risk-return profiles to meet the demand of investors, financial intermediaries, and entrepreneurs for liquidity and safety. The process of securitization to enhance marketability, negotiability, marketability, and return on assets is a prime candidate for financial engineering. With increased globalization, integration and linkages have become critical to the success of capital markets. Such integration becomes seamless and transparent when financial markets offer a wide-array of instruments with varying maturity structures and opportunities for portfolio diversification and risk management. Financial engineering in Islamic finance needs to focus on the development of products that foster market integration and attract investors and entrepreneurs to the risk-return characteristics of the product, instead of the product being Islamic or non-Islamic. New financial innovation is also needed to satisfy market demand on the two ends of maturity structure — i.e., short-term and long-term. Money markets that are *Shariah*-compatible do not exist at present and there is no equivalent of an Islamic inter-bank market where banks can place, overnight funds, or where they can borrow to satisfy temporary liquidity needs.

Another operational difficulty facing Islamic finance is the availability of an equity-based benchmark or reference rate (reflecting the rate of return on the real sector) for pricing assets and evaluating portfolio performance, or comparing various investment alternatives. In the absence of such a reference rate or benchmark, a questionable, but common practice has been to use the London Inter-Bank Offered Rate (LIBOR) as a proxy. Whereas usage of an interest-based benchmark may be sanctioned by *Shariah* scholars as a temporary measure, the system would operate more efficiently if an index representing returns on profit-loss sharing instruments is developed and used as benchmark.

Islamic Banking

Islamic financial institutions have performed well during the high growth period of the industry but, with a rapidly changing global financial landscape, maintaining sustainable growth is becoming one of many challenges. So far, Islamic banks have capitalized on a demand-driven niche market growing at a fast pace but, with a large number of existing Islamic banks and growing interest from conventional institutions (both Western and non-Western) tapping into this emerging market, the industry is becoming highly competitive. Current Islamic financial institutions have maintained a competitive advantage in a market which was characterized until recently by high entry barriers for conventional institutions which were less knowledgeable in *Shariah*. However, with increased awareness and recognition of Islamic financial instruments, advances in technology, globalization and market integration, more experienced and professionally more advanced conventional institutions, will create tough competition in the future. Here are some of major challenges facing Islamic financial institutions:

Two-way Intermediation
As impressive as the record of growth of individual Islamic banks may be, the fact is that, at present, those banks have mostly served as intermediaries between financial resources of Muslims and major commercial banks in the West. In this context, this has been a one-way relationship. There is still no major Islamic bank that has developed methods of intermediating between Western financial resources and demand for them in Muslim countries. While there is considerable room for competition and expansion in this field, the long-term survivability of individual Islamic banks will depend on how rapidly, aggressively, and effectively they can develop techniques and instruments that allow them to carry on a two-way intermediation function. They need to find methods of developing marketable *Shariah*-based instruments by which asset portfolios generated in Muslim countries

can be marketed in the West as well as marketing *Shariah*-based western portfolios in Muslim communities.

Risk Management

Financial markets are becoming more integrated and interdependent, thus increasing the probability of expeditious contagion effects. Further, insufficient understanding of the new environment creates a greater risk perception even if the objective level of risk in the system is unchanged or reduced. The current wave of capital market liberalization and globalization may prompt the need for enhanced risk management measures, especially for the developing economies and the emerging Islamic financial markets. Whereas financial risk management is widely practiced in conventional financial markets, it is grossly under-developed in Islamic financial markets. Islamic financial institutions need to take immediate steps to devise an infrastructure for implementing proper risk measurements, controls and management, and to innovate instruments to share, transfer and mitigate financial risk so that entrepreneurs can concentrate on what they do best — managing exposure to business risk in which they have a competitive advantage.

This requires Islamic financial intermediaries to adopt appropriate risk management not only for their own portfolio, but to provide innovative risk management services to their clients. A financial institution which can offer guarantees, enhance liquidity, underwrite insurance against risks, and finally develop hedging tools for a fee, can and should be established. If the basic building blocks of the Islamic financial system are viewed as set of "asset-backed" securities, derivatives can be created synthetically and can be used to share, transfer or mitigate financial risk. Both on- and off-balance sheet hedging instruments should be developed using the basic building blocks of the Islamic financial system by applying techniques of financial engineering.

Islamic financial institutions need to realize the importance of operational risk — risk due to failure of controls and processes. Currently, there is a serious lack of a risk management culture and of enterprise level sponsorship of active risk management. Formulating a strategy for risk management in Islamic financial markets will require:

- comprehensive and detailed discussion of the scope and role of derivatives within the framework of the *Shariah*;
- an expanded role of financial intermediaries with special emphasis on facilitating risk sharing;
- the applicability of *Takaful* (*Shariah*-compliant mutual insurance) to insure financial risk; and

- the application of financial engineering to develop synthetic derivatives and off-balance sheet instruments.

Standardization

Another operational challenge for Islamic banks is to standardize the process of introducing new products in the market. Currently, each Islamic bank has its own religious board examining and evaluating each new product without coordinating the efforts among other banks. Each religious board may have its preferences or adherence to a particular school of thought. This process should be streamlined and standardized to minimize time, effort and confusion. There should be proper post-product audit by audit committees to make the institutions comply with the *Shariah* guidelines defined by the religious board. Some Islamic banks have already started using such audit committees.

Consolidation

Due to the large number of small-sized institutions, Islamic banks do not enjoy efficiencies of economies of scale. Many Islamic banks use the facilities of conventional banks as intermediaries for treasury management, foreign exchange, portfolio services and investment banking, which reduces their profit margins. It has been suggested that it is time for Islamic banks to seriously consider merging into large financial institutions, in order to enjoy economies of scale and reduced overhead costs through efficiency gains.

Governance

In principle, the governance model in Islamic financial system is similar to that of a stakeholders-based incentive system through participation of *Shariah* boards, public policy institutions, regulatory and supervisory institutions which monitor the performance of an Islamic financial institution and its faithfulness and commitment to contracts that protect interests of all stakeholders. In the case of Islamic financial institutions, governance issues are similar to those raised in the case of an "insider" system of governance, where the institutional investor plays an active role in the governance process.

Whereas increased monitoring by investment account holders through increased transparency is highly desirable, their representation in the organs of governance raises several operational and implementation concerns. The majority of investment account holders are individuals who may not organize themselves collectively to perform the necessary monitoring. Under such circumstances, the responsibility of regulators and *Shariah* boards increases to ensure that an adequate monitoring mechanism is in place to protect the rights of investment account holders. A second implication of the role of investment account holders in Islamic financial institutions is that the financial institution, as the custodian and manager of investment accounts, becomes an institutional investor with a vested interest in the governance of the institutions that are the recipients of funds. This implies that investment account holders are stakeholders in the financial institution, and that the financial institution itself becomes a stakeholder in the enterprises that depend on the funds that it provides. This issue is not highlighted in the current discussion of corporate governance.

Finally, the role of *Shariah* boards in sound governance is also critical. It is common practice in current governance structures for each institution to maintain a *Shariah* board or *Shariah* advisor. This practice leads to inefficient decision-making due to duplication of effort, and lack of standardization. Instead, a system-wide board of knowledgeable religious scholars who are also specialized by training in Islamic economic and financial principles would be more efficient. Ideally, a *Shariah* board would be composed of a group of scholars and experts in *Fiqh*, banking, economics, accounting and finance. This structure of governance with a system-wide religious board will be more efficient and cost-effective because:

- stakeholders will not require duplicate monitoring;
- institutions will not need to maintain their own boards;
- boards will consist of knowledgeable experts in *Shariah* as well as finance,
- there will be uniformity of expected behavior which will set the standards to be followed by individual institutions.

Such a system-wide *Shariah* board can work closely with the regulators and supervisors to ensure that effective monitoring and supervisory controls are devised to protect the rights of all stakeholders with whom the financial institution has explicit or implicit contracts.

Endnotes

1   Rajan, Raghuram G., (2005), "Has Financial Development Made the World Riskier?"

2   Fukuyama, Francis (1996), *Trust: The Social Virtues and the Creation of Prosperity*.

3   Interestingly, also in the same paper, Mehra reported that the real worth of one dollar invested in 1802 in equity would have been nearly $560,000 in 1997, whereas the real worth of the same $1 invested in 1802 in Treasury bills would have been $276 over the same period.

4   For further details see Minsky, Hyman (1982), *Inflation, Recession and Economic Policy*, and Khan, Mohsin (1987), *Islamic Interest Free Banking: A Theoretical Analysis*.

References

Chapter 1

Chapra, M. U. (2000), "The Future of Economics," The Islamic Foundation, UK.

Khan, Tariqullah (1996), "An analysis of risk sharing in Islamic finance with special reference to Pakistan," Doctoral Thesis, Department of Economics, Loughborough University, UK.

Kuran, Timur (1995) "Islamic Economics and the Islamic Subeconomy," *Journal of Economic Perspectives*, Fall 1995, 9:4, pp. 155–173.

Islamic Development Bank (IsDB) and Islamic Financial Services Board (IFSB) (2005), *The Islamic Financial Services Industry: Ten-Year Master Plan 2006–2016*, Islamic Development Bank, Jeddah, Saudi Arabia.

Chapter 2

As-Sadr, Mohammad Baqir (1982), *Iqtisaduna: Our Economics*, World Organization for Islamic Services, Tehran, Iran.

Jain, L. C. (1929), *Indigenous Banking in India*, MacMillian & Co., London, UK.

Chapter 3

Birnie, A. (1958), *The History and Ethics of Interest*, William Hodge & Co., London, UK.

Chapter 4

Abu-Lughod, J. (1989), *Before European Hegemony. The World System AD*, Oxford University Press, New York, pp. 1250–1350.

Ayoub, M. (2002), *Islamic Banking and Finance: Theory and Practice*, (State Bank of Pakistan: Karachi, Pakistan)

Firestone, Y. (1975), "Production and Trade in an Islamic Context," *International Journal of Middle East Studies*, Vol. 6, No. 2, pp. 185–207.

Gerber, H. (1981), "The Muslim Law of Partnerships in Ottoman Court Records," *Studia Islamica*, Vol. 53, p. 114.

Goitein, S. D. (1955), "The Cairo Geniza as a Source for the History of Muslim Civilization," *Studia Islamica*, pp. 168–197.

Goitein, S. D. (1962), *Jewish Education in Muslim Countries*, Based on Records of the Cairo Geniza (Hebrew), Jerusalem.

Goitein, S. D. (1961), "The Main Industries of the Mediterranean Area as Reflected in the Records of the Cairo Geniza," *JESHO*, 4, pp. 168–197.

Goitein, S. D. (1954), "From the Mediterranean to India," *SPECULUM*, 29, PP. 181–197.

Goitein, S. D. (1964), "Commercial and Family Partnerships in the Countries of Medieval Islam," *Islamic Studies*, Vol. 3, pp. 318–319.

Goitein, S. D. (1967), "A Mediterranean Society, The Jewish Communities of the Arab World as Portrayed in the Documents of the Cairo Geniza," Vol. I, *Economic Foundations*, Berkeley and Los Angeles.

Yousuf DeLorenzo, Yusuf Talal (2002), "The Religious Foundations of Islamic Finance," in Simor Archer and Rifaat Ahmed Abdel Karim (ed.) Islamic Finance: Innovation and Growth, *Euromoney*, London, UK.

Udovitch, Abraham L. (1970), "Commercial Techniques in Early Medieval Islamic Trade," *Islam and the Trade of Asia*, ed. D. Richards, pp. 37–62.

Udovitch, Abraham L. (1967), "Labor Partnership in Medieval Islamic Law," *Journal of Economic and Social History of the Orient*, Vol. 10, pp. 64–80.

Udovitch, Abraham L. (1967), "Credit as a Means of Investment in Medieval Islamic Trade," *Journal of the American Oriental Society*, Vol. 87, No. 3, (Jul.–Sept), pp. 260–264.

Udovitch, Abraham L. (1970), *Partnership and Profit in Medieval Islam*, Princeton University Press, Princeton, USA.

Chapter 5

Chapra, Umer and Tariqullah, Khan (2000). "Regulation and Supervision of Islamic Banks," Occasional Paper no. 3, Islamic Research and Training Institute: Islamic Development Bank, Jeddah, Saudi Arabia.

Jensen, M. C. and Meckling, W. H. (1976), "Theory of the Firm: Managerial Behavior, Agency Costs and Ownership Structure," *Journal of Financial Economics*, October, pp. 305–360.

Presley, John R. and Sessions, John G. (1994), "Islamic Economics: The Emergence of a New Paradigm," *Economic Journal*, Vol. 104, No. 424 (May), pp. 584–596.

ul-Haque, Nadeem and Mirakhor, Abbas (1989), "Optimal Profit-Sharing Contracts and Investments in an Interest-Free Economy," in Khan Mohsin and Mirakhor Abbas (eds.), 1987, *Theoretical Studies in Islamic Banking and Finance*, IRIS Books, Houston, USA.

Chapter 6

Khan, Mohsin (1987), "Islamic Interest-Free Banking: A Theoretical Analysis," in Khan Mohsin and Mirakhor Abbas (eds.), 1987, *Theoretical Studies in Islamic Banking and Finance*, IRIS Books, Houston, USA.

Chapter 7

Archer, S. and Ahmed, T. (2003). "Emerging Standards for Islamic Financial Institutions: the Case of the Accounting and Auditing Organization for Islamic Financial Institutions," mimeo, The World Bank, Washington, D.C. USA.

De Nicoló, Gianni, P. Bartholomew, J. Zaman and Zephirin, M. (2003) "Bank consolidation, internationalization and conglomeration: trends and implications for financial risk," *International Monetary Fund Seminar Series (International)*; No. 2003–121:1–49, May 2003.

El-Hawary, Dahlia, Grais, Wafik and Iqbal, Zamir (2004), "Regulating Islamic Financial Institutions: The Nature of the Regulated," *World Bank Working Papers, No. 3227*, Washington, D.C. USA.

Group of Ten (2001), *Report on Consolidation in the Financial Sector*, BIS, IMF, OECD.

Hassan, K. and Bashir, Abdel-Hameed (2004), *Determinants of Islamic Banking Profitability*, Working Paper, Islamic Development Bank, Jeddah, Saudi Arabia.

Hughes, J. P., Lang, W., Mester. L. and Moon, C. G. (1998), *The Dollars and Sense of Bank Consolidation*, Working Paper 10, Federal Reserve Bank of Philadelphia.

Hussein, K. A. (2003), "Operational Efficiency in Islamic Banking: The Sudanese Experience," Islamic Research and Training Institute (IRTI) Working paper Series No. 1, Islamic Development Bank, Jeddah, Saudi Arabia.

Iqbal, M. (2000), "Islamic and Conventional Banking in the Nineties: a Comparative Study," *Islamic Economic Studies*, Vol. 8, No. 2, April 2001.

Kahf, M. (1999), "Islamic Banks at the Threshold of the Third Millennium," *Thunderbird International Business Review*, Vol. 41, No. 4/5, July–October 1999, pp. 445–460.

Majid, M. A., N. G. M. Nor, Said, F. F. (2003) "Efficiency of Islamic Banks in Malaysia," Conference Proceedings: The Fifth International Conference on Islamic Economics and Finance, Vol. II, Bahrain, Oct. 7–9.

Marcus, G. (2000) "Issues for Consideration in Mergers and Takeovers from A Regulatory Perspective," *BIS Review 60*, pp. 1–12.

Metwally, M. M. (1997), "Differences between the Financial Characteristics of Interest-free Banks and Conventional Banks," *European Business Review*, 97 (2), 92.

Samad, H. and Hassan, M. K. (1999), "The Performance of Malaysian Islamic Banks during 1984–1997: an Exploratory Study," *International Journal of Islamic Financial Services*, Vol 1, No. 3.

Yudistira, D. (2004), "Efficiency in Islamic Banking: An Empirical Analysis of Eighteen Banks," *Islamic Economic Studies*, Vol. 12, No. 1, August 2004.

Chapter 8

Iqbal, Z. (1999), "Financial Engineering in Islamic Finance," *Thunderbird International Business Review*, Vol. 41, No. 4/5, July–October 1999, pp. 541–560.

Chapter 9

Ul-Haque, Nadeem and Mirakhor, Abbas (1997), "The Design of Instruments for Government Finance in an Islamic Economy," IMF Staff Papers, International Monetary Fund, Washington, D.C. USA. October.

Chapter 10

Khan, Tariqullah and Habib, Ahmed (2001), "Risk Management an Analysis of Issues in Islamic Financial Industry," Occasional Paper No. 9, Islamic Development Bank, Jeddah, Saudi Arabia.

Sundararajan, V. (2004), "Risk Measurement, Risk Management, and Disclosure in Islamic Finance," *Seminar on Comparative Supervision of Islamic and Conventional Finance*, December 7–8, Beirut, Lebanon.

Warde, I. (2000), *Islamic Finance in the Global Economy*. Edinburgh University Press, UK.

Chapter 11

Archer, S. (2004), "Capital Adequacy for Institutions Offering Islamic Financial Services: Regulatory Rationales and Key Conceptual Issues," Seminar on Comparative Supervision of Islamic and Conventional Finance, December 7–8, Beirut, Lebanon.

Basel Committee On Banking Supervision (BCBS) (2003), *Consultative Document-Overview of the New Basel Capital Accord*, April, Bank for International Settlements, Basel, Switzerland.

Calomiris, C. (1999), "Building An Incentive — Compatible Safety Net," *Journal of Banking and Finance*, Vol. 23 (1999), pp. 1499–1519.

Chapra, Umer and Khan, Tariqullah (2000), "Regulation and Supervision of Islamic Banks." Occasional Paper no. 3. Islamic Research and Training Institute: Islamic Development Bank, Jeddah, Saudi Arabia.

El-Hawary, Dahlia, Grais, Wafik and Iqbal, Zamir (2004), *Regulating Islamic Financial Institutions-The Nature Of The Regulated*, Policy Research Working Paper No. 3227, The World Bank, Washington, D.C. US.

Evanoff, D. and Wall, L. (2000), "Subordinated Debt and Bank Capital Reform," *Federal Reserve Bank of Chicago*. WP 2000–07, Chicago, US.

Marston, David and Sundararajan, V. (2003), "Unique Risks of Islamic Banks and Implications for Systemic Stability," paper presented at international conference on Islamic banking, Jakarta, September 30–October 2, 2003.

Sundararajan, V. and Errico, Luca (2002), "Islamic Financial Institutions and Products in the Global Financial System; Key Issues in Risk Management and Challenges Ahead," IMF working paper WP/02/192, IMF, November.

van Greuning, Hennie and Bratanovic, Sonja Brajovic (2003), *Analyzing and Managing Banking Risk: A Framework for Assessing Corporate Governance and Financial Risk*, 2nd ed., The World Bank, Washington, DC, US.

Zaher, T. and Hassan, K. (2001), "A Comparative Literature Survey of Islamic finance and Banking," *Financial Markets, Institutions and Instruments*, Vol. 10, No. 4, pp. 155–199, November.

Chapter 12

Ahmed, Mushtaq (1995), *Business Ethics in Islam*, The International Institute of Islamic Thought: Islamabad, Pakistan.

Bashir, Abdel-Hameed M. (1999), "Property Rights in Islam," Conference Proceedings of the Third Harvard University Forum on Islamic Finance, Harvard University, October 1999, pp. 71–82.

Boatright, J. (2002), "Contractors as Shareholders: Reconciling Stakeholder Theory with Nexus-of-Contracts Firm," *Journal of Banking and Finance*, Vol. 26, pp. 1837–1852.

Clarkson, M. B. E. (1995), "A Stakeholder Framework for Analyzing and Evaluating Corporations," *The Academy of Management Review*, Jan. 1995.

Donaldson, T. and Preston, L. E. (1995), "The Stakeholder Theory of the Corporation: Concepts, Evidence, and Implications," *Academy of Management Review*, Vol. 20, No. 1, pp. 65–91.

Freeman, R. E. (1984), *Strategic Management: A Stakeholder Approach*, (Pitman: Boston, USA).

Grais, Wafik and Iqbal, Zamir (2006), "*Corporate Governance Challenges of Islamic Financial Institutions*," 7th Harvard Forum on Islamic Finance, Boston, US, April 22–23.

Grais, Wafik. and Pellegrini, M. (2005), "Corporate Governance of Business Offering Islamic Financial Services: Issues and Options," Working paper, The World Bank Group, Washington DC, US.

Hart, Oliver (2001), "Norms and the Theory of the Firm," National Bureau of Economic Research, working paper 8286, http://www.nber.org/papers/w8286.

Imam Zayn al-Abidin Ali ibn al-Husayn (1990), *Risalat Al-Huquq*, trans. William C. Chittick, *The Treatise on Rights*, (Foundation of Islamic Cultural Propogation in the World: Qum, Iran).

Iqbal, Zamir and Mirakhor, Abbas (2004), "A Stakeholders Model of Corporate Governance of Firm in Islamic Economic System," *Islamic Economic Studies*, Vol. 11, No. 2., March 2004.

Islahi, Abdul Azim (1988), *Economic Concepts of Ibn Taimiyah*, The Islamic Foundation: Leicester, UK.

Islam, Muhammad W. (1999), "Al-Mal: The Concept of Property in Islamic Legal Thought," *Arab Law Quarterly*, pp. 361–368.

Jensen, M. C. and Meckling, W. H. (1976), "Theory of the Firm: Managerial Behavior, Agency Costs and Ownership Structure," *Journal of Financial Economics*, October, pp. 305–360.

Mirakhor, Abbas (1989), "General Characteristics of An Islamic Economic System," *in* Baqir Al-Hasani and Abbas Mirakhor, *(ed.) Essays on Iqtisad: The Islamic Approach to Economic Problems*, (Nur Corp., MD, USA), pp. 45–80.

Mirakhor, Abbas (1995), "Outline of an Islamic Economic System," *Zahid Husain Memorial Lecture Series No. 11*, State Bank of Pakistan, Islamabad, March 1995.

Van Greuning H. and Z. Iqbal (2006), "Banking and the Risk Environment" in Archer S. and R. A. Karim (eds.) *Islamic Finance: Regulatory Challenges*, John Wiley, Asia.

Zingales, L. (1997), "Corporate Governance," Working Paper No. 6309, National Bureau of Economic Research (NBER), Cambridge, US.

Chapter 13

Fukuyama, Francis (1996), *Trust: The Social Virtues and the Creation of Prosperity*, Free Press Paperbacks.

Khan, Mohsin (1987), "Islamic Interest-Free Banking: A Theoretical Analysis," in Khan and Mirakhor (eds.), 1987, *Theoretical Studies in Islamic Banking and Finance*, IRIS Books, Houston, TX,

Mehra, Rajnish, (2004), "The Equity Premium: Why is it a Puzzle?" *Financial Analysts Journal*, pp. 54–69.

Minsky, Hyman (1982), *Inflation, Recession and Economic Policy*, Wheatsheaf Books, London.

Prescott E. C. and Mehra, Rajnish (1985), "Equity premium; a puzzle," *Journal Of Monetary Economics (Netherlands);* Vol. 15, No. 2, pp. 145–61.

Rajan, Raghuram G., (2005), "Has Financial Development Made the World Riskier?" *NBER Working Paper 11728.*

Bibliography

Ahmad, Mahmud (1967), "Semantics of the Theory of Interest," *Islamic Studies*, Vol. 6, No. 2, June, pp. 171–96.

Al-Amine, Muhammad, Al-Bashir Muhammad (2001), "The Islamic Bonds Market: Possibilities And Challenges," *International Journal of Islamic Financial Services*, Vol. 3, No. 1.

Al-Dhareer, Siddiq Mohammad Al-Ameen (1997), "Al-Gharar Contracts and its Effects on Contemporary Transactions, Eminent Scholars," Lecture Series No. 16, Islamic Development Bank, Jeddah, Saudi Arabia.

Al-Harran, Saad Abdul Sattar (1993), *Islamic Finance: Partnership Financing*, Pelanduk Publications, Selangor Darul Ehsan, Malaysia.

Ali, Salman Syed (2005), "Islamic Capital Market Products: Developments and Challenges," Occasional Paper No. 9, Islamic Development Bank, Jeddah, Saudi Arabia.

Al-Saud, Mahmud Abu (1993), "Islamic View of Riba (Usury and Interest)," in Saad Abdul Sattar Al-Harran (ed.), *Islamic Finance: Partnership Financing*, Pelanduk Publications, Selangor Darul Ehsan, Malaysia.

Al-Saud, Mahmud Abu (1993), *Islamic Finance: Partnership Financing, Pelanduk Publications*, Selangor Darul Ehsan, Malaysia.

Al-Zarqa, Anas Muhammad (1993), "An Islamic Perspective on the Economics of Discounting Project Evaluation," in Saad Abdul Sattar Al-Harran (ed.), *Islamic Finance: Partnership Financing*, Pelanduk Publications, Selangor Darul Ehsan, Malaysia.

Archer, S. and T. Ahmed (2003), "Emerging Standards for Islamic Financial Institutions: the Case of the Accounting and Auditing Organization for Islamic Financial Institutions," mimeo, The World Bank, Washington, D.C. US.

Archer, Simon and Rifaat Abdel Karim (2002), *Islamic Finance: Growth and Innovation*, Euromoney Books, London, UK.

Ayoub, M. (2002), *Islamic Banking and Finance: Theory and Practice*, State Bank of Pakistan, Karachi, Pakistan.

Black, Fischer and Myron Scholes, "The Pricing of Options and Corporate Liabilities," *Journal of Political Economy*, 81:3, 1973, pp. 637–654.

Chapra, M. Umer (1989), "The Nature of *Riba*," *Journal of Islamic Banking and Finance (Pakistan)*, Vol. 6, pp. 7–23 July–September.

Chapra, M. Umer. (2000), "The Future of Economics," *The Islamic Foundation*, UK.

Chapra M. Umer and Tariqullah Khan (2000), *Regulation and Supervision of Islamic Banks*, Occasional Paper no. 3. (Jeddah, Saudi Arabia: Islamic Research and Training Institute, Islamic Development Bank).

Chapra, M. Umer and Habib. Ahmed (2002), "Corporate Governance in Islamic Financial Institutions," Occasional Paper No. 6. (Jeddah, Saudi Arabia: Islamic Research and Training Institute: Islamic Development Bank)

Cizakca, Murat (1995), "Historical Background," Encyclopedia of Islamic Banking and Insurance, Institute of Islamic Banking and Insurance, London, UK.

Creane, S., Rishi Goyal, A. Mushfiq Mobarak and Randa Sab (2003), Financial Development in the Middle East and North Africa, (Washington, D.C. USA: International Monetary Agency).

De Nicoló, Gianni, P. Bartholomew, J. Zaman and M. Zephirin (2003), "Bank consolidation, internationalization and conglomeration: trends and implications for financial risk," International Monetary Fund Seminar Series (International); No. 2003–121:1–49, May 2003.

El-Gamal, Mahmud (2000), *A Basic Guide to Contemporary Islamic Banking and Finance*, Rice University, Houston, TX, USA.

El-Hawary, Dahlia, Grais, Wafik and Iqbal, Zamir (2004), "Regulating Islamic Financial Institutions-The Nature Of The Regulated," Policy Research Working Paper No. 3227, The World Bank, Washington, D.C. US.

Errico, Luca and Mitra Farahbaksh (1998), "Islamic Banking: Issues in Prudential Regulations and Supervision," IMF Working Paper WP/98/30, (Washington, D.C. US: International Monetary Fund), 1998.

Fadeel, Mahmoud (2002), "Legal Aspects of Islamic Finance," in Simon Archer and Rifaat Abdel Karim (eds.) *Islamic Finance: Growth and Innovation*, (London, UK: Euromoney Books).

Fukuyama, Francis (1996), *Trust: The Social Virtues and the Creation of Prosperity*, Free Press Paperbacks.

Grais, Wafik and Iqbal, Zamir (2006), "Corporate Governance Challenges of Islamic Financial Institutions," 7th Harvard Forum on Islamic Finance, Boston, USA, April 22–23.

Gray, Robert (2005), *Islamic Capital Markets*, Presentation made on 10 Year Master Plan for Islamic Financial Services Industry, HSBC Bank plc, UK.

Haque, Zia-ul (1995), *Riba — The Moral Economy of Usury, Interest, and Profit*, Ikraq, Kuala Lumpur, Malaysia.

Hasanuzzaman, S. M. (1981), The Economic Functions of the Early Islamic State, International Islamic Publishers, Karachi, Pakistan.

Hasanuzzaman, S.M. (1993), *Indexation of Financial Assets: An Islamic Evaluation*, Research Monograph Series No. 4, International Institute of Islamic Thought, Islamabad, Pakistan.

Hasanuzzaman, S.M. (1994), "Conceptual Foundations of Riba in Quran, Hadith and Fiqh," *Journal of Islamic Banking and Finance* (Pakistan), Vol. 11, pp. 7–15.

Hasanuzzaman, S.M. (2001), "What is Mudaraba?," *Journal of Islamic Banking and Finance* (Pakistan), Vol. 18, No. 3 & 4, pp. 65–82.

Hussein, K. A. (2003), "Operational Efficiency in Islamic Banking: The Sudanese Experience," Islamic Research and Training Institute (IRTI) Working paper Series No. 1, Islamic Development Bank, Jeddah, Saudi Arabia.

IFSB (2005a), "Guiding Principles Of Risk Management For Institutions (Other Than Insurance Institutions) Offering Only Islamic Financial Services," Exposure Draft No. 1, Islamic Financial Services Board (IFSB), Kualalumpur, Malaysia.

IFSB (2005b), "Capital Adequacy Standard for Institutions (Other than Insurance Institutions) Offering only Islamic Financial Services', Exposure Draft No. 2, Islamic Financial Services Board (IFSB), Kualalumpur, Malaysia.

International Institute of Islamic Economics (IIIE) (1999), *IIIE"s Blueprint of Islamic Financial System*, International Islamic University, Islamabad, Pakistan.

Iqbal, M. (2000), "Islamic and Conventional Banking in the Nineties: a Comparative Study," *Islamic Economic Studies*, Vol. 8, No. 2, April 2001.

Iqbal, Zamir (1997), "Islamic Financial Systems," *Finance and Development*, International Monetary Fund, Washington, D.C. June.

Iqbal, Zamir (1999), "Financial Engineering in Islamic Finance," *Thunderbird International Business Review*, Vol. 41, No. 4/5, July–October 1999, pp. 541–560.

Iqbal, Zamir (2004), "Financial Intermediation and Design of Financial System in Islam," International Seminar on Economics, Malaysia, Sep. 22–24, 2004.

Iqbal, Zamir. and Mirakhor, Abbas (1999), "Progress and Challenges of Islamic Banking," *Thunderbird International Business Review*, Vol. 41, No. 4/5, July–October 1999, pp. 381–405.

Iqbal, Zamir and Mirakhor, Abbas (2002), "Development of Islamic Financial Institutions and Challenges Ahead," Simon Archer and Rifaat Abdel Karim (eds.) *Islamic Finance: Growth and Innovation*, (London, UK: Euromoney Books).

Iqbal, Zamir and Mirakhor, Abbas (2004), "A Stakeholders Model of Corporate Governance of Firm in Islamic Economic System," *Islamic Economic Studies*, Vol. 11, No. 2., March 2004.

Iqbal, Zamir and Tsubota, Hiroshi (2005), "Emerging Islamic Markets," *The Euromoney International Debt Capital Markets Handbook*, Euromoney Publishing, London, UK.

Iqbal, Zubair and Mirakhor, Abbas (1987), "Islamic Banking," Occasional Paper No. 49, International Monetary Fund, Washington, D.C. USA.

Jensen, M. and Meckling, W., "Theory of the firm: Managerial behaviour, agency costs and ownership structure," *Journal of Financial Economics*, Vol. 3, 1976, pp. 305–360

Kahf, M. (1999), "Islamic Banks at the Threshold of the Third Millennium," T*hunderbird International Business Review*, Vol. 41, No. 4/5, July–October 1999, pp. 445–460.

Khan, M. Fahim (1994). "Comparative Economics of Some Islamic Financing Techniques," *Islamic Economic Studies*. Vol. 2, No. 1, December 1994.

Khan, Mohsin (1987), "Islamic Interest-Free Banking: A Theoretical Analysis," in Khan and Mirakhor (eds.), 1987, *Theoretical Studies in Islamic Banking and Finance*, *IRIS Books*, Houston, TX, US.

Khan, Mohsin and Mirakhor, Abbas (1987), *Theoretical Studies in Islamic Banking and Finance*, IRIS Books, Houston, TX, USA.

Khan, Mohsin S. and Mirakhor, A. (1992), "Islam and the Economic System," *Review of Islamic Economics*. Vol. 2, No. 1, pp. 1–29.

Khan, Tariqullah and Ahmed, Habib (2001), "Risk Management an Analysis of Issues in Islamic Financial Industry," Occasional Paper No. 9, Islamic Development Bank, Jeddah, Saudi Arabia.

Labib, Subhi Y. (1969), "Capitalism in Medieval Islam," *The Journal of Economic History*, Vol. 29, No. 1, The Tasks of Economic History, pp. 79–96.

Levine, Ross (1997), "Financial Development and Economic Growth: Views and Agenda," *Journal of Economic Literature*, Vol. 35, No. 2, pp. 688–726.

Lewis, Mervyn K. and Algaoud, Latifa M. (2001), *Islamic Banking*, Edward Elgar, Cheltenham, UK.

Majid, M. A, N. G. M. Nor, F. F. Said (2003) "Efficiency of Islamic Banks in Malaysia," Conference Proceedings: The Fifth International Conference on Islamic Economics and Finance, Vol. 2, Bahrain, Oct. 7–9.

Mehra, Rajnish, (2004), "The Equity Premium: Why is it a Puzzle?" *Financial Analysts Journal*, pp. 54–69.

Merton, Robert C. and Zvi Bodie (1995), "A conceptual framework for analyzing the financial environment," in Dwight B. Crane et al., Eds., *The Global Financial System: A Functional Perspective*, (Boston, MA: Harvard Business School Press), pp. 3–32.

Metawally, M. M. (1985), "The Role of the Exchange in an Islamic Economy," *Journal of Research in Islamic Economics*, Vol. 2, No. 1, pp. 21–30.

Mills, Paul S. and John R. Presley (1999), *Islamic Finance: Theory and Practice*, Palgrave Macmillan Ltd, Hampshire, UK.

Minsky, Hyman (1982), *Inflation, Recession and Economic Policy*, Wheatsheaf Books, London.

Mirakhor, Abbas (1983), "Muslim Contribution to Economics," first presented at the Midwest Economic Association Meeting, April 7–9, and reprinted in *Essays on Iqtisad* by Al-Hassani and Abbas Mirakhor, Global Scholarly Publication, New York, N.Y., USA.

Mirakhor, Abbas (1987), "Analysis of Short-Term Asset Concentration in Islamic Banking," IMF Working Paper (WP/87/67), International Monetary Fund, Washington, DC, USA.

Mirakhor, Abbas, (1989), "General Characteristics of An Islamic Economic System," *in* Baqir Al-Hasani and Abbass Mirakhor, *(ed.) Essays on Iqtisad: The Islamic Approach to Economic Problems*, (Nur Corp., MD, USA), pp. 45–80.

Mirakhor, Abbas, (1989), "Theory of an Islamic Financial System," *in* Baqir Al-Hasani and Abbas Mirakhor, *(ed.) Essays on Iqtisad: The Islamic Approach to Economic Problems*, MD, USA: Nur Corp.

Mirakhor, Abbas (1994), "Equilibrium in a noninterest open economy," *Journal of King Abdulaziz University: Islamic Economics*, Vol. 6, pp. 3–24.

Mirakhor, Abbas, (1995), "Outline of an Islamic Economic System," *Zahid Husain Memorial Lecture Series No. 11*, State Bank of Pakistan, Islamabad, March 1995.

Mirakhor, Abbas (1996), "Cost of capital and investment in a non-interest economy," *Islamic Economic Studies*, Vol. 4, No. 1.

Mirakhor, Abbas (1999), "The design of instruments for government finance in an Islamic economy," *Islamic Economic Studies*, Vol. 6, No. 2.

Mirakhor, Abbas (2005), "Globalization and Islamic Finance," Keynote lecture at the 6th International Conference on Islamic Economics and Finance, Jakarta, Indonesia, November 21–23.

Mirakhor, Abbas (2005), "A note on Islamic Economics," Lecture delivered at the Islamic Development Bank for Research in Islamic Economics, Saudi Arabia, April.

Nyazee, Imran Ahsan Khan (1995), *The Concept of Riba and Islamic Banking*, Niazi Publishing House, Islamabad, Pakistan.

Prescott, E. C. and Mehra, Rajnish (1985), "Equity premium; a puzzle," *Journal Of Monetary Economics (Netherlands);* Vol. 15, No. 2, pp. 145–61.

Presley, John R. and Sessions, John G. (1994), "Islamic Economics: The Emergence of a New Paradigm," *Economic Journal*, Vol. 104, No. 424 (May), pp. 584–596.

Rajan, Raghuram G., 2005, "Has Financial Development Made the World Riskier?," *NBER Working Paper 11728.*

Saeed, Abdul (1996), *Islamic Banking and Interest*, E.J. Brill, Leiden, Netherlands.

Saleh, Nabil A. (1992), *Unlawful Gain and Legitimate Profit in Islamic Law: Riba, Gharar, and Islamic Banking*, 2nd Ed., Graham & Trotman, London, UK.

Samad, H. and Hassan M.K. (1999), "The Performance of Malaysian Islamic Banks during 1984–1997: an Exploratory Study." International Journal of Islamic Financial Services. Vol. 1, No. 3.

Shabsigh, Ghiath (2002), "Comments: Regulation of the Stock Market in as Islamic Economy," in Munawar Iqbal, ed., Islamic Banking and Finance: Current Developments in Theory and Practice, (Leicester, UK: Islamic Foundation, 2001.

Siddique, Shahid Hasan (1994), *Islamic Banking*, Royal Book Co., Karachi, Pakistan.

Sundararajan, V. (2004), "Risk Measurement, Risk Management, and Disclosure in Islamic Finance," Seminar on Comparative Supervision of Islamic and Conventional Finance, December 7–8, Beirut, Lebanon.

Sundararajan, V. and Errico, Luca (2002), "Islamic Financial Institutions and Products in the Global Financial System; Key Issues in Risk Management and Challenges Ahead," IMF working paper WP/02/192, IMF, November.

Udovitch, Abraham L., (1981), "Bankers without Banks: Commerce, Banking and Society in the Islamic World of Middle Ages," Princeton Near East Paper No. 30 (Princeton, NJ: Princeton University Press).

ul-Haque, Nadeem and Abbas Mirakhor (1989), "Optimal Profit-Sharing Contracts and Investments in an Interest-Free Economy," in Mohsin Khan and Abbas Mirakhor (eds.), 1987, *Theoretical Studies in Islamic Banking and Finance*, IRIS Books, Houston, TX, USA.

van Greuning, Hennie. and Iqbal, Zamir (2006), "Banking and the Risk Environment," in Archer S. and R. A. Karim (eds.), *Islamic Finance: Regulatory Challenges*, John Wiley, Asia.

van Greuning, Hennie and Bratanovic, Sonja Brajovic (2003), *Analyzing and Managing Banking Risk: A Framework for Assessing Corporate Governance and Financial Risk*, 2nd ed., The World Bank, Washington, D.C.

Usmani, Taqi (1999), *An Introduction to Islamic Finance*, Idaratul Ma"arif, Karachi, Pakistan.

Visser, Wayne A.M. and Alastair McIntosh (1998), "A Short Review of the Historical Critique of Usury," *Accounting, Business & Financial History*, 8:2, (Routledge, London, UK), July, pp. 175–189

Vogel, F. E. and Hayes, Samuel L. (1998), *Islamic Law and Finance: Religion, Risk and Return*, (Cambridge, MA, USA: Kluwer Law International).

Warde, I. (2000), *Islamic Finance in the Global Economy*, (Edinburgh University Press, UK).

Yudistira, D. (2004), "*Efficiency in Islamic Banking: An Empirical Analysis of Eighteen Banks*," Islamic Economic Studies, Vol. 12, No. 1, August 2004.

Index